RESEARCH FOR DEVELOPMENT

RESEARCH FOR DEVELOPMENT

A Practical Guide

SOPHIE LAWS
WITH
CAROLINE HARPER & RACHEL MARCUS

Los Angeles | London | New Delhi
Singapore | Washington DC

SAGE Publications Ltd
1 Oliver's Yard
55 City Road
London EC1Y 1SP

SAGE Publications Inc.
2455 Teller Road
Thousand Oaks, California 91320

SAGE Publications India Pvt Ltd
B 1/I 1 Mohan Cooperative Industrial Area
Mathura Road
New Delhi 110 044

SAGE Publications Asia-Pacific Pte Ltd
33 Pekin Street #02-01
Far East Square
Singapore 048763

British Library Cataloguing in Publication Data

A catalogue record for this book is available
from the British Library

ISBN 978-0-7619-7326-3 (hbk)
ISBN 978-0-7619-7327-0 (pbk)

Library of Congress Control Number Available

Typeset by C&M Digitals (P) Ltd, Chennai, India
Printed in Great Britain by
CPI Antony Rowe, Chippenham, Wiltshire
Printed on paper from sustainable resources

FSC
Mixed Sources
Product group from well-managed
forests and other controlled sources

Cert no. SGS-COC-2953
www.fsc.org
© 1996 Forest Stewardship Council

Contents

Acknowledgements

The writing of this manual has been possible only because of the help and support of a large number of people. Thanks are due to the members of the advisory group: Rachel Baker (Edinburgh University), Sara Gibbs (INTRAC), John Harriss (London School of Economics), Perpetua Kirby (independent researcher), Pat Kneen (Joseph Rowntree Foundation), Robert Lamb (Institute of Development Studies), Bridget Pettitt (independent researcher), Fiona Power (ID21), Alan Thomas (Open University). We also took advice from development practitioners working in many countries, and are especially grateful to: Nicola Chapman, EI Khidir Daloum, Clive Hedges, Tina Hyder, Lina Fajerman, Wendwessen Kittaw, Maddy Lewis, Peter Little, Robert McFarlane, Le Thi Minh Chau, Pham Thi Lan, Lu Yiyi.

Others who kindly read and commented on drafts were Roger Adams, Simon Mollison, N.K. Phuong, Joachim Theis, Chris Thornton, and Roy Trivedy. Liz Kwast and John Wilkinson helped with websites.

Many people kindly assisted in providing case studies. Some of these are referred to in the text and all informed our thinking. Thanks are due to: Mike Bailey, Ranka Bartula, Jo Boyden, Emma Cain, Olivera Damjanovic, Chris Eldridge, Irada Gautam, Yang Hai Yu, Guy Hatfield, Jutta Heering, Vanessa Herringshaw, Amanda Heslop, Andrea Hitzemann, Louise lllingworth, Edda Ivan-Smith, Victor Karunan, Sharfuddin Khan, Anne LaFond, Sheri Lecker, Pierre Lorillou, Maeve McAnallen, Isobel McConnan, Neil MacDonald, Chris Mclvor, Ianthe Maclagan, Dumisani Mnisi, Anne Mulcahy, Rahat Orozova, Sue Paganga, Jenita Rose Mary Perera, Peter Poore, Ranjan Poudyal, Jasmine Rajbhandary, Vijay Rajkumar, Helen Roberts, Judy Roberts, Shirley Robinson, Eddie Strong, Patti Strong, Sue Stubbs, Eddie Thomas, Chris Thornton, Kadiatou Touré, Mandal Urtnasan, Raya Ushurova, Andy West.

We are grateful for permission to reproduce the following material from other sources:

The example of a mobility map in Chapter 17 is reproduced from Theis, J. and Grady, H.M. (1991) *Participatory Rapid Appraisal for Community Development*. London: IIED and SCF Federation.

The matrix scoring and ranking charts and the wealth ranking map in Chapter 17 are reproduced from Britha Mikkelsen: *Methods for Development Work and Research: A guide for practitioners*. © Britha Mikkelsen 1995. All rights reserved. Reproduced with the permission of the copyright-holder and the publishers, Sage Publications India Pvt Ltd, New Delhi.

The children's drawings in Chapter 17 are reproduced from Boyden, J. and Ennew, J. (eds) (1997) *Children in Focus: A manual for participatory research with children*. Stockholm: Rädda Barnen (Save the Children Sweden).

The triangulation diagram in Chapter 16 is reproduced from Denscombe, M. (1998) *The Good Research Guide for Small-Scale Social Research Projects*. Buckingham, UK and Philadelphia, USA: Open University Press.

The action research diagram in Chapter 18 is reproduced from Wadsworth, Y. (1997) *Do it Yourself Social Research*, 2nd edition. St Leonards, Australia: Allen and Unwin.

The diagram of sampling strategies in Chapter 19 is reproduced from Blaxter, L., Hughes, C. and Tight, M. (1996) *How to Research*. Buckingham: Open University Press.

Permission has also been given for extensive use of material from the following sources:

Theis, J. and Grady, H.M. (1991) *Participatory Rapid Appraisal for Community Development*. London: IIED and SCF Federation.

Mikkelsen, B. (1995) *Methods for Development Work and Research: A guide for practitioners*, New Delhi: Sage Publications India.

Boyden, J. and Ennew, J. (eds) (1997) *Children in Focus: A manual for participatory research with children*. Stockholm: Rädda Barnen (Save the Children Sweden).

Denscombe, M. (1998) *The Good Research Guide for Small-Scale Social Research Projects*. Buckingham, UK and Philadelphia, USA: Open University Press.

Bell, J. (1987) *Doing your Research Project*. Buckingham, UK: Open University Press.

Hall, D. and Hall, H. (1996) *Practical Social Research: Project work in the community*. Basingstoke: Macmillan.

Craig, G. (1998) *Women's Views Count: Building responsive maternity services*. London: College of Health.

Wadsworth, Y. (1997) *Do it Yourself Social Research*, 2nd edition. St Leonards, Australia: Allen and Unwin.

O'Laughlin, B. (1998) 'Interpreting institutional discourses', in Thomas, A., Chataway, J. and Wuyts, M. (eds) (1998) *Finding Out Fast*. London: The Open University/Sage.

Blaxter, L., Hughes, C. and Tight, M. (1996) *How to Research*. Buckingham: Open University Press.

Ritchie, J. and Spencer, L. (1994) 'Qualitative data analysis for applied policy research', in Bryman, A. and Burgess, R.G. (eds) *Analyzing Qualitative Data*. London: Routledge.

Dyson, S. 'Interviewing by conversation', *Sociology Review*, April 1994. University of North London course texts (1998–9) *Introduction to Data Analysis for Social Scientists and Research Methods*. Applied Social Science Scheme, University of North London.

Pratt, B. and Loizos, P. (1992) *Choosing Research Methods: Data collection for development workers, Development Guidelines No. 7*. Oxford: Oxfam Publishing, 274 Banbury Road, Oxford OX2 7D.

Nichols, P. (1991) *Social Survey Methods: A field guide for development workers, Development Guidelines No. 6*. Oxford: Oxfam Publishing, 274 Banbury Road, Oxford OX2 7DZ.

Kirby, P. (1999) *Involving Young Researchers: How to enable young people to design and conduct research*. York: Joseph Rowntree Foundation.

Finally Save the Children thanks the Department for International Development for essential financial support to this project.

The UK Department for International Development (DFID) Support policies, programmes and projects to promote international development. The DFID Provided funds for this study as part of that objective but the views and opinious expressed are those of the authors alone.

O N E Managing Research for Development: How to Use this Book

Introduction – Why Use Research in Development Work?

This book consists of two parts. The first concentrates on managing research – giving practical advice on all the issues that arise in making research for development work happen. The second part gives guidance on how to actually do the research itself.

Often the same people manage research and carry it out, and there may be no clear line where one stops and the other starts. But experience tells us that much of what goes wrong in research for development work relates to planning and management. And most of the books about how to do research concentrate on the methods themselves, and neglect the many 'real life' issues which have to be decided in setting up research projects. Part One aims to put this right.

Throughout the book, each chapter finishes with a checklist summarising the main points, and there are other checklists throughout the text. Some key tips are highlighted, as are common pitfalls. Activities are suggested for readers who would like to think actively for themselves abot the issues – most of these could usefully be carried out with a group of colleagues. If you want to read further, a few recommended texts are listed at the end of each chapter. A glossary aims to help you through the jargon of social research.

What are you looking for?

When we consulted development workers on how they might use a book like this, someone said something which rang very true. He said he would look at the manual when he had a problem, and would want to find the answer to his question in half an hour. For this reason the book is full of checklists and tips, and has a good index.

Of course we hope that you will want to read the whole book, but just in case you don't have time, here are a few shortcuts:

? *New researcher starting work tomorrow?* Look at how to supervise them, Chapter 8, and skim the whole of Part One.
? *Looking at a blank page, trying to write a research brief?* Chapter 6 tells you what should go in it.
? *A good idea of an area to look at, but a bit foggy about the details of the project?* Chapter 5 should help you to clarify your thinking, then read Chapter 16 and skim the rest of Part Two, when you are ready to choose methods.

? *Not sure if research is the right approach in this situation?* Chapter 1, especially 1.6.
? *Piles of data and a dead computer?* Chapter 20 to the rescue.
? *Worried about whether your sample is good enough?* Chapter 19 should help you.
? *A colleague has suggested you do some participatory research – but how?* Chapter 3.
? *Heard there's some really good information on your subject on the Internet?* Chapter 12.2 and the Appendix will get you started.
? *Wondering how to make sure your respondents are really happy to take part in your project?* Chapters 13 and 15 discuss consent.
? *Working in a language you don't speak?* Chapter 14.6 offers advice.
? *Want to know what a focus group is?* Chapter 17.3 will tell you.
? *Need to do some needs assessment? Puzzled by PLA? Stuck on stakeholder analysis?* Development-specific approaches untangled in Chapter 18.
? *Under pressure about your general approach?* Check on different philophies of research in Chapers 1 and 2; and think about the quality of your work using Chapters 4 and 11.
? *About to consider hiring a researcher?* Read Chapter 7, but don't forget to check that the brief is clear (Chapters 5 and 6)
? *Draft report on your desk, but it's not quite right?* Chapter 21 will give a framework for revisions, and Chapter 10 will help you to plan a strategy to promote your findings.
? *Want to build your organisation's capacity to use research in its work?* Chapter 9 suggests some approaches.

Part One: managing research for development

Part One starts with a discussion of why development workers can benefit from using research, and gives ideas on how to tell when research is the best approach to a problem. Chapter 2 looks at the main research approaches, and at the two main types of purpose for which research is used in development work – to inform programme planning and to influence policy. Participatory research is discussed in depth in Chapter 3, as an important type of research that fits in particularly well with development programmes.

Quality is a key issue in determining how much influence your research can have, and Chapter 4 discusses what is meant by quality in research work, across the broad spectrum of different types of research.

The next four chapters are very practical – the first two concern the process of writing the research brief. Chapter 5 discusses how to go about it, and emphasises discussion with all relevant stakeholders. It offers advice on defining the research focus and the key research questions, which set the groundwork for writing the brief itself. Chapter 6 sets out an outline for a research brief, and takes you through the necessary sections with advice on each area.

Chapter 7 discusses the issues involved in deciding who will do the research. This chapter looks at the pros and cons of doing research yourself as a development worker, and then gives detailed advice about the process of hiring research staff.

Chapter 8 offers help on how to supervise research work, and how to estimate costs and timetables. It also discusses some other important aspects of managing research work – negotiating access, managing participatory research and last but not least, relating to funders.

In Chapter 9 we look at how to help people to learn more about research, suggesting a range of ways in which you can build up skills and knowledge. Training workshops are discussed, but learning by doing, with advice from more experienced researchers, is recommended.

The last two chapters of Part One concentrate on two important areas for managers of research projects to consider – promotion and evaluation. Both need to be considered throughout the life of a research project, not just at the end, and practical tips are offered on a range of ways of both promoting and evaluating your work. While the quality of your research itself does have a part to play in how much impact it will have in the world, it is also very important to think positively about putting forward the results of your research in ways which will reach your target audiences.

Part Two: doing research for development

Part Two is a basic guide to how to actually do research. It starts with a chapter on the first step for most research projects – finding out what is already known about your subject. Ways of approaching this task are discussed, including using libraries and the Internet, and seeking out information informally.

Chapter 13 looks at the ethics of research for development work, including detailed discussion of responsibilities to respondents as well as wider accountability.

Chapters 14 and 15 both address crucial matters which determine the quality of the work you do. Communication with respondents is discussed in Chapter 14 – general issues of language and style, how to demonstrate listening and respect – and also more specific issues in communicating with children, with people who are not literate, who are disabled, or with those whose language you do not speak. Advice is given on working with an interpreter, and on techniques for research with children. Chapter 15 then moves on to look at the practical measures you need to take to ensure your data-gathering process, whatever form it takes, is of good quality. Effective ways are described, for example, of ensuring that respondents are able to give informed consent to participation; of protecting confidentiality; of recording data; and of ensuring 'trustworthiness' in your work.

In Chapters 16 and 17 we arrive at the point where people often try to start – the choice of research methods, and a description of the techniques themselves. Chapter 16 suggests that it is useful to distinguish between broad approaches to research and the specific techniques that you will use to gather the data. It is recommended generally to abandon the search for a single perfect technique to use, but to use the approach known as 'triangulation' – looking at things from a number of angles, using a variety of different techniques.

Chapter 17 describes seven tried and tested research techniques, giving information on their strengths and limitations, and when it is appropriate to use them. The first section offers advice which is relevant to many techniques, on how to ask questions – what kinds of questions to avoid, and how to evaluate the questions you want to ask. Then the chapter deals with interviews, focus groups, documentary sources, observation, questionnaires, ranking and scoring exercises and visual methods – maps, diagrams and drawings. A final section looks briefly at some other possible approaches, including creative techniques like photography and drama, and market research methods.

The techniques described in Chapter 17 are used in a huge range of different types of research. In Chapter 18, we look at some packages of methods that are particularly relevant for development workers. Often they use techniques drawn from those described already, but they are put together in a particular way, often with a specific philosophy behind them. Needs assessment, stakeholder analysis, action research, consultation, baseline studies, case studies, Participatory Learning and Action, and Household Food Economy Assessment are discussed in this chapter.

How to choose a sample is discussed in Chapter 19 – talking to the right people. Different kinds of sampling are discussed, including both quantitative and qualitative approaches. A special section offers advice on how to include 'hard to reach' people in your study.

Continuing through the life cycle of a piece of research, we reach the analysis stage in Chapter 20. Development research projects have been known to collapse at this point, when the enthusiasm of the data collection process is past, and suddenly it is not at all obvious how to proceed. After a discussion of problems of interpretation, practical guidance is given about how to deal with your data. There is detailed advice is given about how to analyse qualitative and quantitative data, both by hand and with a computer. Finally you are encouraged to step back and consider how to bring together your findings and clarify what they really mean overall.

The last chapter, 21, guides you through the process of writing up the research – looking both at what to write and at how to write it. It contains sections on what needs to go into your report and on how to present quantitative data clearly. This chapter should be read alongside Chapter 10, which encourages you to look at how to get your message across, both in writing a report, and in communicating your research findings in a variety of other ways.

To help you to get the most out of the Internet for your work, Appendix 1 gives some pointers to useful websites for development and research issues. And finally the Glossary can help with any unfamiliar terminology

1 How to use this book

What is research? What is the best approach to research for development work? What are the different ways in which research is used in development work? This chapter aims to lay the foundations for the rest of the book by attempting to answer these questions.

This manual is written for development workers, and is intended to give you the tools to use research as effectively as possible in your work. For development workers, research is one approach to making social change. Ideas are proposed to assist in deciding when a research approach is the best one to take.

Research is used in development work for a variety of purposes. It may set out to explore an issue in order to plan a programme; it may, more broadly, ask people in an area about their own needs; or it may aim to collect in-depth information about a specific issue, to make a case for change. Research methods are also used in programme monitoring, evaluation, and review. What we call research can range from very small local pieces of work (perhaps just reviewing existing information) to major international projects.

Chapter 2 gives some of the theoretical background the reader will need to feel confident in working with researchers, briefly describing some important schools of thought about research. It moves on to focus on research for policy influence – when does research really have an influence? Chapter 3 looks at participatory research – an important kind of research in development work.

1.1 Some effective research for development work

So what can be achieved through using research in development work? 'Research' can refer to a wide range of activities, some very rigorous and technical, some quite small scale and simple. It involves collecting new information in a systematic way, and good research questions received wisdom, challenges ideas that are taken for granted. This section aims to show what can be achieved, through some real-life examples.

In the following example, research into the situation of children stitching footballs in Pakistan gave information which could be used both to plan Save the Children's own programme of work, and to influence policy on child labour internationally.

EXAMPLE

Child Labour Project, Sialkot, Pakistan

Save the Children's research into the situation of child football stitchers in Sialkot, Pakistan, was the foundation for its involvement in a coalition working to phase out child labour in football production. The research provided detailed information about the reasons children stitch footballs, their working conditions, the problems they and their families face and the kinds of measures that would be needed to ease children's transition out of the workforce. It challenged some of the myths that were floating around, for example, that child stitchers were prevented by their work from attending school, and revealed for the first time the large numbers of women football stitchers. On the basis of this new and important information, Save the Children was able to plan its own contributions to a programme to assist children's transition out of the workforce.

The research was also very timely. The initial findings were available at the same time that the International Labour Organisation was planning its own programme, and the completed research was ready by the time most of the partners in the Sialkot programme started to plan their activities. It was thus possible to use the research to influence other partners' activities so that they promoted family welfare – for example by finding ways that women could continue working after their children stopped. This research has also provided the basis for broader advocacy on child labour issues with industry, international organisations and consumers, among others.

In Pakistan, and internationally, the research played an important role in establishing Save the Children as a credible actor on child labour issues. The fact that it was rigorous, based on a carefully thought out methodology, and was widely seen to be impartial have all been important factors in the ability of the Save the Children to exert an influence on the programme and to speak with authority on the issue (Save the Children, 1997).

Research is also important simply in ensuring that development programmes are appropriate to the needs they aim to address. In addition to carrying out research themselves, development organisations would greatly benefit from encouraging the greater use of existing research. Especially in emergency situations, there is often a failure to seek out relevant research on a group suffering a crisis – for example work produced by anthropologists – and this can compromise effective intervention.

EXAMPLE

Appropriate aid for nomads in Somaliland

A failure to read ethnography in the immediate post-conflict phase on Somaliland led agencies to build schools in pastoral nomadic communities that would normally move continuously with their herds to water sources. Schools created a focal point for settlement, but also provided a target for grenades and by bringing people together rendered them more vulnerable to attack.

Development agencies are increasingly using participatory research methods that enable community members to have a say about the issue itself, and about how the research is carried out. Participatory work can contribute to programme development, as well as to influencing policy at the national or international level.

what do the harms tell us?

EXAMPLE

The contribution of older people to development – Ghana and South Africa

Older people are often invisible when development issues are discussed, although they make up an increasing proportion of the population of developing countries. HelpAge International carried out a major study of the contribution of older people to development, with two studies completed in Ghana and South Africa. The purpose of the research was to improve the responsiveness of policies and services to the needs and capabilities of poor and disadvantaged older people in African and other countries.

The study involved fieldwork in a number of locations within each country. Methods included interviews, focus groups, and techniques drawn from Participatory Learning and Action (PLA), a development from the tradition of Participatory Rapid Appraisal. These techniques emphasise visual approaches – mapping, diagramming, ranking and scoring exercises, which enable participants to share information together, and to debate its meaning as a group. Reports were published in both countries, which drew together the findings of the research in different local areas. The project again involved older people directly at the point when the research findings were presented to government officials at national level.

Important findings drew attention to the different kinds of contributions made by older women and older men. In addition to income-generating roles, older people made important social contributions, for example as health care providers, asset managers, educators, mentors, and carers. The research began the process of feeding older people's views into policy discussion on ageing in Ghana and South Africa. HelpAge saw the research as representing a catalyst for developing processes for including older people in mainstream decision-making about issues that affect their lives (HelpAge, 1999).

The next example shows what can be done through re-analysing publicly available information with particular questions in mind.

EXAMPLE

The South African Children's Budget

A number of South African civil society organisations advocate for public spending policies that target children. To support their efforts, Idasa: Budget Information Service and the Youth Development Trust completed a study analysing government spending on children in South Africa. First Call: The South African Children's Budget (1997):

- monitors the link between government policies and expenditures intended to benefit children;
- tracks government spending on children in key socio-economic sectors;
- provides recommendations for improved socio-economic delivery to children; and
- suggests indicators to monitor shifts in spending to children.

The Children's Budget Project fulfils an important function in providing key technical analyses and support on government spending on children in South Africa to both the government and the civil society children's rights advocates. The statistical information and analyses compiled in the Children's Budget study have made a critical contribution to the children's rights policy debate in South Africa.

  Certain children's rights organisations, such as the South African National Council for Child and Family Welfare, have used the Children's Budget statistical information and analyses extensively in their policy advocacy campaigns on key child welfare issues. And the government has appended First Call to the 1997 South African Government Report to the United Nations Committee on the Rights of the Child. At the international level, the Children's Budget Project has co-ordinated and made significant contributions to an international seminar on Macroeconomics and Children's Rights, aimed at replicating similar studies in other developing countries.

1.2   So what is research?

A major challenge in writing this manual is that what we mean by research covers a large and diverse group of processes. And everything about research is argued over. There is fierce debate between researchers, and those who use research, about the validity of different research approaches. It is hard to find a place to stand where the ground does not shift beneath your feet. It would be so much easier to explain something like plumbing, where it is so much less a matter of opinion whether things work or not.

  When we consulted practitioners on what they would like to see in this manual, they asked for clear statements on the questions: What is research? What are the 'rules of the game' if you are doing research? Reasonable questions! But huge piles of books have been written debating the answers.

And the discussion is not just an academic one: it emerges regularly in daily life for those doing research for development work.

EXAMPLE

Evaluating community health development projects: the debate

Save the Children in the UK and internationally regularly sets up community development projects which aim to improve the health of a group of people. Usually these aim to work as partnerships with government health services. All such work needs to be evaluated, so at a certain point SCF staff meet with health service research staff, often doctors of public health medicine. A discussion then ensues about how the evaluation will be done.

Typically, the public health people will insist that the only valid evaluation would compare objectively measurable 'health gain' – children growing taller, people living longer – for the area where the intervention will occur with a 'control' area, where no such development work is going on. The model is the randomised controlled trial (RCT), which is the best method of assessing medical care. Many issues arise: What are appropriate measures of success? How could the effect of the intervention be isolated from other changes in the area? How can the cost of such a major study be met?

An alternative approach may then be suggested, which concentrates attention on the community members' views about the development work, on the issues which they raise as important to them. Development is about the empowerment of community members, and not about fulfilling aims set by outsiders. And the process of carrying out an intervention may be valuable in the long term, as much as the direct outcomes. Importance is placed on learning throughout the life of the project rather than making a judgement at the end.

A complex discussion then takes place, which community development workers usually find enraging. Questions of values, practicalities, cost, validity, philosophies of knowledge (what counts as a real effect? whose opinion counts?), and the detail of possible research methods all fly around the room in a chaotic muddle.

The medical model of research is particularly well-defined. Also, of course, doctors hold great authority in most societies, and may have an influence on the survival of health-related projects in their area. This makes negotiations of this sort particularly fraught. It is crucial to any partnership process to agree an approach to evaluation that will be acceptable to the key partners. But sometimes there seems to be no way through the conflicts which present themselves. Focusing on evaluation and research does not soften any differences of approach, rather it usually sharpens the outlines of the matters at issue.

Similar patterns can crop up in dealings with many other kinds of professionals, for example economists, agronomists, psychologists and others.

This book has been prepared by professional researchers who have frequently supported development workers in situations like this. There is no simple solution. Arguing about whose truth matters is important – it is part of the process of development to ensure that the voices of less powerful people are heard (for example, Holland with Blackburn, 1998). Equally it is essential to argue about how we can measure the success of our work in a way that is convincing to those who need to be convinced (for example, Oakley and Roberts, 1996; Sinclair, 1998).

What this manual hopes to achieve is for development workers to feel more confident when they take part in this kind of discussion.

1.3 'But I'm not a researcher' – the contribution of the development worker

This handbook is written for development workers: there is no intention to turn you into a researcher. What the manual aims to do is to give you a greater sense of control in using research within your work. Looking at things from a more research-oriented point of view can avoid mistakes in the design of programmes by avoiding wrong assumptions about a situation.

EXAMPLE

Why were children missing school? Northern Iraq

Save the Children was concerned about low school attendance within a Kurdish community in Northern Iraq. The organisation had assumed that the cause of the problem would be the parents' lack of money. However when researchers talked with the children, they found out that teachers were beating the children so severely that they were afraid to go to school. There were also allegations of sexual abuse. Save the Children was then able to discuss with the local authorities a programme of teacher training which addresses how children should be treated as well as how to convey information.

EXAMPLE

Identifying an effective intervention – Child Labour Project, Sialkot, Pakistan

The research into children stitching footballs in Pakistan was partly aimed at clarifying what would be the most useful intervention for Save the Children and other organisations to make. Some campaign groups were pressing the industry to build more schools. However the research established that it was not lack of schools which was preventing children from going to school. The key factors were the high cost and low quality of schooling, as well as their families' need for income. It would have been ineffective to set up more schools.

Activity 1.1

How do you feel about research?

Without thinking too much about it, jot down the feelings, ideas and images which come up for you when you think 'research'.

What about the words 'enquiry', and 'investigation'?

What do these feelings mean for you in thinking about how you will use this manual?

Where do they come from? Experience at work? Your schooling?

This could usefully be done with a group of people, discussing people's different responses.

In their ordinary work, development practitioners do some similar things to researchers. They are very likely to undertake needs assessments. They investigate people's opinions and probe their explanations for problems in their lives. They work with people to help them to analyse their situation – to make sense of things, beyond the individual.

Development workers also use some of the same methods as researchers, but the way in which things are done will be somewhat different. Both may conduct interviews, undertake observation, hold group discussions, and ask groups what is most important to them. Development workers generally specialise in being with people in an informal way, so that trust is built up. This makes it possible for people without the confidence bred by an extended formal education to discuss issues of importance to them, and to ask questions about why things are as they are.

It is not the intention of this manual to simply re-label development workers' methods as research. Even though there are many schools of thought about research, all of them have a set of rules that define the quality of information which is regarded as 'good data'. Development work has its own standards and priorities, which are different.

Take the example of a development worker discussing an issue such as unemployment with a young person. Like a researcher, they are likely to be listening for themes in what the young person says which they have heard also from other young people they have talked to, so as to understand what is important to the whole group. But the development worker will also be observing the conversation for ways in which they can enable the young person to feel more in control of her life. They might let contradictory statements pass, if they were at the stage of building trust with the person.

A researcher would be much more concerned to record things exactly as the young person puts them. If they are engaged in work of any depth, and they hear apparently conflicting points of view held together, they will gently ask questions to tease out the way the person is thinking. The researcher is not trying to effect change in the young person, but to understand the situation.

If the young person says something which offends the development worker's principles, for instance blaming themselves for events the worker regards as caused by wider social forces, the development worker is likely to challenge that interpretation. Depending on their school of thought (see below, Section 2.2), a researcher may simply record such a comment, or they may put forward a different view, usually in a neutral way, such as 'some people might say...' and then record the response.

In encouraging development workers to learn more about research, the hope is that they will take from the disciplines of research the things that could be most useful to them. Doing research does change your point of view.

The skills and knowledge of the development worker have a great deal to contribute towards research processes. One key role is that of identifying issues on which research is required. With their knowledge of the situation and needs of a group of people, combined with an understanding of broader social processes, development workers can frame research issues which are 'live' and meaningful to those concerned. Secondly, the development worker's skill in building relationships of trust with people, including those who face discrimination, is invaluable in facilitating research which actively involves community members.

Key aspects of a researcher's approach include:

- A questioning approach to everything, including everyone's pet theories.
- Concern to understand what people say very accurately, to hear them without bias.
- Appreciating that how we ask questions can determine the answers we get.
- An analytical approach – that is, looking for patterns in things, probing behind surface appearances.
- Trying to get inside how people make sense of things – especially when the sense is not immediately obvious.
- Becoming ever more conscious of the researcher's own impact on people and their responses.

Research methods can be seen as a set of tools which you can use in various ways – but they are complex tools, and there are risks attached to their use. Like many tools, it is important to learn to use them properly in order to avoid accidents.

Some types of research are best left to experienced research professionals. Large-scale surveys, complex statistics, and indeed some subtle qualitative research on sensitive issues, are best done by researchers with specialist training. Development workers may wish to commission this type of work, and Chapters 5 to 7 aim to help them to do so effectively. But there are many kinds of research approach which are straightforward to use, and can enable development workers to understand the issues they are working with in more depth, and represent people's views more accurately.

1.4 Who should do research for development work – the broader issues

This section discusses some wider questions arising from choices made about who does what research in development work. Development workers are in the business of creating social change, and need to take a pragmatic approach to the use of research in their work. At times, it may well be that an expert view from a famous university is exactly what is needed. However there are some broader issues to be considered, beyond the immediate piece of work.

The traditional model of research concentrates internationally recognised expertise in a few centres. A situation has developed where research knowledge and skills belong to an élite. For example, much of the research into the issues for the South is carried out by people who are based in the North. Frequently, research is done by highly paid academics or consultants who make brief visits to poverty-stricken areas and then return to their base, taking their data with them. This pattern has several consequences:

- Concentration of knowledge and skills in the North or in élite centres, not in the countries or among the people in question.
- Few opportunities for Southern people or non-academics to learn from research processes.
- Data may never return to the country or place it relates to.
- Perception that answers lie with outsiders, experts, and not with those directly involved.

A similar situation arises where knowledge in any country is concentrated only in élite centres.

There are, of course, more and less sensitive ways in which researchers/ consultants can operate, but the power imbalance seems an inevitable part of this pattern. One purpose of this manual is to encourage development workers to play a role in supporting researchers in the South and in disadvantaged communities in the North. In this way, it will be possible for more research to be done closer to those who are the 'objects' of the research.

CHECKLIST **For developing research skills in disadvantaged communities**

✓ Where possible, hire researchers from Southern countries/disadvantaged groups

✓ Build in some training and development work for local workers to any research brief, so that they learn from a variety of research processes (See Chapter 9 on learning how to do research for development work.)

✓ Seek to develop research ideas which are locally generated and owned, and there will be demand to keep the data locally, even if research is conducted by outsiders

✓ Ensure that if data is removed from its context, it is copied, or returned to those who can use it for development purposes (unless there are issues of confidentiality which prevent this)

✓ Require appropriate feedback of findings to local agencies and the community members[1] themselves as well as to decision-makers

✓ Ensure that research processes are carried out in an open way, and demystified for all participants

✓ Organise participatory training workshops in research skills as part of your ongoing staff development work

✓ Ensure that where relatively inexperienced researchers are employed, they have a clear brief (see Chapters 5 and 6) and sufficient support – coaching and supervision – from those with relevant experience (see Chapter 7)

1.5   Research and social change

Development work usually aims to create social change of some sort. It might, for example, aim to assist a minority community in moving out of poverty, or it might be directed towards increasing educational opportunities for children and adults across a whole region. There are many theories of

---

[1]'Community member' is used as a very broad term to refer to those the development worker/researcher relates to. They might, for example, be villagers, young women, or disabled people. It is recognised that community links and support may be strong or weak.

how social change takes place, and on top of these many more theories about how development workers can and should intervene in these processes. One way of thinking about the use of research-type activities within development work is to focus on how research can contribute towards processes of change.

There are a number of different ways of looking at this, all of which are used in development work. Perhaps the dominant model is what you might call the rationalist, or engineering approach (Bulmer, 1982). This suggests that we have a social problem (and its definition is straightforward). Information is needed to understand the problem better in order to solve it. Research collects such information, and then policy will change in light of such findings. Researchers are seen as being like engineers, providing technical data to solve technical problems.

not for slavery

However there are a lot of problems with this model. In reality, things are much more complicated. There may not even be agreement about the nature of the problem. Policy change does not automatically follow from relevant research information – the process is more difficult and contradictory than that. The assumptions behind this model see governments, and the powerful generally, as benignly and openly seeking to improve things. All the complexities of political reality are left out.

Much participatory research works with a quite different model of the links between research and social change (See Chapter 3). Ordinary people are seen as important actors, and research aims to empower them to better understand their situation, and hence to take action to change it. Information is not seen as neutral, but as reflecting people's different standpoints. The key is to give voice to the experience and knowledge of oppressed people.

Non-governmental agencies (NGOs) also sometimes think in terms of campaigning as a route to social change – in this case research is seen as providing ammunition for campaigners. This is really a kind of engineering model, but it sees public opinion as important, whereas the traditional model aims to influence decision-makers directly, simply through the strength of the evidence.

Which approaches are chosen depends upon many things. This may be a tactical choice, depending upon the issue in question and the kind of change which is desired – whether it be, for example, legal, economic, or a change of ordinary people's attitudes. But this choice also springs from professionals' own beliefs about how change takes place. Some place their faith in parliamentary processes, others in grass-roots education and action.

Suppose for example that the aim is to influence some aspect of professional practice, perhaps in social welfare work. Some see the best hope of achieving this through scientific-style research which aims to 'prove' the success of a particular method of work. Others would want to directly engage with the professionals in co-operative enquiry. Others still would give information to service users or the general public to encourage them to pressure the professionals to change their practice.

It is worth reflecting on these issues in reading this manual, so that you can be conscious of the framework you are working within. It is not surprising that the research we do in NGOs is so diverse, when it is performing a number of very different functions in the organisation's work for change.

Activity 1.2

What model of change do you use?

In the table below, list projects which you are familiar with which you think fit into each of these approaches. How many fit squarely in one category?

If you can involve some colleagues, ask two other people to fill in the table separately, and then discuss any issues which arise.

If the fit is bad, can you think of a better way of describing the model of social change behind your work?

Model of research for social change	Projects fitting this model
1. Rationalist/ Engineering	
2. Empowerment	
3. Campaigning	

1.6 How to tell when research is the best approach to a problem

Obviously development workers have other tools at their disposal and there is no intention in this manual to suggest that a research approach is appropriate to all situations. It has certain built-in disadvantages in many development situations. Where many people do not read or write, or have been taught not to criticise but to accept 'truths', research approaches are difficult for them to get to grips with. Although there are many methods which can enable non-literate people to contribute to data collection and to some extent analysis, a research approach will tend to introduce barriers to their full participation. This does not mean that research is illegitimate in these situations – agencies need information for their own reasons. But research is unlikely to be the best method when the key aim is to empower people directly in this situation.

If you are planning a participatory project, remember that there are many different ways of working alongside community members to investigate their issues and help them to express their needs and views.

EXAMPLE

Making videos about dynamite fishing in Tanzania

Dynamite fishing is a major problem on the coast of Tanzania. In 1994, a group of Tanzanian fishermen and women learnt at a conference that the authorities typically blamed the environmental destruction on the local fishermen's ignorance. During the next six days, a video film was made in which they explained their perceptions of the true situation to fellow villagers and to 'an establishment of anonymous decision-makers'. Participants were able to exert control over the production of the video by watching and approving the results of the day's shooting every evening. 'People... want to speak loud and clear. Many of those who have never had access to modern, public fora seem to love the concept of being seen saying something for the records'. The participants revealed the dynamiting of fish and the destruction of the local marine environment, even giving the names of corrupt police and dynamite dealers.

When Johansson returned to Tanzania in 1996, he discovered that the video had had an extraordinary impact. It had not produced a miracle policy shift protecting future fishing grounds and coral reefs. But it had engendered community mobilisation on a massive scale, bridging regional and ethnic divisions between villagers and instilling confidence and inspiring action, only for them to be let down time and time again by corrupt local police and fisheries officers. Johansson writes that 'the video really did make policymakers listen to villagers, even when they seemed unable to act. Many politicians and officials came from the mainland... and had no idea what a reef is (they thought it was just rocks). Fishermen showed them blasted and intact reef from a boat through a mask. They came back full of stories of how corals grow like a forest, that it's a fragile structure, home of the fish. We have an amazing video statement of an almost shocked MP who makes analogies with burning a forest or bombing a village.' (Johansson, 1994; Holland with Blackburn, 1998).

A range of creative approaches can be effective, as can more traditional community development methods.

Some poor and disadvantaged communities, both in the UK and in parts of the South, complain of too much research being done on them. Researchers appear regularly in people's homes, asking similar sets of questions, and nothing seems to be done as a result. This syndrome obviously adds insult to injury for the community members, and is a scandalous waste of resources. There is no excuse for undertaking research, especially with people who are as hard-pressed for time as are those living in poverty, without first making sure that the information you need is not already available.

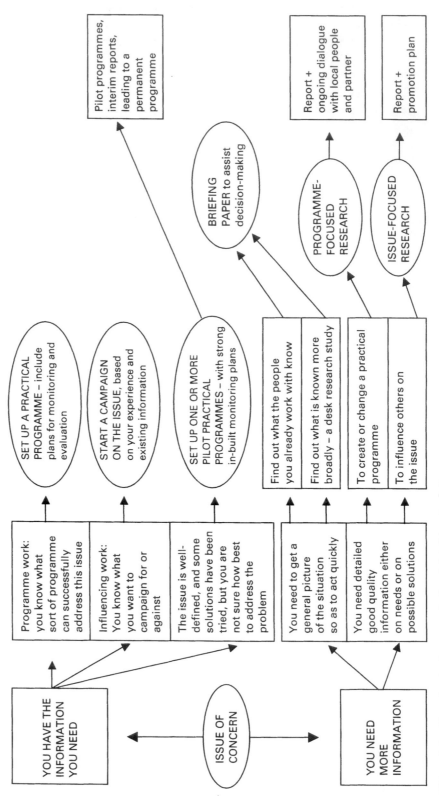

Figure 1.1 Flowchart – is research the right thing to do?

Table 1.1 Conditions for research

When research may be an effective approach	When research is not likely to be helpful
When no one has much information on a situation	When it is clear what needs to be done, but no one is getting on with it
When there is only 'anecdotal' evidence of a 'hidden' problem	When your programme is trying to decide where to start, in a known environment
When the group you are working with feels that their point of view has not been heard	When political conflict or state repression is particularly intense
When policy-makers, e.g. in government, are considering a policy change and want to investigate its possible impact	When communities have already been the subject of many research projects
When it is important to show that you have accurately represented people's views	When the primary concern is to increase people's participation, and build their personal development, rather than to act upon research findings (Kirby, 1999)
When you know that past attempts to address this issue through programmes have made mistakes	Where there are no resources to follow up research with any action
	To avoid making a decision

What role will your research play?

Research can fulfil different roles in a process of working for change. It will be helpful to be clear where in the process you think you are, and what you hope to achieve through the research – See Table 1.2.

Each of these situations has its own key requirements for how the work is carried out. You need to think of the research work as closely linked into either advocacy processes, perhaps an organised campaign to influence policy, or to programme planning and development. To be an effective part of development work, research needs to be planned and carried out in co-operation with others with related responsibilities.

If in doubt …

Perhaps you are not sure that research is the right approach to the problem you hope to address? Research is not the only way of investigating a question,

Table 1.2 Different possible roles for research in development processes

Policy-focused research	Programme-focused research
Raising a new issue in the public domain	Investigating the needs of a community, or specific group of people
Putting forward a new perspective on a 'live' issue	Investigating the need for a particular programme
Producing strong evidence of the benefit or harm of a particular policy	Demonstrating convincingly the effectiveness of a particular programme (evaluation)
Drawing together learning from different studies to support a policy position	

and it may not be the most useful one for some purposes. At times, a much simpler investigation is all that is required, more like what a journalist might do to gain some greater understanding of an issue, or to dramatise it for their readers. Calling it 'research' can over-complicate the task you need to undertake.

If in doubt before starting a full-scale research project, you could try:

- **Small-scale internal fact-finding:**
  Find out what people inside your organisation and those working closely with you already know about the issue – and what they think should be done. This can be done more or less formally (a meeting, a short questionnaire), as appropriate.
- **A mini-literature search and review:**
  Spend some time collecting existing research on the issue you are interested in, and write a summary of what you have found out. Make an effort to contact people who have grappled with the same types of problem in different geographical areas.
- **Carry out a small pilot study:**
  After clarifying the research questions you want to investigate, carry out a small study to get some general impressions of the information you could collect. For example, carry out five interviews with local people on the issue you are interested in; or raise it as an issue at a group meeting which is already scheduled, and facilitate a short discussion on the subject. Make sure you record the data you get properly, as you may need it later, if you proceed to do larger research.
- **Test the idea for the research project:**
  If you are concerned about committing your organisation to a research project, it may be helpful to carry out a SWOT (Strengths, Weaknesses,

Opportunities, Threats) analysis on the project, making guesses about future outcomes (Gosling with Edwards, 1995), and to do the same for any alternative strategy you can think of.

The amount of energy you put into research-type exercises should depend upon the use you intend to make of the material you collect. There is no one recipe for research for development work – what you do needs to be appropriate to its purpose (see Chapter 5: Planning for Effective Research – Preparing to Write the Brief).

Key points from this chapter

This chapter has aimed to show the positive contribution that research can make to development work. It suggests that development workers have an important role in identifying issues that require investigation, and in planning and carrying out research. The contested nature of ideas about research is discussed, and readers are encouraged to aim to understand these issues sufficiently not to be intimidated in defending their methods. It is important to be conscious of the various issues of power inequality that are involved in research work. Different approaches to research in development work are considered in relation to what they say about how change comes about. There is also discussion of how to tell when research is the best approach to take to a problem, and what other courses of action might be considered.

CHECKLIST   Using research in development work

✓ Research can be a powerful tool in working for social change, and can be used in a variety of different ways

✓ Development workers need a good understanding of research because it is important in their jobs whenever they need to produce, or assess, evidence for any claim about what is really going on here

✓ There is debate about most research issues!

✓ Development workers do many similar things to researchers, but their training leads them to approach these tasks in different ways

✓ A research perspective can contribute a questioning attitude, a concern to hear people's views accurately, an analytical approach, and can help us to reflect on how our own actions determine the responses we get

✓ It is very important to build research capacity in the South and in disadvantaged communities in the North

✓ Research is only a useful approach in some situations – there are others where it would be useless, wasteful, and possibly harmful

✓ If in doubt as to whether research is needed, there are a number of things you can do, short of a full-blown research project, which will give you a better sense of the issues in question

Further Reading

Mikkelsen, B. (1995) *Methods for Development Work and Research: A guide for practitioners.* New Delhi, Thousand Oaks, London: Sage.

This book was written to help development practitioners whose research proposals were being rejected by Danish research funders due to lack of knowledge of research methods. Based on long experience, it offers practical guidance and critical reflection on methods for development work and for research.

Thomas, A., Chataway J. and Wuyts, M. (eds) (1998) *Finding Out Fast: Investigative skills for policy and development.* London: Open University/Sage.

A collection of articles aimed at development managers who use policy-related research in their work. Helpful discussion of the place of research in policy processes.

Bulmer, M. (1982) *The Uses of Social Research: Social investigation in public policy-making.* London: George Allen and Unwin.

Offers models for thinking about the relationship between research and decision-making in public policy.

2 How is Research Used in Development Work?

This chapter gives some of the background the reader will need to feel confident in working with researchers, briefly describing some of the ideas behind some important schools of thought about research. It suggests that rather than searching for the 'right' methods of research, we should accept that a wide range of approaches can be useful for different purposes.

In development work, research is undertaken for two main types of reason – firstly to inform the programme (either as needs assessment before starting or as monitoring and evaluation as the programme develops), and secondly to learn more about issues with a view to influencing policy. This distinction is explored, and will crop up throughout the manual, as the primary purpose of the work has important consequences for the way in which research needs to be carried out.

Next, we will look at some of the issues involved in research for programme development and finally at what is known about research that has influence on policy, and how this is done.

2.1 So what's the right approach to research for development work?

This manual would have been a lot simpler to write if it was setting out to sell a particular set of research methods. Participatory methods, for example, are clearly of great value for development work, and it would be quite straightforward to advocate these, and explain how to use them.[1] But actually there is value for development workers in a number of approaches to research.

At times, for example, an agency needs to argue an unpopular case at the political level. Then it is helpful to use evidence which will be accepted as valid by a variety of powerful players. It is not a good idea to set up a situation in which you have to defend the case itself and at the same time the validity of the evidence, where an issue is hotly contested. It can be worth using more conventional methods where they can make an important point convincingly.

---

[1]See recommended reading for Chapter 3.

A musical interlude

Perhaps we can think of research as a bit like music. Having the privilege to live in a multicultural society, in our house we have different music for different moments. We might put on reggae to put people at ease, classical Indian flute music to create calm, some Scottish folk music to give us energy. There is, to me, no point in arguing the virtues of one type of music against another – they are not in competition, and each obeys its own rules. Each kind of music can be played well or badly, and even those of us without any great musical training can tell the difference.

There are of course people who only appreciate Mozart or Bob Marley. And most of us find traditions very remote from those we grew up with difficult to tune into. But if we don't try, we miss a lot that is going on in the world.

Research and music are both about communication and coherence – if it doesn't try to reach you, if there's no emotional link to anything you know about, you won't listen to it. Equally, if it doesn't hold together, and make sense in itself, it is unattractive, and the listener turns away.

My point is that we need to appreciate a wide range of styles of research, and that, conversely, researchers of all sorts need to make efforts to make their work accessible to a wide audience. The most traditional methods, for example the census, asking very simple questions, may be totally appropriate for some purposes, for instance to establish what the balance is in the numbers of females and males in the population. But to begin to explain any imbalance, it would be important to investigate many factors in a variety of ways. What social structures surround the survival of girls and boys? Are there any medical reasons behind any imbalance? Is female infanticide occurring? Finding answers to these questions obviously involves a more subtle approach.

In offering examples here, I am always aware that there are objections which can be made to any given approach. For example, it is now well shown that records of deaths are not in fact necessarily the 'simple facts' we might expect them to be. A suicide or indeed an infanticide will often not be recorded as such, for understandable social reasons. The fact that such statistics are unreliable does not mean that they are meaningless and should not be collected. Research is always imperfect. It is part of the scientific tradition, and a very valuable part, that we treat any 'truths' we arrive at as provisional, and open to question. Quality is defined by the internal logic of a piece of research, and by how well it is defended. There is no absolute standard of right and wrong out there.

2.2 Two major research approaches

Research is all about the power to define reality. To say that you are doing research suggests that you are undertaking systematic investigation with a

narrative
is, top

view to making some claim about the world. But different research traditions see this issue differently. Traditional scientific research tends to deny the power dynamics around research. It claims that *the scientist is a disinterested, unbiased observer, who can produce objective truths about reality*, a reality which straightforwardly exists out there to be observed. Social science which follows this tradition, such as mainstream psychology, aims to make social research as similar as possible to the natural sciences, such as physics or chemistry. Social research of this type is often called 'positivist' research (see Glossary for definitions of unfamiliar terms).

More recent approaches in the social sciences take a different view entirely. They challenge the view that a truly objective science is possible, showing how the observer's standpoint affects what is seen at every level. We tend to see what we are looking for. Hence, reality is to some extent constructed by our views of it. These traditions go by many names, which are inclined unfortunately to be rather daunting to the uninitiated. A few widely used ones are social constructionism, phenomenology, critical theory, grounded theory, and postmodernism.

What these traditions have in common is that they are interested in *the ideas people themselves generate*, rather than looking at social reality through categories determined by the researcher. Definitions are often challenged. They aim to reduce bias through what is called 'reflexivity' – open reflection on the researcher's own point of view and how it influences their perceptions. Background assumptions about people and situations can be brought to the fore and examined. The 'taken for granted' aspects of people's lives can be brought into question. 'Hidden' issues can be brought into the public sphere in a relatively safe way.

There are many elements to the inequalities of power which create, and are created by, poverty and disadvantage. Economics, social structure, and access to natural resources are important. But part of the problem for less powerful groups of people is that their reality is not visible to others. Often, when people are asked about their situation, oppressed people will say that one of the worst things about it is other people's view of them. For example, disabled people find others' attitudes just as oppressive, and perhaps more personally damaging, than inaccessible buildings and transport systems.

Naming something can in itself have an important impact. When feminists began to look at women as an oppressed group, it enabled women to reconsider issues they had thought of as individual personal problems, and see them as part of a wider social system. This released a huge amount of energy and creativity. Having a name for one's situation can help to make sense of it and perhaps change it.

To give a simple example of how these different approaches affect research processes, let us take the case of a development worker who wants to commission a study of the situation of children in a longstanding refugee camp. A traditional, positivist approach might weigh and measure children, and would be likely to use well-tested questionnaires or checklists to see how the children are faring in relation to standard measures of child development.

These would include standards for psychological adjustment, social behaviour, educational achievement etc. They might interview parents and/or those who work with the children, looking for evidence of maladjustment, on standard indicators. They would want to know how many children go to school, how many suffer from physical or mental illness, how many commit offences, how many teenage pregnancies occur.

These are measures of quality of life which are pre-defined by other (powerful) people who are removed from the particular situation. Teenage pregnancy is one example of a measure which is widely taken in the North to be obviously a 'bad thing', but where the young women involved may not agree that it is a problem (Phoenix, 1991).

A 'social constructionist' researcher might instead spend time in the camp getting to know the people and observing the situation. Whilst they might seek broad information about indicators of health and welfare, they would concentrate on what the children themselves and their parents think about their situation. They would ask open questions about what children and adults consider to be the benefits and drawbacks of life in the refugee camp for children. Keen to avoid making assumptions, they might not take it as given that life in the camp is worse for the children than the place they came from, but would ask questions about this. Aware of power dynamics, they would try a variety of ways to enable children (and mothers) in particular to voice their point of view, away from the 'community leaders' as well as the camp authorities.

Both approaches have their strengths. Since expert views, and international standards of child welfare, are valued within donor agencies, a positivist report might be effective in attracting funds to a particular programme. On the other hand the second approach is more likely to generate action by the refugees themselves, and might identify issues which could be missed by an approach that makes assumptions about what the problems are for people.

Quantitative and qualitative research

The major divide in research approaches is sometimes presented as between quantitative and qualitative research.

As can be read from the words used, the first is seen as concerned with numbers and the second more with meanings. A quantitative approach asks how many people share a particular characteristic, or hold a particular view. A qualitative one looks more at what people think and feel, and why. However it is not usually helpful to debate the virtues of one approach against the other. Most research for practical purposes contains some element of both, and this is how it should be. It will be more useful to understand the philosophical basis for each general approach – positivism and social constructionism – as discussed above. These issues will be explored further in Chapter 16: Choosing Methods.

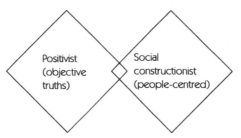
2.3   Types of research for development work

Many kinds of activity that could be called research are undertaken as part of development work. People use a variety of terminologies to refer to these different activities, and there is a tendency for new jargon to be invented every few years, describing different methods or packages of methods. Do not be downhearted! With a grasp of the most common methods and the key issues which surround them, it will be easy enough to understand any new 'magic formula' which comes along.

Choosing one of many ways of dividing up this complex field, I suggest that there are fundamentally two types of research that are commonly carried out in development work: that which relates primarily to the programme itself, and that which addresses issues beyond the programme. Issue-focused research is usually undertaken with the intention of having an influence on policy. See Figure 2.1 for a visual representation of its typography.

Within each of these circles, there are a great variety of kinds of research, but they all share some key characteristics, related to the final purpose of the exercise. Is it fundamentally to inform the programme? Or does it seek to influence policy more broadly by gathering information on issues? Participatory research may fit into either of the two circles. There can be a greater or lesser degree of participation within research for the programme or research for policy influence. In participatory research, as in all other research, it is still important to keep a focus on the final purpose of the exercise.

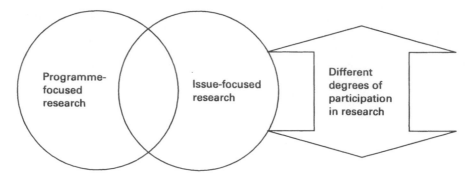

Figure 2.1 The two main types of research for development work

However the diagram shows two overlapping circles, because there are important areas of overlap between programme-focused research, and research on issues.

You cannot always put a piece of work in one category or the other. One common area of overlap is where needs assessment or community profiling research is undertaken with a view to broader influence as well as to plan a specific programme of work. NGOs often hope to demonstrate the impact of national or international policy on people through a study of a particular community. Another case in point is where evaluation research is designed not only to enable the organisation itself to learn the lessons of a project, but to demonstrate the value or problems of a particular way of working to a wider audience. This manual will therefore include further guidance on these areas.

The reason why it is helpful to look at the two types of research separately is that the main purpose of the project should dictate many things about how the work is undertaken. If you sit on the fence and hope that it will achieve everything, you may find that neither purpose is properly served.

This manual will focus mainly on research for policy influence, because Save the Children's *Toolkits: a practical guide to assessment, monitoring, review and evaluation* (Gosling with Edwards, 1995) offers guidance on many areas of programme-related research. The key task for this new manual is to assist development workers in undertaking research on issues, and it will avoid duplicating material already published in *Toolkits*.

This chapter focuses on the purposes of research rather than how it is carried out, so I have divided up research approaches in relation to the reason for undertaking it, not its technical features. For example, in the category 'research for advocacy', you might find anything from a public opinion poll, to an ecologist's study of environmental damage in an area, to peer research by young people. Equally community-needs assessment can be undertaken in a wide variety of ways, from large-scale surveys to focus group meetings.

This is a different kind of distinction from the one discussed above in Section 2.2, where we looked at the difference between positivist and social constructionist approaches. The latter 27 refer to whole intellectual traditions – theories of knowledge and methodologies. In this section we are focusing, more pragmatically, on the reasons for undertaking the research, the uses you wish to put it to. You can have research for either programme or policy purposes which works within either tradition. Equally both types may use qualitative and/or quantitative methods – either may involve surveys, interviews, focus groups, or observation.

Programme-focused and issue-focused research

The next section looks at some of the characteristics of the two types of research for development work. Many, many different terms are used to describe different types of research work used for practical purposes. Programme-focused research includes:

- Needs assessment
- Community profiling
- Stakeholder analysis
- Action research
- Programme evaluation
- Participatory research – people defining their own issues
- Participatory Learning and Action – PLA (was Participatory Rural Appraisal).

EXAMPLE

Assessing the needs of young people and of disabled children in Serb Sarajevo

The aim of this project, looking at the needs of young people and of disabled children, was to demonstrate a model of community-based social welfare that includes partnership between the statutory agencies and the communities they serve. The project was conducted in Serb Sarajevo, Republika Srpska, where close to one-third of the population is still internally displaced. The project was initiated by Save the Children UK in the context of an agreement for action by an adviser on Child Welfare and Protection, seconded for one year to the Ministry of Health and Social Welfare, Public Fund for Children Protection, and the Centre for Social Welfare in Serb Sarajevo.

Using a community profile approach, the first step was to carry out research within the community that would assess the needs, and present solutions to the needs, of youth and of disabled children, as seen by them and by others in the community. The priority was not to produce some academic research, but to facilitate a process whereby local people gained self-confidence, learned about their community, could be involved in assessing local needs and used the results to progress action.

The research ensured that it recruited a cross-section of representatives from the youth community and parents as advocates for children with disabilities. The youth group consisted of ten young people aged between 16 and 21, five female and five male. They were from varied backgrounds in terms of academic achievements but all shared the problems of being displaced and living in the area. The advocates for the children with disabilities consisted of six parents – five mothers and one father. None of them had any experience in any kind of research work. Training was provided in peer research.

The training involved a basic grounding in research methods including questionnaire formulation, interview methods, ethics, an understanding of the difference between quantitative and qualitative research, and an introduction to concepts of community. It was based largely around group discussions and involved sessions in which the groups talked of their own views of the area they lived in and consciously reflected on their ideas about important local issues.

Each of the groups chose a method they felt was appropriate to the task to be undertaken. The youth group decided upon a semi-structured interview approach based upon a questionnaire and with some assistance agreed a set of open-ended questions. They carried out their interviews in cafes, in the street, in public buildings, and in people's homes.

The youth research team conducted their research amongst others who were of a similar age or younger than themselves. Their sample was selected by convenience and by 'snowballing', which is a method that reaches out from their own circle of friends to the wider community making contacts by word of mouth. The young people conducted a total of 175 semi-structured interviews. The sample for the children with disabilities group was taken from a list provided by the Centre for Social Welfare, and in total 24 families with disabled children were visited and interviewed by the group.

The group of parents decided that more in-depth interviews would be appropriate for their work with parents of children with disabilities. After some discussion and assistance they selected relevant questions as prompts. They carried out the interviews in the respondents' homes, where the respondents might feel more at ease.

When the interviews were completed, the field researchers analysed the information they had collected, first grouping the responses, then quantifying the data and selecting illustrative quotes for inclusion in the report. The report, 'Community appraisal of life in Serb Sarajevo for young people and children with disabilities', gave an impeccable often painful description of the life in the community seen through eyes of its members. It highlighted precisely and in the most subtle detail the life problems for disabled children and youth; at the same time it offered realistic and practical solutions. The issues of unemployment, poor accommodation, criminality, education, and transportation were the most important ones.

After being published the report was presented to the representatives of the local community and potential donors. For Save the Children UK it was the guiding light for projects that followed and are still going on. The direct and immediate impact of the research was the establishment of an organisation of youth and disabled children 'Return our smile' that in the course of two years evolved into a reliable partner of Save the Children UK work in the region of Serb Sarajevo. This organisation now runs a computer school, gym, playroom for disabled and non-disabled children, issues a monthly bulletin for young people, organises plays with a local theatre, and does many other things. They got the space from the community – a ruined building in need of reconstruction and 100m² for young people to use in a local school. They are building and re-building links within the community with authorities and institutions, making their voices heard and respected. One of the parents said:

"I like that the parents had a chance to give their opinion and that they, during our visits, showed their interest in something being done for these children. If we as parents would organise ourselves, we could, with somebody's help, improve the standard of these children in some way. The parents are really embittered with the work of the local authorities to date, who do not care much about these children. I do hope that some changes will be made with the help of our research."

Issue-focused research for policy influence can include:

- Research for campaigning – to 'prove a point'.
- Thematic research looking at experience in a number of countries.
- Reviewing what is known on an issue.
- Making the voices of less powerful people heard by decision-makers.
- Reframing an issue – new ways of seeing.

EXAMPLE

Influencing policy and practice – the Child Labour Project, Sialkot, Pakistan

In 1996, following media campaigns by US-based and European pressure groups against child labour in Pakistan's football stitching industry, Save the Children was invited to join a coalition of organisations working to solve the problem. Initial visits to the area – Sialkot district in the east of Pakistan – and discussions with children, families, local NGOs and industrialists called into question some of the claims on which campaign work had been based. For example, early discussions showed no evidence that children were working as bonded labourers.

Although several other organisations had commissioned studies of child labour in football manufacture, it was clear that none had discussed the issue in any depth with child football stitchers, nor with women who make up a high proportion of stitchers. However, there was strong pressure to act fast and there was concern that action might well be taken on the basis of incorrect information and thus lead to an ineffective programme, or worse, one that actually undermined children's and families' wellbeing. It was important to undertake an in-depth, rigorous situation analysis to check the accuracy of early impressions, and of the different claims being made about the situation of child football stitchers.

Furthermore, child labour is a politically and emotionally charged issue at the best of times, even more so in this case with a constant western media spotlight. This meant being sure the research was rigorous – carefully designed so that it provided an adequate basis for drawing conclusions, carried out accurately and carefully analysed to be sure that the findings were based on the data that had been collected. One of the main audiences, the international and local football manufacturers, was particularly interested in the numbers of children involved. It was therefore important that the research was carried out on a large enough scale to provide a basis for estimating the numbers involved. Because football stitching takes place throughout a district of 2600 sq. km, Save the Children felt it was important to interview people from a sample of towns and villages across the district, to illuminate differences in working conditions, rather than concentrating on those closest to Sialkot city, as other investigations had done. Finally the researchers were aware that numbers carry weight. Overall 428 households were surveyed in 30 villages and 2 towns, and 745 children and 1004 adults were interviewed. These villages were selected on a stratified random basis to give coverage of the entire district.

The survey had two parts: one collected detailed information about family size and income, numbers of children stitching, their ages, how long they had worked, how much they earned, and their school attendance. The second asked respondents more open-ended questions, such as what is your view on children stitching footballs?, or what would be the effects of phasing out child labour? In Pakistan, as in many other cultures, it is common for male heads of household to answer questionnaires on behalf of their families. It could be difficult to find out women's and children's views of their situation through the survey. Save the Children also wanted to provide opportunities for people – men, women, and children – to discuss issues related to child labour, education and the football industry more freely. Forty-six different focus group discussions were therefore organised. The groups were based on gender and involvement in football stitching and in the case of children also age and school attendance. For example, some of the group discussions included girl stitchers aged under 10 who attended school, or boy stitchers aged 10–13 who did not; mothers and fathers of child football stitchers, and community leaders. (Save the Children, 1997).

EXAMPLE

The impact of water metering on low-income families in England

Since the privatisation of the water industry for England and Wales in 1989, there has been increasing concern about access to water in these countries for families on low incomes. Water prices rose steeply while benefits levels increased only modestly. An adequate supply of clean water is essential to health. Access to clean water has been a cornerstone of the UK's public health policy since the mid-nineteenth century. However government policy was moving towards introducing metering more and more widely, which Save the Children feared would have serious consequences for low-income families. Obviously using the price mechanism to press customers to save water puts far greater pressure on those on low incomes. It seemed likely also that the stress would be greatest for those with more children.

The study aimed to investigate the impact of water metering on children in low-income families. It was primarily qualitative in nature, seeking to find out to what extent families change their behaviour when their water is charged for on a metered basis. We asked for parents' own views and also looked at their water bills. Seventy-one low-income families living on two newly built estates in outer London were interviewed – meters are now installed with all new building.

Families reported on their water bills, whether they used less water now that they had meters, what they cut down on, the effects on children, their views on metering, and problems they had in paying the bills. The report gives statistical information about the actual bills people were paying, the extent of their debts, and their accounts of whether and how they save water. It also quotes their opinions about being forced to save water in this way.

The research attracted a great deal of media attention when it was launched, and it has been quoted repeatedly in Parliamentary debates on the subject. Legislation introduced which addressed some of the problems the research highlighted. (Cunningham et al, 1996).

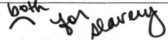

Table 2.1   Key features of programme- and policy-focused research

Key features of programme-focused/ needs-assessment research	Key features of issue-focused research for policy influence
• Should lead to action for change in the immediate area	• Should lead to action for change beyond the local area
• Appropriate focus dictated by practical aspects of the programme, not by theory	• The more clearly defined the research question the more effective the research will be
• Joint working with partner agencies likely to be most productive	• Crucial to be clear about the audience and what is required to influence them
• Participation by 'the researched' will lead to greater ownership of the findings and hence greater likelihood of action being taken	• May involve direct participation by 'the researched', or may be carried out to support a participatory advocacy process
• Research process needs to be managed close to the programme	• Researchers need to be or become knowledgeable about the broader context of the issue in question – ie investigate what is known already beyond the local area
• Researchers need to have an understanding/experience of the issues faced by practitioners	

One key message to be drawn from dividing up research for development work into these two types is that the overall purpose of the exercise needs to be the central factor in deciding on the methods to be used and how the research is undertaken. Throughout this manual, there will be reference back to the distinction between research focused on informing the programme and research on issues aimed at policy influence. Because of the different audiences involved, and the different level of scrutiny which can be expected, these two types of research have different needs at many stages of the research process. Table 2.1 describes some of the key differences.

> **COMMON PITFALLS 2.1**
>
> Expecting policymakers to be interested in research you do for your own programme planning purposes

> **COMMON PITFALLS 2.2**
>
> Expecting a study of an issue to automatically tell you what the programme should be doing about it

We will next discuss consultation with communities, and some other activities that are a bit like research, but which may not exactly be research. After that, the following two sections look in more depth at the two main types of research for development work – for programme development and for policy influence.

2.4 Consultation with communities – is it research?

Consultation is an important activity for development workers. It is a core element of their day-to-day work to seek to involve local people in decision-making of various kinds. A consultation process is not the same as a research process. A dictionary definition of 'to consult' is 'to have regard to; to ask the advice or opinion of; to refer to; to deliberate together; to serve as a consultant'.[2] Consultation is about taking advice from people, asking their opinions, and not just about recording their experiences or collecting information.

In the UK, the Labour government has promoted community consultation on a range of issues, for example on health service priorities. Consultation, or user involvement, where service users are actively engaged in giving feedback on decisions relating to a service, often uses research-type methods, but it is not the same thing as research. It is a directly political process, and its constraints are about political realities – research has different priorities. One important distinction to keep in mind here is that in some cases the intention is to consult people because they have had a particular experience, and in others simply as members of the public. However there is some common ground between the two kinds of process, including the necessity of:

---

[2] WWWebster Dictionary, Meriam-Webster, Incorporated 1998, World Wide Web.

- being fair about who is involved;
- asking questions in a way which is seen to be unbiased;
- ensuring that people are consulted in a way which enables them to participate properly – clear communication;
- reporting findings accurately and honestly.

Thus research traditions may have many useful things to teach those involved in consultation, but consultation exercises can be killed stone dead if they are turned into research projects. Research ideas can impose unnecessary constraints on consultation processes. Their 'life' comes from the real engagement of people with the issues. For example for a consultation process it may be appropriate to consult with people who are easier to contact than others, while a research project which aimed for findings which could be generalised to other populations would need to be more rigorous in its sampling processes. 'Calling it research' can create problems rather than help people. Organisations need to do the consultation they can afford, and will be able to listen to – there is no point in elaborating these processes so that they become overwhelmingly difficult and expensive.

Many of the methods described in this manual could be useful for consultation processes. Consultation can be done both for programme development and for policy influence. The key question in assessing consultation as well as research is this: how confident do you feel about taking action on the basis of this evidence?

See also Chapter 18.4 for more on consultation.

2.5   Using research for programme development

The most common reason for development workers to use research in their work is to inform the planning for their programme. They may want to look in more depth at what issues are perceived to be important by local people, or to understand more about why things are as they are. Sometimes this will mean a broad look at a wide range of issues seen to be affecting a community, sometimes research will be targeted at a particular issue, for example health care for young children. Increasingly, development workers like to engage the community directly in the process of deciding priorities for their work, rather than regarding it as primarily a technical exercise.

Included here are processes like stakeholder analysis, where a development worker systematically investigates the views and plans of agencies, individuals, and groups which have a 'stake', an interest, in a particular issue (See 18.2). This stands on the borderline between research and planning. It can be done in a more or less formal way. There are texts giving specific guidance on many approaches within this category of work, for example on community profiling (Burton, 1993; Hawtin et al, 1994) and on Participatory Learning and Action PLA (see 18.7 below).

At times, programme-oriented research is required to investigate the impact of interventions. It cannot be taken for granted that aid efforts are effective, and there can be unintended consequences.

This area of work is covered in Save the Children's *Toolkits: a practical guide to assessment, monitoring, review and evaluation* (Gosling with Edwards, 1995), and this manual will not repeat material contained there.

The next section looks at the use of research to influence policy, a type of research which is increasing in development work, and which is more fully described in this manual.

2.6   Using research to influence policy

So when and how does research influence policy? This is not an easy thing to find out, as it is difficult to identify what degree of influence particular research evidence has on particular decisions.

Activity 2.2

Which research projects have influenced you?

Let us start by drawing on your experience of research within your own work.

Either alone or with a group of colleagues, brainstorm a list of research projects which have had an influence on you. What has really affected your thinking? It may be helpful to include areas outside your immediate professional concerns – think also about research which may have influenced choices you make in your own life. Then think about why this research was able to influence you.

Brainstorm:
What research has influenced you?
Why did it have this influence?

Activity 2.3

Assessing the influence of research projects

Identify three issue-focused research projects aimed at influencing policy that you are familiar with. They need not be ones you undertook in your own organisation, but they need to be finished, as we want to focus on the influence they have had. They can be at local, national, or international level. Consider what evidence you can use to assess what influence these projects had on policy. For example, they may have led to a change in the law, or to changes in the allocation of resources. Think about what features of these research projects, in your view, helped them to have an influence.

	Evidence of influence on policy	Features which enabled this research to have influence
Project 1		
....		
Project 2		
....		
Project 3		
....		

Was it difficult to assess influence? Or perhaps you had difficulty in identifying projects you were confident had an influence. You may like to make a note of ways *not* to have an influence!

Features which prevent research from having an influence	How could influence be increased?

If you can involve some colleagues in this activity, ask them to make their own assessments of the same projects. Discuss together the ways in which you have judged influence. Consider what this means for planning for influence.

Some researchers have studied the issue of the influence research has on policy (Weiss, 1977; Finch, 1986). Academic research often has less impact than researchers might hope. However it may be that those directly engaged in development work are in a better position to set up research which is relevant to important issues, and to feed findings into policy processes in a way which increases their influence.

In a study of various research projects, Weiss and Bucuvalas (1977) found the following factors increased the influence of research:

- Research quality
- Action orientation (that is, research having direct and practical implications for action, and clearly formulated recommendations)
- Challenge to the status quo
- Conformity to user expectations
- Relevance
- Timeliness

Quality

Quality is a key issue in terms of research utilisation. This is not only a formal issue of adherence to rules, but much more fundamentally it is the question of whether the research can be believed. In relation to research for development it may be more useful to talk about credibility or 'trustworthiness' (Oakley, 1999), than about the standard technical terms 'validity' and 'reliability'. Chapter 4 will look in more detail at the importance of quality in research for development.

Timing

Timeliness is also important. The following example, taken from an impact assessment report by the Department for International Development on a project which looked at DDT use in Zimbabwe, shows how scientifically excellent research can miss its time in terms of having an influence.

EXAMPLE

Too late: DDT use in Zimbabwe

DDT was widely and successfully used to control tsetse fly in Zimbabwe in the 1960s and 70s. By the 1980s its use there had become controversial, partly because of the effects of its residues on non-target wildlife and partly because of its persistence in temperate climates where it was already banned. The objective of the research was to produce a better understanding of the environmental costs of using DDT vis-à-vis alternative insecticides for ground spraying against tsetse. The project was implemented between 1987 and 1992 at a cost of £866,000.

The evaluation of the project found that it was successful in terms of its immediate scientific objectives, but not to have achieved benefits commensurate with its costs. It is unlikely to have a significant impact on tsetse control policy and practice. Higher level policymakers were insufficiently involved, and the research design was too narrow to be as useful as it might have been. However even if the project's shortcomings had been recognised and addressed, it was set up too late to influence decisions on DDT use within Zimbabwe, and might never have been able to do so because of the public prejudice against DDT. The policy debate was too far advanced to allow the research findings to have any impact (Department for International Development, 1998).

Challenge to the status quo versus conformity to expectations

Looking back at the factors identified by Weiss and Bucuvalas (1977), there may seem to be a contradiction between the factors 'challenge to the status quo' and 'conformity to user expectations'. The conformity factor is defined by Weiss and Bucuvalas as dealing with support to the individual policymaker's values and construction of reality, their own experience and knowledge. The challenge factor relates to existing assumptions and institutional arrangements as well as research which implies the need for a major change in philosophy, organisation, or services, and raises new issues or offers a new perspective.

Weiss and Bucuvalas were surprised at finding that research which offered a challenge to existing ideas was felt by the decision-makers (in the US government) whom they questioned to be more useful than work which reinforced their expectations. They comment that

'These findings suggest ... that research is useful not only when it helps to solve problems – when it provides ideas and information that can be instrumentally applied to recognised problems – but research is also useful when it questions existing perspectives and definitions of the problematic ... Even if the implications are not feasible or politically acceptable at present, such research helps to develop alternative constructions of reality. In time, these alternative images of reality can yield new ways of addressing policy problems and new programmes and procedures for coping with needs.

'Thus the definition of "use" is broadened. Research that challenges accepted ideas, arrangements and programmes obviously cannot be put to work in a direct and immediate way ... Yet, decision-makers say it can contribute to their work and the work of other appropriate decision-makers. It can *enlighten* them.' (Weiss and Bucuvalas, 1977; emphasis in original)

Giving a new perspective

Finch (1986), similarly, concludes that qualitative research can be particularly important in reframing an issue, so that it is looked at in a new way. An interesting Northern example of this is Mayer Hillman's work on children's safety and freedom (Hillman et al., 1990).

EXAMPLE

Are children safer, or just less free?

Hillman noted that road accident rates for children have actually fallen in the last twenty years in England and Germany, despite the huge increase in car ownership. The explanation he proposed lies in the great restrictions which parents now place on children's independent mobility. Children of about nine and a half in these countries had in 1990 only the freedom (for example to go to school on their own) which children of seven had twenty years ago. 91 per cent of UK 7- to 11-year-old children own a bicycle, but only 35 per cent are allowed to come home from school alone. Hillman drew attention to the cost to children's health and sense of self of the restrictions traffic imposes on them (Hillman et al,1990).

A piece of work which is still controversial, but has had an important impact by reframing an issue, is that of Fairhead and Leach (1996) on environmental change in West Africa.

EXAMPLE

Deforestation in West Africa – is it a problem?

Parts of Guinée in West Africa feature patches of dense, semi-deciduous forest scattered in the savanna. These tend to be around villages. Orthodox thinking about the West African environment has viewed these as relics of previously more extensive forest cover. This has been regarded as the result of farmers destroying vegetation. This belief has been dominant since the 1890s, and has been used to justify repressive measures against the inhabitants' land-use practices.

Fairhead and Leach looked at the historical evidence in relation to the Kissidougou prefecture of Guinée, particularly air photographs and more recently satellite pictures, from 1952 up to 1992. They found that 'in many zones, the areas of forest and savanna vegetation have remained remarkably stable during the 40 year period which today's policy-makers consider to have been the most degrading. Where changes are discernible these predominately involve increases in forest area' (p 107). They looked further at landscape description and maps from earlier periods. These 'clearly falsify assertions of more generalised forest cover'.

The researchers further collected oral information from local inhabitants, who described how village forest islands are usually formed through human settlement and management. This could be confirmed by observation of more recent settlements. People value the forest islands around their villages for a variety of reasons, and habitually do a number of things which positively encourage their development. Fairhead and Leach suggest that rather than being half-empty, the landscape should be seen as half-full. This challenges the notion, which they trace to colonial times, of African farmers as ignorant and careless of their environment. It also challenges current policy towards farmers.

EXAMPLE

Simple targets or sustainable change in the health sector?

Save the Children's study of the sustainability of health sector improvements in very poor countries contained a critique of 'parallel programmes'. At the time, donor agencies were directing
their efforts through programmes on a single health issue, eg immunisation; HIV prevention;
family planning. However there was no support to the general infrastructure of health services,
and efforts were duplicated. By framing the issue in terms of sustainability, which everyone
agreed to be essential to progress, the project effectively focused attention on the problems
(Lafond, 1994; Smithson, 1994).

Better policy-oriented research

Janet Finch's work, which focused particularly on qualitative social research,
takes the view that the influence of such research has historically been
limited, and that this type of research has not yet fulfilled its potential for
informing policy decisions. Writing in 1986, Finch set out to say what a more
highly developed version of policy-oriented qualitative research would look
like, and her list of criteria included the following:

-   'It will not necessarily serve the agenda of those in power and those who
    'make' policy
-   It will tend to develop 'policy-oriented research' which is critical, chal
    lenging and oppositional, but not necessarily allied to a party-political
    position
-   It may well contain a specific commitment to the democratisation of
    knowledge and the skills through which it is created
-   It will be concerned with policy at all levels, including grass-roots policy
    change' (Finch, 1986)

This prescription should reassure researchers working in the voluntary
sector. It is striking that although it comes from the academic world, it high-
lights the importance of both sharing research knowledge and skills more
widely, and of the grass-roots level of change, as indicators of quality.

Effective policy-oriented research, then, can usefully learn from the
development tradition, in that it requires relationships to be built at all levels.
People learn best from processes they are actively engaged with, and this
goes for high-level policy-makers as much as it does for you and me. An
interactive approach at the planning stage and throughout the research
process, drawing in those you hope to influence, as well as those you hope
will benefit from any changes you bring about, will set a strong base from
which to build your project.

It may make us anxious to let powerful people see the 'inner workings' of a research project, but a transparent process is much more convincing than one where key processes are obscured. A strategic approach is required: analyse at what level the decisions you hope to influence are made, and then work out what sort of evidence could have influence, and who needs to be consulted. It simply does not work to carry out research, however excellent, in isolation from those who need to learn from the research and then expect them to be interested in it.

EXAMPLE

Street children in China – the importance of working in partnership with government

The phenomenon of increasing numbers of children living or working on the street, often separated from their family, has become an issue for government in China. The national Ministry of Civil Affairs and the Civil Affairs Bureaux at provincial and other levels has the responsibility of developing a response to this issue. In 1999 Save the Children UK began to work with departments of Civil Affairs at Ministry and provincial levels on street children's problems.

One site for the partnership between Save the Children and the government is the province of Xinjiang in north-west China. This is an autonomous region, with a high percentage of ethnic minority people, especially the Muslim Uighurs. The west of China is also a poor area, and many people migrate eastwards. Children are part of such migration both within the province and moving out: many are also trafficked. In order to understand the situation better, it was decided to carry out research in addition to testing out different methods of work.

The work on street children is a partnership using ideas and resources originating locally as the foundation for development. For research to be recognised and used in the future, and for methods of work to be sustainable and maintained it was crucial to involve government in the process of design and implementation. Save the Children facilitated a multi-sectoral meeting of interested government departments, mass organisations, and academies, such as the police, Civil Affairs Department, Street Children Centre, Women's Federation, University, Academy of Social Sciences. Participants then decided and agreed an approach to the research and the work.

The research was commissioned by Save the Children, with the Street Children Centre, and conducted by the Academy of Social Sciences. The initial results were fed directly back to Civil Affairs and other officials, and influenced the next stage of work. The involvement of a range of government departments ensured a wider awareness of the issue, and the research results heightened this further. The partnership approach meant that the results were keenly awaited and taken up for policy and practice. Without this involvement, the research would have had to be first completed, then presented to officials and government persuaded to pay attention and take it up. The involvement of local agencies in the research gave them a stake in seeking out responses to the issues raised, and to the parents and children who participated (West, 2000).

In summary, here are some key points which we can draw from the literature, and from Save the Children's experience, on the question of what makes for influential research.

CHECKLIST   For research to influence policy

   ✔ Research is of high quality
   ✔ Challenging to current assumptions, offering a new perspective
   ✔ Implications for action are clear
   ✔ Relevant to its audience
   ✔ Timely
   ✔ Clearly expressed and well-promoted
   ✔ May involve the researched in speaking for themselves
   ✔ Involves policy-makers with the research process

Activity 2.4

Assessing research projects using indicators for influence

Choose three research projects that you are familiar with. It may be helpful to use the same ones you used for Activity 2.3, but it will be best to use projects you feel did have a substantial influence. This exercise aims to help you to use the indicators identified above in practice, to consider your own experience of research for policy influence.

The table below asks first for your assessment of the overall influence of the project, and then asks you to assess it in relation to each of the items from the checklist above of factors leading to influence.

For each factor and for overall influence, enter HIGH or LOW.

	Project 1	Project 2	Project 3
Overall assessment of influence			
Research quality			
Challenge, new ideas			
Action needed made clear			
Relevance to audience			
Timeliness			
Clear expression			
Strong promotion			
Participation			

In reflecting on this activity, consider the patterns which emerge. Obviously these are complex issues, and experience will not necessarily fit tidily into boxes. Did you think of new factors that do not appear in our summary?

What did *you* think important in determining the influence the projects have had? Can timeliness be more important than quality? Challenging ideas more important than promotional effort?

If you can involve some colleagues in this activity, ask them to make their own assessments of the same projects. Discuss together the issues which arise. Make a note of ideas that arise as to how to improve the influence of your research work.

Key Points from this Chapter

A key distinction is made in this chapter between research for the programme and research on issues, for policy influence. These two broad types of research have different requirements in a number of respects. Research for policy influence is then further discussed, asking what factors lead to effective influencing work. Some findings from research into this question are presented, and readers are asked to consider this issue in relation to their own experience.

CHECKLIST   For understanding research for development work

✓ Many different approaches to research may be appropriate within development work, for different purposes

✓ Both positivist and social-constructionist research traditions can have their place in research for development work, but it is important to understand how each operates

✓ It is helpful to distinguish research aimed at informing programme development from research aimed at policy influence – the final purpose of the exercise should determine how the work is done

✓ Consultation is not the same as research, but those carrying out consultation exercises can learn from research on some issues

✓ In order to have policy influence, research needs to be of good quality, relevant, timely, oriented to action, and to present new, challenging ideas, but within a framework recognised by policy-makers

---

Further Reading

Gosling, L. with Edwards, M. (1995) *Toolkits: A practical guide to assessment, monitoring, review and evaluation*, Development Manual 5. London: Save the Children.

Concentrates on methods relating to programme planning, management, and review. Each methods section gives strengths, weaknesses, and prerequisites for success. Includes sections on involving the right people; working with issues of difference; planning in emergency situations and; setting terms of reference (oriented to programme-related exercises). The tools that are described include PLA, surveys, logical framework analysis, and cost-effectiveness analysis.

Finch, J. (1986) *Research and Policy: The uses of qualitative methods in social and educational research*. Lewes: Falmer Press.

Reflects on (primarily British) experience of research on practical policy issues, and its success or failure in influencing policy.

3 Participatory Research

Participatory research has become established in recent years as a powerful tool for development workers. This kind of research aims to enable people who traditionally have been merely the 'subjects' of research to take an active part in making their own voices heard. Participatory research may be embedded within a process of development work in a way in which traditional research would not be.

In this chapter we will look at the wide range of ways in which participation in research is possible, then at the different purposes pursued through this practice. There will then be a discussion of how to decide how much participation is appropriate, and some of the issues and problems of participatory approaches to research.

What is called participatory research covers a wide range of practices and derives from a number of different sources both in the North and in the South (Harper, 1997; Reason, 1998). This type of work goes by many names in different parts of the world – action research, practitioner research, participative inquiry, Participatory Learning and Action/Participatory Research and Action (PLA/PRA), Participatory Action and Research (PAR). It is widely recognised as a powerful way of making change in complex situations. Many of the guidelines throughout this manual come from these traditions. The core process is to enable participants to share their perceptions of a problem, to find common ground and then to engage a variety of people in identifying and testing out some possible solutions. There is a process of shared learning for all concerned. This can be particularly powerful in situations where local professionals have not felt empowered to take action about an issue. This type of work may or may not involve community members, the 'end-users' of services. However participatory research of all sorts follows some unifying principles.

At its heart is the validation of the knowledge and intelligence of ordinary people. Research and learning are seen as essentially intertwined, and attention is focused on the processes by which people actually learn, rather than on an idea of facts or truth as something that exists in the abstract. The other key common thread is an orientation to action. Participatory research has a better chance of leading to solutions to problems, because it actively involves those who best understand, and have the greatest stake in, the issues – community members themselves. The process of the research itself may be seen as more important than its outputs, in the sense of written reports and so on.

Participatory research takes a facilitative approach to respondents[1], rather than aiming to extract information from them. Researchers need to be conscious of the impact of their own attitudes, behaviour, and feelings and to have a commitment to hand over power and initiative to others. The intention is to build people's ability to understand their own situation, and to take action on their own behalf. A very wide range of different methods are used in participatory research, including pretty much the full range of methods used in the social sciences, adapted to a participatory approach. Even large-scale surveys can feed into a participative process. Participatory Learning and Action (PLA), developed for work in the South, uses an eclectic collection of methods, specialising in ones which enable people without literacy skills to express their views and knowledge.

Development workers have several major advantages in undertaking participative research. In many ways participatory research approaches are a natural group of methods for them to use. They are likely to be skilled in working with people in a facilitative way. Their orientation, too, is towards action for change. Indeed another way of looking at this area is to consider participatory research as one of a range of methods used to facilitate community members' greater participation in decision-making. It will not always be the best method to empower community members, since a research orientation (ie towards finding out information) brings with it some difficulties as well as some opportunities.

3.1   Participation for...?

Like the policy-oriented research discussed in the last section, participatory research explicitly aims to make change in society. But the way in which change takes place is seen differently, as we saw above in Section 1.5. Community members' own learning and growth in self-confidence is seen as crucial to enabling them to act more effectively on their own behalf. The key outcomes of such research may relate more to the empowerment of those concerned than to formal reports or high-level policy change – but often both types of outcomes are desired.

Participatory research may fall into either of the broad categories of research identified above – it may be programme-focused/needs assessment or policy-focused research on issues. A piece of work with either type of core purpose may fall anywhere on the continuum illustrated in Figure 3.1 below, and involve greater or lesser community participation.

---

[1]'Respondent' is used here to refer to all those people who give information as part of research exercises. They may be interviewed, take part in a group discussion, or fill in a questionnaire themselves. Their participation may be very active or minimal.

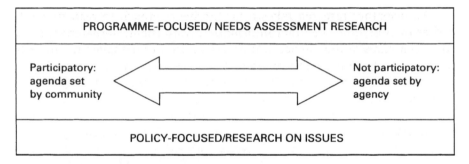

Figure 3.1   The continuum of participation in research

Since the overall aim is empowerment, it is actually key to participatory research processes to seek to make links between local communities and the larger policy framework – to influence the forces which structure people's lives. As Figure 3.1 shows, it is possible to use participatory approaches in both policy-focused projects and in programme-focused ones. We should not assume that participation is only relevant to small, local studies. The study of the contribution of older people to development (see 1.1) is an example of a highly participatory process linked to policy change at the national level.

For example, Participatory Learning and Action (PLA) has been very important internationally (see Chapter 18.7) (Theis and Grady, 1991; Gosling with Edwards, 1995). It developed out of Rapid Rural Appraisal, which was oriented towards local needs assessment processes. But increasingly it is being used in broader policy-oriented processes, for example to build up national Participatory Poverty Assessments (Holland with Blackburn, 1998).

Participation may also simply help to gather more accurate information.

EXAMPLE

The impact of HIV/AIDS on children in New Delhi, India

In some research by Save the Children in New Delhi on the impact of HIV/AIDS on children, it was felt that the involvement of children and practitioners from partner agencies helped in getting richer information. For example, the involvement of a female street educator provided information on the sexual behaviour of girls living in the streets and what sex means for them. The involvement of street boys helped to find out how information about HIV/AIDS does not translate to behaviour change, because the boys lack control over these behaviours (eg condom use in commercial sex) and over the circumstances they live in. Some of this information had never been documented before. The children were involved in getting access to other children, in collecting information, and in framing questions to be asked to other children.

3.2   Participation by...?

So whose participation are we talking about? Often, when people refer to participatory research, they are talking about community members – who might be villagers, street children, people with experience of mental health services, or women traders, for example. But it is also important to foster participation in research for development work by people involved in organisations whose support would be needed to find a solution to a problem. These may be local or national government agencies; local NGOs; professionals like doctors, nurses, or teachers; politicians... the list goes on. See the example of researching street children's problems in China, presented in Section 2.6

One of the major issues for participative research is that the inequalities of power between different groups within the community in question need to be handled with care. In any community, it is likely that women, children, and disabled people will have difficulty in getting their point of view heard. The poorest people out of any group will be in the same position. Plenty of other social groups are similarly excluded from full social participation. Declaring that you are doing a piece of work where everyone's view is important will not be enough to make it possible to overcome these problems. It is crucial that specific measures are taken to counter-balance social inequalities, or else participation can simply mean that those with the loudest voices get their way once again. These issues will be discussed in depth in Chapters 14, 15 and 19.

3.3   Participation in...?

Participatory research is not a method but more an approach, a way of working. Participatory research can involve the use of a wide range of methods, qualitative and quantitative. The term is often used to refer to research that uses methods which enable respondents to meet together and discuss issues, or which take an interactive approach, so that respondents' own point of view comes through clearly. However participation can occur in a number of different ways, such as:

- Setting the broad agenda for the research.
- Clarifying the detailed research focus.
- Responding to research which uses interactive methods.
- Undertaking fieldwork – interviews, group discussions.
- Analysis of data, making sense of findings.
- Promotion of findings.
- Appointing researchers.
- Managing the research, eg membership of advisory groups.
- Advocacy using the results of the research.

Involvement of each type has different consequences for the way in which the research needs to be conducted, for example in terms of the support offered to participating people. There is no one recipe for successful participatory research. Judgements must be made with knowledge of the purpose of the exercise, the resources available, the skills of those involved, and the nature of the issue in question.

EXAMPLE

Views on primary health care – Cowgate, England

A group of women worked together with a researcher based in a Save the Children community project in Cowgate, an isolated estate in the North East of England. The women were concerned about the standard of primary health care available in the area. After much discussion they decided to undertake a structured self-completion survey of their area, asking views on the local doctors' services. The researcher tried to persuade them to take a sample, but the women insisted that as many community members as possible should have the chance to take part, so as to give their work more credibility. Twelve hundred households were involved. The women were also actively involved in analysing the data.

   The report was very critical of existing services, and caused a stir. The group won an agreement to appoint a salaried general medical practitioner based on the estate (a very unusual arrangement), and local people were involved in the selection of the doctor. In this case the research methods used were quite conventional, but all the work was directed and to a great extent carried out by local women themselves (Dodson and Hares, 1994).

This project used particularly traditional research methods. Participatory research often uses methods which are seen as especially suitable for engaging community members' active involvement. Research within the Participatory Learning and Action (PLA) tradition uses a wide range of methods, including visual methods such as mapping, model building, and various ranking and scoring techniques (See Chapters 17.7 and 17.8, and 18.7 for more details). It aims to encourage the involvement of people who cannot read or write.

EXAMPLE

The South African participatory poverty assessment

The South African Participatory Poverty Assessment undertaken in 1995/6 aimed to improve analysis at the level of national policy. The project followed a national quantitative poverty assessment, and was characterised by a concerted effort to build participation and stakeholder inclusion into every stage of the research process, from research design and methodology to management, facilitation and synthesis. The approach entailed a partnership, albeit unequal, between community participants, NGOs, professional researchers, the national government and donor agencies.

A broad framework was set by those planning the PPA, and then proposals were invited from individuals and organisations wishing to carry out investigations into particular poverty-related issues. Research had to be qualitative and participatory, broadly within the PLA tradition, but a wide range of methods were acceptable – the key requirement was that the agencies proposing pieces of work already had a relationship with the community/ies they proposed to work with.

Nine proposals were chosen, and different types of organisations and individuals then carried out the work. A criticism was that people in poverty did not have a direct input into the agenda. Perhaps some of the proposals were shaped by organisations' engagement with those in poverty, but this was a rather indirect type of influence.

Once fieldwork was completed and reports received from the different projects, synthesis was undertaken in an open and participatory way. The key challenge was to interpret the reality reflected by the research into a useable framework for policy formulation without losing the voice of the poor. The PPA was felt to be a broadly empowering experience, although some weaknesses were identified, for example a tight timescale (initially just one year but extended to 15 months) guided by the World Bank (Attwood and May, 1998).

Other approaches use the creative arts, such as drama, photography, or video – issues are raised through these techniques, and then discussed within the community.

EXAMPLE

Local women take photographs – public health needs in Yunnan, China

A participatory needs assessment process with women in Yunnan, China, used a range of methods but included the innovative use of photography, called Photovoice. Fifty-three local women were trained in photography techniques, and the project used photographs:

–   to record and reflect the community's strengths and concerns,
–   to promote critical dialogue and knowledge about important issues through group discussion of photographs, and
–   to reach policy-makers.

This project was concerned with public health promotion. Women took photos, for example of farmers fetching water, and of babies squirming on blankets in the fields while their mothers undertook heavy manual work. These pictures brought to the fore issues for which local women had been unable to gain attention in the past (Wang et al, 1996; Wang and Burris, 1997).

get for chapter on photography

3.4   Peer research

Peer research is a special type of participatory research, which has developed in recent years as a valuable way of working within development work in the North and the South (Kirby, 1999). Essentially, people from the group in question – perhaps street children, users of mental health services, disabled people – are engaged as researchers to work alongside professional researchers to investigate their own situation. The community members are offered training in research methods, and work together to identify key issues, to develop research tools (questionnaires, focus group topic guides, etc), and to carry out fieldwork. They are usually paid for their time.

Peer research has been particularly developed in work with children and young people, perhaps because young people can feel a greater distance from older researchers. It may be particularly useful as an approach to work with people who share some sort of minority, stigmatised status, because of the bonds between 'people like us' where there is an assumption that their experience is outside the mainstream.

The peer researchers may be involved in a number of ways – their experience and knowledge is drawn on to decide on the focus for the research, they choose the research methods, and they carry out the fieldwork. Peer researchers have used a variety of methods including interviews, questionnaires, focus groups, and observation (for example, Abebaw et al, 1998; Broad and Saunders, 1998).

EXAMPLE

Peer research with young people in England – leaving care, and mental health services

Save the Children has carried out two peer research projects in England with young people which have used a similar methodology, one with care leavers and one with young people with experience of using mental health services. In each case, a small group of young people was offered research training delivered in a small number of two- to three-day workshop sessions, with practical exercises in between. A focus group interview with the peer researchers was used to draw out the key issues, and then the group itself decided the specific focus of the research and the methods to be used. A questionnaire was developed and tested, and then interviews carried out by the young people themselves. Analysis and writing was led by professional researchers, with some input from the young people, limited by time and external pressure (West, 1995; Laws et al, 1999).

EXAMPLE

Lao young people look at their lives

A recent project in Vientiane, Laos, looked broadly at the views of young people on their lives – to give a 'snapshot' view for decision-makers on the views of young people on a range of topics that affect them. 20 young people between 17 and 22 were trained in research methods, especially on how to run focus groups with their peers. The training lasted a week, which was felt in retrospect to be too short a time – group works skills are not easy to learn quickly. Information was collected on the good and bad things in life; relationships with families and friends; what it means to be a Lao person; money and the future; crime and punishment; and the environment.

Focus groups were tape-recorded, where they gave permission, and this means that quotations from the young people bring the report to life. The groups were also given some structured tasks to do, such as lifelines for each young person, case studies to discuss, statements with which to agree or disagree. The report is 'owned' by five organisations, and is felt to be successful in having an impact on policy issues. The trained young researchers hoped to continue their work at the end of this project with a piece of work on Life Skills and HIV/AIDS (Lao Youth Union Vientiane Municipality et al, 1998).

Peer research approaches are attractive to development workers, as they build the skills of community members in a number of areas, as well as producing a piece of work which is fully informed and owned by them. It can be a good way of showing what community members can do. Sceptics cannot help but be impressed with how readily community members will grasp the basic issues involved in research. And a peer research process yields at the end informed and motivated people who are excellent advocates to promote the findings of the research.

However it is important to realise that the peer researchers will require considerable support throughout the life of the project, if they are to fully participate in the decisions that are made. Research can be a long drawn-out process, and this can create problems for people with turbulent lives – it may be worth trying to concentrate the work into a short period. It is, of course, also true that people-problems affect all types of research. We should not assume that peer researchers will 'naturally' find it easy to show empathy with others like themselves.

EXAMPLE

Children as evaluators: children in female-headed households in Tajikistan

The 1992 civil war in Tajikistan destroyed homes and infrastructure, and created many female-headed households. In 1994 Save the Children began a project in Khatlon Province, in the south of the country, which aimed to reduce the vulnerability of children in female-headed households.

As the project's objectives directly concerned children it was decided that children would be the best judges of whether or not they had been achieved. It was hoped that if children were approached by other children they would open up and say what they thought.

The evaluation was carried out in 1998. Fifteen children, aged 12 to 16 years, were involved. Eight were boys and seven were girls, and all came from families that were benefiting from the project. Only two days were available for training and six for the fieldwork. (With hindsight, project staff agreed that this was not enough time, and that ideally, a pre-sessional stage of the evaluation would have begun a month in advance, giving time for the purpose of the evaluation, its context and all the interviewing techniques and methods to be discussed and practised.) Field workers were the main trainers. They explained the basics of interviewing, such as the difference between open and closed questioning and the use of pictures as a dialoguing tool, and covered issues such as body language, and the need to pace questions.

Pilot visit interviews were made and role-plays carried out, but the initial interviews did not go well. The child evaluators did not empathise with the children they interviewed, but were unsympathetic and inquisitorial. This was an unforeseen problem – staff had assumed that the child evaluators would 'connect' with children in the same circumstances as themselves. The child evaluators' use of other techniques also began to unravel. They did not use the pictures properly; certain children dominated; they rushed through questions; and important questions were missed out.

The need to empathise was explained to the child evaluators in depth and a variety of role-plays were performed. This was the turning point in the week. Their whole approach changed, and they went about their subsequent interviewing more sensitively. Verbatim recording of the child evaluators' interviews (which programme staff felt was an invaluable source of qualitative information) showed that after this point, the child evaluators called women 'dear aunt' and children 'my dear sister/brother'. Once this barrier had been overcome, the children felt increasingly confident. They took on the role of interviewing school directors and committee members, something many had been too shy to do at the beginning of the evaluation.

Some of the adult staff had originally had misgivings about children as evaluators, but by the end of the process, all staff felt it had been worthwhile. Three gave a similar reason: that children are truthful. One quoted the Tajik proverb, 'If you want to know the secrets of a house, ask a child.' (Parry-Williams, 1998)

Research is complex work, and the training needed to produce research of reasonable quality is considerable. No one wants to see people used as tokens, sent out to undertake work they do not fully understand, and this means a commitment to giving a high level of support to the peer researchers. If other community members are to be enabled to give their views in an open way, peer researchers need to learn the relatively complex skills involved in qualitative fieldwork.

Particularly where the issues being researched are sensitive and personal, it is important to remember the needs and rights of the respondent as well as those of the peer researcher. Some respondents will be encouraged to participate by the fact that it is 'someone like them' doing the research. But others may have concerns about their privacy and anonymity, since they will be talking to someone from their own community, not a researcher who will disappear at the end of the project. It may be appropriate to offer some choices to respondents about how they participate in the project.

Should peer researchers be paid?

If peer researchers are working alongside professional researchers or development workers, carrying responsibility for the outcomes of the research project, should they be paid for their work? Practice varies. Some projects have paid a weekly wage for a short period, others have paid expenses at a good level, others have given a grant to the peer researcher for the project and others have not paid at all. There are many issues to consider. Where the peer researchers are children, there are further issues. Are we encouraging child labour if we pay, for example, street children who work with us on research projects to compensate for lost earnings?

In deciding on this matter, you obviously need to take account of the context you are working in. Employment opportunities are of course valuable to people, but you need to think through exactly what is entailed in constructing the peer research in this way. It does increase the distance between the peer researchers and other participants considerably. On the other hand it creates a deeper level of engagement from a small group of people. Projects have grappled with these issues in different ways.

See also Chapter 19.3, which discusses the broader issue of paying incentives to respondents in research.

Table 3.1 Advantages and disadvantages of payment for peer researchers

Advantages of payment for peer researchers
- ✓ Recognises the peer researcher's contribution
- ✓ Peer researchers feel valued
- ✓ Not paying may mean that peer researchers will suffer directly as a result of taking part in the research, because they may be unable to make money or could even lose their employment
- ✓ Professionals can take the peer researchers more seriously
- ✓ Increases motivation and interest in the project
- ✓ Helps to ensure tasks are completed
- ✓ Can bring the peer researchers into an organisation's internal decision-making structure, and give them more influence in this way

Disadvantages of payment for peer researchers
- Payment can be a form of control, dictating how peer researchers are to 'participate' rather than supporting them to work to their own agenda
- Payment changes the relationship between peer researchers and professional staff, increasing the power imbalance – staff become managers and direct what peer researchers do
- If peer researchers volunteer, they can 'vote with their feet' more easily, making workers more accountable to them
- Some peer researchers may participate in the project for the money, and not because they are interested in the work
- Paying peer researchers can set a precedent whereby they will want to be paid for any similar future work, which may not be sustainable

Sources: (Boyden and Ennew, 1997; Kirby, 1999)

EXAMPLE

Issues in paying peer researchers – street children study experiences of incarceration in Dhaka, Bangladesh

A peer research project with street children who had been incarcerated in jail or correction centre carried out in Dhaka, Bangladesh, by Save the Children found that it was making increasing demands on children's time. The girls especially, mentioned that they have to have regular paid work for their survival. It was decided to offer children a daily amount equivalent to the average income of a street child, only to be paid for the days the children worked on the research.

After some days some difficulties emerged, with children asking to be paid for days when they were not working. The issue was taken to the group of children to discuss. They agreed that they should only be paid for days they worked. In favour of their decision they mentioned that Save the Children or the partner agency Moitree Parishad would not support them for their whole life. They will have to depend on their own capacity. Before the research they were on their own and they would be on their own after the research also (Khan, 1999).

Table 3.2 Strengths and limitations of peer research

Peer research – strengths
- Peer-led research will focus on those issues of priority to community members themselves
- Facilitates strong community participation in, and ownership of, the project
- Builds peer researchers' skills and confidence
- Can 'reach' very disadvantaged, alienated groups of people

Peer research – limitations
- Participation by the small group of peer researchers does not automatically facilitate participation by the wider community in question
- Peer research is demanding on the peer researchers – they need support, and the difficulties of their own lives may affect the research process (this is also true of professional researchers, of course!)
- Requires considerable resources to undertake properly
- Access to respondents/the wider community not necessarily guaranteed by involvement of peer researchers
- Targets for influence may not accept the validity of peer research

CHECKLIST   For good practice in peer research

✓ Recruit peer researchers with appropriate skills and attitudes – research is demanding and responsible work
✓ Recruit enough peer researchers to allow for some to drop out as time goes on
✓ Consider carefully how peer researchers will be recompensed for their time, in light of their existing situations
✓ Ensure that enough time is spent on the training to enable peer researchers to make genuine choices about the research focus and methods
✓ Include ethical issues of consent and confidentiality in the training process
✓ Provide easy access to support and supervision during fieldwork
✓ Work on ways of involving peer researchers more fully in analysis and writing processes

3.5 How much participation is appropriate?

There is a danger for 'participation' to become such a 'hooray word', that it is assumed that the higher the level of community participation in any piece of work, the better it will be for all concerned. But participation has costs, not least in terms of the time of the community members concerned. And positive outcomes cannot be guaranteed. As with any research decision, the level of participation that is appropriate depends upon the final purpose of the exercise.

Much writing about participation refers to the concept of a 'ladder of participation' (Arnstein, 1969; Hart, 1992), which starts from decorative or tokenistic participation, and rises to the group in question initiating and being fully in charge of a process. Many versions of this ladder have been produced. The virtue of this image is that it demonstrates how some processes that are claimed as participatory involve minimal or no change in power relations. However there are problems with this hierarchical imagery. It tends to suggest that whatever the situation, greater participation is desirable, with the final goal being autonomous organising by the group in question. However there are many situations where this would be an entirely unrealistic goal, and it seems a pity to judge less intense participation wanting by comparison to it. Many valuable pieces of work facilitate participation in one or two aspects of a process, and this may be all that is wanted by the stakeholders. It should not be assumed that participating in these processes is necessarily a desired goal for community members.

Consider instead a wheel of participatory research (see Figure 3.2 below), where participation in different aspects of a piece of work is given value as appropriate within any particular piece of work. The key reason why participation is important is that community members gain greater power. There is some transfer of control of decision-making. Thus, important participation can take place in a number of different ways, at different stages in a process.

A community group might request that a piece of research be done (perhaps an investigation of pollution to their water source), but not want to take much role in the details of the process. Or in another project (perhaps a needs assessment to set priorities with people with AIDS), researchers might use strongly qualitative methods which would enable respondents to very fully consider their responses and to get their own questions answered. This can enable those individuals to 'have their say' and be heard more fully. A third project might involve community members as researchers, using a simple self-completion questionnaire. This might give the respondents less space to put forward their views, but would engage community members in actively investigating an issue, building their confidence to take action. These different types of participation should not be seen as more or less valuable, but each as valid in its place.

The wheel also suggests the idea of travel, and reminds us that research is a means to an end, and not generally an end in itself. It is also important to acknowledge that the practice of participatory research is evolving as people learn more about how it works.

It should be remembered that participatory research is a partnership process. While professionals need to be conscious of the power they

Figure 3.2 The wheel of community participation in research

have, and make every effort to facilitate community members in having a say, it is not helpful if professionals feel inhibited from contributing their own skills as well. Researchers should not get too agonised about the power they take, for example in undertaking analysis of data, researchers' skills and insights can be useful too, and community participants can often more easily take a view when some suggestions are made to react to.

There can be valid and meaningful participation in any or all of the different elements of the research process represented as spokes of the wheel. It is not necessary to see it as an ideal to involve community members in all aspects of the process – this may not be at all appropriate to the particular situation.

What are the factors to take into account in deciding the level and type of participation which is appropriate to a particular project? This is a complex matter, which cannot easily be reduced to a checklist. Development workers will have experience of assessing situations to make similar decisions about what is possible with a particular group. However there are perhaps a few points worth making. First of all, do not make too many assumptions about what people are capable of – try and check this by undertaking some exploratory exercises. The questions to ask may be more about what you are able to support them to do, and what they might *want* to do.

And a key factor is your organisation's existing relationship with potential participants. It is much more difficult to start out on participatory research 'cold' than it is where some trust already exists between the community and the agency. This is usually based on some kind of service provision, some sort of positive, practical engagement with the community.

Time is often the central factor in deciding these questions. A very short time-scale inevitably limits participation. Wherever possible, negotiate to extend deadlines, to enable greater participation to take place.

Factors to consider in deciding appropriate types of participation in research include:

- The wishes of community members in relation to participation in this process – level of commitment.
- The issue the agency wants to investigate, and its match to local concerns.
- Existing relationships with stakeholders – is there some trust already there?
- Time available (both worker time day by day, and time in which the process needs to be completed).
- Level of support available.
- Skills of those working with community members.
- Current skills and experience of community members.

Figure 3.3 could usefully form the basis for a discussion with community members about which elements of a research process they would wish to be involved in.

Figure 3.3   For use in planning how community members will participate in the research

1)   Indicate what level of involvement community members will have at each research stage
2)   Indicate who will carry out the required tasks at each stage

STAGES IN THE RESEARCH PROCESS	1) Level of involvement • None • Being informed • Expressing a view • Shared decision • Main decider	2) Who will carry out the tasks? • Community members • Staff • Partner agency
Initiate research		
Set budgets		
Decide the research topic		
Set aims and objectives		
Recruit researchers/other workers		
Advisory group		
Choose research methods		
Create research tools		
Collect information (fieldwork) – Data from community – Data from professionals – Data from existing material		
Provide research data (ie own experience/views)		
Analysis		
Choose recommendations		
Write report		
Produce other product (eg presentation, video)		
Disseminate research findings		
Access to research findings		
Development and campaigning		

(Adapted from Kirby, 1999)

3.6   Issues in Participatory Research

The process of undertaking participatory research is always challenging, as it requires us to question many taken-for-granted practices.

As we have seen, a key issue for managers is that the first step in participatory research involves enabling the participating group to set the agenda – to decide what the research will be about. There is usually a need to reconcile stakeholder priorities with agency priorities. This can be a particular issue where the intention is to use a participatory process to develop research aimed at policy influence. The imperatives involved in policy-focused work to be very clear about audience and message are hard to follow if you are also working with a community-led agenda. However a middle way can generally be found, as community members are realists too.

One issue to consider is that of the distinction between public and private realms or issues. The PLA type of process, which emphasises open discussion within a local community, is likely to be most suitable to investigate issues which are already identified as shared community problems. A high level of community participation is likely to make it more rather than less difficult for those with less power within the community to raise issues which may be seen as 'private', for example relating to inequalities within households, like violence against women or children.

PLA practitioners often make efforts to enable women's and children's voices to be heard, for example by meeting separately with them. But the essentially public process of the PLA does not allow individuals to speak confidentially about their situation. It may be argued in response to this point that issues which people cannot raise publicly cannot usefully be addressed by development workers. However in terms of research, more formal research methods can have the virtue of distancing the respondent from the findings, so that issues can be raised in a generalised way without people being obliged to 'own' a particular experience.

Another question which has been raised (Laws et al, 1999), particularly about peer research, again relates to issues which are sensitive and personal. It may be true for some people that they would prefer to discuss personal matters with others 'like themselves'. However for others, the loss of privacy involved in talking to someone from their own community will be a problem. Traditional 'neutral' researchers who are distanced from the community may in fact be easier to trust with very personal information. It may be appropriate to offer a choice of interviewers, rather than assuming that peer researchers are the best for all respondents.

EXAMPLE

Who judges what is best? Child workers in Bangladesh

A tricky ethical issue arose in research Save the Children did with children who work in cigarette factories in Bangladesh. There are very few other economic opportunities for either young people or their parents in the area, and the children felt that they need to do this work to support the family income. The young people also felt that if they work, perhaps their younger siblings would not have to.

So should the organisation accept the young people's judgement, and not intervene, despite the very damaging conditions which this work involves? The dilemma is particularly acute given the difficulty of stimulating alternative economic opportunities in the area – there is no guarantee that efforts to provide alternatives would produce enough income for children to stop working. It is a real problem in all kinds of research for development that people facing great oppression are likely to have low expectations in terms of what they hope for in life. But it will be a more acute issue still where the aim is to take the lead from community members themselves.

Participatory research has a great deal to offer to development practitioners, but it is no easy option.

Key Points from this Chapter

Participatory research has a particularly important role in development work, and this chapter looks at the principles behind such approaches, and at the different levels at which participation can take place. Issues about who should participate, in what, and for what purpose are discussed. The image of a 'wheel of community participation' is proposed, suggesting that there may be a variety of different kinds of participation in research processes, which are equally appropriate in different situations. Some of the problems of participatory research are also raised.

The next chapter looks at quality in all types of research work.

CHECKLIST   For understanding participatory research

✓ Participatory approaches can reveal more about a problem
✓ Participatory research is oriented to finding solutions
✓ Careful thought needs to be given to involving a range of people – perhaps including community members themselves, and local service-providers
✓ Community participation is possible at many different points in the research process, from identifying the research focus, to doing interviews, to promoting the findings – consideration needs to be given to how much participation is appropriate, and at what point/s in the process
✓ A balance needs to be struck between community priorities and agency agendas
✓ It should not be assumed that the participation of some community members, for example in fieldwork, will automatically facilitate full participation by others
✓ Participatory research requires strong facilitation skills, an interest in research rigour and an interest in solutions

Further Reading

Wadsworth, Y. (1984, 2nd edition 1997) *Do It Yourself Social Research*. Victorian Council of Social Service, St Leonards, Australia: Allen and Unwin.

A nicely written straightforward guide for community organisations carry out their own research. A best seller, for good reason.

Theis, J. and Grady, H.M. (1991) *Participatory Rapid Appraisal for Community Development: A training manual based on experiences in the Middle East and North Africa*. London: IIED and Save the Children Federation.

Covers one group of methods. Enthusiastic and clearly written. Includes useful guidance on general training approaches and techniques. Lots of individual methods simply explained, including depth interviews.

Mikkelsen, B. (1995) *Methods for Development Work and Research: A guide for practitioners*. New Delhi, Thousand Oaks, London: Sage.

Includes a good deal of material about PRA – 'how to' and reflection on experience.

Holland, J. with Blackburn, J. (eds) (1998) *Whose Voice? Participatory research and policy change*. London: Intermediate Technology Publications.

Reflects on the development from local Participatory Rural Appraisals to the use of participatory methodologies in work intended to have influence at the national and international policy levels. A collection of articles, many of which discuss Participatory Poverty Assessments, promoted by the World Bank in the 1990s.

Boyden, J. and Ennew, J. (1997) *Children in Focus: A manual for participatory research with children*. Stockholm: Rädda Barnen.

Rädda Barnen, S-107 88 Stockholm, Sweden. Tel: (+46) 8-698 90 00. Email: info@rb.se

Focused on research with children, but covers a lot of generic research issues. Particularly good examples given throughout, including visual ones. Strong on ethical issues, and of course on specific issues in work with children.

McKeown, C. and Hedges, C. (1996) *Skills in Community Research Training Pack* Newcastle: Save the Children. For further information contact: Save the Children, North East Development Team, Unit 3 Blackfriars, Dispensary Lane, Newcastle upon Tyne, NE1 4XN. Tel: 0191 222 1816.

A well-organised training pack with a clear framework of learning objectives for the participants, and suggestions of exercises to use in teaching a wide range of research skills. Written for training UK community members.

Perpetua Kirby (1999) *Involving Young Researchers: How to enable young people to design and conduct research*. York: Joseph Rowntree Foundation.

Practical guide to peer research with young people, based on a group of nine projects undertaken in England by Save the Children.

Worrall, S. (2000) *Young People as Researchers: A learning resource pack*. London: Save the Children.

Training pack linked to the Kirby manual.

Mental Health Foundation (1999) *The DIY Guide to Survivor Research: Everything you always wanted to know about survivor research but were afraid to ask*. London: Mental Health Foundation.

Aimed at users (survivors) of mental health services, this pack is based on a sequence of training days offered to participants in the Strategies for Living project.

4   Quality in Research

How can development workers ensure that research they undertake is of good quality? For that matter, what is meant by quality in research work, if, as we have seen in the last chapter, there are many approaches to research which follow different rules? This chapter argues that it is crucial that development organisations recognise the value of good quality research work. There are quality issues to be considered in relation to the process of research as well as to its products.

Some quality standards are proposed, in checklist form, which summarise the key issues that require attention. Finally some guidance is offered as to the practical steps to take to ensure that your research meets these standards.

4.1   Why does quality matter?

Perhaps it is obvious that the quality of the research we do affects the extent to which it is taken seriously. But at times NGOs have perhaps hoped that their research will be accepted as valid more because they are 'on the side of the angels' than because of its quality. There is never enough time or money to do the perfect piece of work, and aspirations have to be scaled down to what is possible.

Research can be expensive, and it is important that research activity is kept in balance with other types of development activity. But it is also important that research is good enough for its purpose. This is really the key – the quality of the research you do needs to be sufficient to the decisions which will rest on the results. It may be better to do one excellent piece of research in a year than to do three 'quick and dirty' ones which may not be taken seriously. In a different situation the reverse may be true. But it is helpful to stand back a little from the immediate situation when planning research. Some of the sense of driving urgency that surrounds development work is constructed by the culture of the organisations carrying it out (Edwards and Hulme, 1995). It should not be assumed that longer term, better quality research is not possible.

It is crucial, for each piece of work, to find an appropriate balance between rigour and relevance (Harper, 1997). Work with more depth takes longer and costs more, but it may have much greater influence. Equally there is clearly no point in doing elaborate academic work on situations which are fast-changing, where information is needed very quickly.

Audience is an important issue to consider when making decisions about what priority to give to quality in research work. Different audiences care about different aspects of quality, and what measures you need to take to assure quality in the work depends very much on who you hope to influence.

If development organisations aim to influence policy, research work needs to stand up to hostile scrutiny in public settings. Journalists will ask awkward questions, and enjoy nothing so much as finding faults in claims made in research work. If journalists, and indeed politicians and other policy-makers, are to take an argument seriously, they need to be convinced that the claims made are credible. If partner agencies are the key audience, it may be that they will highly value the genuine participation of community members in the process of the research.

4.2   What does quality in research mean?

Activity 4.1

What do you value in research in your field?

This activity asks you to think about what qualities you look for in judging the value of research for development work. What does quality mean to you?

Brainstorm a list of features which tell you when research you come across in your work is of good quality.

When you have completed your list, see if you can put these features in order of importance, by labelling the most important one with an A, the next with a B and so on.

You may like to do this brainstorming exercise with a group of colleagues.

As we have seen in Chapter 2 there are important differences among the different research traditions. One person's good quality research may not be another's. But whilst there are differences of view about methodology, it is possible to identify some standards which are very widely accepted. The essential integrity of a piece of research is readily identified, whether or not it is undertaken within a tradition one is particularly sympathetic to.

A common misconception about research is that the more statistics are included in a piece of work, the more authority it has. There are several problems here. For example, it is widely believed that many countries manipulate their population statistics for political reasons. In the UK, unemployment figures have been 'massaged' by governments over many years, by excluding various categories of people from them, to bring them as low as possible.

It is important to have confidence in the integrity of any source of figures that you use. Another common problem is that you must be sure that a sample is large enough to sustain any complex statistical procedures you want to try.

> **COMMON PITFALLS 4.1**   Claiming more from a piece of research than can really be supported by the findings

---

It is particularly important to avoid claiming more than can be shown from the data you have produced. It is better to say less than to have your whole argument destroyed by one false over-blown claim. A common mistake is to try to generalise from small and/or unrepresentative samples. For example, a study of the members of an organisation for parents of sick children might find, perhaps, that 80 per cent were dissatisfied with the help they got from professionals. You could not then claim that 80 per cent of all parents of sick children are dissatisfied. People may have joined the organisation precisely because they were unhappy. The data is useful in itself, and it describes a real issue for those people, but it cannot be generalised to the wider population.

Perhaps it is worth saying that quality is not the same thing as size! A large sample will get you nowhere if the questions set are unclear or ambiguous, or if they are so superficial as only to state the obvious. It depends entirely on the purpose of the research what its scale needs to be. See below, under 'generalisability, 4.5'.

It can be difficult to decide how much time and money to spend on research-type exercises, whether they are a needs assessment process or a piece of work aiming at policy influence. There are real limits to what can be achieved for a very small budget. Research is not something that it is wise to try to 'hurry up' with, as below a certain level of quality it is simply of no use. It is worth taking some advice about what exactly could be done at different levels of resourcing. A rule of thumb might be to think about the research effort in proportion to the resources involved in the programme or policy decisions which will depend on its findings.

> **COMMON PITFALLS 4.2**   Assuming that elaborate statistics impress policy-makers. You may trip yourself up, and some of your readers may not understand your message

---

One important aspect of quality goes beyond the individual research project – it is about making sure that your research makes sense in the context of what is already known about the issue in question. Knowing the field more broadly, and drawing on existing information, gives much greater authority to reports of research projects. The findings from a small-scale study can be greatly supported by reference to research undertaken by others.

4.3   Quality standards for research for development

Table 4.1 is an attempt to summarise some key indicators of quality in research for development work. There are undoubtedly other important aspects. Space has been left for the reader to add points which seem to them of key importance in the context in which they work. It will be seen that these are not the same as the rules of academic research – development work has different priorities. Of course research of different types has different key imperatives – this is an attempt to give a simple checklist for the non-specialist.

You might want to use this list of standards when:

– discussing practice issues with a newly-appointed researcher;
– forming a research team for a particular project;
– assessing a completed piece of work before publication;
– assessing a whole body of research work, with a view to developing better practice.

To assess some of the issues listed in Table 4.1, there is no substitute for getting advice from an experienced researcher. For example on sampling, if you wish to make generalisations from your sample it is essential to talk to a statistician *before* you do the fieldwork to ensure that you have sufficient numbers, and that the structure of the sample is suitable. Equally you may wish to seek advice on ethical practice in research if you are not familiar with the ways in which researchers practically go about protecting respondents.

The standards listed above are summarised in an activity in Chapter 11.1 suggesting, as one approach to evaluating research for development work, to look at these standards and assess the strengths and weaknesses of your project in relation to them.

> **TIP**   Consult a researcher now![1]

4.4   On consulting researchers

This manual advises you to consult an experienced researcher at a number of points in the process of carrying out or commissioning your research, as a way of improving the quality of your work. It is a good idea to show someone

---

[1]Some development workers will find researchers employed within their own or others' organisations who can be asked for advice on research matters. If such help is not available, researchers who work in universities or research institutes will often give advice to people from development projects.

Table 4.1 Some quality standards for research in development

1. RESEARCH PLANNING

- Should be about an important issue
- Should be needed, that is
  - not duplicate other research
  - not be a substitute for action
- Should be relevant to the organisation's mission – an issue on which it could follow through with further work if appropriate
- Should be aware of where the idea for the research came from, and prioritise ideas which come from 'the researched'
- Should have a clear brief, including aims and objectives and suitable research question/s
- Should be planned in co-operation with relevant other agencies and representatives of community members affected by the issue
- Should have organisational structures which are transparent and make researchers answerable to all those with a legitimate interest in the research, including the subjects of the research
- Should be planned with a view to increasing local or national research skills as one of its objectives
- Planning should include a strategy to promote learning from the findings

2. RESEARCH PROCESSES

- Research should question taken-for-granted ideas and explanations
- Researchers should interact with respondents with respect and a concern for clear and open communication
- Where research is participatory, researchers should aim to enable participants to have a say in the original design of the project, and in identifying key issues from their point of view, as well as in data collection and analysis

Continued

Table 4.1 Continued

RESEARCH PROCESSES (*Continued*)

- The sample should be adequate to the purpose of the research
- Research tools should be piloted and revised before use
- Data collection should be systematic, and care taken to preserve the integrity of the data, that is

  - questions should never be 'leading'
  - recording should be as exact as possible
  - quotations should not be taken out of context so that meaning is distorted
  - the process of gathering the information should be systematically observed and recorded

- Should be planned with an awareness of the impact of power inequalities, both between different groups in the population and between researchers and respondents. Power relationships in the 'private sphere', within the family – gender and age hierarchies – are especially important to take into account

- Ethical issues in research should be actively considered as problems arise, and in particular procedures should ensure

  - that respondents' consent is properly sought, and that they understand what they are agreeing to when they give it
  - that no pressure is applied to respondents to participate in research
  - that where undertakings to protect confidentiality of data are given, they are fully complied with
  - that where respondents wish to be anonymous, their identities should be protected throughout the life of the project, from initial contact to publication and subsequent promotional activity

- It is essential to establish good communication with respondents. Where different languages are involved, interpreters must be used who understand the research process and are able to give accurate and full translations

- Exact procedures involved in drawing the sample should be explained in reports, and there should be reflection on the strength and weaknesses of the sample used
- Researchers should be reflective and open about their own perspectives and the influence these have on the research process
- Statistical procedures should be briefly explained for a lay readership, and the meaning of their findings clearly expressed
- In quantitative research, checks should be made on the validity and reliability of research tools, that is
  - that they measure what they claim to measure, and
  - that responses are consistent if, for example, a questionnaire is repeated with the same people at a different time

3. INTERPRETATION AND ANALYSIS

- In interpreting findings
  - researchers should take great care to avoid overlaying their own interpretations onto respondents' comments
  - uncertainty of meaning should be acknowledged where this occurs
- Analysis should include consideration of alternative interpretations of the data, and reasons why these do not hold
- Analysis should have regard to the policy context, including research information beyond the current project and should comment on its relevance to the issue at hand
- Claims made must not go beyond what can be supported by the evidence

Continued

Table 4.1 Continued

4. PROMOTING RESEARCH FINDINGS

- Reports should be concise, but should include all the information necessary to assess the quality of the research
- A summary of the final report is essential to having an influence
- Recommendations should be based on the findings
- Findings should be fed back to the subjects of the research, and to all agencies and individuals who contributed towards it, in formats which are accessible to them
- Other research which is quoted from or referred to should be identified as such, and fully referenced, to enable readers to locate the item
- Research findings should be disseminated in a targeted way, with special attention to ensuring that those with related policy responsibilities are informed of relevant research results

with more experience a draft of any research brief, and to consult on your choice of methods, or on sampling issues. And you may well want them to read drafts of a final report.

However a development worker who read a draft of the manual reminded me that consulting a researcher may not always be the happy experience I might wish it to be. Researchers are inclined to offer strong criticism of what they are shown – and this can be crushing to someone inexperienced. Experiences like this can make people dread the very idea of consulting researchers on their work.

There is a wide cultural difference between the ways in which researchers and development workers typically expect to operate. Development workers tend to emphasise support over criticism, and to give feedback in a gentle way, minimising any negative comment. They may encourage self-reflection/criticism rather than giving direct feedback. However one of the key features of survival in a research culture is that one's work must be capable of standing up to criticism. Obviously all research is imperfect, but as a researcher you must learn to build in defences against obvious lines of criticism in whatever you write. Researchers are trained to analyse and criticise everything they read. Therefore, if shown a draft, researchers will typically point out *all* the possible problems they can see in it – and take some pride and pleasure in the exercise! It does not mean the work is bad, necessarily, if there is a long list of problems – it may just be particularly interesting.

Of course, at times such criticism will really be negative. If you consult someone who is out of sympathy with the philosophy behind your work, they are unlikely to give useful feedback. Though they should have the grace to explain that this is the problem, it cannot be guaranteed that they will tell you this. Some researchers do believe that only highly structured, quantitative research is meaningful, and will argue against others types of work as if it was simply bad research. It is well worth checking what school of thought anyone you consult subscribes to – no researcher will mind being asked this. If they do not give a reply you can understand, it may be a bad omen for your future relationship!

But usually, researchers' criticisms will be useful to you. You may want to get more than one opinion. And of course you do not have to take the advice you are offered. But the principle of defending your work against likely criticisms is a useful one, and experienced researchers can help you to do that.

You may or may not, in any case, have easy access to an experienced researcher with knowledge of your field. Some large NGOs have research sections either in regional offices or at their headquarters, but you may also find appropriate people in independent research institutes, universities, or local or national government research units. Some work on a freelance basis. Some researchers will see it as part of their role to offer help to those doing research in NGOs – though of course they are likely to have only limited time to offer unless you are able to pay them. You could, for example, ask an experienced researcher to give you just a few days' worth of advice, spread over the life of your project. If you will need to pay someone for their help, please refer to the guidelines in Chapter 7 for assistance.

CHECKLIST   For successfully consulting a researcher

✓ Ask for an overall response to the work as a whole, before starting to look at the details
✓ Expect to hear criticism
✓ Explain clearly the purpose of your research, and the needs of its audience – researchers may be more oriented to an academic audience
✓ Find out what school of thought (see 2.2 above) the researcher belongs to early on – if they use obscure terms, get them to explain in straightforward language
✓ Ask questions to establish what level of decision any criticism relates to – for example is the problem in the research focus or the research questions themselves, the methods proposed, the sampling scheme?
✓ Don't despair!

CHECKLIST   For researchers giving feedback to development workers

✓ Remember to praise the good things about what you are shown
✓ Give comments which are as specific as possible – avoid generalisations
✓ When you criticise, make suggestions for what would be better, taking into account the research capacity of the agency in question
✓ Remember this is not an academic exercise, and the research design needs to be adequate to its practical purpose
✓ Give development workers information about your own background and perspective
✓ Do not expect development workers' research plans to fit into your agenda
✓ Ask for feedback on your feedback!

The next two sections look at some sticky issues in relation to the quality of research work – the ideas of objectivity and of generalisability.

4.5   Some key issues in research quality

A note on objectivity

The idea of objectivity in research is very important to the mainstream tradition of scientific research. Researchers are seen as disinterested and able to rise above human conflicts of interest. This idea remains powerful, and it is important where an organisation is aiming to have influence on policy in a highly contested area to take this into account. NGOs are by definition committed to a certain set of values, but may still be seen as non-partisan in some respects and in some situations. It may be that research commissioned from academics will more readily be seen as objective.

As has been discussed already, there is an alternative strand within research which challenges the notion of a value-free social science. This tradition draws attention to the inevitable biases which human beings introduce into research simply through the way in which perception is influenced by one's expectations.

In the international development field in recent years, the tradition of the use of large-scale surveys, seen as accurate and objective, has been questioned. Where no account is taken of local knowledge, questions may be entirely irrelevant to real life, and survey results can be meaningless and simply wrong. A more interactive approach, where the people being studied are engaged with as equals in an investigation, is seen to produce more useful, and probably more accurate, information. The practice of first Rapid Rural Appraisal (RRA) and now Participatory Learning and Action (PLA), and Participatory Rural Appraisal, Participatory Research and Action (PRA) have developed (Holland with Blackburn, 1998). In these methods the researcher's attitudes and behaviour are key to the success of the research, and emphasis is placed on hearing the views of all those involved, and of negotiation between different perspectives, rather than attempting to identify an over-arching truth about a situation.

Another important group in this area of work (for example, Roberts, 1981; Stanley and Wise, 1983; Jayaratne et al, 1991) has been feminist researchers, who have argued that the whole notion of valuing objectivity and rejecting one's subjectivity as a source of knowledge comes from a male view of the world. It has masked much sexist research, and inevitably creates a hierarchy between the knowledge of the researcher and that of their respondents/'subjects', which is inappropriate. Feminists have argued for a social science that acknowledges the subjective as well as the objective.

These approaches have been an important corrective to some traditional research thinking, which has elevated the idea of objectivity in such a way as to suppress new ideas, and in particular ideas coming from relatively powerless groups. It is too easy for the point of view of the powerful to be seen as the objective one.

However there is a danger, following this line of thinking, of arriving at a position where there can be no knowledge beyond the opinion of an individual, and the only question is who you believe. Everything is relative, no 'truth' is possible. In practice, most of us actually operate with a pragmatic sense of reality which allows us to see that differently located people will have different perspectives on an issue. However we at the same time accept that there can be evidence for or against claims made about an issue, which go beyond the individual. We evaluate evidence on the basis of how it was produced as well as on the basis of who has produced it.

Some rules of the scientific tradition thus make intuitive sense, for example the requirement that the processes followed in undertaking a study should be revealed so that another investigator could in principle repeat it and see whether the same findings emerge.

The social constructionist tradition (see Section 2.2) accepts that there will always be an influence on research from the researcher's own values, beliefs, and interests. Its method of dealing with this inevitable bias is for researchers to be open about where they are coming from, to allow the reader to evaluate their work on that basis. This is known as reflexivity. In interpreting data, qualitative researchers will also follow a number of procedures which put a check on the extent to which their expectations influence their interpretation of their data. The categories that a researcher identifies are questioned repeatedly, and a trail is left to show any other researcher how each categorisation of data was arrived at and what material is regarded as fitting into each category. Thus interpretations could be challenged.

So there are different ways of looking at the issue of objectivity in research. A conscious decision needs to be taken for each project on how this issue will be addressed, and this made clear in the final report.

What is reflexivity?

Reflexivity is a key idea in qualitative research. Many social researchers do not believe that there can be a truly objective social science, because everything we observe is affected by the fact that it is us observing it. The concepts that we use are also a part of that social world. We cannot stand outside of our world to avoid our perspective being contaminated by it. So we have to accept that our interpretations are our interpretations. Someone else might see it differently. Therefore the best way to make our work 'honest' and trustworthy is to say, 'OK, these are my interpretations, but here is some information about who I am – this will help you to decide what view to take of my way of seeing things.' You can take account of this in reading my work. Researchers will also openly reflect on the ways in which who we are may have an impact on our work.

Our own standpoint is made up of all the many elements which influence us, including things like nationality, gender, ethnicity, and age, but also our beliefs and values.

You are being reflexive when:

* You think about what is influencing the way you interpret what people tell you.
* You discuss with colleagues your different ways of seeing the same piece of data.
* You ask respondents for their reflections on their experience of the research process – 'How did you feel about this interview?'
* As a researcher you are open about your viewpoint on or involvement in an issue – this might include your personal

    - beliefs
    - interests
    - experience of the topic
    - expertise.

To give an account of how these matters might have a bearing on their findings, the researcher is likely to need to draw on personal details, for example their

– social background (class, family, environment)
– age
– sex
– ethnicity
– religion
– sexuality (hetero- or homosexuality, marital status)
– education and qualifications
– work experience and skills

(see also Denscombe, 1998).

EXAMPLE

Gendered judgements? Polygyny in South East Asia

Research on the practice of polygyny (men having two or more wives) among a South East Asian minority group by male researchers consistently produced relatively positive and sometimes glowing accounts of the practice. Female researchers, working closely with local women, produced startlingly different, negative accounts. The gender of the researcher was of paramount importance in terms of what they saw, what they were told, and how they interpreted it (Cooper, 1984).

This is not about trying to 'match' researcher to respondent – whatever you did, there would be inevitable differences. It is about trying to make conscious the social processes going on underneath the research interaction.

Activity 4.2

How does an interviewer's identity affect findings?

Think of a controversial topic about which you are informed and happy to discuss – eg abortion, political characters, privatisation. Select two people to interview you who are known themselves to have differences in gender, their own views, their training, etc.

Allow a wider group to observe the interviews. Discuss how the interviewer's characteristics or background may have affected the interview. Discuss how the interviewer can make his or her conclusions 'objective'.

A note on generalisability

Some statements on quality standards in research include 'generalisability of findings' as a key standard. Indeed, the UK National Health Service's research and development funding system will only fund research which allows generalisation. The intention is that research should always enable statements to be made about a broader population than the one directly studied. This is an important principle of sampling for quantitative research.

However it is not appropriate to apply it to all research. Qualitative research which explores meanings and aims to generate ideas about a social phenomenon can be valuable without being generalisable. Case study research will also not usually allow generalisation. Any research on minority groups, or research about socially hidden phenomena, will have problems if it is required to be generalisable. Minorities are often under- or mis-represented in official statistics, for a variety of reasons, and this makes generalisations problematic. Any group which fears officialdom can best be researched by working through friendship networks and trusted organisations, a process which cannot yield a strictly representative random sample. Of course the minority of people who are in touch with such organisations may not be entirely representative of those who are more isolated. But there may be no choice. It is better to learn something about hard-to-reach groups than to let a purist approach block such learning.

It is of course essential not to generalise from samples which cannot support generalisation. But this does not mean that work on specific groups is invalid.

4.6   Quality: product or process?

When we think about quality in research, we tend to first focus on quality of product. That is, does the final report succeed in persuading readers of its argument? Does the methodology (the whole approach to the problem, including methods) hold water? Is the material well-presented and credible? Are the recommendations firmly based in the evidence presented?

But it is also important to think about the quality of the *process* of the research work. In a development context, this is likely to include issues like the quality of the involvement of community members at each stage of the research – conception, development, data collection, and analysis. Some issues to consider are:

*   Who defines the research objectives? Have 'the researched' had a say?
*   Are relevant partner agencies fully on board?
*   If you are from a Northern or international agency, are you building research capacity among Southern partners as well as investigating the issue?

And of course for all research projects a key question is about ethical standards of conduct in relation to respondents – that the research does no harm, and takes proper care in relation to consent and confidentiality.

Activity 4.3

Assessing quality of process and of product

Consider the overall quality of a piece of research you are familiar with, looking in broad-brush terms at its strengths and weaknesses in relation to the quality of the product and the quality of the process. Make notes in the following frameworks of issues which arise.

	Strengths	Weaknesses
Quality of product		
Quality of process		

A strong process should produce a strong outcome. However it can be an issue in development work that concern for process overtakes concern for the final product. Equally, traditional research may sacrifice ongoing relationships with stakeholders in pursuit of the perfect final report. You need to consider the priorities for your particular piece of work to decide what is most important to you – though ideally of course process and product should not be in conflict.

EXAMPLE

Local ownership matters – the Mozambique Participatory Poverty Assessment

The experience of the Mozambique Participatory Poverty Assessment (PPA) suggested that there were trade-offs involved between local ownership and the quality-control demands of the World Bank. The idea for the exercise originated in Washington with the World Bank, and was initially met with a lukewarm response from the Poverty Alleviation Unit in the Mozambique Government's Ministry of Planning. It was essential to build local ownership, and to distance the World Bank from the PPA. The Universidade Eduardo Mondlane (UEM) was invited to carry out the work. Enthusiasm increased as UEM became increasingly responsible as facilitators of the process.

From the point of view of the World Bank, there were a number of issues about the quality of the work, for example in relation to recruitment and preparation of the research team, aspects of how the fieldwork was carried out, and in the writing up of the research. Presentation of an overall poverty assessment or a summary of policy implications was severely delayed. However much learning had taken place in the course of the fieldwork, and from early interim reports. Changes in policy were occurring, although the formal process was incomplete. The process was unsatisfactory from the Bank's point of view, but perhaps the way in which it was done increased the likelihood of creating a sustainable commitment to this approach of poverty monitoring in Mozambique in the future (Owen, 1998).

4.7   In practice – assuring quality in research

So what do you need to do to ensure that your research is of good quality? The whole of this manual is intended to assist you in this, of course, but a summary here of the practical steps you can take may be helpful. Assuring quality depends very much on working with people who have a clear sense of external quality standards, so there is no substitute for building in some role for more experienced researchers. This may be quite remote, in the sense of looking at terms of reference or reading draft reports. But more positive involvement, such as giving a researcher a professional supervision role throughout the life of the project will be even more helpful. Very briefly, some key points are as follows:

CHECKLIST   Of practical steps to assuring quality in research work

✓ Good early planning
✓ The brief/terms of reference is clear and shared with all those involved
✓ Good research questions have been defined, and the methods selected match the research questions
✓ Staff have sufficient relevant experience
✓ Project allocated sufficient resources to undertake research of adequate quality
✓ Supervision by experienced researcher
✓ Advisory group established, involving policy-makers from relevant agencies; research advisors; representatives of the researched group
✓ In participatory research, participation planned for throughout the project
✓ Promotion planned for throughout the project
✓ Final reports read and commented on by a range of people
✓ Build in evaluation and feedback on the research process

There is more detail on all of these points in Chapters 4 to 8

We should not always be in the position of working out how to run successful research projects as we go along – organisations should aim to ensure that a wide group of people learn from the experience of each project they undertake. For this learning to take place it is essential that a record be made of how things were done, difficulties and what were encountered and how these were dealt with. Some kind of group discussion at the end of the project will assist people in learning the lessons for next time.

EXAMPLE

Learning from consultants' visits – Ethiopia

Save the Children in Ethiopia has a policy that whenever a foreign consultant comes to work in the country, they aim to assign a member of staff to shadow them. They have the task of writing up an account of the work that was done. They learn from observing the way the consultant works, even if their methods are not successful, and they are able to share that learning with colleagues long after the consultant has left.

Key Points From this Chapter

This chapter has urged concern for quality in research in development work, both in relation to the products of research work and in relation to the process followed. Some relevant quality standards have been proposed. The complexities involved in identifying quality standards are briefly discussed, particularly in relation to the notions of objectivity and of generalisability. A checklist of practical steps which managers could take to ensure the quality of research work is suggested.

Further Reading

Denscombe, M. (1998) *The Good Research Guide for Small-Scale Social Research Projects*. Buckingham, UK and Philadelphia: The Open University Press.

Gives pragmatic advice on how to do 'good enough' research with limited resources. Very useful general guidance on how to use a number of research methods and approaches.

Robson, C. (1993) *Real World Research: A resource for social scientists and practitioner-researchers*. Oxford, UK and Cambridge, USA: Blackwell.

Contains a useful discussion of how to establish trustworthiness.

Harper, C. (2001) 'Do the Facts Matter? NGOs, Research and International Advocacy', in Edwards, M. and Gaventa, J. (eds), *Global Citizen Action*. Earthscan.

5 Planning for Effective Research – Preparing to Write the Brief

So you've decided to do some research? This chapter aims to help you to manage the process in the most effective way possible. A certain mystique tends to surround research work, but do not be deceived. The first step is to realise that research needs to be managed, just like any other activity you undertake within your work. Whether or not you are undertaking the work yourself, the development practitioner or manager must ensure that proper planning and management systems are set up for any research project. This chapter and the next one offer help in writing a research brief. This one concentrates on the key tasks of defining the research focus and the method questions, and Chapter 6 discusses all the other issues you need to consider in writing a brief.

Chapter 7: 'Who should do the research?' and Chapter 8: 'Managing Research' go on to look at the ongoing management of research work, including how to estimate costs and time-scales, and at decisions about who will do the research.

5.1   Getting to Grips with Research

There are a number of processes you need to undertake, which may need to be done in a different order in different projects. Key research management tasks include:

- Conceiving the idea.
- Drafting the brief.
- Agreeing the brief with other stakeholders, including community members.
- Considering who you want your research to influence and how it will do this.
- Considering whether and how this project can enable more people to learn research skills.
- Deciding who will undertake the research.
- Working out the time-scale.
- Negotiating access to information/respondents.
- Estimating costs.

- Arranging appropriate support and supervision for researchers.
- Setting up an advisory group.
- Applying for funding.

For most research exercises, the most difficult parts of the process are at the beginning and the end. This chapter and the next one concentrate on the issues which arise at the start of the process – writing the brief and agreeing it with all those with a stake in the project. Later chapters pick up the other issues listed above in more depth, for example costings and supervision are discussed in Chapter 8. The key to successful research is to work out a good brief, with clear aims and a coherent and achievable plan of work. We talk about research proposals, terms of reference, and briefs. These all refer to the same document. I have chosen the term 'brief' because it expresses the idea that the document communicates a job to be done.

> **COMMON PITFALLS 5.1**   Starting out on a research project without a written brief

To write a good brief, you will need to consult with a wide range of people – partner agencies with an interest in the topic you hope to research; staff (and/or external researchers) who may be involved in carrying out the research; and perhaps funders. The process of writing the brief involves setting out the assumptions you are making as well as your plans, and this will lead to fruitful discussions.

> **TIP**   Working out a research brief is a major piece of work, and time needs to be allowed for it.

Particularly if you hope to attract funding from research-oriented funders, considerable work will be required to satisfy them that you both know the existing research and are competent to undertake the work you propose. Most research proposals go through several drafts, with major changes being made, before they are agreed – it is important not to be put off by critical comments from colleagues on early drafts of the proposal. Time spent on this at an early stage will certainly pay off in the long run. Proposals for major projects can take anything from two weeks to several months to prepare.

5.2   The Process of Writing the Brief

It is best to start writing the brief as early as possible in the process of planning the project, and to expect to revise it many times before it is completed. You could start out with just some notes about the purpose of the exercise, before you are ready to write about the methods in any detail. Do not put off committing your thoughts to paper for too long – it is the best way of enabling other people to become involved, if they can see what you are thinking. You can always add the more technical details at a later stage.

Who should write the brief?

The main drafting of the brief should be undertaken by the person with the clearest view of the research which is being planned. This may be a manager, but equally it may be a development practitioner, or an in-house researcher, though external consultants should generally not be asked to write briefs for their own projects. Whoever does the main writing, responsibility for ensuring that the brief is adequate to its job remains with the manager in charge of the project. If the brief does not make sense in terms of its contribution towards the overall goals of the development work the agency is undertaking, there will be a problem.

Research briefs are often collaborative efforts, but development practitioners need to think through the implications of their agency's involvement, at whatever level it may be. Where a proposal is being submitted to an academic research funder, it may be planned jointly with academic or independent researchers. In this case, it may be that the researchers will take lead responsibility for writing the brief, and approach a development organisation to be a partner in the bid. Where this is so, the development agency needs to concentrate on clarifying what will be expected of it as a result of its involvement in the research. For example, will the agency be used as a link to community members? If so, do frontline staff members agree that this will be feasible and acceptable? Have any ethical issues been properly addressed? Are the researchers expecting the agency to provide administrative help, and can this, in fact, be delivered? And will the agency be expected to do any of the analytical work?

Does there always need to be a written brief?

Yes! It is the surest way of guarding against surprises. Even small-scale in-house research projects need clear guidelines if they are to be successful. Many projects develop out of programme planning, but another common way in which research takes place in development projects is when one of the members of staff is undertaking some further education or training, and a research project is part of the requirements for the course. Even in this situation, there can be important implications for the development programme, and there should be formal agreement as to what is planned and what is expected of whom. Frequently the required outputs and time frame demanded by an academic course are quite different from those needed by a development agency. Clarity of outputs for different parties is essential.

Ensuring the brief is owned by key stakeholders

It is not unheard of for development projects to feel that the brief for a piece of research has been imposed on them wholesale. It is very important to realise when this is what people feel, and to do something about it. Research in development is always part of some sort of change process. Often the intention is to influence policy or practice, either within an agency or more broadly. People are much more likely to be influenced by a piece of work if they have some feeling of ownership of it than if they merely read about it later. No one likes to hear about research in their 'field', especially if their help will be required, only after all the main decisions have been made. Key stakeholders need to be involved from the start of the process for maximum impact.

It is important for staff within the commissioning agency to be happy with the brief, and to see that it makes sense in relation to the other work

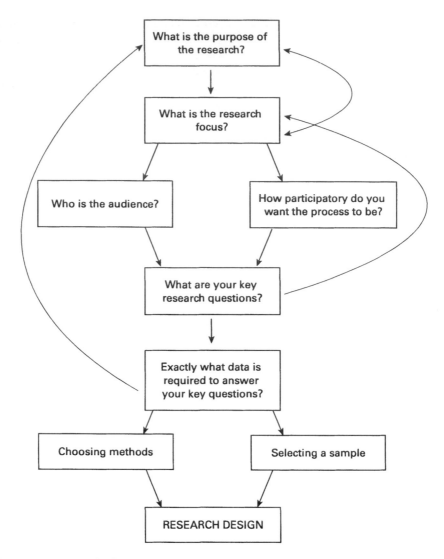

Figure 5.1 Research planning flow diagram – the key questions

that they are doing. Partner agencies should also be consulted, as it is likely that they will be involved, either in assisting in contacting informants, or in implementing recommendations. This also, of course, applies to members of the local community, and where possible community organisations should be shown a draft brief for comment. You might want to call an open meeting for community members to discuss your plans. Support at a later stage is much more likely to be forthcoming if people have some ownership of the project from the start.

People are sometimes worried that research may be critical of their work, particularly where there is an element of programme evaluation. Trust can be built by operating with openness. It is also important to realise that many people will find a formal research brief a daunting document to get to grips with. It may be useful to summarise the key points, taking account of the interests of those you are writing for, and being clear about what outcomes are intended to follow from the research. It can help to present key points in visual form – for example with a flow diagram to show how the research will inform policy and practice, or to show how different workers will relate to each other.

5.3   Defining the Research Focus

Getting the research focus right is the central task to be accomplished in writing a research brief. You will certainly know the broad area you want to work in, but in order to clarify your proposal you need to convincingly link the problems you want to investigate to your research strategy. Begin to think in terms of questions which can be answered through research – Section 5.4, below, looks at how to define research questions.

Try to remain open minded for as long as possible about exactly how you will focus the research. A decision will have to be made, of course, but the process of discussing the issues with others will throw up new possibilities, and you may find that your original ideas need to be reconsidered to get to a project which is both feasible and appropriate to your purpose.

Although actually writing the brief does not lend itself to group work, it can be very helpful to work with a group of colleagues to clarify the focus for a piece of research. This is also something that experienced researchers can helpfully advise on, as they will have a feel for what will be involved in different research approaches.

You may also want to directly consult policy-makers, and look at how your ideas fit into wider frameworks.

EXAMPLE

Essential National Health Research in Africa

In a growing number of African countries, organised attempts to formulate a broad health research agenda are already under way. The Essential National Health Research (ENHR) movement is bringing health researchers, policy and programme managers, health care providers, and community representatives together to identify priority research problems. One of the overall aims of this activity is to establish and promote a national research agenda that:

– pays particular attention to the most vulnerable population groups (women, children, the poor);
– strengthens the links between research, action, and policy;
– cuts across and brings together diverse disciplines and social sectors.

People sometimes seem to start their thinking about a research project by drafting a questionnaire. Researchers' hearts sink when they are consulted by someone bearing a questionnaire, but who has not thought clearly about the overall purpose of the exercise, or even about who exactly is to fill it in. The time to develop the research tools is logically somewhere in the middle of a research project, not before it has begun. Do not decide on the methods that you want to use before you are clear about the focus of the research. Methods should not drive an investigation. Sometimes researchers have become so focused on particular techniques within PRA that they have carried out transect walks, drawn out matrices with beans, or done mapping exercises with no clear idea of why they were doing it.

What follows are six activities or thinking points, to assist you in finding the right focus for your research project. So many are given, as this is a crucial step and every project is different. You may want to try one or two of these activities to test your ideas, before moving on to the next step.

Activity 5.1

A brainstorming workshop to help define the research focus

Invite some colleagues to a workshop, briefing them that it is not a decision-making meeting, but to generate and explore new ideas. Schedule it for one hour at the most. As well as those who know most about the research problem, invite people who do not know much about the problem but are good at asking critical questions.

At the start, give people a very brief introduction to the issue you want to research – just a few sentences. Then ask each participant to write down separately three ideas which come to their minds as ways of researching this issue. Pin their ideas on the wall and have everyone look at them and respond. Ask whether these are statements about things you already know, or whether research is needed.

A similar process could be carried out at a distance by post or email, though people are less likely to engage so readily with your question at a distance.

(Adapted from Robson, 1993, p 27)

TIP   Ways of looking at sorting out the research focus:

Picture those you hope to convince of your case:

What evidence would they need to see to be persuaded?
Think ahead to what you want to report:

What is the story you want to tell?
This last question may seem to suggest a cynical approach to research, where the results are seen as wholly predictable, which is the wrong spirit in which to start a research project. However, in practice, research for development is often planned for its (hoped-for) impact – it is intended to make

more visible a particular experience, or demonstrate a point about how the world works. In working towards a clear research focus, the question 'What is the story you want to tell?' is useful in drawing out people's motivations, and in checking the context of a proposal. You can decide later whether it will in fact be possible to tell that story from this data.

COMMON PITFALLS 5.2   Starting on a research project and then finding that another group of researchers have just published something very similar. Can be very embarrassing.

Sorting out the research focus may involve you in quite a lot of work, and it may be helpful to think of it as a mini-project in itself. Two types of approach may be worth considering:

Activity 5.2

Do a thorough search for existing information

Find out in depth what is already known about the subject you are looking at. Failing to collect relevant literature before starting on a research project is extremely wasteful. You may even find you do not need to collect new data.

How to do this will be discussed in detail in Chapter 12. Make sure you have clear questions in mind when you are looking at the literature. You should include library research, using the internet, and seeking up-to-date information through statutory or other voluntary agencies.

EXAMPLE

Locating crucial existing data – solvent abuse in the UK

Members of a small UK voluntary organisation working on the issue of solvent abuse came to visit a larger agency, aiming to persuade the agency to prioritise the issue. They said that it was a priority for their organisation to get research done to establish the extent of solvent abuse in children. A researcher at the larger agency had recently read a published study containing exactly this information, alongside data on children's substance use more broadly. This was already strong evidence to support the argument for action on solvent abuse issues. Small organisations do not have dedicated research staff but it is worth their while to prioritise some library research at regular intervals.

One risk of doing an extensive literature review is that you can become over-taken by the way in which the issues you intend to research have been framed by other researchers. Keep hold of your own perspective.

Another risk is that desk research may be carried out as a way of post-poning a decision. Doing a search for existing material can look like the line of least resistance, from everyone's perspective except the unfortunate person who is given it to carry out. Be sure that the findings will be of real use – literature reviews are hard work.

Activity 5.3

Do some exploratory fieldwork

Before writing the research plan, it may be useful to jump in and try out some of the your ideas in practice. Spend some time talking to people and observing, and see how much you can find out about the issues that you want to investigate.

This should enable you to introduce the research to communities, partners, and authorities; clarify the focus and questions of the research; begin to identify the type of sample you will use; test out methods, and above all identify logistical problems. The practicalities of research are often overlooked in writing a brief, and it is best to identify the problems as early as possible so as not to set up unrealistic expectations.

This may be particularly helpful when the matters you hope to research are sensitive ones, where you can check out the acceptability of the language you intend to use. For example, a study of stepfamilies in the UK found that no one volunteered to take part in the research when they used the term 'step-parents', and it went better when they talked about family change.

Be aware, though, that there are some risks involved here too. You could raise expectations inap-propriately, or you could cause confusion and anxiety in a community. Ensure that those undertak-ing exploratory fieldwork are sensitive to community concerns and have good communication skills.

Activity 5.4

Take it apart and put it together again

Write down the question which comes to your mind most readily, and then take it apart. Try to define each of the important terms of the question, and consider the issues this raises.

For example, in studying child labour, a number of issues of definition need to be considered:

- What counts as work?
- When is work damaging?
- What age group are we talking about?
- Should studies focus on work in a particular sector (eg mining), or include other work? Only paid work? All work?

For example, you want to study the physical punishment of children in your country. Some questions might be:

- What do you mean by physical punishment? At home? At school? In other institutions?
- What do you mean by children? Babies? Teenagers?
- Are you looking at opinions, or trying to get evidence of what is actually happening?
- Whose views are of interest?

Often we use jargon or include assumptions in the questions that we think of setting for research. One project began with the aim:

- To understand civil society's attitudes to education.

After discussion this was changed to the much more focused aim:

- To study why few girls go to school.

The first aim was huge, and the broadness of the question would have made it difficult to address properly what was the key concern of the investigators. 'Civil society' is difficult to define for research purposes. However the key issue about the first 'aim' is that it does not identify any problem or question – it simply seeks to understand more. The second formulation is much more specific and reveals the problem of concern very directly.

FOR EXAMPLE

An agency may wish to review the way in which it does its work. But some questions will be more helpful to ask than others. You could ask:

- What are the best types of health projects?

Or

- What can we learn from our health projects?

But these are extremely broad questions, where both the general field of study (health projects) and the specific issue (what is best? what can we learn?) are not closely defined. A better question might be:

- What are the key institutional factors which determine the success of immunisation programmes?

This specifies immunisation programmes as a more limited field of study, and directs attention particularly towards 'institutional factors' – those which are (to some extent) under the control of the organisation itself, and of government health agencies. A more transparent term than 'institutional factors' would be better still.

Having taken it apart, you will need to put it together again. The intention is not to push the project towards more and more abstract questions. NGOs are not in the business of fundamental theoretical research, but this procedure will help you to be conscious of the assumptions you are making, which helps to define good research work.

It is worth considering whether there is a comparison with some sort of standard or other situation implied by your question? Can you find a way of making this an explicit part of the study?

Activity 5.5

Look at it from another angle

There is a tendency for research to examine the powerless more than the powerful. But answers may not lie with those at the bottom of the heap – at times it is more useful to find out more about those with the power.

EXAMPLE

Researching employers of child domestic servants in Bangladesh

A Bangladeshi organisation, Shoishob, carried out a large survey of households where there was known to be a child domestic servant employed. Employers were asked questions about how they treated their servant. This survey generated an overwhelming amount of data, and problems were experienced in analysing it. However simply by carrying out the survey, the issue of these children's welfare was effectively raised.

Activity 5.6

Beyond the project: researching large subject areas

In talking about research, we tend to think in terms of individual projects. But this may make us think too big or indeed too small to cope with the problem we are grappling with. It may be more appropriate to think in terms of developing a *research strategy* which involves a series, or a net-work, of different pieces of work that contribute towards elucidating a shared set of questions.

EXAMPLE

What works in child welfare interventions?

Barnardos (a major UK child welfare voluntary organisation) have in recent years been working with a broad strategy to review the evidence on 'What works' in relation to child welfare inter-ventions. They have looked at early years provision, help for families with disabled children, and support on leaving care, amongst other issues. They are looking at the methodological issues in evaluating these services as well as what is known about the issues themselves.

On the other hand, when a piece of research looks daunting, it may be useful to break it down into smaller chunks.

EXAMPLE

Child labour in Vietnam – breaking down the problems

A Save the Children study of child labour in Vietnam was carried out as a set of distinct one-week case studies of specific kinds of child labour, for example work in gold mines, work in coffee plantations. Each was written up separately, using a standard outline format, and then an overall report was compiled based on this information.

EXAMPLE

Child poverty in Africa

Save the Children wanted to undertake a study of child poverty in Africa, addressed to donors who support the World Bank on poverty alleviation. This daunting task was broken down into eight country papers, each focusing on a particular theme, plus an overview paper to draw the findings together. For example, the paper from South Africa tackled budget setting, from Uganda the impact of conflict on child poverty, and from Ethiopia and Kenya, issues relating to different local economies such as that of pastoralists.

5.4   Setting the Research Questions

The activities above should help you in defining the focus of your research. The next stage is to define the research questions for the project. Research focus and research questions are of course closely linked. Once you are clear on the general focus of the research, the next important task is to identify the key questions to be asked by the research. These are not the same as the questions which may be asked to respondents as part of the research, they are the big questions which the research as a whole seeks to answer.

It is essential to identify a set of questions which the research will address. These need to be *researchable questions*. In fact they need not only to be researchable in principle, but also to be capable of being answered by methods which are feasible for you to use. The broad issue the research is concerned with (the research focus) needs to be broken down into sub-problems (the research questions), which can be expressed specifically, and which can be addressed with the evidence which will be collected. Do not expect your research to answer too many questions – ensure that the scope you set for it is achievable within the resources at your disposal.

COMMON	Setting too many research questions, and questions that are too broad to
PITFALLS	answer within your resources
5.2	

It is a good idea to have some detailed discussions within the research team to clarify the research questions. It may be worth making a 'long list' of all the questions you would ideally like answered, before narrowing it down to the questions you will be able to address in this project.

EXAMPLE

Clarifying the research questions – the impact of water metering on low-income families in England

Save the Children in the UK decided to undertake a study of the impact of water metering on low-income families. For many years water charges had been based on property values, with people paying a fixed charge each year. There was a move to change to metering with charges based on how much water is used, and in some areas this was being implemented. There were anecdotal reports that large families on low incomes were taking drastic measures to save water, and suggestions that this might have an impact on children's health. In a relatively water-rich country, should economic pressure on consumers be the main mechanism by which water is conserved?

In working out how to research this issue, given the resources the researchers had, they produced a whole series of sub-questions. These are just some of them:

What measures do people take to save water?

Is water-saving in fact linked to income?

Do charging systems in fact influence people's behaviour?

Have individual families' behaviour changed with the change in charging system?

Are people aware of the system being used to determine their water costs?

Are families using measurably less water as a result of the economies they report?

Is there harm to children's health resulting from sharing baths or flushing the toilet less often?

Are epidemics of diarrhoeal diseases occurring more frequently in areas where water is metered?

What do people/parents think about water metering?

Are some families more affected than others? Those with more children? Those with medical conditions requiring extra washing? Those with young babies?

To investigate different questions in this list would require very different procedures. For example to get an objective detailed measure of people's water use would involve the researchers in putting measuring devices on each appliance, which seemed excessively invasive and expensive, though some such studies have been done. Other questions could only be investigated through medical records, which would rely on these being very complete and up to date. The best sort of study for these purposes would have been a comparison between metered and un-metered families. This was not possible, and it was decided to study people's own accounts of their behaviour and views, and their actual water use. However the total volume of water used per household could also be established, through people's water bills (Cuninghame et al, 1996).

In setting research questions consider whether a question can be answered:

- Are you looking at a question, or is it really a statement you wish to make?
- Are the different factors involved defined in a clear and unambiguous way?
- Can items of evidence (ie data you could collect) be identified which would answer the question?
- Are there value judgements embedded in the question which make some factors problematic to measure? (For example 'a good education'; 'a healthy lifestyle'.)
- Is a comparison implied by the question? If so, this needs to be made explicit. Is information available to enable comparisons to actually be made?
- List some possible answers to the question you have set. Will this type of answer meet your needs?

TIP   If in doubt, consult a researcher

Hypothesis testing

Many texts on research will tell you that all research needs a hypothesis. Much traditional scientific 'positivist' (see Chapter 2, Section 2.2 for a discussion of positivism) research sees its central aim as attempting to disprove a hypothesis. A hypothesis is

> 'a logical supposition, a reasonable guess ... It may direct your thinking to the possible source of information that will aid in resolving the problem.'
> (Leedy, 1997)

We make simple hypotheses all the time. For example, since I can see that the sun is shining, I hypothesise that I may be able to get my washing dry outside today. We also make much more complex hypotheses, for example, one broad hypothesis might be that it is possible for famine to occur in countries where sufficient food is present, but where social divisions prevent its distribution to those in need. In principle, these are both testable hypotheses.

Hypothesis testing essentially deals with 'why' questions – explanations – and is highly relevant to much academic scientific research, which aims to develop generalisable theories about the world. It looks at cause and effect in a very focused way.

However researchers working in non-positivist traditions reject the idea that all research needs a specific hypothesis, and the sort of research development workers most often carry out may not require a formal hypothesis. Research can bring to bear a new perspective, perhaps describing a situation from the point of view of the people concerned, rather than setting out to 'prove a point'. The investigation may be at too early a stage for it to be appropriate to test hypotheses – it may be more a matter of generating some relevant hypotheses that could be tested later.

However it is a good discipline, when you are working to clarify your research plan, to try to turn your research focus into a set of hypotheses. If you do this, you will make explicit the theories which lie behind your way of seeing the problem, clarifying the assumptions you are making.

For example, let us look at some ways of writing a research question, structured as a hypothesis, and then structured in a more open way:

Hypothesis:

That significant physical violence and abuse towards children is more common in families where there is physical violence towards adult women (usually the mother).

Non-hypothesis question:

What are the effects on the incidence and type of violence or abuse of children of the presence or absence of violence towards adult women in the family?

These are both of course difficult issues to investigate, due to social norms of 'family privacy'. Both formulations beg many questions about definitions. Using a specific hypothesis encourages researchers to define terms as tightly as possible before starting their investigation. This has its pros and cons. For example, might sexual abuse or neglect be missed, in our example, if questions were very tightly directed towards physical violence?

Key Points from this Chapter

The last two sections, on setting the research focus and selecting suitable research questions, are intended to assist you with the most difficult task involved in writing a research brief. However there are still a number of important issues to sort out to complete the brief. The next chapter offers guidance on all the other areas you need to think about in undertaking this task.

CHECKLIST   For effective research planning

- ✓ Expect to actively manage the process of initiating and overseeing a research project, as you would any other project – allow time for this
- ✓ Writing a good brief is the key to planning effective research
- ✓ Research briefs should be thoroughly discussed with all concerned before they are finalised
- ✓ In drafting the brief, defining the focus and key questions for the research is the central task, and should be given time
- ✓ Work out a project timetable and budget which allows realistic resources for each of the tasks involved

> ✔ Ensure recognition and support from your organisation's management
> ✔ Community involvement should be considered in relation to every aspect of the project from identifying the research focus to promoting its findings

Further Reading

Hall, D. and Hall, I. (1996) *Practical Social Research: Project work in the community*. Basingstoke, Macmillan.

Written for students doing research as part of their degrees, often on placements with a voluntary organisation. Gives guidance on negotiating an agreement between the researcher, their agency and the organisation where the research is taking place.

Blaxter, L., Hughes, C. and Tight, M. (1996) *How to Research*. Buckingham, UK: Open University Press.

Aimed at people involved in small-scale research projects at college or at work, this helpful book includes good advice about how to focus a research project.

Wadsworth, Y. (1984, 2nd edition 1997) *Do It Yourself Social Research*. Victorian Council of Social Service, St Leonards, Australia: Allen and Unwin.

A nicely written straightforward guide for community organisations to carrying out their own research. A best seller, for good reason.

6 Planning for Effective Research – What Should Go into the Brief?

This chapter takes you through the process of writing a research brief in some detail. Any researcher who has worked in NGOs will tell you that a large proportion of the problems people encounter in research work could be avoided by writing better briefs at the start of research processes. For this reason a lot of space has been given to this process here. The last chapter concentrated on discussing the *process* of writing the brief, and the key first step in writing it – defining the research focus. This chapter discusses the issues you need to consider in writing each section of the brief.

Research planning documents

A lot of different terms are used for the various documents we use in planning research work. Table 6.1 aims to clarify the distinctions between different kinds of document.

Table 6.1 Research planning documents

Type of document	Also called	Definition	When written
Brief	Proposal; terms of reference	Describes and justifies the research plan	During planning stage, often before applying for funding
Protocol		Detailed plan for carrying out the research	Start of implementation stage
Contract		Formal agreement of roles and responsibilities when employing staff – may refer to the brief	If employing staff specifically for the research project

6.1   Writing the Brief

Table 6.2 gives a framework for a research brief, which can be adapted to different needs. There are sections in the text corresponding to each element of the brief. It is followed by some thoughts about different areas to emphasise in different types of research project.

Obviously a research brief needs to reflect the scale of the research being proposed in terms of how elaborate it is.

The contents and style of the brief will need to reflect the purpose of the research. Different types of research need different emphases in the brief:

- Research that is essentially part of developing a programme of development work needs a brief which emphasises the practical *outcomes* which are desired and encourages regular, appropriate *feedback* to partners.
- Research aimed at influencing policy requires consideration of exactly *who the work is addressed* to, and *how the research fits* into an influencing strategy. The methodology chosen needs to be convincing to the audience. The participation of key stakeholders in the planning and conduct of the research should be defined in the brief. The role of the researcher/s in writing up and *dissemination* should be specified as part of the brief.
- If *capacity sharing* through developing the research-related skills of staff or partners is part of the purpose of the exercise, this should be made explicit and time allowed for it.

Table 6.2   An outline research brief/terms of reference

	Where discussed in detail
Introduction and background, setting the scene – existing information, gaps and rationale	See 6.2.1 below
Aims and objectives	6.2.2 and Chapters 1 and 2
Research focus and research questions	Chapter 5.3 and 5.4
Audience	6.2.3 and Chapter 10
Methods	6.2.4 and Chapters 2, 3 and 15 to 18
Analysis	6.2.5 and Chapter 20
Outputs – reports, presentations, interim reports, training sessions, etc	6.2.6 and Chapters 21 and 10
Plan for dissemination/ influence/ implementation	6.2.6 and Chapter 10
Accountability – support and supervision	6.2.7 and Chapter 8.1, and 13.3
Advisory group	6.2.8 and Chapter 3
Time-scale	Chapter 8.2
Budget	Chapter 8.2
Ethical considerations	6.2.10 and Chapter 13

• If the research is very participatory, with end users defining the research questions, then this needs to be specified in the brief, identifying empowerment explicitly as an important outcome.

If you plan to seek external funding for your project it is crucial that you obtain the guidelines for research proposals used by the funder/s you have in mind. Many funders, for example ESCOR (Economic and Social Council on Research, the research arm of the UK Department for International Development – DfID) and the Joseph Rowntree Foundation provide detailed guidance on the format in which they wish to see proposals written. DfID requires that the project plan be set out in the Logical Framework Analysis format.

Do you need a research protocol?

Some research projects require a **protocol** in addition to the brief. This gives full details of the procedures to be followed as part of the research and is written once the research is under way. It may include research instruments, eg questionnaires, along with an account of how they are to be used. Essentially it tells you in detail how the objectives set out in the brief will be addressed in practice.

It can be very helpful to write a protocol where many people are involved in undertaking a large and complex piece of research. It may give a useful structure to the process of agreeing on a research plan where community members are participating in research.

Research projects have a way of changing from what was intended by the original brief once the logistical issues involved in the research become clear. Writing a protocol gives an opportunity to set down in writing what will actually be done, at the point when you are starting to do it, which may be some time after the brief was written. How adaptable you are about changes to the research procedures after the protocol is written depends upon the style of research you are undertaking. Traditional scientific research follows its protocol exactly – more interactive processes may take the protocol as a broad guideline.

A research protocol includes:

• Background to the study
• Aims and objectives
• Research focus – key question/s
• Methods in detail:

    – The sample, and how it will be drawn. How many? Who exactly?
    – Exact plans for procedures to be followed in, eg, administering questionnaires, interviews, focus groups, observations etc
    – Research instruments to be used, eg questionnaires etc
    – Procedure to be followed in obtaining consent from respondents
    – Procedures to protect confidentiality of data

- Notes on how any special ethical considerations for this study will be dealt with, eg making information or help available to respondents after interviews, etc.
- Timetable and resources required
- Methods to be used in analysis of data – as much detail as possible
- Outputs, dissemination plan.
- Procedures for monitoring the progress of the research, timings of team meetings, supervision and outputs.

If a well-worked-out research brief is available, it may not be necessary to duplicate information that is contained in it – or you can incorporate aspects of the brief into a protocol document. The protocol should give those carrying out the research a quick reference point to be clear about exactly what they should be doing. It is particularly important where a consistent approach is needed in carrying out fieldwork.

Contracts

If an external consultant is to undertake the research, you will also need to set a contract defining the relationship between the consultant and the organisation. Save the Children and other large agencies have model contracts which you can use for these purposes. More details on setting contracts will be discussed in Chapter 7.3 looking at commissioning research.

It may also be useful to set out some kind of contract or terms of reference for particular team members, for example where staff are seconded from one or more agencies to act as fieldworkers on a project. It is best to be clear about exactly what is required.

6.2   What to Think about in Writing a Research Brief

The next section looks in more detail at the issues you need to make decisions about as you work on the brief for your research project. We have already looked at the key issues of setting the research focus, and identifying the research questions, in Chapter 5. These lay the basis for writing the brief, and you need to refer back to Chapter 5.3 and 5.4, if you have not already worked through those processes. The material below helps you to think about the other important issues involved in writing the brief.

(1)   Setting the scene

It is easy to feel that the introduction to a research brief is unimportant, as you are probably very familiar with the material which needs to go into it. But to the reader it is crucial. The introduction needs to answer a number of questions:

- Why is this research important to the development work your organisation is involved in?
- What is the wider background to the subject? Is there national or international legislation or guidance which relates to this issue? Looking to the future, are key decision points coming up?
- What do we already know which is relevant to the questions you are raising?
- Why this research now?

(2)   Aims and objectives

Research for development needs research questions for intellectual clarity. But this type of research is done for practical purposes, and so also needs aims and objectives, similar to those you would set for any other sort of project. This is a matter of making explicit the outcomes you hope to achieve by carrying out this piece of work.

- An aim is a broad statement of what the research hopes to achieve.

  An aims statement answers the question: why are we doing this piece of work?

  For example:
  'To find out how maternal mortality is affected by distance from health centres and if this is a primary factor.'

- An objective is a specific, realistic, and measurable statement of the change you want a particular piece of work to achieve.

  A statement of objectives answers the question: what do we hope to achieve?

  For example:
  'Using the information obtained make recommendations to the Ministry of Health and donors on the location and efficacy of health centres in relation to reducing maternal mortality.'

   In setting objectives, it is particularly important that they be concrete and capable of assessment. It should be possible to tell whether or not the objective has been achieved at the end of the project.

EXAMPLE

Some simple objectives – the Child Labour Project, Sialkot, Pakistan

The Sialkot study set out its objectives as follows:

The situation analysis will be designed to provide baseline data on the lives of children in Sialkot District and the work that they do in the sporting goods industries and other forms of work. It will also gauge the opinions of the children, their families and their communities on the changes needed to ensure the best possible future for children involved in child labour.

In short the situation analysis will seek to answer three questions:

What is the problem and how big is that problem for children?

If the problem exists, **why** does it exist?

What can be done about the problem?

These are broad objectives, and the study specified its focus in more detail in the research questions, though these were also many and broad. However it was a major study which was able to carry ambitious aims.

A common confusion is to mix up methods or activities with objectives. Thus you get an objective reading 'To carry out a survey ...' or to 'Run five focus groups with xyz ...'. This is unhelpful as it does not tell us what purpose is being pursued by carrying out the survey or running the groups. Methods or activities are the ways in which you pursue your objectives, they are not ends in themselves. This distinction is very important, as if we fail to make it, we can get hooked into doggedly continuing to carry out particular activities as if they were an end in themselves, even when they are not working well. It would be better to step back and look more broadly for other ways in which the aims we have in mind could be reached. Methods will be specified later, but they are a way of achieving the objectives, not objectives in themselves.

Objectives should relate to the content of the research and to its process. For example, it is important to assess whether objectives that relate to capacity sharing – outcomes from the *process* of the research – are possible. For example, the project working with young people with experience of using mental health services as peer researchers could have as a specific objective to increase the confidence of at least four young people in speaking up on mental health issues.

It may also be helpful to include more wide-ranging objectives relating to the way in which you wish the research project to relate to local communities and to partner agencies. For example, an objective might be to build co-operation between your agency and the provincial department of social welfare.

Objectives should not be seen as fixed once they are set on paper, though they should be taken seriously. They are key management tools, and if circumstances change and the working objectives being pursued by staff change, it is best to formally redraft the written objectives to reflect this. It may be necessary to get agreement to this from all stakeholders. If this is not done, staff can feel that the brief sets them up to fail.

Some agencies, eg DfID, require proposals to present their objectives in the form of a logical framework analysis. This format is explained in *Toolkits* (Gosling with Edwards, 1995), in relation to practice – the same principles apply to research proposals.

(3) Audience

Who is the research for? Research is all about communication, and most research undertaken as part of development work has quite specific audiences. These are, however, diverse. They range from community members to politicians at national and indeed international levels. What is needed to convince these different groups of a case may be very different. Some audiences are much more wedded to traditional research methods than others. You need to think about your audience in relation to the design of the research itself, and also in planning the promotion of the findings – a different writing style will be needed for different audiences.

The standard and style of your research needs to be fit for its purpose, and part of that purpose is defined through a consideration of audience. List out all the possible audiences for a particular piece of work. But do not stop there. You need to decide which audience/s have top priority in relation to this piece of work. It may be that the same data will be of interest to a very wide group of people, but even if this is so, it is likely that you will need to use different methods to communicate your message to different groups. For example, politicians will require less detail than professionals who may also want information on the methodology used.

Busy senior managers and politicians do not read long and complex research reports. It is essential that the findings be summarised, if they are to be read by people with decision-making power. It is also crucial to realise that people bring their own agenda to your research. Take account of the terms in which powerful people are thinking – what they think the problem is. You need not agree, but to get their attention you need to relate the problem as you define it to their specific understanding.

EXAMPLE

Meeting prejudice half way

In an Asian country, where Save the Children works, senior Government officials believe HIV is a foreigners' problem. This research, looking at HIV prevalence needs to look at both foreign and national populations to gain the interest of decision-makers, even if it is likely that HIV is not significantly prevalent among foreigners.

Table 6.3   Some audiences for research

Research into child labour in the sports goods industry in Pakistan	–	The sports goods industry
	–	International donor agencies
	–	Pakistani government and NGOs
	–	International Labour Organisation
	–	Campaigning NGOs
	–	Private sector working in developing countries
Needs of young people and disabled children in Serb Sarajevo	–	Local people: parents and other adults; children and young people
	–	Potential donors
	–	NGOs
	–	the Ministry of Health and Social Welfare
Sustainability in the health sector	–	UNICEF, WHO, World Bank
	–	UK Department for International Development
	–	Other international donor agencies, especially in the health sector
	–	Governments of countries studied
	–	Other Southern governments
	–	Academics in development studies
Studies of child sexual abuse in Pakistan, South Africa	–	Adults in the community
	–	Children themselves
	–	Local NGOs
'Leaving care' research	–	The UK Government
	–	Young care leavers
	–	Politicians with an interest in young people leaving care
	–	Local authorities
	–	Social workers

It is equally important to think about audience in relation to research which is primarily addressed to a local community or a particular group of people. At times the key purpose of a research project is to raise the issue publicly amongst a community. For example, some HIV-related research has been of this nature. Another example would be research that shows how people are not taking up benefits such as pensions and disability benefits to which they are entitled. In this case the accessibility of the methods used is absolutely central, and thought must be given to how this particular group can best contribute to and learn from research.

Respondents themselves are always one of the audiences of a research project. The research in Bangladesh on child domestic servants (see 5.3, activity 5.5), which asked questions of their employers, is an example of how research can have an impact on respondents simply by raising new questions. People who were employing children as domestics found that filling in the questionnaire drew their attention to the children's welfare in a new way.

Getting clear about audience may also enable you to think about who to involve in advising you about the research. It is helpful to have people like those you hope to influence – or indeed those people themselves – directly involved with the research. This enables ongoing dialogue about what evidence is seen as important and relevant, and what is not.

(4)   Methods

The research brief should give a general idea of the kinds of method which will be used for the research. But do not feel that you have to specify every last detail. If the brief is to be used to employ an experienced researcher, it is a good idea to leave them some room to advise you on the methods they think would be most appropriate to your research questions.

In participatory research too, it will be best to leave choices of exact methods to those who will be carrying out the research. Often there are several possible approaches which could be taken, and there is no need to specify too early on the methods which will be used.

You may want to state roughly the scale of the research, for example how many people will be interviewed. But until you are clear about the difficulties you may encounter, it is worth leaving some leeway. In proposals for quantitative research you will need to give some specific figures, but consult an experienced researcher on sampling first.

Ensure that you remember to pilot any research tools (eg question- naires, focus group topic guides) before they are used. Time needs to be allowed for organising a small pilot study and for reflecting on the results and making the necessary changes.

See Chapters 16 and 17 for more on research methods.

(5)   Analysis

Yes, I know you don't want to think about analysis yet! It is at the point when data collection is complete, and analysis and writing should start, that many research projects threaten to collapse. This can be a huge waste of resources.

Analysis is the process of organising the information you have collected, relating your data to the research questions. It requires you to interpret what people have said, and to decide on the categories you will use to organise your material. It is not a good idea to plunge into the process of collecting data before you are clear about how you are going to analyse it. While you may be able to hire somebody to make sense of the data once it is in, it is far preferable to involve anyone who will be analysing the data in the early planning stages. If you do not, it may not be possible to get from the data the information you require. Questions asked in slightly the wrong way can be impossible to analyse.

This applies to both quantitative and qualitative research. Analysis is part of the design of research work, and any research materials like questionnaires should be designed with a view to the final methods of analysis. There is nothing like knowing that you yourself will be responsible for writing up the research to make you focus on getting the right data in the first place.

Many research projects include an element of both quantitative and qualitative data collection. It is usually best to think about the analysis of these two elements separately, though you will need to bring them together again in the end, of course. Where a large amount of data is to be collected, careful thought needs to be given to the technicalities of analysing the data. You may need to use a computer, and should identify the package you will require, and the hardware it needs to run it. Or else you need to find someone who has suitable computer facilities and skills who can help you.

If you hope to get funding for the project, research-oriented funders will want to see a clear and detailed statement of the procedures that will be followed in interpreting and analysing the data.

Computer software exists for both quantitative and qualitative data analysis – but don't be bounced into using it just because it looks good on your proposal. Chapter 20 includes a discussion of the advantages and disadvantages of computer analysis for the different types of data. Remember that qualitative analysis always takes considerable time and skill, whatever technology you use to help you. Quantitative analysis can be very straightforward or extremely subtle, depending on the type of project.

It is quite difficult to anticipate how you will need to analyse your data, and therefore how you should collect it. This is something one learns from (sometimes bitter) experience. Ask someone who has been involved with two or three completed research projects to have a look at your plans and comment on how best to make the data collection process suitable for the analysis you intend to undertake.

See Chapter 20 for more on analysis.

(6)   Outputs and dissemination plan

You may need a conventional research report. But few people are filled with joy at the thought of reading such a report, even if it is about something they are extremely interested in. Think creatively about how you would like to see the research reported. Think about how you yourself have learned about research findings – what communication methods reached you?

Some projects need to produce two or more reports – one, perhaps, for those most directly involved with the community group in question, and one for a wider audience of policy-makers. The wider audience will want less detail about, for example, the history of a particular programme, but may need more background information to put the findings in context. The people who were the 'subjects' of development research should have access to its findings – and be able to respond to them. You may want to write a shorter, more direct report for them.

Indeed, written reports may be irrelevant, and feedback better given in person, whether through talks to groups of community members or workshops for partner agencies. Video can be used to present a project's main findings, with human stories interwoven with evidence, but they are expensive.

EXAMPLE

Getting the message across: the needs of young people leaving care in the UK

Save the Children's peer research on leaving care in the UK[1] was reported in three ways. A report was produced, and also a short summary on a single folded sheet of paper. Both were attractively produced with photographs as illustrations, and much use of direct quotations from the young people. Alongside these, a video was produced which recorded the process of developing the research with the young researchers, and illustrated the main themes which had been identified by care leavers as causing them problems. The research was also presented in person to various audiences, including a meeting in Parliament, with the young researchers presenting their work themselves.

The project succeeded in drawing Parliament's attention to the issue, as an all-party group of MPs attended the launch event and agreed to take the issues forward. Legislation has now been introduced which strengthens local authorities' obligations (West, 1995).

An important way in which people learn from research is through articles, either in journals or in less academic magazines and newspapers. All professional groups have publications on which they rely to keep up to date, and it is important to publish in these if you want to influence these groups. The internet is becoming an important source of information, but busy professionals will only see information that presents itself readily.

It can be a good idea to write this into the brief from the start. If employing someone, you can specify that you wish them to write articles and present seminars as well as to write a report. Too many research projects only employ researchers up to the point when the 'long and boring' final report is complete, leaving no one whose job it is to present the findings in more accessible ways. It is important to employ a researcher with the writing skills you need – see Chapter 7: 'Who should do the research?' An alternative is

---

[1] Care leavers are young people who have been looked after by the state, through local authorities, either in children's homes or now more often through fostering in families. They often experience difficulties at the point when they are expected to become independent.

to split these roles, and ask someone with journalistic skills to carry out the promotional element of the work.

Reports often go through several drafts, and if they are published, there will be further work involved in getting the design right. Incorporating changes required by readers of a first draft can be a substantial piece of work, and this should be acknowledged in the brief.

For reports aiming to influence policy, it is important that recommendations are written in an appropriate way. You may want to specify something about the type of recommendations you require in the brief. Recommendations should include not only 'what' but also 'how' changes should be made. For example, you may want guidance on action that a particular agency, or arm of government, could take in the short or the longer term. Development-related projects do not generally want to see recommendations which call for further research! It may be a good idea to expect researchers to work with hands-on development workers and managers to draft appropriate recommendations.

See also Chapter 10 for more on promoting findings of research.

(7) Accountability, support, and supervision

Research does not look after itself. As was stated at the start of this section, it needs managing just as much as any other project. The research brief should state to whom the researcher is accountable, and where they will get support and supervision. Sometimes some of a researcher's accountability will be through an advisory group, but this can lead to confusion. Generally it is best to have a clear line of accountability through an individual who is responsible for overseeing the research as a whole, and for linking this project with other related activities. The line manager should be a member (or perhaps chair) of any advisory group which is established, and shares responsibility with the researcher for ensuring that discussions at this group produce clear decisions to enable the research to proceed.

Researchers should receive regular supervision in relation to their progress towards meeting their aims and objectives, just like any other staff. They may also need support and supervision from another researcher with experience of the type of work in question, in addition to management supervision.

CHECKLIST   For research management arrangements

✔ Establish a clear line of accountability, preferably to an individual rather than a group
✔ Set up appropriate research and managerial supervision arrangements
✔ If necessary, buy in professional research supervision
✔ Establish regular liaison to ensure that confusion does not arise between the advisory group, any external supervisor, and the line manager

See also Chapter 8.1 on supervision.

(8) Advisory or steering groups

Beyond the smallest piece of investigation, all research projects benefit from setting up an advisory group to assist the staff through the various stages of the research. As well as offering support and a sounding board for the researchers, an advisory group also ensures that partner agencies which may be affected by the research process or findings have an opportunity to be represented. Those the project hopes to influence can be invited onto the advisory group, where they will learn from the project as it goes along, and can ask questions and satisfy themselves if they have doubts about any aspect of the research. The research should be accountable to those whose lives it concerns – community members, including perhaps children and young people. Finally funders may well wish to be represented, and have a say in how the research proceeds.

EXAMPLE

The Joseph Rowntree Foundation

The Joseph Rowntree Foundation, a major UK research funder, insists as part of the conditions of its grants that projects it sponsors have an advisory group chaired by a member of Rowntree's staff. The Foundation have a say in who is invited to join the group, along with those running the project.

These groups are sometimes called steering groups, but this implies that they are responsible for managing the project. It is difficult to be accountable to a group. What happens if members disagree? Perhaps the term 'steering group' sends the wrong message to members. To call the group 'advisory' makes it clear that members' views will be taken account of, but that it may not be possible to do everything they suggest.

Members might include:

* Representatives of funding organisations.
* Researchers/policy experts in the substantive field of study (eg on early years education).
* Researchers with experience of a range of relevant methodologies.
* Representatives of partner agencies – government departments, other NGOs, local authority or health authority managers.
* Representatives of community members/ those being studied.
* Senior management of the 'host' organisation.
* People who are, or are similar to, the people you hope to influence – they can guide you on how to do so (eg someone from the Ministry of Health).

It may be that all members of the research team will attend meetings, or one or two people will represent the others. It is important that information flows freely between the advisory group and all members of the research team itself. The researchers should feel confident to bring any problems they encounter to the group.

Groups do not need to meet frequently – three or four times in the life of a project may be enough. Staff should not feel that they have to refer every small decision to the group, as this can seriously impede progress. People can be consulted at a distance by post, email, or telephone if the people you need are unable to attend meetings.

Outline terms of reference for a research advisory group

The following is an extract from the Joseph Rowntree Foundation's Guidelines, reproduced by kind permission of JRF. These are oriented to research which specialises in issues to do with disabled people and support for them in the UK. Other kinds of work will have different specific concerns in enabling 'the researched' to participate fully.

Purpose and function

- As the title suggests, a project advisory group is advisory and does not have management responsibility for the project, its staff and its finances. Responsibility for the management and successful completion of the project rests with [the designated project manager].
- The functions of advisory groups are varied and include:

    - Advice/support for the work as a whole
    - Help with specific aspects of the work (eg research design and methodology)
    - Providing information about work in progress elsewhere, or policy and practice developments, as a context for the project
    - Reviewing the progress of the project, its timetable and future plans
    - Providing a channel for the funder to keep in touch with the work
    - Providing a forum to focus on dissemination.

- The intention is that groups will be supportive. Even very experienced research and project staff have found that groups can provide positive assistance and useful inputs, as well as providing some structure and 'discipline'.
- Advisory group members can be particularly helpful towards the end of the project when methods of dissemination are discussed, particularly when it is felt that a number of different ways need to be found to get the messages from the project across.

Setting up the group

- The aim is to balance the group's membership so that all relevant contributions and activities are covered. The [funder] particularly encourages the membership of [community members/representatives of those the research is about] where appropriate, and would like to see a greater representation of members of black and minority ethnic groups. Groups sizes vary but usually include between 6 and 10 external members.

The meetings themselves

- The project staff are responsible for organising and servicing meetings, and for circulating papers beforehand.
- Wherever possible, the venue for the meeting should be accessible to wheelchair users and people with limited mobility. [Access of other sorts also needs thought, eg interpreters for different languages etc.]
- In managing the meeting, project staff and chairperson need to ensure that the way in which it is organised and run enables all members to participate fully. Particularly where [community members] are members of the group, this involves careful preparation of the papers for the meeting. It is also important to ensure that there is time at the meeting for users and carers to make points relating to their own agendas, as well as contributing to discussion focused around the project's concerns.
- The [funder] is happy to meet the expenses of those attending advisory group meetings, including any costs not normally incurred for care arrangements which enable a service user or carer to attend the meeting. Group members who are unwaged or in receipt of income support can be offered an honorarium, but the [funder] is not able to meet the costs of loss of earnings for members working in a freelance or self-employed capacity.

EXAMPLE

A multi-agency research management committee: pre-school education in Mongolia

In Mongolia, Save the Children assisted in developing a study of the pre-school sector, using a management committee to ensure ownership of the project by those with a stake in the work. A management committee was established consisting of all those involved in pre-school work from the Ministry of Health and Education, to the National Children's Centre (a quango) and pre-school specialists. The committee was empowered with money and the role of writing the terms of reference. Save the Children provided only advice on the terms of reference, procedures, and research methods. The resulting research was owned by the committee and the expertise was retained in country. The committee itself brought together a group of people who would not have previously spoken, but were instead locked in competition with each other over retaining resources for the pre-school sector. As a result of the committee they were working together to raise funds and are committed to common objectives and to taking the whole process forward.

Chapter 8: Managing Research, gives more details on managing research projects, including advisory groups.

(9)   Time-scale and budget

See below, 8.2, for a full consideration of these issues.

(10)   Ethical considerations/code of conduct

In writing a research brief it is important to discuss any ethical issues which you see arising in this project. You should describe any procedures you intend to use to overcome any likely ethical problems for the project. Ethical issues can arise at any point in the life of a research project, and these will be discussed in more detail in Chapter 13.

A key ethical issue is how you ensure that people who choose to take part in the research do so on a genuinely voluntary basis. This is called 'informed consent', drawing attention to the need to ensure that respondents understand what the research is, and what their participation means. There may be concern about how informed consent will be obtained from respondents if they have limited experience and understanding of what research is, as may be the case with children or people without formal education. The brief should explain how you hope to ensure that respondents understand what they are being asked to do.

It may be appropriate to refer to standard statements of ethical practice produced by professional associations. The Social Research Association,[2] the Association of Social Anthropologists of the Commonwealth,[3] the British Sociological Association, and the British Psychological Association have all produced Codes of Practice. However demonstrating that potential ethical problems have been considered and addressed would create greater confidence than simply referring to a standard code.

The central ethical issue to consider at the outset is whether any risks or costs to participants which are involved in the research process are justified in relation to the benefits to be gained from the project as a whole. Ethical issues in research are discussed more fully in Chapter 13.

---

[2]The Social Research Association is currently consulting on a revision of its existing Ethical Guidelines. This is published annually in its 'Directory of Members', and is available on the SRA's website: http://www.the-sra.org.uk/index2.htm

[3]Association of Social Anthropologists of the Commonwealth, Ethical Guidelines for Good Practice, as revised in 1999. Available at the website: http://www.asa.anthropology.ac.uk/ethics2.html

Key Points from this Chapter

CHECKLIST   For writing a research brief

✓ Before starting on the brief, do some work on defining the research focus (See Chapter 5.3)

✓ A research brief needs to include a standard set of headings (see Table 6.2)

✓ Don't let early decisions about methods lead the research process – concentrate on clarifying the aims and objectives and research questions

✓ If you want your project to have influence, consider carefully the audience for the research

✓ Think ahead about how your data will be analysed and how the results will be promoted – plan for influence throughout the life of the research

✓ Include in the brief any arrangements you plan to make for an advisory group and for supervision and support for the research team

This chapter has concentrated on the practical aspects of managing research for development. It has looked in detail at the different elements which need to be included in a research brief. The next chapter moves on to look at the ongoing management of research, and includes ways of estimating costs and time-scales for research, as well as the issues of negotiating access, sharing research capacity, managing participatory research, and relating to funders.

7 Who Should do the Research?

This chapter aims to assist managers in making decisions about how a particular piece of research is to be undertaken. The key decision is often whether to undertake the research in-house, using existing staff, or whether to hire researchers specifically to carry out the work, either as employed staff or as freelance consultants. And then if you are clear that you need to bring in new people, it will be important to think through the issues about how to go about doing this. Researchers are a variable breed, and who you hire will have a major impact on the piece of work you end up with. The later part of this chapter looks at the process of commissioning research, and describes the different ways in which you can employ researchers.

This chapter falls into three sections. The first looks at the issues involved in the decision about whether a piece of research should be undertaken in-house or commissioned from others. Ways of dividing up the work are considered. The second section looks at managing in-house research and includes an analysis of the skills required for research work, to assist in thinking about staff skills as against specific research skills. The third part looks at employing researchers, both as employees and as freelance workers. Selection processes are discussed, and some tips given on how to choose the right person. Some possible items for a person specification are proposed. The issues involved in working with academics, and with freelance consultants are discussed, and finally the matters which need to be covered in the contract are described.

This chapter focuses primarily on the paid staff who are needed to undertake research exercises. Projects may involve greater or lesser degrees of participation by community members. However such participation does not reduce, and indeed is likely to increase, the staff time involved in carrying out a piece of work. Participatory research may require different types of staff.

7.1 Who can do the Research?

There are a number of choices to be made in deciding who will carry out a piece of research. Who you need to do it depends on what type of research it

is – is it primarily programme-focused research, like needs assessment, or is it focused on issues and aiming to have a wider influence on policy? How much community participation will you aim for? It is likely that more than one person will be involved in the project. Table 7.1 shows some of the possible options. You might like to use it in planning a research project, to identify the roles of the various participants.

You can divide up research tasks in a number of different ways. Some projects are essentially carried out by one person, for example desk studies or small-scale qualitative studies. A participatory project is likely to involve community members, a researcher/research advisor (who may be one of your staff or an external consultant), and at least one other worker to support the community members in their research work. Sometimes a development worker will run the whole project themselves. But a large-scale survey might involve many people – a lead researcher, a supervisor and/or manager, interviewers, administrative staff doing coding and data entry, perhaps a specialist transcriber, a statistician to advise on data analysis... A cast of thousands!

As with all projects, the more complex the division of labour, the greater the need for co-ordination. It is this complexity which makes it advisable to contract out any very large survey work to an organisation which is geared to delivering this sort of project.

Table 7.1   Who can do the research?

	Lead researcher	Super-vision	Field-work	Writing and dissemination	Enabling participation	Admin support
Development staff						
In-house research staff						
New research staff						
Community members						
Freelance researcher						
University academic						
Research agency commercial or voluntary sector						

The Sialkot research project gives an example of a fairly complicated set of arrangements for a major project, which worked well overall.

EXAMPLE

Who did what? – the child labour project, Sialkot, Pakistan

The research was planned and designed by a team from Save the Children Pakistan comprising three managers, all of whom had some research experience, and an experienced researcher/advisor from Save the Children London.[1] The project also drew on the advice of a member of Save the Children's regional South Asia team with considerable experience in participatory research.

The project manager with responsibility for overseeing the research and developing Save the Children's programme in Sialkot played a key role. He was a member of the core team who developed the methodology. He was responsible for the logistics for the entire research, including the recruitment of enumerators for the survey, engaging a consultant to analyse the statistical data, and ensuring there was adequate transport and accommodation. He and a short-term

---

[1]It would be preferable to have support from someone in country, where this is possible.

consultant who worked with the team for the first part of the research played an important role in training enumerators and facilitators of focus group discussions, and developing the sampling frame for villages and households. They also checked questionnaire forms to ensure that data was plausible and discussed inconsistencies with the enumerators, and ensured that data was being correctly entered into the database. The project manager who had a research and community development background also undertook some of the interviews and facilitated focus group discussions.

Forty young people carried out the research, half male, half female, most of whom were high school or university students. Many of them came from the Sialkot area. Staff of two local NGOs were also involved.

The statistical analysis was contracted out to a consultant, and the tables he produced using SPSS (Statistical Package for the Social Sciences) were interpreted by the project manager and research advisor. Translators were paid to translate the notes of the focus group discussions into English. These were then analysed by the project manager and the research advisor.

The report was written by the core team and edited by the research advisor. Each member of the core team wrote a section. The whole team agreed the conclusions and recommendations.

Deciding between doing research in-house and commissioning – factors to consider

Obviously this decision depends upon the nature of the research itself, so will be easier if you have a clearly defined, agreed, brief for the project. This checklist sets out some factors to consider, which are then discussed in more detail below.

CHECKLIST   **Should research be done in-house or not?**

✓ Capacity – research skills
✓ Capacity – workload
✓ Credibility
✓ Audience and level of risk
✓ Methods to be used
✓ Benefits to the programme – and potential for role confusion
✓ Is capacity-sharing an aim for this project?

Capacity – research skills

As has been discussed above (Chapter 1), it is increasingly common for development agencies to undertake research themselves. The larger agencies, like Save the Children, employ professional researchers and they also expect their development practitioners to carry out some types of research as part of their jobs.

Research skills overlap with those of development workers in many ways. However there are also elements of the skills involved which are quite distinct from those needed for most development work. The face-to-face communication skills involved in the two types of work are broadly similar, but some areas, particularly analysis and writing, are very different.

There are also differences of approach, which development workers need to be aware of. A key area is that of avoiding leading questions or putting words into the mouths of respondents. Researchers are carefully trained to ask questions in a neutral way, so that this becomes second nature after a while, but it is not an easy style to adopt, when you also want to present yourself as 'on the side' of your respondents. Where development workers are otherwise in a leadership role in the community, it may be difficult for them to adopt a neutral, listening role. (See Chapter 1.3)

Where there are sensitive issues about confidentiality and consent, you need to be certain that staff appreciate the particular issues thrown up by research as opposed to practice. It is necessary to approach people differently when you want to engage them in research work than you would if you wanted to involve them in a practical project, or offer them a service. It should not be assumed that research will benefit the participant personally, even when it is participatory research, and therefore every effort must be made to avoid putting pressure on people to take part in research. Research should adopt a higher standard in relation to confidentiality of information than might be relevant to development projects, for the same reason.

Whether or not there is *potential* to develop appropriate skills in an individual, for the purposes of a particular project, you need to decide whether or not they are able to undertake it now. Because research projects have their own particular logic, those without practical experience of actually undertaking research are likely to find it substantially more difficult than those with such experience. The planning stage, especially, requires experience.

Many staff will have some knowledge of research methods, from their training. However knowing how to evaluate and criticise research and knowing how to actually carry it out are two very different things!

If you are hoping to undertake a piece of research within your current staffing set-up, the first step will be to match the skills profile of existing staff with the requirements of the task. Table 7.2 sets out the core skills involved in undertaking research. It was developed by the University of North London to assist with focusing the work of the year-long placement which its Social Research students undertake as part of their degree. It could be used by managers in development work in several ways, for example:

• In planning a project you could make a chart which identifies which members of staff you believe have strong skills in relation to the different areas identified.

Table 7.2 Skills for research

1. **Library/Information Searching**
   - Identifying and locating relevant information sources
   - Making effective use of sources
   - Compiling annotated bibliographies
   - Contacting outside organisations/informants
2. **Summarising/Precising Skills**
   - Organising and condensing information into a coherent form
   - Summarising the essence and content of a body of writing/research
3. **Work Planning and Organisation**
   - Planning a work schedule
   - Keeping a research diary
   - Time management
   - Working under pressure
   - Management of research files
   - Organising meetings
4. **Teamwork**
   - Work constructively and critically within a group
   - Learn to give and take criticism
   - Work towards collective goals
5. **Research Design Skills**
   - Define appropriate and relevant data for a study
   - Design a questionnaire
   - Plan a research project or research strategy
   - Devise/implement appropriate sampling strategies
     (quantitative/qualitative)
   - Design a programme of fieldwork
6. **Interviewing Skills**
   - Locate and recruit informants
   - Conduct a series of interviews (structured/
     semi-structured/unstructured)
   - Organise/conduct group discussions
   - Develop appropriate recording skills
7. **Observation Skills**
   - Negotiate access to field of observation
   - Prepare theoretical grounds for watching
   - Select appropriate observational role
   - Carry out observations (participant/non-participant)
   - Develop field recording skills (field notes)
8. **Analysis Skills**
   - Process and organise a body of data
   - Develop an analysis strategy (quantitative/qualitative)
   - Analyse and interpret data
   - Describe and summarise a data set
9. **Report-Writing**
   - Plan a dissemination strategy
   - Plan report contents
   - Write a research report/article/document to deadlines

Continued

Table 7.2   Continued

10. **Research Presentation and Communication**
    – Organise and conduct a briefing session
    – Effective verbal communication (to colleagues, outside agencies, respondents)
    – Clear and concise writing skills
    – Presentation of research findings at seminar/conference
11. **Computing Skills**
    – Use and application of computers (eg word-processing, databases, statistical applications)
    – Skills in the use of specialist software
    – Computerised data-processing and management
12. **Numerical Skills**
    – Processing and analysing numerical information
    – Applying statistical techniques
    – Presenting data in graphical form
    – Skills in specialist statistical techniques
13. **Other Research Skills**

(Adapted with kind permission from University of North London research placements profiling document)

- It could be used to give to staff who are being asked to undertake research-related tasks, for them to reflect upon their strengths, areas they may need help with, and where they want to learn more.
- It may be helpful for the staff member who aims to develop their research skills to score themselves against this list, and use it to identify priorities for their learning in the future.

Please note that it is not suggested that everyone who is involved in research must have this whole range of skills developed to a high degree! This model is offered as it may help you to anticipate the range of skills that will be needed for a project, and arrange for support or training as necessary.

It may be helpful to refer to Chapter 1.2 where we discuss the boundaries of what should be defined as 'research'.

Capacity – workload

Don't underestimate the work involved in your project. Development organisations frequently report being surprised by how much work is involved in a piece of research – for managers as well as for practitioners. If in-house staff are to take a leading role in a research project, it must be accepted that this will have a major impact on their existing workload. The project must be seen as a key objective for them for the next period of time.

EXAMPLE

Estimating time-scales: the impact of income-generating projects, Belize

Research examining the impact of income-generating projects, involving about 250 people in 8 villages in Belize in Central America, took approximately three months of the lead researcher's time and four weeks each for two research assistants/interviewers. This did not include the planning stage, which took about one month of discussion with local government officials.

A number of elements of the research process can be difficult to fit in with other major commitments. The fieldwork stage is often best undertaken intensively, and analysis and writing are extremely difficult to complete if one can only work on it in fits and starts. Concentrated quiet time is essential.

Credibility

Will your research have credibility if it is carried out by staff of your organisation? Whatever you believe about objectivity in research, the people you need to influence may wish to see someone they regard as independent, as without a vested interest, taking a key role in the research. University academics tend to be seen as independent. For example, the important report *Adjustment with a Human Face* gained credibility because it was written by independent academics, in collaboration with UNICEF (Cornia et al, 1987–88).

On the other hand, an element of the credibility of evidence from the point of view of decision-makers depends upon the general reputation of the organisation or individual researchers producing it. Where an agency is held in high regard, and known to be expert in a particular area of work, its research may be seen as having credibility for this reason.

Audience and level of risk

In thinking about who should undertake a piece of research, it is important to consider what will be convincing to your target audience. Will the intended audience of the research accept as valid findings that come from those you plan to carry out the research? Development workers may be better at communicating with community members or with partner agencies (often important targets for research); more experienced researchers may be needed if high-level policy-makers are the key target audience.

The politics of a piece of research are also a key factor. How much pressure will be placed on the integrity of the research findings? Where an issue is highly controversial, the agency needs to be very confident that its research findings can be defended. Even research on issues that are not immediately perceived in the charity world as risky can draw unwelcome attention. It is important that you have research done by people who can assure the level of quality you need, given the scrutiny this piece of work will be under.

EXAMPLE

Press scrutiny – child poverty in the UK

A right wing British newspaper went through a Save the Children report on child poverty in the UK with a fine-tooth comb, aiming to support their headline story that the research was 'shoddy'. The report in question looked at nutrition, and aimed to show that there is food poverty in the UK through a combination of focus group discussions with project users (carried out by a professional research agency) and a literature review, carried out by a professional researcher. Attention was focused on the problems of isolated communities where only more expensive, less healthy food is available in local shops, and travel to better shops is too expensive for families on low incomes. Fortunately the report had been well-researched. The same newspaper has since attacked other children's charities' research.

EXAMPLE

Unpopular findings – the child labour project, Sialkot, Pakistan

The research that Save the Children carried out on child labour in the sports goods industry in the Sialkot area of Pakistan also came under close scrutiny. The research looked in some detail at children's work stitching footballs and what impact this had on their general welfare and education. The findings were unwelcome to lobby groups that campaign to ban child labour altogether, who called the methodology into question in their criticism of the project. They claimed that the sampling frame was 'unscientific'. The sample was in fact large and appropriate, the methodology of the study strong, and the information was triangulated in various ways (ie supported by evidence from other sources).

Methods to be used

Another issue to consider is that some research methods are more difficult to use than others, and may require greater experience. However it is important to use the methods which are best suited to your research question, and not to let the methodology of a study be determined by the competencies of those concerned.

Practitioners may be familiar with interviews and group work for development purposes, but research interviewing and focus group research require a somewhat different approach, and some different skills. (See Chapter 1.3 above for more on this).

In some cases it is simply not economic sense to expect development workers to undertake certain types of research. For example, very large-scale surveys can be carried out much more efficiently by organisations that do them frequently. They employ professional recruiters and interviewers, and have systems for questionnaire design and analysis ready and waiting.

Benefits to the programme – and potential for role confusion

There may be clear benefits for development workers in undertaking research themselves. For example, if a needs assessment is undertaken as a way of consulting local people on what they hope for from a development project, it may make perfect sense for the workers to do the work themselves. This can also have benefits further down the line, when it comes to reviewing the impact of a programme. If the hands-on workers themselves undertook the original needs assessment study, they will have a much more vivid image of the changes they hope to see from their intervention. The monitoring of the programme can then start from a good grasp of the baseline situation (the situation before the programme began). Assessments in emergency situations are one example where it is much better for those who will follow through to do the research.

However there are situations where problems could arise from people performing different roles with the same community. Obviously where there is an element of evaluation of a project's work, it may be inappropriate for those responsible for delivering services to also enquire about people's views of them. Service users may not feel free to make critical comment, and may feel that their access to services could be affected if they were to give negative feedback. More subtly, if an organisation is involved in providing personal support to an individual, it could be very difficult for the person to refuse to assist with research they asked them to participate in. People must have a free choice in whether or not to participate in research.

A broader issue about roles arises where a development worker has been engaged with a particular group of people for a while. If the worker then decides to undertake some research, they are taking up a different role in relation to those individuals, and this could have long-term consequences, for example if they are trusted with sensitive information as part of their research role.

Is capacity-sharing an aim for this project?

Supporting national researchers in the South is a very important development aim in itself, with potentially long-term spin-offs beyond the life of any project. If you are bringing in expert researchers, it is good to ensure that local staff shadow them, or that they formally train local researchers.

Beware of throwing people in at the deep end, however. Plan to offer adequate support if new researchers are relatively inexperienced at research work. Ensure that research supervision is provided, and in particular get advice on the brief at an early stage. It may be helpful to encourage staff to register for further qualifications that include formal research training, so that they have built-in support while they undertake research work, if they see their careers taking this direction in the longer term.

Table 7.3 aims to assist managers in identifying the best way to divide up tasks in a research project.

Table 7.3   Staff skills and roles in research

In-house staff skills and experience	Possible role in research project
Staff have research training and have successfully completed previous similar projects	Could carry out the project independently – may still benefit from supervision by someone more experienced
Staff have some research training and experience	Varies, depending on the specific skills needed for this project
Staff have studied research methods but have never undertaken any themselves	Should not be lead researcher – but could carry out much of the data collection, if communication skills and confidence are strong
Staff have good communication skills and a clear understanding of the purpose of research	Could undertake most of the data collection – interviewing, focus groups. Will need specific training and support
Staff are good at accurate, detailed record-keeping	Could carry out data entry – may be able to administer a self-completion survey, where respondents are literate. Valuable for data management
Staff have good rapport with potential respondents and a clear understanding of the purpose of research	Very helpful in gaining co-operation in the research, gathering a sample
Staff are good at analytical, critical thinking – making out a case	Helpful in framing research at the start, in data analysis and in working out recommendations
Staff have good writing skills	Without research knowledge, most useful role may be to edit and assist in writing final report/s
Staff have good verbal communication/presentation skills	Important in communicating research to policy-makers

You may want to use Table 7.1 to consider how different people's roles could or should fit together.

In this decision-making process there is often a chicken-and-egg problem. The decision about who should do a project depends upon the brief. However clarifying the brief is often the first task to be undertaken. The skill of negotiating better research briefs is one which is learnt over years of research practice. It may be worthwhile asking advice on defining the brief from an experienced researcher, while reserving judgement on who will carry out the work itself. You could pay a small fee for such advice on a consultancy basis, or seek advice from in-house research staff.

We will now look briefly at the benefits and costs, first of carrying out research with existing development workers, and secondly of employing researchers.

Benefits and costs of developing in-house staff's research skills

Research skills are quite complex and diverse, and there are definitely costs for an organisation if it decides to develop these amongst its existing staff. It is worth thinking out a strategy to develop an appropriate level of research skills within a staff group. A single afternoon's training workshop will not do it. If research-type activities will be regularly needed, it may be best to recruit at least one experienced researcher, but it may also be useful to offer some formal training, and expect to offer ongoing coaching, for other staff as they learn these skills. Regular supervision (research and managerial, see Chapter 8.1) needs to be provided, whether those undertaking the work are experienced researchers or development workers learning research skills. An advisory group can be very helpful, but does not offer the safe space to work out problems provided by one-to-one supervision – both types of support are required.

The benefits of developing better in-house research skills are considerable. The research will be firmly based in an understanding of the issues as encountered in 'real life'. Where an agency wants to influence policy on the basis of its practical experience, research-type approaches provide very useful tools for capturing this knowledge. Many of the skills involved (see Table 7.2) are transferable from and to other areas of development work. In general, research teaches a questioning, analytical approach which is also very useful in programme management activities.

Benefits and costs of employing researchers

The key benefit of employing a professional researcher is obviously that they come in already in possession of most of the skills that you need. They have had lengthy professional training, and work experience, carrying out research. Some may have weaker skills in working alongside community members to encourage participation, but many are learning to work in this way. Some universities now teach participatory research alongside traditional methods.

Researchers usually have strong analytical and writing skills, which others can find difficult to develop. They will also have the practical skills, and will understand the discipline needed to record data properly, and to be careful in interpreting it.

You may be able to recruit researchers who also have a strong knowledge base in a particular policy area, which can take years to develop and may be crucial to positioning the research appropriately.

The downside of hiring a researcher for a particular project, especially on a short-term basis, is that when their contract finishes, they leave, and may take with them important learning which the organisation needs. While they may well have written a report, organisations are notoriously bad at learning from written reports. The other concern that employing agencies often have is that an 'outside' person may misinterpret the brief they are given, and could be difficult to manage. On the other hand, the discipline of explaining fully what is required to someone not steeped in the ways of a particular agency may be a useful process to go through early on in a project.

Is there a middle way?

It may be possible to divide up the work to take advantage of the abilities of in-house staff, while also benefiting from the input of a more experienced researcher. This can be done in several different ways. One way is to employ a research advisor to oversee the whole of the research process, and have development workers do most of the data collection and be involved in the analysis and writing. Another is to have a development worker lead the project, but provide them with regular supervision from a research advisor/consultant. Some projects are led by development workers but use professional researchers to collect the data, so that, for example, someone neutral comes in to facilitate focus groups or conduct in-depth interviews. It may be that a development worker and a researcher can usefully work alongside each other throughout a project, but roles and responsibilities need to be clearly defined. However it is not advisable to plan to involve someone more experienced only at a late stage in the research. Most of the key decisions about the research process are made early on, and these determine the quality of analysis which will be possible. An experienced researcher should be consulted on the brief, and also at the point of drafting research tools (questionnaires, focus group topic guides, etc).

7.2   Managing In-House Research

It is helpful to treat all pieces of research the same, and set them up with a degree of formality, even if in-house staff are undertaking quite small-scale exercises. As has been discussed above, this means writing a brief, agreeing it with all stakeholders, and setting up formal objectives and supervision which is appropriate to the task. It is best to go through all the processes detailed in Chapters 5 and 6 to set up a research management framework for your project.

> **COMMON PITFALLS 7.1** Expecting novice researchers to cope with a vague brief, and without support.

Supervision is particularly important. To promote wider learning, as well as to ensure that a piece of research reaches appropriate quality standards, it is good practice to organise research supervision for staff, relating specifically to the research task. (See 8.1, 'Supervising research work')

7.3   Employing Researchers

The other way of organising in-house research is to hire researchers onto the staff, either as permanent staff or on contracts relating to the particular piece of work. Increasingly, as the need for research work grows, agencies find it economic to employ researchers as permanent staff. One of the virtues of this is that other staff in effect receive coaching on research methods as an ongoing part of the researcher's presence in the work team. However it is also still appropriate at times to appoint researchers to work on a specific project, particularly when you need them to bring in specialised knowledge as part of their contribution to the project.

Employed or freelance?

There are a number of issues to be considered in choosing between employed research staff and using freelance workers, hired to undertake a specific task. For example:

- Will you still need research capacity when this project is over?
- How long will the piece of work take? Really?
- How specialised is the knowledge you need them to have?
- The skills?
- Over what period of time will you need to call on the researcher? It may extend into the dissemination phase.

You need to consider the market locally in terms of the supply of suitable researchers. This is very variable. There can be difficulty in finding researchers skilled in using qualitative or participatory methods, especially in parts of the South, where investment in this type of skills training has been minimal. Consultants with strong skills of this sort need to be booked up early.

If you need a high level of experience, and cannot afford a high-level full-time post in the long term, you may need to have the work done on a freelance basis. When employing freelance consultants, it is important to look into the tax situation in the country in question, and establish what your responsibilities are as an employer. Fees (often quoted as a daily rate) asked by freelance workers tend to look high compared to salaries. Some of the reasons for this are that self-employed people get no contribution from employers towards any National Insurance payments or pension, and must make their own arrangements to cover sickness and holidays. They also carry the expenses of their own office base, office equipment, telephone and so forth. Freelances may be good value where you need someone who can work intensively on a particular task, and who has strong specific experience, skills, and/or knowledge which will enable them to undertake the task efficiently.

Increasing numbers of researchers now work on a freelance/consultancy basis. However recruitment processes can be costly, and if a sequence of research work is planned, it may be best to avoid a whole series of short appointments.

In addition to employing individual researchers, there are several other options to consider:

- Academic institutions
- Commercial research agencies
- Voluntary sector research agencies
- Small research organisations – a group of consultants who work together.

It may be appropriate to set up a contract with a particular agency rather than with an individual. Many, though not all, independent research agencies, including commercial ones, do high-quality work. However if you decide to commission work from another organisation, make sure you know who exactly will undertake the work. Sometimes work is delegated to someone more junior than those who negotiate for the contract.

Selection processes

Appointing research staff is just like appointing staff to any other sort of job. Whether you are appointing people as staff or on a freelance basis, some sort of selection process will usually be needed.

> **COMMON PITFALLS 7.2**   Giving a piece of work to a nice man someone has met at a workshop, who was saying all the right things, without ever seeing anything he has produced

There are several ways of going about this – you can treat the process more like other jobs, or focus very much on the piece of work. It may be helpful to produce a person specification, in addition to the job description, to help you to focus on the particular skills and knowledge you require for the job.

TIP   To get the decision right is this: look for *evidence* that they can produce work to the standard you require

CHECKLIST   **Selecting the right person**

✔ Ask candidates to show you some written materials they have produced, preferably published, and which are not jointly authored with others. Obviously younger people will have less to show, but anything written can give an indication of what the person will produce. Look for independent thinking, clarity of expression, sound, well-grounded conclusions, and honesty

✔ If the job includes giving presentations, persuading people of your case, you could ask candidates to make a short presentation as part of the interview process. Exercises like this should be as realistic as possible, without creating an unreasonable amount of work for candidates

✔ If working closely with community members or other stakeholders such as policy-makers is involved, it can be helpful to involve these people in the selection process – they can be asked to assess particularly the candidate's attitudes to and ability to communicate with people like them

✔ Ask for references, and take them up. Where interpersonal skills, and the skills of promoting participation, are as important as writing skills, this can be the best way of judging them. You can ask if referees can be telephoned rather than written to, and can ask specific questions about the referee's experience of the person

✔ Writing a person specification at the start of the process can help you to focus on the key skills you require. This can help you to avoid being distracted by fine qualities and impressive qualifications, which candidates have but which may not actually be relevant to the task in hand

✔ Don't be afraid to ask directly about researchers' opinions on the issues in question, or about their perspectives on research methodology

✔ Ask them to talk about an example of a piece of work they have done which involved a particular method you are interested in

✔ Attitudes and values are important to a person's suitability for a job, but concentrating too much on this area can distract attention from a focus on the skills necessary to carry it out

Experience shows that many more people are good at talking about the issues around research in an interview than are able to deliver finished work to tight deadlines. Writing is nearly always an essential task for which you will rely on the researcher, so if they cannot produce anything which approximates the qualities you require, you should not employ them. Looking at material they have written should also help you to understand their perspective, which will be very important in how they carry out the tasks you require, as well as enabling you to see what quantity and quality of work they have actually produced.

Involving community members in appointments processes

Where research is a participatory process, it can be a good idea to involve community members in the work of selecting a researcher, whether they are to work with you permanently or on a short-term basis. You can, of course, simply invite someone from your group onto the appointments panel and have them work through the process alongside the professional workers. However it is important to think about how to enable them to have a real say in what may be an intimidating and formal process.

Participating community members can be consulted about what criteria should be on the person specification, whether or not it is possible to involve them in the interviews.

Remember that the participants may feel very responsible for the decision in relation to others in the community. It is helpful to offer training to explain how your appointments procedures work, including on equal opportunities issues. If your organisation offers formal training or written guidance on appointments procedures you should make this available to the participating community members. These are useful processes to learn about.

CHECKLIST   For involving community members in appointments procedures

✓ Involve more than one community member
✓ Involve them in setting the criteria for the person specification, not just in the interviews
✓ Ensure that they are offered appropriate training and opportunities to discuss the issues
✓ Make sure you send them any paperwork as early as possible
✓ Remember they may be nervous and give them space to take part
✓ Agree a clear role for them, perhaps paying particular attention to candidates' face-to-face communication skills

---

EXAMPLE

Young people help select staff

Save the Children's Lifechance project in Oxford, England, routinely involved young people in selecting youth workers and researchers to work with them. Their method is to regard the young people as responsible for assessing a number of the criteria on the person specification, those concerning attitudes towards young people and communication skills, and to do this process separately from the interview with professionals. The young people are briefed that their top choice may not get the job, but that their views will be taken into account. Two or three young people interview candidates before or after professionals interview them on the remaining criteria. The two panels then meet to make their decision.

Writing a person specification

The following items might be useful to adapt to your needs in setting a person specification for a research task:

- Experience of using a range of research methods/a particular method.
- Knowledge of a particular field.
- Analytical skills.
- Ability to write to a high standard/for particular audience(s).
- Experience or knowledge of your type of organisation.
- Excellent communication skills (verbal and written)/specify for what particular purpose?
- Ability to encourage the participation of community members.
- Ability to work to deadlines.
- Commitment to relevant values (eg participatory research, equality of opportunity, children's rights, community development approaches...).

As with all person specifications, if you ask for *experience* in a particular area of work you are setting a much higher, and more assessable, standard than if you just ask for *knowledge*. You need to decide whether, for example, having taken a course which covered a particular issue, would be regarded as evidence of sufficient knowledge. You may want to require that people have direct experience of using a particular type of research method. However beware of setting unrealistic person specifications.

It will be helpful to formulate points to specify for what purpose skills are needed. For example, 'Excellent communication skills' could be broken down to specify groups of people the person should be able to interview, or whether group work skills are needed; any negotiation skills needed; and the type of writing needed.

You should of course pursue the same types of equal opportunities employment practice in relation to research posts as to other types of work. Only essential characteristics should appear on the person specification, as any extra ones will disqualify people who could in fact do the job. Setting exercises such as a presentation, and asking to see examples of written work should reflect requirements of the post and focus the selection process on the specific needs of this job.

Note that if the researcher you are employing will have significant unsupervised access to children through their job with you, you should consider child protection issues within your selection process – see Chapter 13.2.

Should researchers' identities reflect those they are researching?

It is well shown that women respondents in many societies are likely to relate better to women researchers than to men. There are some subjects men may prefer to discuss with other men, though in some cultures men seem to be more comfortable talking to women. Matching ethnic identity and background can also be helpful in breaking down barriers. Language skills are of course also a major consideration.

This question has been much debated in the research world, influenced particularly by feminism. It is clear that people are more readily put at ease by researchers who share important characteristics with them. Especially where people feel their identity may be felt to carry stigma or attract prejudice, for example lesbians and gay men, or Gypsies and Travellers, respondents are much more likely to agree to participate if the researcher comes from the same group.

However belonging to the same group is not enough. An insensitive interviewer from your own community is worse than a skilled one from a different one. Communication skills and respect for others are more important than group identity as such, and on issues which are controversial within a community, people may actually prefer to talk to an 'outsider'.

Employment law does not generally allow you to advertise for people on the basis of gender or ethnic origin as such, but you can ask for experience of work with a particular group, or an understanding of the issues which affect them, and test candidates on that.

Invitations to tender

Where you are appointing someone to do a defined task, rather than to fill a post, it may be appropriate to invite a number of individuals or organisations to make proposals to you, saying how they would carry out the task. You need to set a clear brief, and then ask candidates to say what methods they would use to carry it out. It is only worth following this procedure for fairly large projects, as it creates quite a lot of work all round.

Some organisations do not specify the amount of money available, and ask those tendering to say how much they reckon would be needed. Others do give a figure, but ask those tendering to say what they would be able to do for that figure. From the point of view of those writing tenders, it is hard to respond if the amount of money available is not specified, as research can generally expand or contract to fit a budget.

Tendering for research work is quite an onerous task, and standard practice is to approach up to three or four agencies or individuals to tender. Do not make the volume of work promised in relation to the fee the main criterion – it is important to establish whether those tendering have the experience to be realistic about what can be achieved.

Managing freelance consultants

Freelance consultants are employed in relation to the task, not to time spent on work. The relationship with them is different in some respects to that of an employer/employee, but it is best to think of them as an employee in terms of providing support and supervision.[2]

CHECKLIST   **Getting the best from freelance consultants**

- ✓ Give them space to advise you on matters of method and style – let them draw on their experience – while you keep an eye on your objectives for the task
- ✓ Expect to work closely with them – meet with them regularly
- ✓ Work out a series of deadlines for the completion of elements of the task, in discussion with the consultant, and take the schedule seriously
- ✓ Include deadlines for interim reports, and require a draft final report well before the absolute final deadline
- ✓ Tie payments to tasks rather than time, where reasonable
- ✓ Set out clearly to whom they are accountable, and expect to offer supervision (See Chapter 8.1 on supervision)
- ✓ And, once again – make sure the brief is clear and achievable

---

Employers of freelancers dread that they will pay them a lot of money and then not have the product they hoped for. The guidelines above should protect from this. If a trusting relationship is developed, the freelance will inform the employer of any problems which are arising in meeting the brief, just as an employee would.

---

[2] Tool 8 in Gosling with Edwards (1995) gives guidance on working with consultants.

The employing organisation is best protected by a contract which ties payment of fees to the performance of particular tasks, rather than to time spent on the job. For example, an element of the fee might be paid only on delivery of a satisfactory final draft of a report. However freelances have to eat too, and it is reasonable to pay some of the fee up front, to keep the person going while work is carried out. With large tasks over long periods, a regular payment is a reasonable arrangement – there should, however, be clear deadlines set for the delivery of particular tasks.

Development agencies report the experience of consultants producing a draft, comments being collected, and then huge delays occurring in getting the changes required incorporated into the report. There are a variety of reasons why this may occur, but it can be anticipated by writing the process of incorporating agreed changes resulting from readers' comments explicitly into the brief. Thus the consultant allows time for it, is clearly paid to do it, and sees this process as part of the brief, not an unlooked-for extra. If this process is expected to be particularly time-consuming, it may be appropriate to tie an element of the fee to completing it to the agency's satisfaction.

Contracts

When you employ either an organisation or an individual to carry out a particular task, you need to set a contract with them to cover a number of issues. This is required in addition to the brief for the project. The checklist below describes the matters which need to be covered.

CHECKLIST   Research contract outline

- ✓ Tasks and responsibilities
- ✓ Basis and timing of payment
- ✓ Who is contracted to undertake the work
- ✓ Fee
- ✓ Expenses
- ✓ Status and liability (tax issues)
- ✓ Insurance
- ✓ Consultant's obligations
- ✓ Employer's obligations
- ✓ Confidentiality
- ✓ Whose property is the data?
- ✓ Termination of contract
- ✓ Copyright

Some issues from this list which require particular thought:

Tasks and responsibilities

This specifies exactly who is responsible for which tasks. This is a matter of putting on paper your assumptions, to ensure that these are clear from the start. In addition to the core research tasks, remember to include other important aspects. For example, do you require the final report from the researcher on disk? In what format? Research generates a great deal of administrative work. Will any administrative support be available to the research staff?

Ownership of data

This requires some thought. Organisations often expect to own data generated in research they pay for. If this is the case the researcher/author has to seek permission to use information elsewhere or publish elsewhere. Researchers like to own knowledge and ideas they feel that they have created. Respondents too have a right to the information they have revealed. Conflicts can arise, and there is often no clear-cut answer.

It may be helpful to distinguish between raw data and published products. Published material is in the public domain, and whoever has paid to have it written, or to publish it, may reasonably expect to have copyright over it. Sometimes authors share copyright with publishers. Researchers should negotiate in advance with the organisation if they wish to publish elsewhere.

In terms of raw data, organisations often want to 'own' it, so that they can use data gathered in later exercises. But do not assume that your organisation should necessarily own the data generated for a study. From the point of view of protecting the confidentiality of respondents it may be appropriate for the researcher to own the data, although the employing organisation is likely to want access to information from it as appropriate. There can also be issues of the integrity of the research, and researchers may need to ensure that data is not taken out of context. Thus it might be useful to build in some requirement that if data is used for other purposes, some check should be made with the researchers.

Where confidentiality is not a concern, for example where the data is in effect already in the public domain as in a PLA-type of exercise, it may be appropriate to take steps to ensure that a community group retains control of the data from a study. Communities have protested at researchers taking away information which community members have participated in gathering, and which the community itself needs for its own purposes, for example to make a case for funding on a specific element of an investigation such as access to clean water.

Working with academics

There are a number of different ways in which NGOs relate to academic researchers. NGOs can simply commission work from them on a fee-for-service basis. There is also often a close relationship of a different kind. An NGO may suggest ideas for research to a university, with the idea that the university would seek funds from research funders to carry out the work.

Example

Ideas for Academic Research

Save the Children has suggested some issues for investigation by academic researchers, for example:

- *Child labour is often seen as taking away jobs from adults. Is it the case that adult and child labour are substituted for each other? What is the relationship between adult and child labour?*
- *Costing the social impacts of economic transition in Mongolia and Bulgaria.*
- *Estimating children's contribution to family and national income.*

Most research carried out in universities is funded by funding bodies specifically oriented towards academic research. These may be governmental bodies like the Economic and Social Research Council or ESCOR (Economic and Social Council on Research, the research arm of the Department for International Development), or independent charities like the Wellcome Foundation (health-related research). These funders rarely give grants directly to voluntary organisations to undertake research, but they encourage academics to work closely with voluntary organisations as 'research users'.

From the point of view of the voluntary organisation, the important thing to remember about academics is that they have an agenda and priorities of their own. They will be pursuing a sequence of research work in a particular area, and they are likely to have a distinctive perspective on the issues involved. If you do a deal with them, make sure that you are happy for their agenda as well as yours to be a feature of the finished work.

Academic careers are advanced primarily by publishing in academic journals and books, and by giving papers at academic conferences. Many academics are also committed to social change, and hence to disseminating their findings to lay audiences, but they are always also under pressure to give priority to academic audiences.

Having said all this, it is also true to say that some of the most creative and influential research around the development field has been carried out by academics. Where academics have the edge is when they have the ability to step back from an issue and re-conceptualise it – reframe it in a different way, and change the way people see it. One example would be Mamdami's (1972) study of an Indian village, 'The myth of population control'. This anthropological study was very important in showing people that a simplistic approach to population control was doomed, due to the economic and social realities of the people seen by planners and policy-makers as producing too many children.

Another example is some research that has been very influential in developing a better understanding of child abuse. Traditional social work thinking in the UK looked upon domestic violence and the abuse of children as very separate types of problem. Liz Kelly's research (1988) looked at women's experiences of domestic violence, rape, and sexual and physical abuse in childhood and showed how these were often part of a 'continuum of violence'. Kelly's work, with others, has led to changes in social work practice to recognise that where there is domestic violence there should be concern for the children as well as for the woman. Men who were violent towards their women partners were likely also to be abusive towards children in the household. Kelly's work was informed by her own participation in Women's Aid, providing refuge for battered women, but her research has had a wide influence which voluntary organisations can find difficult to achieve.

Managing problems

What to do when a researcher, either employed or freelance, is producing unsatisfactory work? As in all things, prevention is better than cure, and the checklist below gives guidelines, at the risk of repeating points made elsewhere. Many of these points are expanded on in the next chapter, but are given here for those who turn straight to this page.

CHECKLIST   **For avoiding problems with research staff**

✓ Write a clear brief

✓ Make a good match between the skills needed and the person appointed

✓ Get evidence of the candidates' skills, eg written work, references, before making an appointment

✓ Ensure that there is a clear line of accountability and decision-making for the project

✓ Give both management and research supervision, regularly (see Chapter 8.1)

✓ Break down the tasks necessary, and in large projects ask for interim reports on progress

✓ Give encouragement and support as well as critical comment

✓ If it appears a task is being avoided, discuss it in detail. Research involves many different processes and people may lack confidence in how to undertake part of the process

✓ Make sure material gets written up as the process goes along – do not allow researchers to leave all the writing to the end

✓ If hiring on a freelance basis, tie some element of the payments to tangible products

✓ Ensure that contracts made with consultants enable you to cease their employment if their work does not reach adequate standards

---

Dealing with problems once they are evident is the same managerial process as it is for any other staff. It is essential to pick up on problems early, and to communicate to the person very clearly exactly what it is that you want to change. Give the person a chance to explain to you what the problem looks like from their point of view. Aim for an agreed, timetabled plan to set things right.

One scenario that arises from time to time is where a researcher has written a report, which is very different to that which was hoped for by those commissioning the work. Obviously the first step needs to be to give comments to the researcher and ask them to make changes. However where the gap between the product and what is wanted is great, experience shows that a long period of stagnation can follow at this point. Make sure you set clear deadlines, and follow through if nothing has happened. Researchers usually do the best they can on their first attempt, and it is likely that they will have difficulty in producing something very different from their first draft. Assess the scale of the problem, and if necessary pay whatever is due for the work done to date, take the work back and give it to someone else.

Key Points from this Chapter

CHECKLIST   **For good decisions on who will do the research**

✓ In deciding who should undertake the work, balance the needs of the particular project with the need to build research skills in your organisation

✓ Consider different ways of dividing up the work to ensure that enough people learn from a project

✓ Think about how the learning from the research will be used in the future – will a local programme be developed from it? Or a broader campaign? Who most needs to hold this learning for the organisation?

✓ Before asking development workers to undertake research, look in detail at the skills required, and ensure that appropriate support is available

✓ In appointments procedures, make sure you look for *evidence* of candidate's abilities, for example ask to see written work

✓ Write a person specification as well as the brief, to help you focus on the needs of this particular post

✓ Invitation to tender is an alternative way of recruiting to research projects

✓ Freelance consultants also require supervision, and it is important to set out a series of deadlines, including for interim reports if appropriate

We have considered the issues involved in sorting out how you should undertake a piece of research, including capacity, credibility, level of risk, methods, and potential for role confusion. See the checklist for making decisions on who should do the research near the start of this chapter for a summary of the main points to bear in mind. The need to increase agencies' research-related abilities has been discussed. Costs and benefits of using in-house development workers and of hiring new researchers are considered. A skills analysis for research work has been presented, which could be helpful in making these decisions.

There are a number of ways in which research can be undertaken by professional researchers – through employing researchers as permanent staff members or on temporary contracts; through employing freelance researchers; or by commissioning the work from academic institutions, commercial or voluntary sector research agencies.

In selecting research staff, it is crucial to look for evidence of their competence at the specific tasks involved. It is advisable to write a person specification to assist in focusing attention on the skills and experience relevant to the post.

Working with academics and freelance consultants is further discussed. Again, managers are urged to take an active role in managing work undertaken by freelance consultants, from the point of view of ensuring that the organisation's objectives for the project are met.

Further Reading

Everitt, A. and Gibson, A. (1994) *Making It Work: Researching in the voluntary sector*. ARVAC: Essex.

Written for a UK organisation of researchers working in/with the voluntary sector. Gives a detailed account of different research paradigms, including postmodernist approaches, and shows how these would influence a project. Also gives 15, 2- to 3-page case studies of research undertaken in the voluntary sector. Includes material on factors to consider in employing a researcher, and on costing research.

Gosling, L. with Edwards, M. (1995) *Toolkits: A practical guide to assessment, monitoring, review and evaluation*, Development Manual 5. London: Save the Children.

Tool 8 gives guidance on Using Consultants.

8 Managing Research

In addition to setting the brief, there are a number of issues that need to be considered in managing research for development. This chapter looks at the ongoing supervision of research work, with suggestions for issues which require attention in supervising research for development. Secondly, we look at how to estimate costs and time-scales – some possible tools for timetabling research work are proposed, and the timing and costs of various aspects of the research process are discussed. Later sections consider the issues around negotiating access to respondents and the particular needs of participatory research. It is important that research is managed in such a way that research skills are built amongst a wider group of people, and Chapter 9 discusses this in more depth.

8.1 Supervising Research Work

This manual is intended to help first-time researchers, as well as those with more experience. This does not of course mean that once they have given them a copy, the manager can wash their hands of the project! Research processes involve making many apparently small decisions which affect the research profoundly, and it is easy to get stuck when these decisions are difficult. To keep a project on track, regular meetings with a supervisor are essential – weekly if at all possible.

Coaching is an excellent way for many people to learn. Where possible, a team should include people with more and less experience. Those who are learning may be good at data collection, while the more experienced can help in setting the framework and organising the material. They will learn from each other over time.

As was discussed above (Chapters 4, 6 and 7), research projects may need two types of supervision:

- Overall monitoring of progress towards the aims and objectives of the research
- Non-managerial research supervision, advising on methodology, and ensuring that quality standards for research are met.

These may, or may not, be given by the same person. It may be appropriate to make special arrangements for research supervision with an external agency, or another part of a large agency, where the line manager is not able to provide this. Even if this is done, however, the line manager should not relax! *Management* supervision is still key to ensuring that the agency's aims are met by the research.

Research is a specialised area of work, and if researchers are to learn from their work and do it most effectively, they need contact with others in their profession, as well as those they work with on a day to day basis. A research supervisor can also assist the researcher in fulfilling the important function of keeping the project in touch with related work elsewhere. Professional, non-managerial supervision is a good way of ensuring that such learning takes place.

If such support is not available within an organisation, it could be arranged externally. It is possible to build into a research project the provision of research supervision on a consultancy basis, or it may be that an appropriate person at a local university will be able to offer supervision as part of their post.

EXAMPLE

Research consultancy: evaluating peer support in schools

An independent researcher supports the evaluation of a peer support project in London schools run by the Mental Health Foundation through meetings every two months with the lead worker for the project. She advised on a suitable framework for the evaluation, then assisted in drafting evaluation questionnaires and in organising the analysis of the data.

EXAMPLE

A 'companheiro critico' – research advice, Brazil

Save the Children in Brazil has a stable arrangement for support on monitoring, evaluation, and research work. It has an independent development consultant on a retainer, for the equivalent of two months of their time per year, and negotiates each year exactly what the content of the work will be. They call this person their 'companheiro critico' (critical companion).

One role of a research supervisor is to encourage self-reflection about the researcher's own role in the research, for example the impact that their

Table 8.1   Management and research supervision

Management supervision	Research/professional supervision
In co-operation with the researcher to...	
• Clarify aims and objectives	• Ensure that professional standards are met in research practice
• Ensure proper links are made with senior managers within your organisation, facilitating wider use of the research	• Assist with identifying relevant literature
• Ensure steady progress towards aims and objectives	• Assist in making links beyond the immediate area with relevant researchers and others
• Set time-scales and targets	• Draw on experience to assist in planning time-scales
• Deal with resources issues	• Advise on research methods
• Manage research advisory groups	• Ensure people with appropriate knowledge are invited onto advisory groups
• Facilitate links with partner agencies	• Consider emotional responses to the process of the research, and their consequences for the work
• Support participatory processes	• Advise on methods of analysis
• Support the process of working out recommendations from findings	• Assist in dealing with ethical dilemmas which arise
• Ensure that feedback to policy-makers and/or community members is in an appropriate format	• Assist with any writing for academic audiences

gender, background, or manner may have on the research process. It should be possible to talk about the emotional impact research can have, and to unpack what this may mean for the work. (See also Chapter 4.5 on reflexivity.)

Table 8.1 suggests a possible division of labour between management and research supervisors. It may be possible for both these jobs to be performed by the same person.

Where managerial and professional supervision are provided by different people, it will be useful for them to meet up together from time to time, with the lead researcher, to consolidate forward plans, and ensure that all are working towards the same ends.

Researchers are often independent spirits, and may expect to work rather separately from others. But in research for development, it is important that research projects are kept in touch with the broader work of the organisation, for learning to occur in both directions. Further, it may be important to involve partner agencies with a research project, and managers who are also involved with the practice side may find this easier to facilitate than researchers. If partners are involved at an early stage it is more likely that they will be influenced by the findings of the research.

Supervision should not be strongly directive in how objectives are fulfilled, but should keep an eye on the larger picture. The supervisor needs to support the researcher in sorting out a sound methodology for the project.

Where a development practitioner is managing a researcher, the development worker can be confident that they have a legitimate, and indeed crucial, role in relation to a research project. However skilled and experienced researchers are, they come to any project from a different perspective to that of the development workers who are permanently committed to their particular area of work. The development worker needs to ensure that *their* needs are met by the piece of work.

CHECKLIST   Managing research for development work effectively

✔ First, check that the brief (especially the aims and objectives), any output or outcome indicators, and the research questions are appropriate

Matters for ongoing monitoring include:

✔ That progress towards aims and objectives is going well

✔ That a set of 'milestones' along the way – interim reports etc – are planned for and then achieved

✔ That written materials (make sure the final report is not the first thing you see) are clearly expressed and appropriate to their audience

✔ That the process of negotiating access to participants is handled tactfully

✔ That appropriate partner agencies have been informed of, or involved in, the research

✔ That an advisory group is convened as appropriate

✔ That people are being kept informed of progress

✔ That if the research is intended to be participatory, there is evidence that people feel that they are able to participate, and value this process

✔ That disadvantaged sections of the population in question are being included

✔ That formalities have been properly observed, eg informing local authorities of the work in hand

✔ That reports include an appropriate balance between description and analysis

✔ How are recommendations to be arrived at? Is consultation on these planned, and appropriate? The draft recommendations must meet the agency's needs

✔ That ethical standards are being upheld – are procedures for obtaining consent and ensuring confidentiality working well?

✔ Finally, remember to give positive feedback to the researcher, whenever possible – research can be a lonely business

Researchers will generally welcome the interest and involvement of development workers and managers. It is well known that for change to occur as a result of a research project, the active involvement of stakeholders is essential.

8.2 How to Estimate Costs and Time-Scales

'Perhaps the most common practical mistake in research proposals is to grossly underestimate the budget in time and money, required for the project ... Research is a messy and chaotic business, even for the experienced researcher, and will be even more chaotic for the researcher with little practical experience. Research budgets that allow no room for manoeuvre, or for any mistakes, can create significant problems.' (Hakim, 1987)

COMMON PITFALLS 8.1	Allowing far too little time and money to carry out your project

A crucial part of the planning process is obviously to sort out the time-scale for the research, and the costs which will be incurred. As with so many things in life, it is a safe bet that when you think it through you will find that a piece of research will cost more than you had hoped. Time and money are tied up together – more of one can be used to balance less of the other, and vice versa.

So let us start with time, and return to other aspects of costing research later in this section. A research project involves a series of tasks which are quite different from each other, but which may overlap in time, and inter-relate in a complex way. In planning a piece of research, it is worth working

Table 8.2 Research planning timetable

	Jan	Feb	Mar	April	May	June	July	Aug	Sept	Oct	Nov	Dec	Jan
Planning, discussion with partners	↑												
Search for existing information	↑												
Draft research tools (questionnaires etc)		↑											
Select and contact respondents		↑											
Pilot tools and revise		↑											
Fieldwork 1. Focus groups				↑									
Fieldwork 2. Interviews					↑								
Transcribing					↑								
Analysis						↑							
Writing										↑			
Editing and publication											↑		
Dissemination												↑	

out a timetable in some detail at the start. You may not be able to stick to it exactly, but at least it will give you a way of looking ahead at the consequences if things start to slip.

Table 8.2 represents just one kind of research process, to give an idea of how to timetable research work. This example gives possible time-scales for a typical (fictional) medium-sized qualitative study using focus groups to clarify the key issues and then in-depth interviews for the main data collection. It is not intended to be prescriptive either of the activities involved or of the time taken for them, but just to demonstrate a way of setting up a planning grid.

Table 8.2 also shows a way of planning research in real time – that is, it estimates how long the different stages of the process will actually take to carry out. Another way of looking at time is to estimate how many days' work each stage will take. This may be a useful way of working out costs.

Activity

Table 8.3 can be used to plan a research budget. The different elements can take very variable lengths of time, so boxes are left empty for you to fill in.

Table 8.3   Research planning

Task	Time Required	People Required	Costs
Clarifying the focus, setting questions			
Literature survey			
Drafting research tools			
Pilot study			
Selecting and contacting respondents			
Fieldwork			
Transcribing (if needed)			
Analysis			
Report writing			
Commenting and editing			
Design and printing			
Presentations			
TOTAL			

COMMON   Thinking that analysis and writing can be done over the weekend
PITFALLS
8.2

EXAMPLE

Planning for a Participatory Poverty Analysis (PPA) in Vietnam

Table 8.4   Tentative schedule for PPA in Ho Chi Minh City
Deadline for final report: 30 June 1999

Dates	Duration	Activity/Event
1–12 February	2 weeks	Preparations for initial PPA workshop
22–24 February	3 days	Meetings to introduce and discuss PPA with city and district officials and to researchers
1–19 March	3 weeks	Preparations for PPAs in three (or two) poor districts (2 wards per district): permits, logistics, teams, team leaders...
22–24 March	3 days	Training of three PPA teams
29 March–9 April	2 weeks	PPA in Ward A (in three districts simultaneously)
12–23 April	2 weeks	PPA in Ward B (in three districts simultaneously)
26 April–8 May	2 weeks	Writing up
10–23 May	2 weeks	Translation of reports: as reports get out, start translation as early as possible
24–31 May	1 week	Review of reports and recommendations for synthesis report
1–30 June	4 weeks	Synthesis report Poverty workshop (after the summer)

Yes, but how long will our research take?

Since this is an important element of planning for research, we will briefly look at some issues that arise in timetabling various parts of the research process. There is more detailed guidance on planning time and resources for research projects in Chapters 6 and 7. This section concentrates on person-time over the life of the project.

- **The search for existing information:** Some of the most valuable information may only be available with some effort. You may need to visit donor agencies or research institutes, or contact other researchers. This may involve writing off to distant organisations, or going to libraries, both of which take time. Sometimes people will need to be talked into assisting you. However it is also important to set deadlines for literature search work. It can take on a life of its own, and needs to be brought to a conclusion within a reasonable time.
- **Planning and drafting research tools:** This takes time as all questionnaires and other tools need to be thought about very carefully, and go through many drafts before they are complete. Piloting is also nearly always a good idea. Designing a questionnaire can take anything from 8 to 24 hours.
- **Contacting respondents:** There can be hurdles to overcome, usually in terms of persuading 'gatekeepers', who control access to other people, of the value of the research. These could be village leaders or official organisations. For example, UK local authority social services departments have formal procedures which they follow in deciding whether or not to co-operate with any request for participation in research, including an apparently simple request such as that an administrator fill in a questionnaire as part of a national survey. Enquiries may be referred to a national body for decision.

Another example would be attempting to do research in a refugee camp, when UN agencies can be very bureaucratic and slow in giving permission for research. In Laos a research project on juvenile justice and the problems faced by disadvantaged children in the capital city was planned by Save the Children. Months of work went into the planning process before it became clear that it was seen as so politically sensitive that the Ministry of Social Welfare would not co-operate with the project and it could not go ahead. At times these problems are unavoidable, but delays and waste may be avoided if an assessment of likely problems of this sort is made at an early stage.

On the other hand development projects may have no problem at all with contacting respondents; if they plan to do their research with the community they already know through their existing service provision. However if the research concerns a sensitive subject (eg mental health, money, domestic violence), people may still be reluctant to take part, even if they have some trust in those initiating the project. Time will need to be taken to put people's minds at rest.

The administrative work involved in organising any sort of research alone should not be underestimated.

> **TIP**   Making contact with respondents is one of the most variable elements in the time research takes. It can both involve a lot of work and be slow to sort itself out

- **Participatory research:** It is extremely common for reports on participatory research projects to emphasise the need for time to be allowed to win the trust of those taking part, and for participants to gain the confidence to act assertively within the research. Where a strong practice base already exists, this may be less of an issue, but where new relationships need to be forged, it will take time for community members' (reasonable) cynicism to be overcome.

   Participating in research can be stressful for people, for a variety of reasons. In particular, if the issues to be researched are close to home for those involved, and perhaps still painful for them, time needs to be allowed to assist participants in coping in a positive way with the feelings that arise.

- **Fieldwork:** A half-hour interview takes about half an hour to arrange plus the time to get there – remember to allow enough travelling time. If you are not filling in a questionnaire at the time, allow another hour to write up your interview notes. Many interviews take longer, and interviewers also need to spend time with respondents before and after the interview to ensure that they understand the research and are comfortable with it. It is a good idea to allow time between early interviews or focus groups to reflect on the process you have followed and make adjustments.

   Arranging a focus group meeting with ten people can take about one and a half hours where telephones are available, and much longer where they are not. The time taken for interviews depends on the type of interview being undertaken, whether you want simple quantitative information or more in-depth responses. About four to six straightforward interviews of up to 45 minutes, three longer qualitative interviews, or two 1 to 1½ hour focus groups can be completed in a day.

   Do not schedule too much fieldwork for each day – it becomes impossible to listen properly after a certain point, and the quality of the information collected will suffer. Group work is more tiring than individual interviews.

   It is important to fit in with people's schedules, so that you may only be able to conduct interviews in the evenings, afternoons, or on days off. There may also be a seasonal cycle which means people are extremely busy at some times of year and much freer at others. For any research where trust is needed it is good to call on people at home or in their workplace to ask whether they will take part in your research, but of course this also takes time.

The business of actually contacting respondents can be particularly fraught with difficulty when working with disadvantaged groups of people. People who have many demands on their time may break or forget appointments. Your research is not their priority. Allow some time for the likelihood that some planned arrangements will fail and you may need to go back a second time to complete an interview.

- **Recording data:** Time must be allowed for this whatever method of recording you are using. Data that is not recorded during or very soon after an interview or group discussion is irretrievably lost.

  The only way to get a verbatim version of what people actually said in an interview or focus group is to tape record it and transcribe it. An hour of tape can take anything from four to eight hours to transcribe. If the researcher who was present at the interview is a good typist, it is helpful if they do the transcribing – it is more difficult to hear accurately what people said if you were not present at the time. It is possible to get transcribing done by freelance typists who specialise in this. It can be a false economy to ask in-house administrative staff to transcribe tapes unless you brief them very well on exactly how you want it done. Whoever does it, expect to check the transcript carefully and make corrections.

  Transcribing is a lot of work. An alternative method using tapes is to listen to the tapes and take notes, and then transcribe the most interesting passages. If you do not tape record your data, you need to allow time throughout the fieldwork period for notes to be written up.

- **Data entry:** Large surveys take substantial time to 'clean' (sort out inconsistencies) and organise the data for analysis, whether by hand or by computer.

- **Analysis/interpretation:** Allow time for this! People often forget about it when planning research, and it is a crucial part of the process. It is a separate process from writing, and qualitative analysis especially can be very time consuming. With quantitative research it is the data coding and entry, and sorting out of any problems that emerge which takes the time – the actual analysis can be very quick. Qualitative analysis requires continual reflection on the categories used, and the management of large amounts of text, and is not a process which can be rushed without seriously compromising quality.

- **Writing:** Again, this needs to be given time. Someone will almost certainly need to take a solid stretch of time with few other responsibilities to write up a research project of any scale. It is a very difficult thing to do in odd moments. One consultant allows about half the time allocated to fieldwork to write up the report. Thus if the project takes four weeks to collect data, at least two will be needed to write it up. Others think that analysis and writing together can be reckoned to take about the same length of time as data collection. This obviously varies with the volume and complexity of the data and how much analysis and writing is done during the fieldwork period.

The time taken for many of these tasks will depend in part on who undertakes them. Experienced researchers will be more adept at avoiding problems and will certainly find tasks like analysis and writing much easier than people without such experience. However it may be important to encourage a wider group of staff and indeed community members to learn research-related skills. In this case, it will be necessary to allow time for them to make their mistakes and put them right again.

Where training is part of the objectives of a research project, it will be necessary to schedule time for this, even if it is not to be undertaken in any formal way.

With experience, researchers get better at estimating how long research will take, and advice should be sought from someone who has undertaken a similar project.

Estimating research costs

Working out the costs of a research project is never easy. Very often the situation is more that you have to work out what can be done for the money you have available, or which you think you can obtain.

Obviously salaries or fees are the largest part of the cost for any such project. The guidance in the section above on working out the time-scale for a piece of research will give the most help in calculating these. However there are some important other costs which may need to be taken into account.

Possible costs of research projects include:

- Research wages or fees.
- Interpreters, translators for research materials or data.
- Travel and subsistence expenses of researchers.
- Payments to community researchers and respondents (See Chapter 19.2 on sampling).
- Computer hardware and/or software.
- Training for staff and/or community participants.
- Purchasing books, journals, and other reference material; fees for use of libraries.
- Tape recorder, tapes, batteries, transcribing machine (with headset and facility to move tape back a little each time it is stopped).
- Transcribing costs.
- Administrative assistance.
- Administrative costs, eg phone calls, postage.
- Costs of advertising to contact potential respondents.
- Incentives and expenses for respondents, eg for attending focus groups.
- Flipchart.
- Other visual aids for group work.
- Data analysis – it can be sensible to pay someone to analyse statistical data, but they need to be involved earlier as well.
- Advisory group travel and other costs.

- Printing and publication costs.
- Costs of making findings accessible, eg translation, short simple version, tape recording, Braille, etc.
- Costs of advertising and distributing the results, eg printing flyers, holding a workshop.
- Other dissemination costs, eg travel to events, conference fees.

What you need to spend obviously depends upon what you already have in the way of equipment, and what you can do without. However beware of false economies. Staff costs are generally the largest item, and if spending on other items can save staff time, it may well be worthwhile. For example, if paying incentives to respondents means that an adequate sample can be contacted in a shorter time, savings may be made on time otherwise spent unable to proceed with fieldwork (see Chapter 19.2 for further discussion of the use of incentives). Equally if there is a large amount of transcribing to complete in-house, getting a machine which makes this easier is well worthwhile.

A note on overheads

Financing overhead costs is often a huge headache for voluntary organisations. Funders like to see concrete results for their money, and prefer only to fund specific projects, not the general costs of running an organisation. The term 'overheads' refers to all the costs you incur simply by being there, whatever it is that you are doing – rent, heat and light, phone rental and someone to answer the phone, someone to pay wages and keep track of finances, management costs, etc.

In a large organisation the overhead costs of research projects, which can be relatively low, may be able to be absorbed into general running costs that are met from central funds. Small agencies are likely to need to specifically allow for a contribution towards overhead costs. You can work out overheads in two ways, and it is worth considering which will be most attractive to anyone you are applying for funding from. One approach is to specify in detail what you will be spending the money on. The other is to add a percentage to the overall cost of the specific project. Some UK universities add 40% or more to grant applications, others 15 or 25%. Some funders refuse to pay any overhead costs on research grants, others set a ceiling to the percentage they are willing to pay. It is generally worth finding out a funder's attitude towards overhead costs before submitting a proposal to them.

Some examples of prices

Since agencies often experience difficulty in estimating the cost of research work, we give here some actual costs of completed projects.

EXAMPLE

Costs: the Child Labour Project, Sialkot, Pakistan

The Sialkot study of child labour in stitching footballs cost $30,000 in 1997. This includes

Costing of Pakistan study team's time		
Lead research advisor/ consultant, including writing up	Salary and overheads reimbursed for about seven weeks' work	$5250
Two sets of flights for her	London to Pakistan	$1460
Fieldworkers	40 people for 3 weeks, including accommodation, food, etc – estimate	$3000
Three consultants on different aspects	1 for 3 weeks – methodology and training @ $60/day	$900
	1 for 4 weeks – institutional analysis @ $200/day	$4000
	Statistical data analysis – one month	$1460
Printing 1,000 booklets		$2600
Training by staff member from SCF Sri Lanka		$875
Hire of computers		$1000

In addition a member of SCF's staff in Pakistan spent most of his time on this study for six months, a manager spent time supporting the project, and three to four drivers and vehicles were made available for the fieldwork period.

EXAMPLE

Costs: desk study on child soldiers

A desk study was undertaken in February 2000 by Save the Children on child soldiers and children associated with the fighting forces, with a view to identifying what was known so as to inform the next steps in the development of generic best practice guidelines. The costs of this exercise were:

EXAMPLE

Budget: Research on access of disabled children to education in Issyk-Kul district, Kyrgyzstan

Period: September–December 2000

This was a study involving interviews with children, parents, and local government officials.

Description of expenses	Unit price, US$	Quantity	Period	Total amount, US$	Explanatory notes
Research fees					
Researcher	500	1	4 months	500	
Research Advisor	700	1	4 months	700	
Field trips					
Transport expenses	41	3 trips	18 days (4 + 9 + 5)	124	Route: Bishkek–Issyk-Kul (17 villages)–Bishkek
Accommodation	1.5	4 people	18 days	108	
Food	3	4 people	18 days	216	
Other expenses					
Polaroid camera and cassettes	30 + 25	1 camera and 3 cassettes		55	Photos for children who were interviewed
Photo film	2	3	6		To make pictures
Dictaphone cassettes	2.5	2		5	To record interviews
Translation of final report	5	60 pages		300	
TOTAL				2014	

15 days' work by a consultant at $220 per day	$3300
Photocopying, printing, internet time, etc – say	$150
TOTAL	$3450

There would be further costs for printing and publication. It should be noted that the efficiency of this type of exercise depends upon the skills of the person undertaking it.

8.3   Negotiating Access – ... Or How to Reach the Parts other Research Does not Reach

'Negotiating access' is a piece of researchers' jargon which refers to the process of getting permission to approach people, or indeed to use archive material or unpublished official statistics, as part of the research process. Discussions of sampling tend to sound as if you as the researcher were swooping down from on high to pluck those you select out of a pool of willing participants… – if only!

As development practitioners, you may have all the contacts you need to undertake research, if you already have a strong presence in the community in question. However any research based wholly on the direct contacts of a particular person or project risks being perceived as biased.

More robust research, needing a more representative sample, requires access to people who are in contact with other agencies or none. People may also be contacted simply as citizens, for example in some countries through the electoral register, or through visiting homes in a systematic pattern.

When we set out on a research project, our own enthusiasm often makes it difficult to remember that others, whether local community members or staff of partner agencies, will not always readily wish to be involved. People meet your research project with expectations of their own, which you cannot guess. There is often some suspicion of your motives, and there is always competition for people's time. Do not underestimate the work involved in gaining people's trust and co-operation.

TIP   Think through, as soon as you can, what you need to do in order to get access to the people you hope to contact, and to set these processes in train early on. And persist

---

EXAMPLE

Studying physical punishment in schools in England

Save the Children wanted to research younger children's views of 'smacking' (physical punishment) in England, to inform debate surrounding proposed changes to the law. It needed to find a number of primary schools which were willing to allow group discussions to be held on this subject. Parents' permission was sought once the schools had agreed. It was difficult to locate schools willing to participate – 500 flyers yielded only 3 replies. In the end personal contacts were used to build relationships with schools. Schools expressed concern that parents would respond negatively, but in fact in every school which allowed parents to be approached some agreed for their children to participate.

EXAMPLE

Juvenile justice in Laos – off the agenda

A planned piece of SCF research looking at juvenile justice in Laos had to be abandoned after much preparatory work because the government had not been persuaded that the issue should be investigated.

It is worth making enquiries at an early stage to establish what the issues are in relation to access to respondents, before a great deal of time is invested in any particular research design. Do not hope to bypass official 'gatekeepers' – those whose permission is needed to contact others – this is rarely possible in practice, and is usually a bad idea. Gatekeepers hold power in different ways – they may be government ministers, the local doctor, the chief of the village, or a respected older woman. The (reasonable) cynicism of ordinary people in impoverished areas towards those claiming to help them can be reflected in barriers thrown up by their leaders. This can entirely block a piece of research if they are unsympathetic to it. It is better to take the time needed to win over any authorities whose permission you require to undertake your work.

Referring to INGO research, Pratt and Loizos (1992) argue:

'The right of an agency to operate in another country depends upon the will of the host country. Permission to do research should normally have been part of a Country Agreement which set out the conditions under which the development agency operates. If for some reason research has been omitted from the agreement, or had conditions attached to it, then negotiations might have to be undertaken with an appropriate Ministry to get permission to do research. If political conditions in the country generally, or in the area you are working in, are good, and your agency has a positive image with the relevant Ministry, research permission should be readily forthcoming. But if the country is riven by bitter internal conflicts, or your agency is operating in a climate of mistrust or suspicion, then a relatively simple research project may present itself to official minds as a major diplomatic issue, and you will need all your patience, tact and persuasiveness to get the project accepted. Under such difficult conditions, research sometimes simply 'isn't on'.

Alternatively, you make take the view that anything which is not explicitly forbidden by your Country Agreement, and which is covered by your general statement of agency aims, is clearly defensible, and go ahead with your research without seeking official clearance. This strategy might initially save you time and trouble. But be prepared for misunderstandings, and be ready to explain you research in a calm, and diplomatic way if an anxious and ill-informed official – from the police, for example – decides that you are engaged in some form of spying activity, or something else harmful to the interests of the government. Social researchers are used to having their inquiries mis-understood; and the idea of the spy has diffused all over the world.

It is a better tactic, if you want to make a rapid start and cut through the red tape, to notify your most friendly senior contacts in an appropriate Ministry informally that you wish to do some research on a specific topic – agricultural productivity, or mother-child health issues – in a particular locality. Then, in the event of misunderstandings, you can say to inquirers "Mr X and Mrs Y at the Ministry know what we are doing here, and can tell you about our work"...

It is inevitable that some of the activities of foreign development agencies, in particular, should arouse a certain amount of misunderstanding and mistrust; and one of the best ways to counter this is by the greatest possible openness. Try to collaborate with sympathetic officials wherever possible.'

What goes for governments also goes for all kinds of other organisations whose permission you may need to carry out your research. In some cases there may be formal procedures for the granting of permission to carry out research. For example, the UK health service has research ethics committees which vet all research involving patients, and you will not be granted access to any list of patients without your research being scrutinised by such a body.[1] Universities have also begun to create ethics committees to look at their own research. More often, a decision will be made by the senior managers of the organisation in question – yet another reason to involve partner agencies at an early stage. Informal authorities within the community can also of course throw up barriers to research. Research processes are generally seen as potentially threatening, and it is to be expected that those in authority will expect to have a say in what happens.

EXAMPLE

Talking to children living in children's homes – Liberia

In researching the views of ex-child soldiers in Liberia on help they had received, researchers wanted to bring together a group of children who had been at particular transit centre. Some

---

[1]The aim, of protecting patients from invasive or inappropriate research, is of course to be welcomed. However these committees often lack experience and understanding of qualitative research (as opposed to treatment trials), and may impede valuable non-invasive efforts to consult patients.

of them were now living in a children's home run by another agency. One day the researchers arrived at the home and asked permission of the senior staff member present for these children to take part in a focus group discussion that afternoon. He agreed, as did the children themselves. The discussion went well and the group agreed to meet again the following day to complete the questions they wanted to cover. When the researchers returned the next day, the supervisor of the home was there, and said that they did not have proper permission to do this. Permission should have been sought from his senior, at head office. This person was in fact scheduled to attend an advisory group meeting for the project the following day, and the group discussion could only continue after that. It was eventually possible to resume the discussion, later in the week, but some momentum was lost.

One lesson is the need always to get proper permission to talk to anyone, especially groups whose own ability to refuse consent might be questioned. Another is to get on with it! It is never wise to assume that you will have further opportunities for discussion with respondents – get your important questions in as soon as you can.

At times, it is simply not possible to undertake research in the ways in which you have hoped, and you will need to be flexible about methods of data collection.

EXAMPLE

Reaching urban child workers – Vietnam

To complement the research on rural child labour, SCF carried out research on child labour in Ho Chi Minh City in 1997. This study focused on children involved in money-earning activities. It required a complete revision of the original research plan, given the differences between rural and urban work conditions and the complexities of labour arrangements in a metropolis of 6 million people. Involving children in the research proved much more difficult than in the rural areas. Children working in factories were under the constant supervision of their employer and were not able to take breaks to participate in discussions, in diagramming, and in listing and scoring exercises. Many children lived far away from their place of work which made it difficult to track down factory workers at their place of lodging. This part of the research therefore relied largely on informal interviews with children at their workplace and on direct observations of working children. More participatory methods, such as scoring and listing exercises and daily routine diagramming, could only be used with working children attending evening classes and with children at their place of lodging.

8.4 Managing Participatory Research

The same guidelines apply to managing participatory research as to any other sort of research – it is just as necessary to be clear about the purpose of the research, and to make explicit agreements with all those involved about the roles they expect to play. As has already been mentioned, experience shows that participatory research requires time to be spent winning the trust of participants as well as in carrying out the work. A flexible approach will be needed.

It is likely that two sorts of staff will be needed to support participatory processes with community members. There will need to be an experienced research advisor to oversee the process from the research point of view, and they will need to work alongside staff who are familiar with working with the participating group. Trust needs to be established to give participants confidence to have their say. If it is possible to use staff who are already known to some of those involved, so much the better. For work with children and young people, those with youth work, childcare, and teaching experience have much to contribute.

EXAMPLE

Working alongside a counsellor

Save the Children's peer research on young people's views of Bolton's mental health services was supported by the project's Counselling Co-ordinator, along with a research advisor. The Counselling Co-ordinator's role included counselling support but was primarily a matter of ensuring that the young researchers were supported in organising their work, for example in contacting respondents. It was felt in retrospect that more time should have been allowed within this post to support the research project.

To enable participatory projects to have an influence on policy, the manager is a key link between stakeholders and decision-makers. It is also important to remember to keep participatory research projects in touch with other relevant developments – and to remind other managers they deal with of the participatory project's work.

When people become involved as community researchers, for example carrying out interviews, issues can arise about what exactly is their status in relation to the organisation. You should usually expect to pay the expenses of those who take part, and you may want to pay them, either as employees, or a small amount to replace lost earnings. This has been done in a number of projects. But what happens if they fail to appear for work? Or behave in some way contrary to the organisation's expectations? You may want to give these issues some thought, in discussion with those concerned. The evaluation of a major peer research programme in England discusses these issues in detail (Kirby, 1999).

8.5   Relating to Funders

Some research which development workers undertake or commission is paid for by their own organisation as part of their work programme. However quite often funding is obtained from another organisation, which may be specifically oriented towards funding research, or may fund research as part

CHECKLIST   On managing participatory research

✓ Consider facilitating participation in the different elements of the research process (see Figure 3.2 in Chapter 3 above)

✓ Allow enough time for real participation at each relevant stage of the process

✓ Reflect on why you are encouraging participation and what participating community members will gain from their involvement

✓ Allocate sufficient staff time to support participating community members

✓ Consider and resolve any issues in relation to remuneration for participants

✓ Take account of social inequalities amongst the group you hope to involve

✓ Make links between the participatory project and other relevant work in your agency, to maximise learning

of a development programme. Funders of development work want to see evidence that problems have been properly assessed.

When we think about research funding, our first image of the relationship with funders that we imagine is very much an 'us and them' situation. They give us money and we give them reports. However successful fundraising depends upon recognising that any funding arrangement is a type of inter-agency deal (Open University, 1993). It is essential to consider what the funding body wants out of its grant giving, and to co-operate with them in that endeavour. It may also be possible to influence their ideas about appropriate directions for their funding based on the agency's experience. But the first step is to accept that funders have a legitimate stake in the outcomes of their funding operations.

Top of most funders' list of criteria will be whether the issue in question is important enough to merit attention. Making this case persuasively is key if funds are to be attracted. Too often, by the time a funding application is written, the issues we want to work on are so familiar to us that we take it for granted that they are important, rather than arguing why in a convincing manner. A study of grant applications refused by the US National Institutes of Health found that 33 per cent were rejected because 'the problem is of insufficient importance or is unlikely to produce any new or useful information' (Leedy, 1997).

Apart from self-funded research, the two main ways in which research is undertaken is on the basis of grant funding, and through contracts. The key difference is that with grant funding, a researcher may be left to make their own decisions on methods, sampling, etc, after the initial grant is given, whereas with a contract, the funder is likely to be actively involved in these decisions (Hakim, 1987). However the distinction between the two approaches is not as hard and fast as it might appear. Practice is very variable.

Different funders take very different approaches to their work, and it is important to get information from the ones you are interested in, and to adapt your ideas to the framework of those you hope to approach. However even if you are dealing with a funder with minimal requirements for feedback, it is wise to keep them informed of developments from time to time. The more you can make a relationship with them, the more hope you have of further funding in the future. On the whole, research funders understand that changes may need to be made to the details of the proposal they agreed to, but they will want to be told about any major changes of plan, and the reasons for it.

Much development research is funded as part of a package which also includes practical development work 'on the ground'. Where this is true, it is essential to make it clear how the work will be relevant to the donor's aims.

Some of the largest social research funders take a very proactive approach. ESCOR, the Joseph Rowntree Foundation, and the Nuffield Foundation publish quite detailed research strategies in their areas of concern, and invite bids to undertake research to pursue particular sets of questions. These funders encourage people who wish to submit proposals outside of these commissioned programmes to discuss them with the funders' staff first. It is a waste of time all round to submit proposals that have no hope of success. ESCOR has a system where smaller bids can be decided without going through the whole committee process, but larger ones must.

When Rowntree, for example, funds a project, it takes a close interest in it throughout its life, and requires it to convene an advisory group which is usually chaired by a member of the Foundation's staff. It also publishes and distributes a short summary of its findings in a standard format.

NGOs may also relate to research funding in a different way, as 'users' of research undertaken by academics. Funding bodies like the UK Government's ESRC are now placing emphasis on involving 'users' of research in discussions about research funding directions. Voluntary organisations are seen as potentially helpful in identifying what information is needed from research. For example, the ESRC's Children Initiative, which funded 22 projects at a cost of £2.4 million, involved a number of representatives of voluntary organisations on its Commissioning Panel, and continues to involve the voluntary sector in discussions about the results of the research.

This initiative, and others in a number of fields, have also encouraged academics to involve voluntary organisations in their research proposals, with a view to ensuring its relevance to practice. Some fruitful partnerships have emerged. However voluntary organisations also complain of a syndrome where they receive a flurry of phone calls from academics the day before the deadline for applications, asking to put the name of the organisation on their bid. This sort of involvement may be completely token, but it can also drain an organisation's resources as it tries to engage with a project into which it has had no creative input.

NGOs need to think carefully about their role in relation to seeking research funding. The perception of many research funders is that only universities are capable of undertaking rigorous research. For some types of funding, for example from ESRC and ESCOR, the research arm of the UK Department for International Development), it may be necessary to form a partnership with a university. See also the section on 'Working with academics' in Chapter 7.3.

Development workers will be best advised to seek funding which draws on their strengths in terms of active engagement with stakeholders, and ability to link needs assessment with participatory processes and service provision as well as influencing policy. Getting academic research funding is difficult for academics and almost unheard-of for those outside academia. However there are other types of funders who want to see research undertaken with communities, which investigates communities' needs and ways of meeting them alongside programmes which address these needs. Some, for example, Comic Relief and the National Lottery emphasise community participation in their terms of reference.

Others, such as DfID, are now looking for an element of seeking policy influence in applications for its funding. NGOs may be in a good position to ensure that this aspect is followed through, compared, for example, to academic researchers.

Key Points from this Chapter

CHECKLIST   For effective research management

✓ Provide management supervision *and* research supervision
✓ Make a careful estimate of the time research will take – this is usually underestimated
✓ It is important to allow enough time for contacting respondents, and, in participatory research, for winning the trust of stakeholders
✓ There is great value in building up organisations' research capacity – consider this as an element of the objectives of projects, and work out appropriate ways of involving people
✓ Participatory research is likely to need both research staff and staff who are familiar with the group you are working with to commit substantial time to a project
✓ Make sure you understand what a funder wants from its grant-giving, and exactly what its remit is, before you write an application

This chapter has argued that research work will benefit both from management supervision, attending to progress in relation to aims and objectives, and from research supervision, assisting with matters of research methodology and professional practice. Some frameworks are offered to assist with timetabling and costing research projects. It draws attention to some important issues involved in managing research for development: the unpredictable work of contacting informants; building research capacity in-house and with partner agencies; managing participatory research; and relating to funding agencies.

Further Reading

Leedy, P.D. (1997) *Practical Research: Planning and design*, 6th edition. New Jersey: Merrill, Prentice Hall.

Written for researchers, but practically oriented and helpful to others also.

9 Learning How to do Research for Development Work

This chapter is for those who want to build research skills for themselves, their colleagues and those they work with. Making effective arguments for wider change is increasingly seen as an inextricable part of practical development work with communities. Research has an important role to play, as it is one way of systematically making the case for change. There are a number of ways in which research skills can be shared, and development workers can be assisted to undertake the work they need to do.

This chapter starts by considering the different aspects of the research process for which you may want to increase skills. Different aspects can be addressed in different ways. There are exercises throughout this manual which aim to help in building skills in the different areas of research work, but the area of general analytical skills is often identified as problematic. A short section suggests some exercises to develop critical thinking. The next part of the chapter looks at some approaches to skill development – training workshops, joint working, coaching and consultancy, and learning as part of a practical project. Finally we step back and look more broadly at how development organisations can support Southern researchers.

One aspect of the need for skills development is shown in the following example, from a study aimed at minimising the impact of HIV in a region of Ethiopia. The problems it describes are typical of those which arise from the lack of skilled people sharing language and culture with respondents.

EXAMPLE

A skills gap – studying the impact of HIV in Ethiopia

Two sets of limitations were identified:

(a) In research and data collection skills: qualitative research demands a high level of skill and precision in data collection. Because of language and cultural barriers it was not possible for the (expatriate) consultant to collect data directly, nor even to supervise the data collection. The Save the Children research team members supervising the work were also new to the particular research skills involved. The time available for training research team members did not allow for sophisticated skills development. As a result the focus group discussion facilitation was more formalised than would be ideal, following a set pattern of questions. The quality and extent of the data collected was limited by this.

(b) Details lost through translation: the raw data from focus groups was summarised and translated from Amharic and Oromo into English for analysis by the consultant. This inevitably resulted in a loss of fine detail, which is reflected in the broad-brush nature of the results.

9.1   Where to Start?

If you are a manager considering the needs of an organisation you will want first to consider at what level you need to improve research skills, and in what ways this should best be done. Are you looking at:

- The whole organisation?
- Some individual staff members?
- Whole teams of staff members?
- Managers or practitioners?

You may want to hire new people who have the skills you need, or perhaps to set up a whole new department. Or you might want to make an arrangement with another organisation which has the skills you need. If you decide that in-house or external skills training is required, you will need to carry out a training needs assessment exercise with the staff concerned. This means looking at job descriptions and tasks required, and comparing what is needed to the existing skills profile of the staff concerned. It is also extremely helpful to consult the staff concerned about their own perception of the skills they need to learn. People rarely get much out of training they perceive as imposed from 'on high'.

As will be clear from this manual, 'research' is a big subject. The skills and knowledge involved are quite broad and complex.

COMMON PITFALLS 9.1   Setting up a one-day workshop on research methods in the hope that this will make the whole team capable of planning and carrying out a major research project.

To plan useful learning, you need to break it down and work out which aspect of research work is most important to you at this time.

Some broad areas to consider might be:

- The role of research in development work, and different approaches to research.
- Planning and managing research.

- How to choose methods for research projects.
- Data collection techniques: interviewing, focus groups, observation, visual techniques, etc.
- Data analysis.
- Writing and promotion of ideas.

Within any of these areas, you may want to take a participatory approach, and this involves some special skills as well. There is also the general area of developing better analytical skills, a critical approach, which may need attention. And of course you may also need to learn about the specific issues involved in research with a particular social group: disabled people, refugees, or children for example.

It is important to realise that while learning practical techniques is useful, the whole area of attitudes and behaviour, within fieldwork and within the planning and management of research, is also crucial. Learning to listen carefully while thinking about the next question, to approach people confidently but respectfully, can be more difficult than one expects. Carrying out new tasks is stressful, and researchers need help to convey a positive attitude and not to share their anxieties with the respondent!

Obviously some research tasks are more difficult than others. Collecting responses to a standard survey is much easier than carrying out a less structured in-depth interview. Focus group facilitation is particularly demanding. Research planning and management sometimes runs really smoothly, with clear aims and skilled researchers, and is sometimes a nightmare. See Chapter 7.1 for ideas about breaking down a research project, and involving different people in different tasks. Having done this, different training or other educational work may be needed by different parts of a research team. As with all learning processes, for inexperienced people it is best to undertake some tasks where success is reasonably easy to achieve before tackling more challenging ones.

The other chapters of this manual suggest within the text some activities to help people to learn about research. Most of these can be done on your own or with a group. An underlying skill which is essential for many aspects of research work is that of taking an analytical approach, and the next section suggests some ways of working on this.

Developing stronger analytical skills

A critical approach is crucial to research – you need to question your own research questions; to question why people are giving the responses they are to your questions; and then to question how you interpret these. Small children ask a lot of questions, but this is knocked out of many of us by authoritarian schooling which in effect teaches a fear of questioning authority. Confidence is needed to ask sharp questions, as one is exposing one's thinking to others' scrutiny, and this confidence must be nurtured carefully. Working in a language which is not one's mother tongue of course adds to the barriers involved.

Organisations can help to increase staff confidence by building a culture where it is OK to make mistakes, to say the wrong thing occasionally, but perhaps less OK to be passive and say nothing. Timid people need not to be slapped down when they do make a suggestion, if they are to gain confidence. Praise is important.

If innovative work is being undertaken, there is an element of risk involved – mistakes will inevitably be made. When trying out new things, it is not likely that it will be possible to get everything right the first time. When mistakes occur, a learning environment should see them as opportunities to learn, rather than seeking to find someone to blame.

Any exercise which encourages people to think for themselves, and then to argue for their point of view, is useful. One effective traditional method is to set up formal debates, with people speaking for and against a motion, to push people to question and defend their ideas. Another is simply to regularly make a practice of reading one another's pieces of work and commenting on them. This can help in learning to accept comments without feeling that any comment means that one has done wrong.

This is a really essential thing to learn – to expect and welcome critical comment on one's work. If no reader has anything to say about what you have written, you need to ask why! It may not mean that it is good – but that it is boring.

EXAMPLE

Learning to defend your argument – Vietnam

A research training workshop was run with Save the Children staff in Vietnam, which aimed to help them to assess a proposed programme of work through some investigation of the needs of the community. The focus was rural development, and a key exercise saw individual members of the team spending a single day finding out everything they could about one of the issues involved in the proposal – pig breeding, micro credit, water/sanitation. They were then asked to prepare a very short talk about what they had found, and to summarise their recommendation in one sentence. The trainer then challenged them to defend their conclusions, and encouraged them to look at the processes involved in offering evidence to support one's argument. By going through this process some of the trainee researchers completely changed their conclusions.

EXAMPLE

Development Studies Schools for senior NGO staff – South and South East Asia

For several years, Save the Children in South and South East Asia ran regional month-long Development Studies Schools for its senior national staff. The programme was demanding, and included reading, lectures, and group discussion – both formal seminars and informal country-group discussions. Participants were required to write short essays, as well as presenting seminar papers, and were given feedback on their performance, with suggestions (where needed) about how to improve. Many participants found this helped them learn how to put forward and defend an argument in a logical fashion, as well as how to identify and take apart the arguments in others' writing.

Activity 9.1

Some fearful words: a game of eight squares

This game is based on one devised by Boyden and Ennew (1997) in response to questions from participants at training events. Many words are used loosely in everyday speech, and then have specific meanings in social science. This can be especially difficult to grasp where people are working in a second language.

The game can be played in two ways. Early on, use the examples given here. Later, during the process of analysis and writing, the game could be adapted using examples from participants' data or writing.

To play the game, facilitators need to prepare three or four large game boards (on stiff card, about the same size as a flip chart sheet), and mark each one up clearly as follows:

Game board for the game of eight squares

Concept	Fact
Theory	Assumption
Explanation	Analysis
Understanding	Description

You should also prepare two sets of cards, 'Definitions' and 'Examples' (using those given on the answers sheet below), for each group, placing each set in a marked envelope. An answers sheet should be prepared for each facilitator, making sure that the participants do not see this.

So each player or group of players has: a game board, a set of 'Definitions', and a set of 'Examples'. The object of the game is to match each word on the game board with the correct definition and example.

It will be helpful to discuss why people have put things in different places, exploring any disagreements that arise. Try to think of other examples perhaps from your own work, for each of the words.

Answers sheet for the game of eight squares

Word on game board	Definition	Example
Concept	An abstract or general idea which is important to how we think about a particular subject	Sexual exploitation is based on situations of power between men and women, adults and children
Fact	A justified, true belief (based on information that has been properly collected and analysed)	Medical tests and records show that children treated with oral rehydration therapy (ORT) tend to recover better from diarrhoea than children who are not given ORT
Theory	Ideas or principles which explain, or seek to explain, something	If children's rights were respected, their welfare would be improved
Assumption	A belief that is taken for granted and (perhaps mistakenly) used as the basis of a statement or research question	People on low incomes lack knowledge about a healthy diet
Explanation	Statements which make sense of something about why things are the way they are	The increase in skin cancer in some areas is caused by thinning of the ozone layer
Analysis	The logical process of examining data to see what they mean	In a study of 450 15-year-old Indian boys, 25% were found to work full time. Of those who worked full time, 85% were found to have

		suffered an illness episode in the past 14 days, compared to 32% of those who did not work. This suggests that full-time work in childhood may be harmful to health
Understanding	Our perception of the meaning of something	Ali's view is that he cannot get a job because employers think he is too old to be worth training
Description	A verbal account of places, events, people, or situations	In the market on Saturdays, there are usually five stalls selling fabrics, all run by women

Adapted by permission from Boyden and Ennew, 1997.

Activity 9.2

What does this mean to me?

The following training exercise is suggested by Boyden and Ennew (1997), to build the confidence of inexperienced researchers in seeing how to incorporate materials from elsewhere in their arguments. The aim of the exercise is to learn how to identify important information within a large body of data, and how to make appropriate comparisons. *Researchers in other fields could think of equivalent documents to use, of relevance to their work.*

Facilitators should obtain the UNICEF Situation Analysis for women and children for the participants' country, and from another country on the same continent, and photocopy for each participant the pages on children in especially difficult circumstances from each volume (usually a small portion of the whole).

Participants should read both photocopies and do the following:

- Using the photocopies only, write a brief account of children in especially difficult circumstances in the foreign country, giving a description of the main points, together with any criticisms or doubts they may have about the information (150 words).
- List the similarities and differences (compare and contrast) between the situation of children in especially difficult circumstances in these two countries.
- Taking one of the differences, write a hypothesis for research to be carried out in their own country.

9.2   Some Ways of Learning Research Skills

People learn in different ways, but for all of us the more actively we are involved in learning research skills, the more likely we are to take in and remember what we have learnt. Some possible approaches include:

- Training workshops
- Reading, learning on your own
- Formal research training, including by distance learning
- Learning as part of a real research project
- Joint working, coaching and consultancy.

We will look at these areas in more depth below. However there are many kinds of initiative you could take to encourage people to learn more about research work, and some are suggested in the following checklist. Don't assume that if you want people to learn about research, a workshop is the right approach – experience shows that other approaches may be more effective.

CHECKLIST   Learning about research through special initiatives

✓ Set up small low-risk projects, part of whose aim is to develop staff and/or community members' research skills – and ensure time is released to carry these out

✓ Arrange in-house training in research skills – offering training in interviewing skills is a good way of introducing broader research issues

✓ Involve people from partner agencies in training workshops, where appropriate – this is especially useful when working with innovative methodologies which need to be 'sold' to partners

✓ Sponsor staff to undertake external research training

✓ Facilitate networking amongst people doing similar work to promote mutual learning

✓ Work through activities from this manual individually or with colleagues

---

Training workshops

First of all, as ever, be clear about the purpose of any workshop you set up. Check which areas of research (see Section 9.1 above) you need to cover. Find out directly from potential participants what they feel their needs are. If you are planning a specific project, it should be possible to tailor the training to address the particular issues raised by that project. It may be best to wait until you are close to the time when the work will be done, so that people can link the abstract ideas taught to the practical tasks in hand. Even if you do not have a specific project in mind, the most effective training includes an element of practising research skills through a practical piece of work.

There is a well-established format for training in Participatory Learning and Action (see Chapter 18.7), and some excellent guides to carrying out such training (Theis and Grady, 1991; Pretty et al, 1995). Boyden and Ennew's (1997) pack explains how to run training in participatory research with children. These all discuss general approaches to training as well as offering some detailed ideas about how to teach specific skills.

One benefit of setting up training is that it can be a way to build a team of people both to undertake a piece or a programme of research, and to support them. It gives a safe place to work out any controversial issues raised by a project.

CHECKLIST   Some guidelines for training in research methods

✓ Acknowledge and build on participants' existing knowledge and skills
✓ Model within the training the approach to people that you want to see in practice
✓ Try to find trainers who are familiar with the local situation and fluent in the local language – if this is not possible, trainers should team up with a co-trainer who knows the area and speaks the language
✓ Involve someone with experience in adult non-formal training techniques
✓ Use active methods like role play, practical tasks, and open debate
✓ Make sure you use examples to practice on that are relevant to participants' own work
✓ Don't try to pack too much into a short time
✓ Include an element of practical research, however small
✓ Evaluate and reflect on the training, as you hope participants will evaluate and reflect on their research practice

---

EXAMPLE

Involving partners in training on participatory research – China

Save the Children's China programme recently set up training on participatory research methods for development workers who were working with them, and invited staff from partner agencies to take part in the training too. The training concentrated particularly on participatory approaches to working with vulnerable children, including street children, those with HIV, and others from poor urban families. It involved national government officials from agencies responsible for social welfare, and others from local and national 'mass' (quasi-governmental) organisations such as the China Children's Development Centre. Advisors from Save the Children's Vietnam programme were involved who could discuss experience of this type of work in a similar cultural and political context. Learning together in this way focused attention on the importance of considering the young people's point of view on any plans to intervene in their lives.

EXAMPLE

Writing workshops – UK

Barnardos in the UK wanted to improve writing skills amongst its fieldworkers. The six best writers were selected from each region, and they were offered a series of short training workshops, with practical work to do between the workshops, to develop their skills.

Reading, learning on your own

There are many useful books which can give guidance on different aspects of research. Reading on the different areas of the research process is recommended at the end of each chapter of this manual. The best approach for most people is to have books with you to refer to when you have particular questions, rather than expecting to work through them from start to finish.

Formal research training, including distance learning

Many professional training courses, especially undergraduate and Masters degrees contain an element of teaching on research skills. Look for courses which require you to carry out a small project yourself.

The UK's Open University provides distance learning opportunities, including under- and post-graduate courses in development studies, and some management courses which are intended for those working in the UK voluntary sector. These are more development-oriented than research-centred, but using evidence to make a case is taught. Most OU courses are only available to those based in the UK or Europe, but a new course has just been launched using electronic tuition – 'Development Management Online'. For this course you need internet access and to be linked to an international development organisation or NGO based in Europe.

It is likely that more and better opportunities for distance learning will develop over the next few years, using paper-based media and also over the Internet. The list of useful websites in Appendix 1 should give you some places to start.

Learning as part of a real research project

Just get started! This manual aims to make the planning process as straightforward as possible. Start with a small and relatively simple project, to build skills and confidence. You could invent a small piece of work to practice on, which would have benefit to your agency's work.

The most useful learning is gained by being involved in a project from the beginning to the end, having some responsibility for the results. Then you learn about the successes and problems of the methods you try in a very direct way.

Joint working, coaching, and consultancy

One of the best ways of learning about research is to work alongside an experienced researcher. This is why there are points throughout this manual where it is recommended to consult such a person. You could make a stable arrangement with someone that they will advise throughout a project, or indeed throughout the year, as research issues arise.

If you normally lack access to an experienced researcher, but hire them in for a specific project, consider building it into their brief that they will work closely with staff who would like to learn from them. You could ask them to run a specific training or feedback event, so that relevant people gain some direct learning from a project as it is happening. Ask them to discuss openly the methodological choices and problems raised by a particular project, and this will assist you when you next have to plan a research project.

CHECKLIST   Some ways of sharing research skills as part of an ongoing project:

✓ Involve people who want to learn as observers, for example note-taking at focus groups, or at interviews
✓ Have in-house staff lead a project, and arrange research supervision from someone more experienced
✓ Enable staff to be involved in projects from start to finish, so that they learn about how their decisions and actions early on affect the final results
✓ Invite relevant people onto research advisory groups – for their contribution as well as for them to learn
✓ Make the task of facilitating the learning of others part of the brief when you involve more experienced researchers

---

9.3   Supporting Southern Researchers

Researchers, and development workers learning research skills, in the South can face a very difficult environment.

'The total number of professional academics in the development studies university sector in anglophone (English-speaking) African countries amounts to no more than 100, of whom fewer than half have PhDs.' (Bennel, 1999)

Development agencies should invest in skills development in a number of ways. Too often, Northern consultants are hired without thought for the long-term consequences. Effort should be made to build links to existing Southern research organisations, and where appropriate to employ or co-operate with Southern researchers. This is one way of generating sustainable change.

EXAMPLE

Commissioning work from African researchers

In preparing a commissioned report on trends in child poverty in Africa, Save the Children's head office staff commissioned contributions from Save the Children staff or researchers in a number of African countries. Each was paid $1000 to $2000 to write a report on a particular theme within the subject, relating to their country, using existing research (which they may have done themselves) and carrying out secondary analysis on official statistics. In this way the money spent on this project contributed to building research skills in the South as well as engaging a wider group in the countries in question with the issues.

Three kinds of capacity sharing should be considered: that within the agency itself, but also that of the people you work with, and of partner agencies. Partners may include local or national government, national research bodies, and universities. Reflections on recent Participatory Poverty Assessments in a number of countries, led by the World Bank, considered that it was an important outcome of the programme that there are now people with experience of the benefits of participatory approaches within the governments and donor agencies concerned (Norton, 1998).

In some countries academic institutions lack the most basic resources. Agencies should consider donating computers and contributing to libraries.

Key Points from this Chapter

CHECKLIST   For learning about research for development work

- ✓ Be clear about which part of the research process you need to learn about
- ✓ Build in learning as part of a real research project
- ✓ Arrange for joint working and coaching from an experienced researcher to gain the most learning from practical work
- ✓ Involve partner agencies and community members, as appropriate, in training workshops you arrange
- ✓ When planning training, ensure that the principles you want to see in the research work are reflected in the training methods
- ✓ Plan to make a contribution to the broad task of supporting the development of appropriate research skills within disadvantaged communities world-wide

Further Reading

Training manuals:

Theis, J. and Grady, H.M. (1991) *Participatory Rapid Appraisal for Community Development: A training manual based on experiences in the Middle East and North Africa*. London: IIED and Save the Children Federation.

Enthusiastic and clearly written. Includes useful guidance on general training approaches and techniques.

Pretty, J.N., Guijt, I., Scoones I. and Thompson J. (1995) *A Trainer's Guide for Participatory Learning and Action*. London: IIED.

Designed for both experienced and new trainers, provides a comprehensive background to the principles of adult learning, as well as detailed guidance on facilication skills and the principles of PLA. Describes the process of organising training both in workshops and in the field. Includes 101 games and exercises for trainers, and helpful examples from real life.

Boyden, J. and Ennew, J. (eds) (1997) *Children in Focus: A manual for participatory research with children*. Stockholm: Rädda Barnen.

Rädda Barnen, S-107 88 Stockholm, Sweden. Tel: (+46) 8-698 90 00. Email: info@rb.se

Includes a framework for training in participatory research with children.

Research handbooks:

Bell, J. (1987) *Doing Your Research Project*. Buckingham, UK: Open University Press.

A particularly simple and clear presentation of the basics of how to do research. Rather oriented to UK students, but valuable for many readers.

Deer Richardson, L. (1992) *Techniques of Investigation*. Cambridge, UK: National Extension College.

Written as a companion text to Bell, above. Very basic, includes study skills. Clear and well-presented. Examples come from the field of education, but the main text is relevant to any field. Includes activities to help in learning.

Blaxter, L., Hughes C. and Tight, M. (1996) *How to Research*. Buckingham, UK: Open University Press.

Aimed at people involved in small-scale research projects at college or at work, this helpful book includes exercises for readers to carry out.

See also recommended reading in Chapter 3.

10 Managing for Impact – Promoting Research Findings

This chapter draws managers' attention to the importance of promoting the findings of research effectively. There are different priorities for promotional work depending upon whether the research is aimed primarily at informing the programme, or at influencing policy more broadly. Ways of reaching the various different audiences involved, including those who were researched, are suggested. Referring back to the discussion in Chapter 2 about how research can have an influence on policy, guidelines are offered on presenting reports, and on promotional work 'beyond The Report'. The issues involved in dealing with the media are also discussed. Managers are advised to plan for the promotion of research results from the start of the project. Issues relating to how to write a research report are discussed in Chapter 21.

COMMON PITFALLS 10.1	Forgetting to plan or budget for any work to promote the findings of the research

This section is included in Part One because the promotion of the results of research is a key role for managers in development work, and needs to be planned for early in the process. Whilst research and other staff obviously need to be involved in this process, it should not be left to them to carry out in isolation. While a few researchers are excellent publicists for their work, many tend to be diffident about this process. They may not have experience of promotional processes – these are not taught as part of the training of researchers. It is also important to budget for the costs involved in promotional work, and obviously managers will need to do this.

We all naturally hope that our research will have an impact of its own accord, and that the power of its findings will speak for itself. But there is plenty of evidence that this does not happen (Finch, 1986). Work is needed to take the information to those you hope to influence, and it is essential to plan this work in the light of clear thinking about who your key audience is.

The chances of your research being used will increase if, in communicating the results, you:

- develop a systematic promotional strategy for reaching different audiences of potential users;
- write timely reports in direct, non-technical language, using a style appropriate for various potential users; and
- give individual and group briefings as part of the promotional strategy.

Your strategy needs to clearly identify:

- individuals and groups targeted as potential users of the research;
- the types of information that are appropriate to each targeted user group;
- the barriers to accepting and implementing the results, and strategies for addressing them (motivating factors need to be identified); and
- the most promising channels for transmitting information to each user.

EXAMPLE

A communication strategy – health service sustainability

A comprehensive communication strategy was devised for Save the Children's major project on health service sustainability. It was launched at an international workshop with the World Bank, UNICEF and the UK Department for International Development represented. Within the five case study countries there were Research Advisory Committees involving government and donor organisations. It was the process of discussing the findings during the life of the project which was found most influential. A plan to return later to the case study countries was not carried out. Papers were published in key journals such as *Tropical Doctor* and *The Lancet*, and a guest issue of *Health Policy and Planning* was produced. Books and reports were also published directly reporting on the project. One area where the researchers felt they had not succeeded fully in their dissemination of ideas was within Save the Children itself.

The promotional work required will be rather different for the two main types of research we have identified as commonly undertaken in development work – programme-focused research and research aimed at influencing policy. There may well be some overlap, in that research for the programme may have implications for policy more broadly (and vice versa), but practical decisions have to be made about where to direct the greatest promotional effort. It will be important to list all the audiences you would like to reach, but then to prioritise – identify the two or three most important groups of people who should hear about this project.

KEY PURPOSE   KEY PROCESSES   KEY AUDIENCES
OF PROJECT

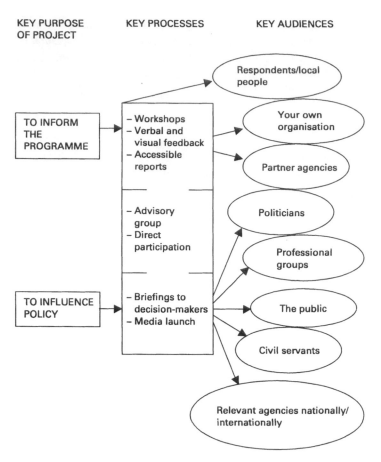

Figure 10.1   Audiences for different types of research, and key promotional
processes

The next two sections look at each arm of this diagram in turn – first
at influencing the programme and then at influencing policy more broadly.

10.1   Promotion for Implementation –
Influencing the Programme

Where a research project has been primarily aimed at informing the practical
work of an organisation, promotion of findings will concentrate on feedback
to four main groups:

• Staff directly involved with the programme.
• Relevant senior managers and others who work with you in different
  sections of the agency.
• Community members/potential users of the programme.
• Managers and practitioners in partner agencies locally and perhaps more
  broadly.

I wonder if you did the activity in Chapter 2.6 (Activity 2.2), that asked you to reflect on which research projects have influenced you? If not, you might like to do it now. When groups of managers and practitioners have done this exercise, people often identify research projects with which they have been directly, personally, involved as having had the most influence on them. This lends weight to the importance of stakeholder participation in research processes.

It is absolutely crucial in this type of work to think about who are the stakeholders in the issue you are investigating as early in the process as possible. These may be a Ministry at government level, an arm of local government, or perhaps other NGOs – the issues are the same. It is only human nature to be less interested in the results of research in which you have had no direct involvement. If a sense of ownership can be built up early on in the research process, it is much more likely that relevant agencies will act on the findings.

It is helpful in the planning stages to consult widely on the brief, asking advice of those you want to influence, with the aim of building a sense of the research as a shared enterprise. Once the research is getting under way, invite relevant people to be on the advisory group, and they will see the process unfold over time. Decision-makers may also be respondents in your research process. You can also of course go further and ask partner agencies to allow staff to participate in data collection and/or analysis, where appropriate.

A useful way of encouraging relevant agencies to get involved in thinking about your research findings is to hold a workshop or seminar at which you present the findings and encourage discussion of their meaning. It is best to avoid focusing exclusively on the research itself, but to use it to open up discussion on the issues it raises. It may be wise to give the floor to key agencies at some point in the day, to give them time to make a response to your findings.

You may like to organise such a workshop in the middle of the project, after some data collection, but well before the final report is written, to present 'early findings', and to ask for discussion of their significance. This engages other agencies with you as partners in the process of understanding the meaning of your work. A workshop like this can be very helpful in working towards recommendations from your research results. It will also act as a form of validation – checking that the findings make sense to others with a good knowledge of the field.

COMMON PITFALLS 10.2   Not involving partner agencies that will need to implement your findings until the research is complete

CHECKLIST   **For feedback to other professionals/partner agencies**

   ✓ Directly involve those you hope to influence throughout the life of the research, and take advice from them on how to reach others

   ✓ Events like seminars or workshops enable people to ask questions and make their own contribution – invite representatives of key agencies to speak alongside you, to respond to your findings

   ✓ Consider how your target audience usually receives information – professional journals may be important

   ✓ Don't forget your own agency – use its communication systems to let people know about the research

Taking findings back to 'the researched'

It is also extremely important to feed back findings appropriately to your research participants, and the general population groups from which they were drawn. This may come 'naturally' to projects which have been participatory throughout, but it is equally important to inform local people of the findings of other kinds of research, which may have been quite technical and carried out at a distance from community members.

EXAMPLE

Making the South African Children's Budget accessible

The South African Children's Budget project (see 1.1) developed a popular version of the Children's Budget in recognition of the need to disseminate the information to a broader range of children's rights advocacy and service organisations. This version is written in easily accessible language, uses innovative layout and graphical designs to represent technical statistics, and is compiled as a loose set of information sheets that are faxable. The layout and design of the product has increased accessibility and affordability of the information. This has enabled smaller children's rights organisations across the country, such as the Thusetsile Creche, as well as the Eastern Cape Legislature Library and the Richards Bay Family Care, to name a few, to obtain and use the research and information from the Children's Budget.

> CHECKLIST   For feedback to community members/respondents
>
> ✔ Consult people from the respondent group about how best to inform their community of your findings
> ✔ You may want to involve them in a working group to promote the messages from the research
> ✔ Plan your strategy to fit in with the ways in which your target group normally communicate – go to them, ask for some space in their events
> ✔ Expect to include some direct verbal feedback to those who are most interested – literacy may be an issue in any group of people: don't make assumptions
> ✔ Consider asking some community members themselves to lead the feedback to their community
> ✔ Reports should have clear simple summaries, and the implications for the real world should be drawn out as fully as possible

There may be a lot of overlap in terms of promotional work between some programme-focused research and that for policy influence – it may be helpful to read the next section as well.

10.2   Promotion for Policy Influence

Chapter 2 considered in detail the mechanisms by which research may have an influence, and identified some key factors to consider, which are summarised here:

> CHECKLIST   For research to influence policy
>
> ✔ Research is of high quality
> ✔ Challenging to the status quo
> ✔ Implications for action are clear
> ✔ Relevant to its audience
> ✔ Timely
> ✔ Clearly expressed and well-promoted
> ✔ May involve people in speaking for themselves

We have seen that it is important to plan for a research project to have an influence throughout its life – that sometimes it is a new way of defining a question which influences people's thinking, rather than the findings themselves. Involving people with policy-making responsibilities in an advisory group, or presenting interim findings informally to small groups, are ways of developing a sense of 'ownership' for the research during its development. This predisposes people to take its findings seriously when they emerge.

Don't miss the boat

FOR EXAMPLE

Changing views of elderly people in Cambodia

For a study of the Situation of Older People in Cambodia, a collaboration between HelpAge International (HAI) and the Ministry of Social Affairs, Labour and Veteran Affairs (MSALVA, now renamed MOSALVY), a research officer worked alongside a research team drawn entirely from the government (national and provincial levels). As a result of this structure, the project had a profound effect on all those taking part and in particular changed their opinions of older people. For example, HAI found out quite incidentally that the research team members had on their own initiative organised and delivered a workshop to their Ministry colleagues with the aim of raising their awareness of the situation of older people. The process also encouraged a particular focus on developing skills in policy-making, for example how to turn raw information into policy recommendations.

There is no doubt that the profile of older people is much higher within government now – for example celebration of 1 October as National Day of Older People is now officially recognised by the Ministry, who also take an active part in these celebrations.

However there is obviously work to be done when the project reports its results. It may be useful to convene a small group, perhaps a different one to the research advisory group, to manage the process of launch and dissemination through to its conclusion. If your organisation has a press office, they will be invaluable at this point.

Activity 10.1

How do you learn about research findings?

(a) Consider your own experience of learning about the findings of research. How have you heard of them? What draws your attention to them?

Think about research you have heard about, which has been of interest to you, and brainstorm a list of ways in which you may hear about such work. Think about research you have heard of recently, and then think about how you worked five years ago – would you have heard about research in any different ways?

(b) Think about the kind of people you aim to influence in your research. Do you think they learn about research in the same way as you do? What do you think they read? Hear? See?

Do this brainstorming exercise with as many colleagues as you can gather together. It need not take long. Notice that different people have different favourite ways of learning.

EXAMPLE

Effective promotion: the Child Labour Project, Sialkot, Pakistan

The Sialkot research was carried out in co-operation with a coalition of organisations working to address the problem of child labour in the area. The report is in English but the executive summary was translated into Urdu. The report was launched in a meeting with representatives of industry, UNICEF, ILO, the Government of Pakistan, and Pakistani NGOs. It was sent to representatives of the sporting goods industry, such as the World Council of Sporting Goods Industries and the Soccer Industry Council of America, as well as to individual sports good manufacturers.

The report created a great deal of interest among organisations engaging with corporate social responsibility. Short articles based on the research and programme work have appeared in Save the Children's supporters' magazine, and in the Development Research Newsletter, *Insights*, produced by ID21 at the Institute of Development Studies among others. The partnership has also formed a case study for an ILO report on multi-sectoral partnerships. Reports on ongoing programme work are posted on a Sialkot project website.

Save the Children staff involved with the programme, including senior Pakistani staff, the London-based research advisor and other members of Save the Children's policy team have made presentations about the research and project to a range of different development and business fora. Over two years after the initial research, the Pakistan team receives numerous requests for information about the programme, as do Save the Children's London-based policy and programme teams.

Whilst it is important to present findings in a way that is acceptable to policy-makers, directly involving community members who have taken part in research can help a piece of work to have a real influence. It is often effective to directly involve people who represent those who were studied in the research in presenting its results. Young care leavers, who had been the researchers on Save the Children's peer research project in England, presented the findings of the research at a number of conferences and to a meeting at the House of Commons. They have the authority of direct experience, and commanded close attention. Young people have also presented material on child labour and on sexual exploitation at major international conferences.

EXAMPLE

Older people speaking for themselves – Ghana and South Africa

HelpAge's research in Ghana and South Africa was presented at national dissemination work-shops which brought together older people from the research communities and a wide range of government, NGO, CBO, academic, and development agency representatives. 'The presence of older people themselves created a unique opportunity for them to have a direct dialogue with policy makers, and this contributed to the success of the programme.' (HelpAge, 1999).

10.3   The Report

First of all, it is essential that the report meet professional standards, so that it will be taken seriously. See Chapter 21 for more advice. Spelling and grammar need to be rigorously checked; references need to be complete and accurate. Claims made need to be clearly supported by the evidence given. These processes require a particularly high level of literacy skills and it will usually be a good idea to get reports read by a number of people with an eye for this type of detail. A good contents list is crucial, and an index is an excellent help to the reader, if the work is complex and lengthy.

Remember that while a small group of people will want to know the details of how you did the research, for the wider audience you must focus on the findings themselves and what they mean for policy.

But the key requirement for impact is a good summary. The process of producing this should be given time, and may need a number of people's involvement. The summary needs to speak to its audience, that is, state the problem which is being addressed clearly, as well as describing the project's findings. But it *must* be short!

The reputation of the agency producing the work, and of the publisher, may also be important to readers. Co-publishing with another agency can enhance the reception of your work, if your own agency has no tradition of high-quality publications.

10.4   Beyond 'The Report'

The messages of research carried out as part of development work usually need to reach many people who will never read a full report of a project, however well written it may be. It is important to think creatively about how to reach these people, and to ensure that the work is done to carry this through.

Again, the lead researcher may, or may not, be the person to do this work. Sometimes a press officer or journalist will be better able to draw out the key points of a report for a lay audience than its author, though it is always important to check any summary with the researcher to ensure that the work is treated with integrity.

It is important to budget to produce publicity material, at least a flyer, for any publication. You may want to produce the key findings or an executive summary as a separate, attractively presented, short paper, which will increase the printing costs, but may be well worth it. Time will be needed to pursue this work for months or sometimes years after the research is completed.

Think about how to 'beat a path to the door' of those you most need to influence. What do they read? Where do they go to discuss issues they are concerned about? Who do they listen to?

Professional groups have their own journals, which are often an effective way of reaching them. The information is given status, in the eye of the reader, simply by appearing in such journals – they are seen as containing what they 'need to know'. A new way of reaching development practitioners is through ID21's Development Research Reporting Service. This website aims to make policy-makers and on-the-ground development managers aware of the latest British development research findings. ID21 offers this service free to users and to contributors.[1]

In addition to specific, focused efforts to promote the results of a particular piece of research, agencies can effectively spread the word by producing materials which integrate a number of different research findings to make an argument. Often a research project can only look at some aspects of an issue, and the significance of its findings are only clear when this evidence is set alongside other information.

Individual and group briefings for key decision-makers

A very effective strategy is to offer personal briefings on your findings and recommendations to key decision-makers. Briefings create a forum for discussion – they are highly visible, allow intensive interaction, and they encourage action. They can be tailored for a specific decision-maker and a

---

[1]ID21 can be found at *http://www.id21.org/*

specific decision. To facilitate discussion, briefings need to clearly convey research results, answer questions, and offer recommendations oriented towards concrete action.

Decision-makers are usually far less interested in the details of your data and its analysis than in the recommendations based on them, though they want assurance that the research is of good quality.

GUIDELINES **For personal briefings**

✓ Understand the audience – find out about their particular concerns and the questions they are likely to ask

✓ Summarise findings in a one-page briefing summary, identifying three key messages from the work

✓ Carefully select the information to present – include only those research results that really matter to the audience

✓ Provide concrete, specific recommendations as to what is to be done, by whom, and when

✓ Choose skilled presenters, and involve also people who have a relationship with members of the audience

✓ Prepare audio-visual aids – and be sure to practice with them in advance. They need to be concise, with no more than seven lines on any one overhead or chart

✓ Bring the findings to life with quotes, personal stories, and accounts of particular situations, as appropriate

✓ Rehearse your presentation and make sure it fits the time-slot you have been given

---

Possible promotional methods could include:

- Individual and group briefings to key decision-makers.
- Presentations or workshops at seminars, conferences on related themes.
- Articles in professional journals.
- Launch events

  - press conference
  - professional conference
  - participatory event.

- Press release targeted to relevant media.
- Exclusive article for one newspaper or journal.
- Articles in academic journals.
- Articles or programmes in media aimed at the general public.
- Radio.
- TV.
- Video.

- Audio tapes.
- Through email lists or post information on a website, eg ID21's Development Research Reporting Service.

10.5   Dealing with the Media

First of all, don't assume that your research needs to get into the mass media to have been promoted appropriately. Some research is addressed primarily to professional or local audiences, and simply is not of sufficient interest to a wider audience. A good test is to consider what would happen if you started to explain about your project's findings in your local bar. Would you have cleared the place by closing time? If it makes a good story, it will make a good story!

It is, however, important to prepare for interest from the media in research you publish, even if you do not plan actively to promote it through the public media.[2] The press may pick it up from a professional conference. The following advice should be relevant to Northern, Southern, or international media.

Preparing a press release can be daunting, but it is an extremely useful process for clarifying the message of a piece of work. The journalist's focus on the questions 'What's the story?' 'What are we really saying here?' gives helpful sharpness to efforts to promote research results.

It is therefore very important to produce a short statement of your key findings, to brief journalists. This may take the form of a press release, or simply be a background paper which can be given to journalists once they contact you. Journalists are lay people, and may not have any specialist knowledge of the field you work in – their audience certainly won't have. Reporters frequently take a very short time to work their story up from your briefing material, so you need to make it as short and clear as possible.

Activity 10.2

Practice writing for a general audience

Write a draft briefing on your research findings to fit on an A4 page in normal type (about 250 words). Test out your draft on anyone you can get hold of who isn't 'in the business' – your friends and relatives, the person in the next office. Get at least two people to read it quickly and then tell you what they think it said. Listen particularly to the questions they ask you about it. Make revisions and try again on someone else.

---

[2]The ESRC has produced a good handbook for researchers on dealing with the media: *Pressing home your findings: media guidelines for ESRC researchers*, From Economic and Social Research Council, Polaris House, North Star Avenue, Swindon SN2 1UJ. Tel: 01793 413000.

It is crucial that the meaning of research results are not distorted in pursuit of a good story. It is often tempting to generalise from too little evidence, but NGOs must be very careful not to appear to make claims they cannot substantiate.

EXAMPLE

How many elephants?

Campaigns around conservation and the environment illustrate this dilemma. The highly charged debate in 1990 around a world-wide ivory ban was confused by contradictions between the World Wildlife Fund's high profile campaign for elephant protection and its low profile support for a more complex solution to sustainable wildlife management. This contradiction became public when conservationists aired their disagreements in the British Journal, *BBC Wildlife* (Princen and Finger, 1994). A later example of the alleged distortion of facts around the same issue was described in *New Scientist* magazine, when readers were told of an elephant over-population crisis with statistics apparently based on animals that never existed (Pye-Smith, 1999). The article accused environmental groups of perpetuating the myth of a catastrophic decline in elephant numbers across Africa, not least because 30 organisations were identified as depending on that myth for their financial survival (Harper, 1997).

EXAMPLE

Tripping up on statistics

Making the results of research meaningful to local media around the country can be a problem for press departments in national charities. Research and Development workers in one major UK children's charity were embarrassed in the early 90s when the results of a national survey were broken down by region in a press statement. The survey had been on parents' views on children's safety. The press office worked out figures for different regions from the general data in the report, and put out a statement to the effect that 'x per cent of mothers in Birmingham do not let children play outside because of fears for their safety'. After these reports, a numerate journalist looked into the research and found that the numbers interviewed in each region were too small to reach significance. This was used to challenge the legitimacy of the claims made by the agency. The lessons from this are that you need to work very closely with your press department, or with press officers to ensure that their legitimate efforts to get your work into print don't rely on illegitimate means.

This case reflects a conflict which can arise between the need to present research findings as 'sexy' enough to get attention, and the need to be scrupulous in presenting them accurately. Managers need to keep control of the presentation of findings from research they are responsible for, as they will undoubtedly be held accountable if there is any negative coverage.

Activity 10.3

Scandal!

Try to think of incidents where you have been aware of controversy over or misrepresentation of research findings – perhaps your own agency's, or perhaps work you have heard of. Conduct a brief enquiry into each incident you can think of. Could the challenge have been avoided? What should have been done?

Compare your thoughts on this issue with those for Activity 2.2, where you were asked to analyse what enables research to have an influence on you. What conclusions might we draw?

The press love statistics, and will always report any claim you make in statistical terms – you need to be sure that you can stand by such statements. If you quote percentages in your report, there is always the danger that press coverage will distort exactly what you said, so you appear to be making wider claims than you intended to. Eg '40% of our sample [of 80 young mothers from an impoverished area] had experienced the death of a child in the first year of its life', can come out as '40% of mothers had babies that died'.

The other issue which often arises is that journalists will want to investigate 'the human story' for themselves, and are likely to ask for access to community members. Save the Children is regularly asked for 'families in poverty' to be interviewed. While people may want to speak out about their situation, it is very important that agencies brief people about how journalists may behave. People may need to be assertive about not giving information they are not comfortable with having published. They need to be aware that their words may not come out quite as they meant them when they are written up by the journalist.

EXAMPLE

'Human interest' stories – protecting people from intrusive questions

One UK study of the situation of children whose parents are in prison was met with considerable press interest. A journalist asked to meet a family who were in this situation, to tell the 'human side'. All the agencies which formed the coalition which had commissioned the study were asked, and refused, to identify users of their services who could be interviewed. There were obvious concerns about the risks involved in revealing a family as related to someone in prison. Finally a probation officer thought of a family who were no longer users of her service, and who wanted to speak out about their treatment. A press officer from Save the Children went along and briefed the family before the journalist arrived about what to expect. She also sat in on the interview, and challenged the journalist when she asked irrelevant questions, for example about what offence the parent was imprisoned for.

Recently there is increasing interest in enabling people (disabled people, survivors of violence, etc) to tell their own stories. Save the Children has produced a booklet with an accompanying tape on interviewing children, for journalists and others (McCrum and Hughes, 1994).

Do not focus exclusively on coverage in the 'serious' press. If you want to have an influence on the public, far more people read local papers and listen to local radio than read the national newspapers. Local media are often short of material and more open to approaches from NGOs. Also remember that the Southern media reaches millions of people – do not just focus on Northern or international media.

It is helpful for the research team to identify a media spokesperson at an early stage in their work. This person should then have media matters in mind as the project progresses. Some large agencies like to put up senior managers to deal with media interest, and this can reinforce the importance of the issue, but this has the drawback that they will not be familiar with the details of the research. There is nothing more embarrassing than a spokesperson who cannot answer sharp questions about a piece of research. It may be best to use the most confident speaker who is directly involved with the research, probably the researcher him or herself. Representatives of 'the researched' themselves may be also excellent spokespeople on the general issues that are raised.

CHECKLIST   On promoting research findings to the media

✓ Don't assume you have a 'story'
✓ Appoint a media spokesperson from your research team
✓ Prepare a press release summarising your one to three (at most) main points
✓ Use any personal contacts
✓ Time the launch carefully

- be ready
- look for a news 'peg' in the timing (eg World Bank annual meeting to release a report on debt)
- but avoid major predictable competing stories (eg national elections etc)

✓ Think ahead about possible hostile questions, and prepare for them
✓ Make sure that spokespeople are fully familiar with the research
✓ Where possible identify and prepare people who represent the subjects of the research to talk to journalists – ensure that you explain how the media works, and the risks involved

---

In undertaking broadcast interviews, remember that you may get a very short time on the air to say your piece. It is helpful for the spokesperson to write themselves a 'script' before any interview, summarising the main points to be made, with reminders of relevant examples to mention. Decide which is the one main point you should make if you do not get time to say more. Use the questions you are asked to make sure you get this point across. If you regularly deal with the media, it would be a good idea to organise some training, involving real journalists, to help staff improve their skills and understanding of this kind of work.

CHECKLIST   For successful broadcast interviews

- ✔ Identify the three main points you want to make
- ✔ Stick to them – do not be diverted onto irrelevant issues
- ✔ Illustrate the main points with well-chosen examples
- ✔ Avoid jargon – imagine a friend or neighbour outside your professional field as your audience
- ✔ Ask journalists what they plan to ask you, before an interview goes on the air
- ✔ Remember that people listen to radio or TV individually, and speak as if to one person, not to a public meeting

---

Margaret Thatcher was noted for her adherence to the rule that she would say what she wanted to say regardless of the questions asked of her. She remained Prime Minister for a very long time! Obviously this policy can be taken to extremes, but it is a good rule of thumb to stick to your 'script' wherever possible.

It is important to be prepared for negative media approaches to your work. In constructing a story, a common strategy for journalists is to identify or generate 'controversy'. This will often not be a problem, indeed we may welcome discussion of the issues. But it is important not to sound defensive in response to hostile questions.

Activity 10.4

Role play a media interview

In preparing for radio or TV interviews, it is very helpful to role play the process with some colleagues. Find someone who would be good at acting the 'journalist', and ask them to take some time to prepare a few tricky questions. They need to have a general grasp of the subject of your research, not a detailed one. Remember of course that most journalists will be essentially sympathetic, and not aiming to catch you out. Ask some other colleagues to be your audience and to give you feedback on how you came across.

You could tape record or video the role play and listen to it later – or not, if you can't face it! If you can, add realism by involving a real journalist.

Key Points from this Chapter

CHECKLIST   For effective promotion of research findings

✓ Plan for the promotion of research results from the beginning of the project, and allow resources for the work involved

✓ Consider a wide range of possible methods of promoting the results – think about how to reach your target audience

✓ Include the costs of promoting the findings of the research in your budget for any project – eg printing, postage, costs of workshops, etc

✓ Ensure reports meet professional standards for clarity and presentation, and include a summary

✓ Involve staff with expertise in promotional/marketing work

✓ Ensure that results are presented in such a way as to maintain the integrity of the research findings

✓ Involve community members in promoting research findings

✓ Be polite! Make sure those who contributed to, or are directly affected by, the research get to see the results early on in the promotional process

This chapter urges managers and development workers to think ahead about the promotion of the findings of their research. Involving those you want to influence as you go along is a very effective way of building ownership of the research, which increases the likelihood that findings will be acted upon. Reports need to be prepared to a professional standard, and to include a summary, which includes some background and the recommendations as well as the main findings. But think beyond the report – only a limited number of people will ever read it.

Consider all of the ways in which people learn about research results, and in particular focus on how you think the people you aim to influence find out information. Your key audience will determine what is most important in promoting your research.

Prepare for press interest in your research. Identify the main points you want to get across and work out how to express them without using jargon. Use examples to illustrate and humanise your message. Where possible, involve community members in promoting the research – they can be more effective spokespeople than professionals.

Further Reading

Pressing Home your Findings: Media guidelines for ESRC researchers.

From Economic and Social Research Council, Polaris House, North Star Avenue, Swindon SN2 1UJ. Tel: 01793 413000.

A good handbook for researchers on dealing with the media, aimed at UK researchers, but helpful more widely.

BOND Guidance Notes (1999) *Introducing Advocacy: Monitoring and evaluating advocacy,* leaflet.

11 Evaluating Research for Development Work

By the time you reach the completion of a research project, there is a natural tendency to want to heave a sigh of relief and move on to the next thing. But if we are to develop better practice in this area, it is essential to evaluate the work we do as we go along. Your evaluation effort should be in proportion to the resources spent on the research project. And how you focus the evaluation will depend upon your key aims for it.

This chapter looks first at some common approaches to evaluating research projects – checking progress against objectives, and comparing performance to a set of quality standards. Next we ask what are you evaluating, product or process? Who needs to be involved, and when should evaluation take place?

The last section looks separately at the specific needs of programme-focused research and at policy-focused projects. It should be noted that this book does not cover the evaluation of programmes themselves in any detail because this is done in Save the Children's *Toolkits* (Gosling with Edwards, 1995).

11.1 Some Approaches to Evaluation

Did it meet its objectives?

The most straightforward way to evaluate research projects, as for other kinds of projects, is to look back at the objectives you set for the project and consider to what extent they have been achieved. Look at each objective in turn and think about how much was achieved, and what difficulties were encountered. Analysing the problems you met will be helpful when you come to plan the next similar project.

Activity 11.1

Evaluating success against objectives

The table below may be useful for thinking these issues through.

	Achievements	Limitations	Issues to consider
Objective 1			
Objective 2			
Objective 3			
Objective 4			

In order to assess success against objectives, you may need to identify a number of specific indicators that you can use to measure how well you have done. Indicators are objective ways of measuring (indicating) that progress is being achieved. For example, a change in national legislation could indicate policy influence.

One problem with evaluation against objectives is that the original objectives may not have been written in such a way as to express clearly all the purposes which were in fact being pursued through the project. In this case, it may be appropriate to add to them or adapt them. You should make sure that the evaluation process you follow is as relevant as possible, to get the most learning out of it.

Look back at the quality standards

Another way of evaluating a project is to compare its performance with a set of pre-defined standards of good practice. You might want to look at your project's success in relation to the quality standards proposed in this manual. These were set out as a list in Chapter 4.3, and are summarised in the following table.

You could use this table in various ways – for a desk-top exercise to focus your own thoughts, or as a basis for formal or informal discussion with others.

Activity 11.2 Does your project meet quality standards for research for development work?

Standard	Strengths	Weaknesses	Notes for action
RESEARCH PLANNING			
• About an important issue			
• Needed			
• Idea came from 'the researched'			
• Clear brief			
• Planned in co-operation with relevant others			
• Transparent organisational structures			
• Developed participants' research skills			
RESEARCH PROCESSES			
• Questioned the taken-for-granted			
• Respectful interaction with respondents			
• 'The researched' had a say in the research design			
• Sample appropriate			
• Research tools piloted			
• Data collection is systematic and accurate			
• Social inequalities taken into account			
• Ethical issues actively considered			
• Good communication with respondents			
• Reports explain sampling methods fully			
• Open reflection on researchers' impact on the process			
• Statistical processes clearly explained			
• In quantitative work – validity and reliability of tools checked			

Activity 11.2   Continued

INTERPRETATION AND ANALYSIS

- Interpretation was accurate and honestly reported
- Analysis included consideration of alternative interpretations
- Broader policy context, wider research findings drawn on
- All claims can be supported by the evidence

PROMOTING RESEARCH FINDINGS

- Reports concise but include adequate information to assess the research
- Appropriate summaries were included
- Recommendations arose from the findings
- Findings fed back to 'the researched' in appropriate ways
- Findings fed back to partner agencies in appropriate ways
- Any research quoted was fully referenced
- Dissemination targeted at those who could make a difference

The next three sections look at the specific issues involved in evaluating the different types of research for development work which we have identified in earlier chapters – what to look at, whom to involve, and when to do it. Then we will look at evaluating programme-focused research, and finally at research aimed at influencing policy.

11.2   What, Who, and When?

Process or product?

As we saw in Chapter 2, the quality of a piece of research relates to both its products and the process through which it was carried out. Activity 2.3, from Chapter 2, could be used to look at the strengths and weaknesses of a piece of work at the end of its life, as well as being useful to undertake during its development.

EXAMPLE

Assessing impact: education for refugee children in London

Save the Children carried out peer research into the educational support needs of refugee and asylum seeker children in London. An assessment was made of the impact of the research, which included information on how many reports had been distributed and to whom, publicity received (presentations given and articles published), and attempted to assess any change in practice which has resulted. Two specific examples of impact in other parts of London could be identified, as well as broader influence, which was more difficult to pin down.

There were also important effects from the process of the research. The individual members of the group gained knowledge of the issues, and skills in conducting research, analysis, writing, facilitating groups, dealing with the press, and public speaking. The group members are highly motivated and want to see change in the situation of young refugees in Britain. They have set up an independent organisation with a constitution and rules of membership, and are producing a newsletter and organising activities for young refugees.

There was also feedback around interest in the peer research methods the project used – they were approached for advice by a group planning to do research with young refugees about the issue of returning 'home'.

Who should be involved in evaluation?

While you could undertake this task alone or with a group of immediate colleagues, it is better to find out what a broader group of people thought of the project. Deciding who is most important to involve depends upon what were the project's central aims – was the important impact to be upon high-level policy-makers, on middle managers, or perhaps on local people themselves?

A short interview with representatives of all the main stakeholders in the research project (including 'the researched') will yield useful information which will usually focus on process more than final impact. You could use the objectives to structure your questions.

It is particularly important to find out what those who were the 'subjects' of the research thought about it. They are the least likely to make their views felt, unless you ask for them. You will usually have to make a special effort to find out what people who were respondents in the research thought of a process. Where you are relating to a community group with its own structures, one way of doing this is to go along to a community meeting and ask people for their views.

You may want to include funders and senior managers who were not directly involved in the project but who should be influenced by it, in your evaluation process. Their view of its success is likely to be important to the future of your work, and even if it is negative, it is better to have this out in the open and discussed. It gives them an opportunity to let you know what they would like to see from you in future.

When should evaluation take place?

While it is useful to undertake an evaluation process at the conclusion of a research project, it is likely to be more helpful still to set up some kind of monitoring system, or 'formative' evaluation process. A formative evaluation helps you to 'form' the project by giving ongoing feedback as the process unfolds.

CHECKLIST   Some ways of getting feedback as a research project develops

- The research Advisory Group should have as part of its role to monitor the progress and impact of the project
- At the end of interviews/focus groups etc, ask respondents how they felt about taking part in the research
- Build in a short evaluation discussion at the end of any group event
- Employ an expert advisor/external evaluator who offers a listening ear and some ongoing evaluation input throughout the life of the project
- Meet together at intervals as a research team, and step back from the day-to-day work to reflect on progress and any difficulties encountered

11.3   Evaluating Different Types of Research

Evaluating the impact of programme-related research

In evaluating research intended to inform the programme, it is likely that looking back at the aims and objectives, as suggested above in 11.1 will be the best approach. You might want to work on the evaluation process together with colleagues and perhaps community members who have co-operated with you on the project. One approach is to set up a workshop session to draw out people's views on the project. You could, for example, have a series of short discussions on to what extent each objective has been achieved.

Another way of doing this is to simply ask people to think about the strengths and weaknesses of the research – process and products. This asks them to identify the criteria they are using, rather than using those defined at the start of the project when the objectives were written.

Where the work has been participatory, it will be very important to learn from community members about what would be their criteria for success for the project. As ever, this is best done early on in a project, as it will draw out any differences of understanding between professionals and community members. You obviously have a better chance of succeeding in the eyes of those you work with if you know what they are looking to see done.

The project's objectives may have included some reference to capacity sharing, but whether they did or not, it will be a good idea to include consideration of this aspect as part of your evaluation process. What learning has occurred? Do people feel more confident about research work? What problems were encountered and how were these overcome? Would you do it differently another time? What could be done to make it easier for more people to learn from research processes as they go along?

To reach beyond those you work closely with, and to give people more space to criticise, if they wish to, you could send out a short questionnaire, or conduct face-to-face or telephone interviews, with key agencies. Questions should start by assessing people's knowledge of the work you have done, and then move on to find out their opinions of it. It would be best for any interviews to be conducted by someone who was not directly involved in carrying out the research project.

The great virtue of conducting some form of evaluation of projects like this is that it gives an opportunity to draw out any problems people see with the work, so that they can be addressed in the future. It can also be a useful way of starting to engage people in thinking what should happen next on the issues you attempted to address.

> CHECKLIST   For evaluating programme-focused research
>
> ✔ Ask community members and colleagues what are their criteria for success for the project – sooner rather than later
> ✔ Structure your evaluation around the project's aims and objectives, *or*
> ✔ Ask people to assess the strengths and weaknesses of the research project's products and process
> ✔ Include questions which invite people to think ahead, to engage with what should happen next
> ✔ Do a small survey – on paper or in person – of key people's knowledge of and views on the project
> ✔ Look at the learning and development of staff and community members which has occurred through the project, as well as the other outcomes

Evaluating the impact of advocacy-related research

For research with broader aims, you need to think about evaluation in a more ambitious way.

Some indicators you might use to assess success include:

Policy/Practice Change

- Direct changes in policy – new legislation; new official guidance; revisions to existing policy documents.
- Direct changes in practice – observable different practice by professionals.
- References are made to your research in policy discussions, eg during debates; in official documents, etc.
- The issue your research addressed appears on agendas it has previously been excluded from.
- Programmes of work have changed in light of your findings.
- Your research has been reported in relevant publications/programmes.

Strengthening participation in policy processes

- Your organisation/NGOs generally are invited to join in more discussions, or at a higher level.
- Community members/those representing them are given greater access to decision-making bodies – eg invited to join important committees.

Institutional learning

- To what extent did people learn – about the issue in question and about research – from this project?
- Evidence that people have gained in confidence as a result of this project.

Financial

- What was the balance in terms of costs and benefits? (Should not be calculated too early.)
- Any effect on your and others' ability to attract funding for work in this area?

With research aimed to influence high-level policy issues it can be particularly difficult to identify what impact a particular piece of work could be said to have had. You may be able to think of other particularly relevant factors for your project.

EXAMPLE

Views changed, but why? The health sector sustainability project

Following Save the Children's major research project on the sustainability of health sector development, UNICEF documents began to use concepts which had been used in that study. Some documents directly referenced the project (UNICEF, 1996) and others did not, but it would appear that there had been some influence. Similarly, a shift in view was identified at meetings at the World Bank on health and education in Africa, where the Bank was beginning to argue that basic primary health care provision should be free at the point of delivery – something Save the Children had proposed. It is difficult to say to what degree these developments arose from the project – other factors may have been more important. What the project certainly achieved was to give greater authority to Save the Children's advocacy work on these issues.

The following monitoring indicators, proposed by BOND (1999), give a practical framework to use in assessing the effectiveness of your advocacy-related research process. It differs from the broader checklist given above in that it offers more direct and specific guidance about how to actually assess the indicators it identifies.

Indicators for monitoring the effectiveness of advocacy work:

Monitoring your target

- Record and observe changes in the rhetoric of your target audience. Keep a file of their statements over time.
- What are they saying about you and your campaign?
- Are they moving closer to your position, adapting to or adopting any of your language and philosophy?

Monitoring your relationships

- Record the frequency and content of conversations with external sources and target audiences.

- Are you discussing new ideas? Are you becoming a confidante or a source of information or advice?

Monitoring the media

- Count column inches on your issue and the balance of pro- and anti-comment.
- Count the number of mentions for your organisation.
- Analyse whether media are adopting your language.

Monitoring your reputation

- Record the sources and numbers of inquiries that you receive as a result of your work.
- Are you getting to the people you wanted to get to?
- How and where have they heard of your work?
- How accurate are their pre-conceptions about you and your work?

Monitoring public opinion

- Analyse the popular climate through telephone polling, or through commissioning surveys.

Key Points from this Chapter

If managers want to learn more about how to run better research for development work, it is essential to make it a habit to evaluate research projects as you would other development work. This can be done using the project's objectives as a starting point, or by assessing the project's strengths and weaknesses against quality standards. Different issues need attention depending on whether the research is aimed at informing the programme or at influencing policy more broadly. The success of any efforts to encourage participation in the research process should also be carefully considered.

CHECKLIST   Of ways to evaluate research for development work

- ✔ Compare achievement to objectives
- ✔ Assess the quality of the product and the process
- ✔ Compare your project with quality standards
- ✔ Ask views of all participants/stakeholders – and let them decide what is important to mention
- ✔ The scale of the evaluation effort should be in keeping with the scale of the original project

Further Reading

Feuerstein, M-T. (1994) *Partners in Evaluation*. London: Macmillan.

A very good general introduction to evaluation. Designed for use in the South – wonderful illustrations. Focuses on evaluating community development-type projects, not research projects. An excellent resource to dip into.

Gosling, L. with Edwards, M. (1995) *Toolkits: A practical guide to assessment, monitoring, review and evaluation*, Development Manual 5. London: Save the Children.

Includes a discussion of project evaluation.

See also further reading recommended in Chapter 4: Quality in Research.

TWO

Doing Research
for Development

12.1 How to Look

Please read this chapter! Development workers are usually, rightly, preoccupied with the here and now, and the prospect of searching out existing information about an issue does not make them happy. They may feel that their own local community's experience is the most important thing. But research is greatly strengthened by placing your new information in the context of what is already known about the issue.

Researchers call this process 'doing a literature search', 'survey', or 'doing a literature review' or 'study'. 'The literature' refers to all the available research on a subject. 'Literature search' refers to the process of finding the material, and a 'literature survey' simply describes the literature which exists. The terms 'review' or 'study' point to the importance of critically assessing the information you collect, and making sense of it in relation to your own research questions.

A good literature review is a key feature by which the quality of a piece of research is judged. It guards against duplication of work which has already been done, and justifies the choice of focus. It should also enrich the arguments which can be made from the new material, and add authority to the whole exercise. Sometimes a whole project is essentially a literature review – mobilising existing information to answer new questions. See also Chapter 17.4 which discusses using documentary sources as a research method in its own right.

EXAMPLE

Situation analysis – children in Mozambique

A situation analysis about Mozambican children looked at existing statistics to investigate a wide range of child welfare issues. Statistics were collected from a variety of sources and presented in a simple way for maximum impact. The analysis showed, for example, that under 18s constitute 54% of the population of Mozambique, that only 8% of the rural population have access to safe piped water, and that 56% of births are not assisted by a health worker. 3,900,000 (42%) children are malnourished, and every hour, 11 children under 1-year-old die (Anon, 1998).

EXAMPLE

Prisoners' families in the UK

The first major publication drawing attention to the problems of prisoners' families in the UK was based on a detailed study of the existing literature, not on original research. Evidence was drawn from Australia, New Zealand, France, the USA, and The Netherlands. This research was important in drawing attention to these issues, which would have been difficult to research directly because of the various sensitivities involved (Lloyd, 1995).

The rhythm of work in development organisations makes it difficult to take the time to seek out and study the literature on an issue. Going to a library, or indeed searching the Internet, does not look like proper work, in the way that other activities might. Often there is little precedent for carrying out these activities. But it really is worth it! The time, and any money, which may be spent, for example on the key few books in the area, will certainly be repaid in the weight it will add to your final report. Looking at it negatively for a moment: if you fail to identify key information in the area you are working on, it will be obvious to others that you are not on top of the existing research material. This can be highly discrediting when you come to use your own findings to argue your case.

COMMON   Ignoring important existing research which could support (or undermine)
PITFALLS   your case – publishing your new research findings in isolation

Of course the difficulty of identifying and locating relevant information will vary greatly depending on where you are based and the degree to which information sources are organised and accessible within the country you are working in. Some countries have desperately inadequate libraries, and it is a real struggle to get information. Obviously you have to work with what exists. But do not assume that no information exists because the local area you work in is very poor, or indeed because none is readily available to you there. Actually some poor communities have been researched very thoroughly! Ask for help from someone located closer to good information sources, or use the Internet (see 'How to use the Internet for research' in 12.2 and the list of useful websites in Appendix 1).

Taking a critical approach

It is important to think carefully about where you look for relevant information. Only some sorts of knowledge 'make it' onto databases and into libraries, and you may be interested in other types of information as well. If you want to locate research which validates the knowledge of people like those you are working with, you will have to search hard to find such material. Sometimes informal networks work better than libraries for this sort of thing. But sometimes the traditional methods work really well – it is always worth a try.

Sue Stubbs (1999) has proposed the following criteria for reading 'the literature' for her own research – it could give pointers to searching on any subject:

1. Are the 'facts' reliable, can they be trusted? How do you know?
2. Are the facts really facts – what definitions (eg of disability) are being used?
3. Are key concepts examined critically?
4. Are concepts considered from a cross-cultural perspective?
5. Have key concepts been exported from the North and uncritically transplanted into other cultures?
6. Are the perspectives of key stakeholders represented?
7. If the writers are 'outsiders', do they write with a self-critical awareness?
8. Is the issue of ownership, participation in and control of research addressed?
9. Is local knowledge and practice acknowledged and drawn upon?
10. Is there a discussion of power and resource issues in relation to global development, including the role and status of multi- and bi-lateral agencies?

Stubbs was seeking information on the education of disabled children in the South, and found that much of the material her literature search threw up was problematic on these criteria. She warns against 'building towers on quicksand' – often the same few academic writers are quoted over and over again, and their work takes on what may be undue authority as a result.

It is important to learn to locate a writer's approach within the field by considering their theoretical assumptions, the sources they cite, and the policy prescriptions they favour (Barrientos, 1998). This will enable you to see patterns in the material you review, and help to decide how much weight to give their work.

Be attentive to what is *not* there, as well as to what you do find. Do not be swept along into the traditional way of seeing an issue, just because that is what the literature concentrates on – if you want to develop a new perspective, you may have to do it without much support from 'the literature'.

Putting your work on the map

To get your work on the map, it is important to deposit your own reports, and those of Southern partner agencies, in the British Library and other 'copyright libraries', which are supposed to hold everything that is in print, as well as in relevant specialist and university libraries. Getting an ISBN (International Standard Book Number) for publications, and generally making sure they 'exist' for the wider world, is really worthwhile. Otherwise a situation,where existing research is not accessible to researchers, is perpetuated. To get an ISBN you need to call the Standard Book Numbering Agency Ltd on 020 7420 6008. You can buy blocks of them or one at a time.

Before you start – getting organised

Perhaps it is self-evident that you need to create a record-keeping system for the information you gather. You need to be able to share information you find with colleagues, and to find it again easily yourself. Also when you cite other people's work in writing, the reader should be able to reliably trace each item from your reference. Just giving an author and date only helps readers who already know the field, and does not inspire confidence. Proper referencing is part of your accountability – it enables others to check your claims for themselves. The references in this book follow the conventions you should use.

But somehow one often hopes to remember things, and it is tedious actually to write down all those details. Don't think you can avoid it, or get anyone else to do it, and don't put it off! As soon as you start reading about an issue, keep notes of your reading, and above all keep exact information on all the sources you use. There is nothing so time-wasting as having to trace your references all over again when you come to write up your work because you did not keep good enough records at the time.

The traditional way of keeping these records is on file cards, and the newer alternative is to put the information onto your computer. In each case the principles are the same – you need to keep the standard set of information which is required to give a proper bibliographic reference. It is also helpful to give each item some key words, so that you can later search or sort by subject. And you may want to write some notes to remind yourself what was interesting to you about the reference, or who suggested looking at it – again, these things are remarkably difficult to remember later on.

For a project of any scale, it is really worth using a computer if you can manage it. You will need to have easy, regular access to the computer to regularly enter and check information as you accumulate references. The computer makes it easy to search for relevant material, or simply to check an

```
┌────────────────────────────────────────────────────────────────┐
│                                                                  │
│  Hall, David and Hall, Irene                        1996         │
│                                                                  │
│  Practical Social Research: Project Work in the Community        │
│                                                                  │
│  Macmillan, Basingstoke, Hampshire, UK                           │
│                                                                  │
│  ISBN: 0-333-60674-4 paperback                                   │
│  Location: (eg Univ of North London library)                    │
│  If library, class mark: 300.72 HAL                              │
│                                                                  │
│  Key words:                                                      │
│                                                                  │
│  Notes: (or put your notes on the back of the card)             │
│                                                                  │
└────────────────────────────────────────────────────────────────┘
```

Figure 12.1   Sample index card

individual record, in a variety of useful ways. You have also got the typing over with, and can draw directly on your computerised records when you come to write up your report.

There are some software packages available which are specially designed for this task. Otherwise you can create a suitable database in any database package. If you find it easier to use word-processing or spreadsheets, you could put the information on either of these, and they will enable some useful searching, although a database is more flexible.

However there is nothing wrong with using index cards. They are more portable and in many ways more flexible to use – and of course very much cheaper than a computer!

What information must be kept? The above (Figure 12.1) shows the key material that is needed.

For journal articles it is important to include the volume and issue number as well as the exact date, and page numbers for the article itself. Articles in edited collections need to be referenced with full details of the article itself, and of the book in which it can be found.

Focusing your literature review

One of the worries about undertaking a literature review is that you might get lost for weeks, wandering amongst a lot of not-very-relevant material. It is important to scan possibly useful books and articles rather than settle down to read every word. Keep a clear focus on the information you need to find. Break down your 'big questions' into sub-questions, and search for evidence relating to these. Refer back to the research focus, the research questions, and the broad aims and objectives of your study at regular intervals to help you to find your way through the material you come across.

You need to identify a number of key words which you can use in searching for relevant material. It may be helpful to make a visual image of

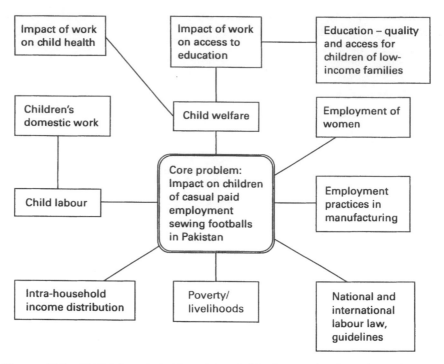

Figure 12.2   Child labour in Pakistan's football industry – breaking down the issues

the field you are looking at, and to make a note of the issues which are related to your central focus. You could draw out a spider diagram like the one above in Table 12.2.

This process identifies related fields, where material you read will not directly address your core problem, but will contain information which may well have relevance. It is worth looking fairly broadly around the topic you are interested in, so as to be aware of the debates which have been taking place to date. This will help you to be confident as to when there is an existing controversy that you will need to relate your work to, and when you are genuinely opening up new areas for discussion.

Writing up the literature review

It is likely that you will want to include a discussion of the existing research as part of your final report. This needs to contribute towards the argument you are making, and should be strongly focused on your own research questions. It should help you make your case. However this can be a difficult task. It is best to start by writing a draft, at an early stage, which has more the nature of you thinking aloud – it enables you to gather your thoughts, and to see what conclusions can be drawn from the existing material. Then when you get to the end of your own research, you can rewrite it into a tighter literature review with greater confidence.

It is really worth writing a first draft which describes the findings of your literature study as soon as you can. Starting to write about the information you have collected is the best way to identify what is most important about it, and to spot gaps which need further investigation. You need to start focusing very tightly on the questions you set out to answer – do not be tempted to simply recount what each source says. This is very boring for the reader!

Leedy suggests that to get the proper psychological orientation, you should:

> 'Consider the review of related literature section in your document to be a discussion with a friend about what others have written in relation to what you plan to do.' (Leedy, 1997)

As with all writing, keep it as brief as possible. It may be best to interweave information from existing research with your own material, rather than to write it as a separate section.

EXAMPLE

Planning a literature review – consulting young people on mental health services

Asked to write a literature review to introduce a Mental Health Foundation report on consulting young people on mental health services in the UK, I took a traditional approach. The review starts with the broadest issues, and focuses increasingly narrowly on the specific issue in question. These are the headings:

- Young people's mental health.
- Definitions and service boundaries (eg of mental health).
- Consultation with users (covering such consultation in the health service more broadly, and beyond).
- Consultation with adult mental health service users.
- Listening to children and young people (again covering issues beyond mentalhealth).
- Consulting with young people on mental health services.

If you locate material which appears to provide evidence which does not suit your argument, do not be tempted to try to sweep it under the carpet. It will greatly strengthen your hand if you discuss what any different findings mean – do they undermine your case? If not, why not?

CHECKLIST   For writing up your literature review

  ✓ Write a draft early, and revise it after doing your own original research
  ✓ Be clear about where you are going in your thinking
  ✓ Have a plan
  ✓ Identify schools of thought within the literature
  ✓ Organise the material into sections which group together related research
  ✓ For each piece of research you introduce, explain how it relates to your own research problem
  ✓ Don't just describe others' work – assess it in relation to your own questions
  ✓ Summarise what you have said – what does it all mean?

12.2   Where to Look

This section will make frustrating reading for people who are working in areas where access to information is a big problem. Libraries in poor countries are of course often poor and sometimes non-existent. Lack of resources of this type is a huge barrier to both scholarship and development in these countries.

But many development workers do or could have access to reasonable library resources, and libraries are so valuable for research, even if you only have a day or two to use them. This section is included to help you to find what you need efficiently.

Using a library

The large development agencies have their own resource centres, which can yield very useful assistance. They will hold some useful material themselves, and the information staff will have good ideas about ways of going about this. However you are likely to need direct access to a library if you are doing research to any depth, though the Internet is increasingly valuable.

It is well worth the effort to get access to a university library. There are many useful resources there, which you may only need occasionally, but which will then be extremely helpful. If you are setting out on a piece of research, you may perhaps already have links to an academic. Ask them whether there is some arrangement that can be made to enable you to use the library of their institution. Anyone who is registered for a course will automatically have access to the library. Otherwise it may be a good idea for your organisation to make some formal link to a department of a university which is interested in the kind of work you do. Many universities welcome links to development organisations.

It is usually a good idea to consult a librarian on the best way for you to search for the information you need. University libraries have subject-specialist librarians who will have good ideas about how to find information on your particular subject. The fast development of new technology means that there is likely to be more change quite soon, in terms of the most efficient way of finding things out.

As well as books and journals, libraries have a number of other facilities that may be of use.

Indexes and abstracts

Every subject has its own huge indexes, which list references for articles on a wide variety of subjects. Many include an abstract, or summary, of the article as part of the entry, so it is easy to assess how relevant the article is to your research problem. Examples include the Index Medicus, the Social Sciences Index, and Social Work Research and Abstracts. These used to be held as very large books, and are now more often found as CD-ROMs (see below).

It is useful to know about *Ulrich's International Periodical Directory.*[1] Volume 3 is an index volume that contains important information that will greatly shorten your search time. A section of this volume is devoted to *serials* (journals) on CD-ROM. Another section gives the serials available online through the Internet. You will also find a section 'Index to Publications of International Organisations'. In the sections devoted to a full listing of titles, you will find all the titles of periodial indexes, bibliographies, and abstracts throughout the world (see Leedy, 1997).

CD-ROMS

CD-ROM stands for 'Compact Disk – Read Only Memory', and CD-ROMs look very like a music CD. You need a computer with a CD-ROM drive to read one – libraries will let you use one. They have been designed to hold huge amounts of information, and are used to hold large reference works, especially reference indexes. Libraries now hold most of their large indexes, for example in education, sociology, food and nutrition, or agriculture, on CD-ROMs.

The other way you may use CD-ROMs, in or out of the library, is in searching databases that are developed by one organisation and then provided to others on a subscription basis. For example, in the UK the National Children's Bureau produces CD-ROMs which give access to its database of references on children's issues. They are currently expanding their information to include useful references for those working outside the UK.[2]

---

[1] *Ulrich's International Periodical Directory: A classified guide to current periodicals, foreign and domestic.* New York: Bowker, annual. Also available online.

[2] Child-data, available from the National Children's Bureau, 8 Wakley Street, London EC1V 7QE, Tel: 020 7843 6000, Fax: 020 778 9512. Website: *www.ncb.org.uk*

Photocopy requests and inter-library loans

This UK-based service enables you to obtain books or journal articles which are not available in the library you belong to from any other participating library, usually the British Library itself. For a fee, journal articles can be photocopied and sent to you – anywhere in the world. Within the UK it is possible to borrow books through this system, via any academic library. You can access these services through the British Library's website: *http://www.bl.uk*

Translations of articles

A useful service for those who read English: where an item you pick up in a literature search is only published in a language you cannot read, it is worth checking whether it has been translated into English. The British Library Document Supply Centre holds a very large number of translations of documents of all kinds, particularly journal articles. They have mainly been translated from Japanese, Russian, French, and German. If you request a particular item, a search will be made to see if such a translation has been made. You can request this through the British Library website: *http://www.bl.uk*

Unfortunately there is no such service relating to translations from English or between other languages.

Out of the library

The most efficient way of finding out what is known on development issues definitely involves asking for help from a number of people.

> **TIP**   Contact a few knowledgeable people directly: most won't mind answering a few questions

Individuals

To get hold of the most relevant and up to date material, there is no substitute for asking advice from someone who knows the field in general and can consider your particular question. Try to locate people who could help you like this – try someone you have some link to, and ask their advice about who else to ask. You could ask for the top five things they think you should read.

Organisations

Many organisations exist which aim to help development workers to access information on key issues – information centres, research units, policy study institutes. They may publish briefing papers which will quickly give you references for the most important published research on an issue. Ask for this assistance – they can only say no! You can look up their website, or just make a phone call or write a letter.

For international development issues – some places to start are: The Institute of Development Studies at the University of Sussex, UK (IDS); ID21's Development Research Reporting Service; International Institute for Environment and Development (IIED); Panos briefings; the Overseas Development Institute (ODI); Bretton Woods Update newsletter. (See useful websites list in Appendix 1 for further information).

In the UK, local authority research departments and health authorities often hold much useful information on local populations. Agencies such as the National Children's Bureau (NCB) and the National Youth Agency both publish briefing sheets, and will undertake targeted searches on their extensive databases and give you a list of references.

Campaigning organisations usually have good information materials. Bridget O'Laughlin (1998) gives detailed guidelines on how to obtain and assess what are called 'grey materials' – unpublished documents which are available from governments and NGOs. She argues that these reports

> are the product of an explicitly political process – though often couched in technical language. The final report is the outcome of a process of negotiation between researchers and the commissioning organisation.'

In using this material, it is essential to locate its choice of questions and conclusions within its particular institutional discourse. She suggests the following steps for best making use of this type of material:

Step 1 *Register the complete reference*.
Step 2 *Study the title page*. Note down the title, date of publication, institutions, etc.
Step 3 *The executive summary*. This is good for reconstructing policy discourses and debates on the issues, but may not reflect the body of the report.
Step 4 *Skimming the substance*.
Step 5 *Survey the quantitative data*. Copy any useful primary data – this may be your only chance to do so.
Step 6 *Review the bibliography*.
Step 7 *Note taking*.

(Reproduced with permission from O'Laughlin, 1998)

O'Laughlin's advice is to leave reading this type of material until you are fairly clear about your field of study and what you are looking for. This puts you in a better position to treat these reports as 'data', and to assess them with a critical mind.

Official publications

These are obviously an important source in carrying out policy-related research work. Governments publish a surprising amount of useful research material, in addition to legislation and guidelines, which you also of course need to know about and take account of. Government documents often contain useful reviews of the literature around a particular policy issue.

In the South, you can usually get copies of government documents that are available to the public from the relevant ministry, or a central information office. Development co-operation offices, eg UNDP, UNICEF, the Food and Agriculture Organisation, or the World Bank, will usually give away copies of documents. Go directly to their office, or check their websites. European Union documents are available from Commission of EU Co-operation offices.

Publications by international bodies can be located in a number of ways. UN agencies usually publish a directory to help you find their publications (and see 'Useful websites', Appendix 1). There is also the listing in *Ulrich's*

International Periodical Directory, as mentioned above, which should give useful prompts for organisations you might not have thought of.

In the UK, many government publications can be obtained from the Stationery Office, but do not make the mistake of thinking that they all can – in fact only 30% of government publications go through this route. Each department or agency can and does publish material itself as well. So first search with the Stationery Office, but then check for other material. A useful reference guide is published bimonthly by Chadwyck-Healey.[3]

Some US government publications can be located through, or even read in full, on the Internet, but it would be unwise to assume that this is a comprehensive list of what is available. However it is worth looking at the relevant website (see below 'Finding useful statistics' and Appendix 1), especially for current initiatives.

Finding useful statistics

Development workers often use secondary data in the search for statistical information on the group of people that a programme is interested in. This section will look briefly at the types of information which may be available to you, but first some words of warning. The quantity and quality of information that is available on a population is extremely variable. In some countries, nothing is published, and requests for information to the government will yield, at best, no more than a few figures on yellowing bits of paper. In the North, and some Southern countries, there is a long tradition of collecting information on the population, and a potentially overwhelming quantity of local and national-level information exists. However the quality of this material is variable – it is essential to treat all official statistics with deep suspicion!

EXAMPLE

A reality check on official statistics in China

A researcher working with county statistics bureaux in China a few years ago learnt that there were many difficulties faced when carrying out census-type research. Births are kept hidden so that officials can report their population as within their allocated quotas. Deaths are hidden in order to continue to claim benefits. Statistics officers may simply count the children they can see when they visit. Whole villages run away. Officials have been lynched in remote villages. A lot of data is guessed at and made up.

---

[3]*Catalogue of British Official Publications Not Published by the Stationery Office*. Cambridge: Chadwyck-Healey, 1980-, bimonthly.

China's fifth national census publicity stresses that information collected 'cannot be used to punish anyone for their past mistakes or population-related matters'. The 5 million census-takers will be backed by another 1 million advisers to check recording technique and accuracy (Gittings, 2000).

CHECKLIST   Questions to ask when faced with a statistic

- Who says so? Or who has undertaken and who has written about the research?
- How do they know? Or what method has been used and what is the sample?
- What's missing? Or what information is not there? What statistics are not given?
- Does the result answer what the question asks?
- Does it make sense? Or has the assumption the statistic is based on been proved?

(Taken from Huff, 1973)

But do not despair! Even if it is likely that the figure you are looking at may be inaccurate by 10% each way, for example, it is worth knowing about. It is well worth spending some time searching for relevant statistics, as they are so helpful in giving context to your own research work. You have to make a judgement on how much time to give this, in light of your knowledge of how likely it is that you will be successful in finding anything useful.

Table 12.4 suggests ideas for what statistics may exist, and some ways of finding them, in the UK and world-wide.

As we have seen, the UN agencies are an important place to start – in many countries there are UN information centres. Get their most recent report, and follow leads you find there. In South and North, it is worth asking for information from local universities and colleges. Specialist NGOs may also be able to help.

A note on the UK Census

For development workers working in the UK, it is worth knowing about what you can get from census data. Censuses are carried out every ten years – the last one was in 2001. Analysis takes some time. This means that the information may be quite out of date, which may be more or less of an issue depending on how much change has taken place in local populations in that period. The other major problem is that despite some effort, there is recognised to be serious undercounting of some groups, especially homeless people. The 1991 Census for the first time asked about ethnic origin (rather

Table 12.1 Some sources of quantitative information

Type of information	World-wide	UK
Demographic – age, sex, ethnic origin, household/family type, etc	Census of population; population surveys; United Nations reports; local births and deaths registration; National Statistics Office; County statistics offices	Census, carried out every ten years – local details from local authority research departments; health authorities' annual reports; General Household Survey
Poverty, income, welfare	Household Living Standards surveys; demographic and health surveys; World Bank Living Standards Measurements Survey (exists for some countries only); World Bank and UNDP Human Development Indicators	Census; Households Below Average Income statistics; Living Standards surveys
Health	Health surveys; maternal and infant mortality data; WHO country reports; Health ministry studies; UN Administrative Committee on Co-ordination Sub-Committee on Nutrition – reports on the world nutrition situation	Department of Health; Health authorities
Child welfare	Ministry of social welfare studies; UNICEF studies, eg State of the world's children (annual report)	Local authority education and social services departments; National Child Development Survey (sample survey)
Economy and labour market	Labour force surveys; World Bank; Agricultural reports (these may include much useful information on other aspects of life, and are sometimes more up to date than census-type data); International Labour Organisation	Training and enterprise councils; Local authority planning and economic development departments; employers' organisations; trades unions
Housing/shelter	Census; UN Habitat reports; living standards surveys	Census; House Conditions survey; Local authority housing and planning departments; Housing advice agencies
Environmental	Agricultural reports, UN Environment Programme reports	Local authority environmental health departments; health authorities

than birthplace) – the figures are certainly not fully accurate, but they are better information than existed before.

Every local authority uses the Census to produce analyses of a range of demographic information, broken down to electoral ward level. This can be very useful. Contact your local authority's research department, or in London, the London Research Centre, to find out what information is available.

Some other sources of information

Newspapers: it is really worth keeping newspaper cuttings which relate to your area of work. These can provide data on how events are perceived, as well as on what is happening.

Anthropologists' reports: these often contain extremely useful information and interpretation on an area, even if their focus is quite remote from yours. May also give you new ideas and lead you to other helpful sources.

How to use the Internet for research

Of course many people do not have access to the Internet, or their access is limited by, eg, power cuts, unreliable telephone connections, etc. But increasingly the Internet is becoming available, and it can be a helpful tool for research for development work. You can easily check up on general information provided by international organisations, and increasingly you can download whole documents – key policy documents but also discussion papers, how-to-do-it guides and so on.

If you have no experience at all of using the Internet, first either plunge in and give it a try, or else get yourself one of the beginner's guides (Kennedy, 2001). Practice on something you are really interested in (your hobbies, holiday destination or other frivolous matter!). You need to learn to use search engines (eg Alta Vista, Yahoo) and bookmarks/favourites to use the Internet effectively.

There is a specific website to help you! It is *Keying into Development – a guide to using computers for research into development studies*, put together at the University of Sussex. You will find it at: *http://www.ids.ac.uk/eldis/kid/kid.html*

Some tips on searching the Net

Most search engines and databases allow you to search in a pretty focused way. If you just enter some words you want to search on, the system will produce everything which matches any word in the phrase, which can be overwhelming. For example, if you enter 'participative research and action', you would get websites identified which feature any of these words. However you can avoid this. The following 'operators' (symbols on your keyboard) enable you to be quite specific about what you want to find:

Operator	Meaning	Example	Results
*	Wildcard	particip*	Matches all words with this element in them: participatory participation, participative, etc
+	Include this term	+ participative + research + action NOTE that first +	Returns results with ALL words
−	Exclude this term	+ amazon − bookstore NOTE there is a space before the −	Must have one but not the other
""	Quote phrase	+ "participative research and action"	Must include whole phrase exactly as written

Using the Internet for research has to be approached somewhat differently from using it for domestic matters. As with less specialist usage, it can be very useful, but it can also be very frustrating. You are not likely to get far without some idea about where to start, as the search engines tend to be unhelpful on professional questions. Their method of searching is too general. The material you need tends to be in large databases, and it is best to start with some idea of where you are going. Web-sites often give very useful links to other related sites, and this can be the best way to find what you need. For this reason this manual includes a guide to some useful websites for research for development work (see Appendix 1).

If you know what organisation you think would have the information you need, but do not have their web address, it is often possible to guess their address. All World Wide Web addresses begin with: *http://www* – however there are a minority of Internet addresses which do not include www, so do not assume all have it. There will then be a dot and either the full name, without any dots, or the initials, of the organisation. Then there will be another dot and a suffix.

The first part of the suffix relates to the type of organisation, the second to where it is located. The first part of this might be '.org' for voluntary and non-profit organisations, '.com' for US companies, '.co.uk' for UK companies, '.ac' for UK universities or '.edu' for US, Australian, and other universities, for example. Government websites have '.gov' at this point.

The last part of the address may give the country the organisation is located in: .vn for Vietnam, .fr for France, .bf for Burkina Faso, .ch for Switzerland, and so on. International organisations may (or may not) use '.int' as their final suffix – many do without one. It is essential to spell each element right, but the web is good at finding addresses which are incomplete.

It's always worth trying a guess at a web address. Otherwise, try a search engine.

TIP   If you can't get into a website, try again at a different time of day, to avoid heavy traffic on the net

---

One of the wonderful things about the Internet is its speed. It is possible to get up-to-date information on fast-moving situations. Many newspapers have useful sites with good indexing, and there are some specialist sites on emergency situations. (See Appendix 1.)

Warning: there is no quality control on the Internet.
Information you access in this way needs to be checked carefully. With statistics in particular, it is essential to find out the source given for any statements made, and check that too.

Access to libraries and bookshops

A very helpful aspect of the Internet is that you can now access many library databases through the net. This means, for example, that if you have a vague reference from someone, with just an author and a rough date, you can search the British Library's website (*http://www.bl.uk*) and have a good chance of finding it. Equally you can go into many university library databases. These can also be searched by key word (ie subject). Obviously there is a risk of getting far too many references, but if you can refine your search to a well-focused set of key words, you can find much useful material.

For a busy person, libraries can now be used much more efficiently. Using the Internet, you can check from your desktop computer what they have, and whether it is on the shelf or out on loan, rather than having to travel there and look for yourself.

CHECKLIST   Use the Internet for ...

- ✔ Searches of specific databases on well-defined subjects
- ✔ Finding up-to-date information on current issues
- ✔ Checking references against library databases
- ✔ Finding out what major libraries hold on a subject

Don't use the Internet for ...

- ✘ General searches on wide subjects (eg environmental problems, poverty)
- ✘ Identifying statistical information which can be quoted with full confidence

CHECKLIST   For locating key literature

✓ Find and study carefully any recent reviews of the 'state of the art' in the field you are working in. These may be found in official documents, or academic publications
✓ Look 'sideways' from your central subjects
✓ Don't confine yourself to searching within one discipline (eg anthropology, nursing, psychology) – there may be relevant data in a number of fields, and you may need to specifically seek them out, as cross-referencing can be weak
✓ Ask people!
✓ Use the Internet when you have ideas about where to look for information – specific sites, or specialist databases

Key Points from this Chapter

CHECKLIST   For reviewing the literature

✓ Do a good search, including both library searches and contacting organisations and individuals who are knowledgeable
✓ Review the literature by critically assessing the material you have collected, and analysing the different approaches it represents
✓ Note what is not there as well as what is
✓ Be aware of the political forces which operate in determining whose knowledge becomes part of 'the literature' and whose does not
✓ Keep the aims and research questions of your own study always in your mind
✓ Use the Internet – appropriately
✓ Write a first draft of your study of related literature as soon as you can – this will help you greatly in your thinking

Further Reading

Leedy, P.D. (1997) *Practical Research: Planning and Design*, 6th edition. New Jersey: Merrill, Prentice Hall.

Barrientos, S. 'How to do a literature study', in Thomas, A., Chataway, J. and Wuyts, M. (1998) *Finding Out Fast*. London: The Open University/Sage.

Peters, Stuart (1998) *Finding Information on the World Wide Web*, Social Research Update 20. (*http://www.soc.surrey.ac.uk/sru/SRU20.html*)

Gash, S. (1989) *Effective Literature Searching for Students*. Aldershot, UK: Gower.

Sharp, J.A. and Howard, K. (1996) *The Management of a Student Research Project*, 2nd edition. Aldershot, UK: Gower.

Aimed at those doing PhDs – useful when you need help with more complete literature searching

Hart, C. (1998) *Doing a Literature Review: Releasing the social science research imagination*. London: Sage/The Open University.

Emphasises the importance of reflection on the material studied.

Bulmer, M. and Warwick, D.P. (eds) (1993) *Social Research in Developing Countries: Surveys and censuses in the Third World*. London: UCL Press.

13 Research Ethics

Questions of ethics are embedded in every aspect of the process of research for development work. Whilst there are some specific issues which are traditionally discussed as ethical dilemmas within research (how to obtain meaningful consent to participation, confidentiality of data), ethical questions are relevant to a much wider field of concern. The subjects of every chapter of this manual have an ethical dimension: is the research worthwhile? Have community members had a say in its focus and conduct? Is it well defined and carefully planned? Is the sample appropriate, including everyone it should? The list goes on. It is not possible to make research ethical by abiding by a particular set of rules of procedure – it is necessary to consider the ethical aspects of the whole undertaking.

Having said that, having noble long-term aims does not justify being careless about the way in which research is done. Protecting the privacy and confidentiality of respondents is a key priority – as a researcher you cannot always foresee what harm may occur as a result of your work, but respondents often can. An open and responsive process is important, but you also need to take care of dull administrative matters like never writing people's names on data, and keeping data secure.

This chapter starts with a brief consideration of existing codes of ethics, then moves on to three major sections covering responsibilities to respondents, wider accountability and responsibilities to colleagues.

13.1   Codes of Ethics

The professional associations for different types of research, including the Social Research Association[1], the Association of Social Anthropologists of the Commonwealth (ASA)[2], the British Sociological Association, and the British

---

[1]The Social Research Association has recently revised its Ethical Guidelines. This is published annually in its 'Directory of Members', and is available on the SRA's website: *http://www.the-sra.org.uk/index2.htm*

[2]Association of Social Anthropologists of the Commonwealth, Ethical Guidelines for Good Practice, as revised in 1999. Available at the website: *http://www.asa.anthropology.ac.uk/ethics2.html*

Psychological Association, have produced a variety of statements of ethical practice which govern their professions. I have drawn on these interesting documents in preparing this chapter, especially that of the ASA. The full documents are available at the organisations' websites and on paper. However ethical guidelines frequently raise more questions than they answer. Ethical practice in research is generally a matter of finding a balance between a number of principles, and is highly dependent on specific context.

Current ethical codes have been criticised by researchers for failing to give appropriate guidance in relation to research with children, participatory and otherwise. Barnardos' (a large UK childcare NGO) publication *Listening to Children* (Alderson, 1995) includes a helpful framework of ten topics to consider on the ethical issues which arise in relation to research with children. The Rädda Barnen pack *Children in Focus* (Boyden and Ennew, 1997) also discusses these issues, and gives some exercises to assist in focusing on the ethical issues of importance to children.

13.2   Responsibilities towards Respondents: Some Ethical Issues to Consider

In this section, the following principles are discussed:

- Avoiding harm to respondents
- Avoiding undue intrusion
- Communicating information and obtaining informed consent
- Rights to confidentiality and anonymity
- Fair return for assistance
- Respondents' rights in data and publications
- Respondents' involvement in research.

Avoiding harm to respondents

As a researcher your paramount obligation is to ensure that you protect the physical, social, and psychological well-being of those you study, and that you protect their rights, interests, and privacy. You need to assess the possible risks or costs to respondents of taking part in your research, try to minimise these, and weigh them up against the benefits to individuals and wider groups. It is difficult to judge the ultimate impact of any research you undertake, and any benefit from it may not accrue to the respondents themselves. If you fear that people may be harmed, do not continue with the research. If you have concerns, at the very least ensure that you have direct discussions with representatives of the group to be researched themselves.

Anticipating harm

Whilst potential respondents may be aware of risks to themselves of your work, you yourself may sometimes be better placed to guess at the possible consequences of participation. Even if respondents consent to participation, it is still your duty to protect them as far as possible from any potentially harmful effects of your research, whether these relate to individuals or whole social groups. Some groups such as ethnic minorities who face prejudice and discrimination may be particularly vulnerable.

Wasting people's time

When you involve people in research, you are often taking time which they would otherwise spend contributing to the household income. You may want to give some recompense for this, but it is also important to make sure that your research is necessary. Be certain that no one has already gathered the evidence you need before embarking on fieldwork. It is shameful that there are impoverished communities in the North and the South, conveniently placed for researchers, which receive a steady flow of researchers enquiring about one thing or another. Their situation has not been transformed by this over-researching.

Raising expectations

A related issue is that of inappropriately raising expectations. It is very diffi-cult for people in need to understand that a researcher is interested in them only for the purposes of broader study, and will not bring any assistance in their wake. This is especially true of community-level efforts like PLA exer-cises, which explicitly ask people to prioritise issues for action. Of course they may have beneficial effects in themselves, but most people want direct assis-tance, not just 'facilitation'.

On the other hand, if we worried too much about raising expectations, we would do nothing. And at times, expectations are so low that they should be raised. The issue is complex, but it must be thought through. In research for development work, the most practical response is to do everything possi-ble to ensure that any research work is embedded within a programme of practical work and advocacy, and to be honest with respondents about likely outcomes.

Working with particularly vulnerable respondents

The issues discussed in this chapter are particularly pertinent where respon-dents are especially vulnerable. This may be because of political vulnerability, such as groups seen as at odds with their own government, or refugees who are unwelcome in the country they have fled to. It may be due to power imbalances of other kinds: because they are children, or have learning difficulties or disabilities which impair communication, or simply that they cannot read or write. Of course this adds up to a lot of people, and people with whom development workers are likely to be involved! Your duty to think ahead about the impact of your work is greater, and in terms of the process of your research you need to pay extra attention to good communication with respondents. More time will be needed to gain valid consent, and to build trust amongst particularly disempowered people.

In planning research, it is a good idea to assess the particular risks of your specific piece of work.

EXAMPLE

Child protection issues in research on child domestic labour in Egypt, Morocco, and Lebanon

Save the Children in the Middle East and North Africa was embarking on research with children in domestic labour and children in institutions in Egypt, Morocco, and Lebanon. The researchers identified the following issues:

- The children are the weakest members of powerful institutions (family, orphanage) which have an interest in maintaining themselves.
- For children in institutions, the institution managers have a strong interest in maintaining the charitable reputation of the institution. Many institutions in the region are closely linked to people of political or religious prestige, who also have an interest in maintaining the charitable reputation of the institution. These factors might make it difficult for a researcher to intervene in cases where children's rights are violated.
- For children in domestic labour, abuses take place in a private sphere which influences the way in which private actors view each other's rights. Continued access to any children involved in the study cannot be taken for granted.

Obviously the risks of different research projects vary widely in nature and intensity – each needs to be assessed specifically.

In terms of dealing with vulnerable individuals, researchers need guidance about what to do if, for example, a respondent talks during an interview about suicide, or harm to others, and the researcher is concerned for the respondent's or other people's safety. Researchers should, at the end of such an interview, talk directly to the person about their concerns, and discuss with them what should be done. Researchers should have available on the spot information about possible sources of help. In some projects, researchers routinely leave behind a package of information for respondents. It is always appropriate for such issues to be shared with a research supervisor, who can advise on the basis of wider experience.

Child protection   Because of children's relative powerlessness, researchers have a particular responsibility for their protection. This obviously includes preventing any harm to children being caused by the research itself, but also giving thought to what you will do if a child should take the opportunity of a research interview to disclose current or past abuse.

Organisations need to discuss this difficult issue and agree a policy, so that individual researchers are supported in any action they take.

One UK organisation, the National Children's Bureau (2000), has the following policy guidelines on this matter:

'We believe that there must be limits to any guarantee of confidentiality or anonymity in situations where child protection is an issue. Where a child or young person divulges that they or others are at risk of significant harm, or where the researcher observes or receives evidence of incidents likely to cause serious harm, the researcher has a duty to take steps to protect the child or other children.

It is important, however, that the researcher does so only after full discussion with the child, ensuring that he or she is aware of the likely consequences and taking very careful account of his or her wishes. If, after discussion with the child, the researcher decides it is necessary to inform others – hopefully with the consent of the child – the researcher must ensure that the child has immediate support and is kept fully informed.

To deal with this possibility, children and young people should be told at the outset, and as necessary during the course of an interview, that confidentiality cannot be guaranteed if information of this type emerges.'

As with adults, the first priority is to have a direct discussion with the young respondent about what they think should be done about the abuse. Often they will know what action they would prefer. It may be helpful if the child can be persuaded themselves to tell someone else whom they trust, who can help to support them and address the situation.

EXAMPLE

Reports of child abuse: children on commercial farms in Zimbabwe

A project investigating the needs of children on commercial farms in Zimbabwe, which offered a rare opportunity for children to have grievances heard, found several instances where abuse was indicated. One group reported: 'We are physically and mentally abused by our stepmothers. They always accuse us of something we have not done. If anything is missing at home, we are always blamed. Some of us girls are given men, whom we do not want. If the men we are given become broke, our stepmothers usually look for another man with money. Some children are abused by stepfathers, when their mothers are away.'

Some children also wanted to report their own physical abuse. These were referred on to a professional counsellor or to members in the community who were judged to be competent and better placed to deal with the issue. One of the adult co-ordinators of the project said: 'The subject of child abuse has not been easy to deal with ... Unless services, professional counselling and legal protection is available, a child who reports abuse can be placed in an even worse situation. There is need to establish an education, protection and care programme in these communities if this problem is to be adequately addressed' (McCartney, 2000).

The fact that in many (most?) parts of the world, reporting child abuse by no means guarantees a sensitive and positive response from the authorities, is of course a huge problem. But this is not a good enough reason to 'turn a blind eye' to what a child is telling you. And while you cannot guarantee a wholly appropriate response from others, it is also true that a researcher by themselves is most unlikely to have suitable skills to assist a child who is in an abusive situation. The child will need help from others, and you should facilitate this, involving the child as far as possible in any decisions you make.

Recruitment of researchers working with children

Remember that it is possible for research staff to take advantage of their position to abuse children. If researchers will be working closely with children and building up trusting relationships, and especially where significant unsupervised one-to-one contact with children is required by the research, there need to be checks to ensure that the risk of abuse is minimised. Police checks should be carried out on anyone in this position. This is not always possible, but every effort should be made to obtain official confirmation of the candidate's integrity in this regard.

It is important to check on the identity of those applying for (or holding) such posts, by asking to see documents such as a birth certificate or passport and by following up references offered. Asking to see qualifications is a simple but practical and effective vetting measure.

Reference requests should seek specific information on the candidate's suitability to work with children. Select referees that have experience of the candidate's work with children and ask for further information from them.

Unless it is essential for the research, if is often best to avoid making plans which involve researchers being alone with children.

Avoiding undue intrusion

It is easy, as researchers, to get very excited about how important our research is, but it is essential to remember that respondents have other priorities. You need to consider how potentially intrusive your research is, and whether this is necessary and justifiable. You have no special entitlement to study all phenomena, and the pursuit of information is not in itself a justification for overriding other social and cultural values.

Having said that, as noted in the example quoted above, many violations of women's and children's rights take place within what is seen as the 'private sphere' of the family. The privacy of family life cannot be allowed to block all research which aims to open up these issues. However these sensitivities need to be considered in choice of methods, sampling, and numerous other research decisions. Informal research methods may be more effective than more structured approaches.

Communicating information and obtaining informed consent

Giving information is closely tied up with the process of getting consent from respondents in an appropriate way. Research needs the freely given informed consent of its respondents to be ethical. It is therefore essential that researchers work out effective ways of ensuring that respondents understand what the research is about: its purpose(s); the anticipated consequences of the study; who are the funders and sponsors; the anticipated uses of the data; possible benefits of the study and possible harm or discomfort that might affect participants; how data will be recorded and stored; and the degree of anonymity and confidentiality which can be afforded to respondents. It is worth having a checklist of the things you need to say to each respondent!

Some approaches to consent

Some researchers give respondents a written information sheet and ask them to sign a form stating that they give their consent to participate in the research. This is good practice where respondents are able to read and understand such written materials, and where it is felt important to have evidence that respondents gave their consent. Certainly a clear, simply written information sheet should be provided, even if only some of the participants can read it. Respondents often think of questions about the research after the researcher has left. But this approach has its problems. One does not want respondents to feel that because they have signed a piece of paper they are obliged to take part in the whole research process, if it later strays into areas they are not happy with. And of course it is inappropriate if respondents cannot read or understand what is written.

It is best to think of consent as an ongoing process, in which you remind respondents of the possible future uses of the information they give you as appropriate, and in which respondents can opt out whenever they wish. With children in particular, who are often given little choice about participating in processes such as schooling, it is important to show them that they do have a choice. One approach is to tell children you are interviewing that whenever they say 'stop', the interview will stop, and show them that this is so.

It can be difficult for potential respondents to understand what is meant by 'research'. People naturally tend to assume that if you are approaching them with a lot of questions, that there is some particular reason why they have been chosen. You need to explain particularly clearly that they will not benefit or suffer personally, regardless of whether or not they take part in the research. (See also Chapter 15.1, which discusses some practical steps to take in relation to obtaining consent).

Activity 13.1

Gaining informed consent

Practice explaining about your research, including all the issues you need to cover, and asking for people's consent to participate, in a role play exercise with colleagues. Think about the particular people you will be researching with, and explain as you would to them. Have the person playing the respondent ask some awkward questions. You can try out draft information sheets at the same time, where appropriate.

EXAMPLE

Informed consent from children with communication difficulties

A joint project between Hammersmith and Fulham Social Services (London) and Save the Children looked at ways of consulting children and young people with disabilities about services for them. The children in the study were aged between 4 and 14 and had a range of disabilities and communication needs. The researchers had a number of concerns about how to get valid consent from their respondents, and how to assure confidentiality. Working closely with practitioners from a day centre that the children used was very helpful in encouraging parents and children to agree to take part, but did it make it difficult for them to decline? It was difficult to maintain the anonymity of respondents with this high level of staff involvement, and on one occasion confidentiality was broken (a staff member told a parent something that a child had said).

In terms of gaining consent, in some cases it was satisfactory, as shown in the following account:

'I said – shall I tell you a bit about why I'm here? She signalled "yes". I got out the leaflet. I read it through to her, showed her the picture, explained that what she says will go in a book but not her name. I said you don't have to say anything you don't want to, I said you can stop when you want. I asked if it was ok to talk to her about [the Centre]. She signalled "yes".'

In other cases it was less clear that the child understood what was being said, and they were not included in the research.

Ongoing consent was also felt to be important. One researcher established a means for a child to indicate that they wished to stop:

'I got out the "Stop" sign, gave it to (child) and explained that if he wanted to stop for a short while, to stop to eat or drink, or just to rest, or stop for today, or stop altogether, he could let me know by holding up the stop sign. I said, "how will you let me know if you want to stop?" and he put up the sign and smiled' (Lewis and Kirby, 2001).

Rights to confidentiality and anonymity

Respondents should have the right to remain anonymous and to have their rights to privacy and confidentiality respected. You should make every effort to protect the identities of those from whom you have collected data. As described in Chapter 15, there are a number of steps you need to take in putting this guidance into practice. As well as changing individuals' names you may need to protect the identities of villages or other geographical areas.

In some situations (such as participatory work within small communities) it is not realistic to undertake to protect the identities of those taking part, and in this case, of course, you should not suggest that you could. Then people can decide for themselves what they say and what they don't say, knowing that their neighbours or local government officials, for instance, may find out what they said.

It is important to be specific about what confidentiality means in any particular study.

EXAMPLE

Consent and confidentiality – studying the problems girls face in Surkhet, Nepal

A study of the difficulties girls face in families in Ramghat and Ghusra villages of Surkhet district, Nepal, produced a video documentary of girls' voices and a 'safe environment for girls project' in Ramghat. How were ethical issues addressed?

Informed consent was obtained from village development committees, schoolteachers, and NGOs before undertaking any fieldwork. Before starting the discussion with the various groups, the objectives of the research were outlined. The individual interviews with adolescent girls were kept confidential and not disclosed in their village. The names of the informants were not given in the report. Pseudonyms are used instead. The individual girls for case study were chosen by the girls themselves and reasons were explained in the group before choosing the individual girls, to reduce the group's expectations.

To protect the girls, the draft video for girls' voices was shown to the children whose ideas were documented in filming. Once it was shown to the children, they requested and were excited to show the video to their parents too. The researchers again returned to the village and filmed the parents talking about the girls' difficulties and then showed them the film of girls' voices. In the video, lots of views were against the parents' behaviour towards daughters. Surprisingly their brothers and parents were convinced by the girls' ideas and agreed that what they said was happening in their village. Then the parents agreed to the video being shown to any audience.

As part of their responsibility to avoid harm to respondents, the researcher has a duty to anticipate ways in which confidentiality may be compromised. For example, it is not enough just to change names, if people remain identifiable from their characteristics or story – the only male teacher in the school, or whatever. Where this problem is difficult to overcome, it can be useful to discuss with the respondent in question what to do for the best. They may want to withdraw consent to use their data, or they may decide they are happy to be identifiable.

In participatory projects, respondents may want to use their real names, getting acknowledgement for their work. Researchers need to think this through, as respondents may not be aware of all the possible consequences of publishing their views or experience openly, if they have little experience of publication. Obviously, again, it is essential to explain the possible effects of such an action in detail with all those concerned.

There are, however, limits to any guarantee of confidentiality in situations where the person may be at risk. See above, under section 1.4.1 on child protection.

Fair return for assistance

There should be no exploitation of respondents, as individuals or as groups (eg a village used for an exercise when training in PLA techniques), and fair return should be made for their help. Why should people spend their time helping you when they could be doing work to put food on the table? This issue is discussed in Chapter 19 the Right people: Talking to – Choosing a Sample, in relation to offering material recompense as an incentive to participate. Particular issues are raised by peer research, where participants may put large amounts of work into a project, and this is discussed in Chapter 3.4.

Respondents' rights in data and publications

It is important to recognise the rights of respondents over data and publications you produce. It is good practice, where possible, to allow respondents to see transcripts of interviews and field-notes, and to alter the content, withdraw statements, and provide additional information if they so wish. The same process can be carried out verbally, explaining what you understood the person to say. However upsetting it is to the researcher to lose good data, if a respondent does not want you to publish it, you should not use it.

The question of feedback and consultation on action or publications arising from the research is also an ethical one. Respondents are entitled to know what you are saying about them!

Respondents' involvement in research

The importance of respondents' participation has been emphasised through-out this manual. Perhaps the most difficult, and the most crucial, point where this should be followed through is at the end of the project. People need to be involved in the process of deciding what will and will not happen as a result of the research project.

Equality issues

The right to active involvement in research processes concerning one's community should extend to all members of the community. It is easy to per-petuate discrimination against groups of people, usually by taking the easy way out and ignoring those whom the majority routinely exclude. For example dis-abled people are often socially invisible, and will not automatically be included by community members in public processes. Some communities will exclude particular ethnic groups. Lesbians and gay men may not be immediately visible or able to speak publicly, but they exist in all populations (Lowe et al, 1991). Development researchers need to ask questions about, and endeavour to involve, people who are not readily visible, as well as those who are.

Another issue to consider, in the conduct of your fieldwork, is how you as researchers will respond if you hear prejudiced or degrading comments about discriminated-against groups, whether these are racist, sexist, anti-gay, or of whatever type. Traditionally, a researcher should not put forward their own view in any circumstances, staying outside the issue. But if you ignore such comment, you can seem to collude with these attitudes. If you inter-vene, you can alienate your respondents or get sidetracked. It is useful for an organisation to consider these issues, so that fieldworkers know what kind of action they should take.

Activity 13.2

Dealing with equality issues

Consider the following situation:

You are running a focus group discussion, and right at the beginning, two participants make strongly prejudiced comments about minority ethnic people in their area, blaming them for all kinds of social problems. Only one other participant appears to disagree, and he is intimidated.

Discuss within your research team what you should do.

13.3 Wider accountability

If you aim to study powerful people, such as the directors of multinational companies, you can be sure that you will be made accountable for your work in a variety of ways. The same does not necessarily apply to those in poverty. Researchers may need to set up structures to assist in making themselves accountable for their actions. An advisory group for the research, involving key stakeholders, is a good start.

At national level

It is important to be aware that there may be national laws or administrative regulations which may affect your research. You should also remember that in most cases, social research data are not privileged under law, and may be subject to legal subpoena.

Research conducted outside one's own country raises special ethical and political issues, relating to personal and national disparities in power, political interest, and national political systems. In some countries the government requires that researchers from other countries affiliate themselves to a local research institution before consenting to their work. This is in any case good practice, as it ensures that the researchers of the country have a chance to contribute towards and learn from the research.

In projects planned from one country and conducted in others, it can be a good idea to set up a research advisory or reference group within any country where fieldwork takes place, perhaps in addition to an advisory group for the whole project. This can have all kinds of benefits, including useful advice on local conditions, building wider ownership of the issues the research is addressing, and perhaps empowering 'the researched'. See also Chapter 8.3 on negotiating access.

Research ethics committees

Because of the particular risks of medical research, there is a well-developed approach within health care to the scrutiny of research proposals for their ethical implications. In the UK, research proposals in the health field usually need to be submitted to a Research Ethics Committee for approval before health service staff will be able to assist in contacting service users or staff. If the research requires access to health service records, or if patients are to be contacted through such records, the project will need to go through this process.

Ethics committees look at the overall quality and relevance of the research as well as direct risks to respondents. These committees have been constructed with clinical research in mind, and social researchers in the health field have at times met with lack of understanding of qualitative research.

Increasingly universities and other organisations are setting up their own research ethics committees, in response to public concern about the need for scrutiny of research practice.

At community level

Researchers' relationship with the community being studied has been discussed throughout this manual. Development work aims to empower communities, and research needs to work in the same direction. This will often mean an increasing level of participation in research processes, but this needs to be appropriate to the particular situation (see Chapter 3.5). Participation in research processes cannot be assumed to be beneficial.

Making information available

If anyone is to learn from your work, it is essential that findings and information about methodology be published or otherwise made available to others. One contribution towards preventing the waste of resources involved in duplicate studies of the same issues and groups is to ensure that key findings are available for future researchers to read.

It is also of course important to publish within the country or area where the data was collected, for the same reasons. And to publish in the language/s of that country, so that your findings are made available to those they most concern.

Failure to publish, or deliberate suppression of information, can be unethical, if you think of the waste of resources and broken promises involved. It is of concern when research data is treated as private property, and people are prevented from publishing by those who commissioned it.

13.4 Responsibilities to colleagues

Research for development work is often very much a team effort. As well as experienced staff there may be research assistants, interpreters, and community workers involved in various capacities. All those involved should be treated with respect, and efforts made to ensure that less experienced staff gain the maximum possible benefit from their involvement (see also Chapter 9).

Northern researchers should take account of the interests and needs of Southern colleagues, considering the disparity in resources available to them. Development research organisations should make every effort to invest in Southern research institutions.

Researcher safety

The safety of researchers while undertaking fieldwork should be given explicit consideration, with discussion encouraged amongst the research team. Researchers should be told that their own safety should be placed above the successful completion of research tasks. Assess the risks of your particular project, plan ahead, and avoid risks as far as possible. In some environments, researchers share some dangers simply by being there – organisations should have their own procedures for protecting all staff in insecure situations, and these should be applied equally to researchers.

A specific code of practice on safety for researchers has been developed by the Social Research Association, and can be found on their website.[3]

Obviously some risks will be specific to the topics under investigation, but a few guidelines apply to many situations:

- Make sure that a research colleague *and* a trusted friend/family member knows where you are and what you are doing each day, and when you expect to return. Let them know when you have returned.
- Consider working in pairs – this has other benefits too in terms of quality of data collection and opportunities to learn.
- In countries where this is possible, a mobile phone is useful for keeping in touch, should plans change, and for calling help if you should need it.
- Think about what will be the safest transport option.
- Ensure that your dress is appropriate. Avoid carrying anything of value with you.
- Carry documentation establishing your identity as a researcher.

CHECKLIST   Ethical issues to consider in research for development work

✓ Is the research necessary?
✓ Is the research well-planned as a project, and integrated into a programme of practical work?
✓ Have you considered the specific ethical issues raised by this project, and how to address them?
✓ How will informed consent be obtained from respondents?
✓ Are you providing accessible information about your project?
✓ What level of confidentiality and anonymity can you offer to participants, and how can they be effectively informed of this?
✓ Is there appropriate stakeholder participation in the project?
✓ Are you offering appropriate return for assistance?
✓ Are respondents able to check your version of the information they have given you?
✓ How will you ensure that information is appropriately fed back to those who were researched?
✓ What systems are in place to ensure that you learn from your experience?
✓ How are respondents to be informed of, or consulted on, the results of the research?
✓ Assess any risks to field researchers and work out ways to minimise them

---

[3]Social Research Association, A Code of Practice for the Safety of Social Researchers, available at the SRA's website: *http://www.the-sra.org.uk/article9.htm*

Further Reading

Association of Social Anthropologists of the Commonwealth, *Ethical Guidelines for Good Practice*, as revised in 1999. Available at the website: *http://www.asa.anthropology.ac.uk/ethics2.html*

The Social Research Association Ethical Guidelines. This is published annually in its 'Directory of Members', and is available on the SRA's website: *http://www.thesra.org.uk/index2.htm*

Alderson, P. (1995) *Listening to Children: Children, ethics and social research*, Barkingside. Essex: Barnardos.

Commissioned by Barnardos, this is a thorough consideration of the ethical issues involved in research with children. It looks at each stage of the research process as well as at questions like what research is done and what is not. Includes a useful summary of 'ten topics in ethical research'.

Boyden, J. and Ennew, J. (eds) (1997) *Children in Focus: A manual for participatory research with children*. Stockholm: Rädda Barnen.

Whole text is strong on ethics of research with children.

14 Communication with Respondents – the Key to Good Research

Social research is all about communication. Sometimes in development research it is necessary to create good communication across a very wide gap in terms of experience, language, and culture. It is crucial to learn to communicate with those you are working with in a way which is comfortable and acceptable to them. You need to learn how people usually greet each other, sit together, converse, and take leave. Anyone who has lived and worked for a period of time with people like those with whom you are researching will have a huge advantage for this reason. But in addition to general cultural familiarity, research requires an active interest in others, and a willingness to ask questions about things that are taken for granted, questions which may seem unnecessary or strange to 'insiders'. And fundamentally it requires listening, giving space to the other, and having patience as they work out what they want to say.

There is a strong power dynamic in research work. Usually the researcher is more socially powerful than the respondent. This has all kinds of effects, for example respondents may feel that they should give answers which will please you. You need to make active efforts to minimise the distance this creates, through how you talk and behave.

In this chapter we will consider a number of issues relating to communication – language, style, and working in non-literate contexts. There will be brief consideration of some issues relating to work with disabled people and with children. We will then look in a little detail at how to proceed when you do not share a language with your respondents.

14.1 Language

We will discuss below the complex issues involved in research with people whose language you do not speak. But it is also important to think about the kind of words you use in your own language. Jargon and technical terms can be very confusing and intimidating to respondents – do not let them creep in to what you say. Use language that you know is familiar to your respondents, and put things as simply as possible.

It is very helpful to check if people have grasped key points by politely asking them to explain back to you. Pay attention to non-verbal signals that your respondent has lost the thread of what you are saying/asking (looking confused, gazing around the room, etc). If you are giving important information, repeat what you have said at least once and ask if it is clear to those listening.

You need also to check that you have understood the other person correctly. It is very tempting to nod and smile and pretend that you are following someone, when really you are not. Be assertive and honest. It can be embarrassing to admit you cannot follow what is being said, but if you don't, you are lost! People know when you are pretending, and they will lose faith in the whole process. Rephrase back to the person what you think they just said, and check on areas you are not sure of.

14.2 Style

How you present yourself in terms of dress, posture, and so on is part of your communication with others. What is informal and relaxed in one setting can be positively rude in another. Equally, dressing in an over-formal way can make you and your different background more conspicuous than it needs to be, and create distance. Aim to be as informal as possible, while dressing formally enough to show respect. Think about the particular group you are working with and what their norms are. But be yourself! You won't blend in by adopting dress or behaviour you are unfamiliar with.

Remember that appropriate body language in different situations is quite culturally specific. In Western cultures, direct eye contact is used to establish a person's honesty and openness. But in some cultures direct eye contact between strangers is avoided, and can be seen as aggressive. There are, in any culture, complex rules around gender relations which need to be negotiated carefully.

If you are interviewing people in their own homes, it is important to balance politely playing the role of a visitor (ie accepting hospitality which is offered), with maintaining the professional role you have as a researcher – and indeed avoiding people expending scarce resources unnecessarily.

You can demonstrate listening and respect by:

- sitting at the same level as your respondents;
- using appropriate eye contact (varies by culture);
- making small encouraging movements (nodding etc – also varies by culture) and noises;
- adopting an open, relaxed posture (avoid folding arms, turning away);
- not interrupting.

14.3 Working in Non-literate Contexts

Obviously it is important to adapt research methods to the abilities of the people you are working with. Interviews and group discussions build on the basic skills of conversation. It can be helpful, whether or not people have literacy skills, to use visual materials as a focus. Participatory Learning and Action (PLA) has developed many methods which are intended to facilitate the active involvement of non-literate people – mapping, diagrams (such as seasonal calendars), and various ranking and scoring techniques (see Chapter 17: Seven Key Research Techniques). These use local materials to create a visual representation of the issues under discussion, or, for example, to describe the area. However they are generally not ends in themselves, but are ways of encouraging discussion about the issues in question. For example, building a map of the area with local people using materials that come to hand is a means to a discussion about local problems, while at the same time affirming local knowledge and skills.

It is important that these techniques are not used rigidly, but are carefully adapted to the local context. People can find diagrams just as puzzling as words on paper, and may not, for example, readily see the purpose of ranking exercises. They should only be used when they are meaningful to participants and when they can produce information relevant to the exercise in hand. Where there is a strong oral tradition, people may actually be very comfortable with discussions, regardless of level of literacy.

COMMON PITFALLS 14.1   Assuming that you should carry out mapping or ranking exercises regardless of the purpose of your study

---

Remember that in addition to those who cannot read or write at all, there are very large numbers of people, in Northern societies as well as Southern, whose literacy is poor, and who lack confidence in this area. You can help these people, and partially sighted people, by using plain language, large print, and illustrations that give prompts about the subject discussed in the text. An audio tape of key information will also help people, where tape recorders are available.

14.4   Communicating with Disabled People

Some disabled people have conditions which mean that their communication is impaired, through deafness, blindness, and/or a learning disability. But most disabled people have difficulty in getting anyone to listen to them, because of negative social attitudes towards disabled people. Assumptions are often made about their abilities that are entirely wrong. There are no different rules for communicating with disabled people – having respect, taking time, observing how they communicate with others – are key. You do not need to be a disability 'expert' to talk with disabled people.

Most people with impaired hearing can communicate successfully through a mixture of lip-reading and signs, which usually build on signs people in their culture use routinely. A minority speak a formal sign language, and can conduct complex discussions through a sign-language interpreter.

Remember that many elderly people and quite a few young people have some hearing impairment. This can become particularly stressful in group situations. Raising your voice is unhelpful. Make sure people speak in turn, and indicate when they are speaking. Speakers may need to turn towards the person with impaired hearing, and avoid covering their mouths, to let them lip-read them. Before you start, think about the layout of the room, where people are sitting and check that everyone can see each other. These measures will be helpful to other people in the group as well.

In order to make written materials accessible to those with a visual impairment, reading them out loud, or tape-recording is the most helpful method. Large print (preferably at least 14pt) will help many. Braille is extremely helpful for the minority who have learnt to read it, but many blind or partially sighted people never get the chance to learn.

EXAMPLE

Funding accessible communication

For a recent project of particular relevance to disabled people, Comic Relief gave separate funding for dissemination through taping and translating into Braille. It is important for this work to be done to professional standards. Actually getting information to disabled people requires promotional efforts beyond just putting the material into an accessible medium. How will blind people, for example, find out that your publication is available to them?

14.5 Working with Children

In recent years a body of work has developed which proposes a new approach to research with children (for example, James and Prout, 1990; Qvortrup et al, 1994; Johnson et al, 1995; James et al, 1998). Rejecting traditional approaches to children which essentially see them as defective adults, the new philosophy suggests that research should see children as 'social actors' in themselves. We should be interested in children's points of view for their own sake, not just to measure them against adults' perceptions. Children are placed at the centre of the process of investigation, and research should seek to take a lead from the children's own agenda.

So what does this mean for how we actually carry out research with children? Do not assume that it is automatically necessary to use special techniques because you are working with children. The whole range of research approaches and techniques discussed in this manual can be used with children – where appropriate. As ever, the key issue is what you are trying to find out through your research, and your respondents' comfort with different kinds of communication. But the way in which any research is carried out is critical – children are excellent observers of adults, and researchers' behaviour and attitudes will come through to children very clearly. It is crucial to show respect to children, and as part of this, to take enough time to develop trust and rapport with the children you want to work with.

It is best to think of children as like other disempowered people, and to direct your efforts to finding ways of equalising as far as possible the power imbalance between researchers and children. The advice throughout this manual about handling different stages of the research process is equally important if working with children. For example, we should be just as concerned not to waste children's time with un-thought-out research that will result in no change, as we would adults'.

Starting out

- **Observe and listen:** it is best, before attempting to act upon a situation by initiating research processes, to spend some time observing how the children you want to work with communicate ordinarily. Then you can plan your research techniques in keeping with what they are comfortable with.
- **Show respect:** make sure you let children introduce themselves to you properly. Sit at the same level as them. Let them talk to you about their concerns, and take time to appreciate what they are getting at. Keep sessions short, and respect children's other commitments.
- **Be friendly and encouraging:** children will tend to look to adults for approval and praise, and you will need to strike a balance between not seeming to judge their responses, and encouraging them when they are working well with you. Any critical comment from you will be taken to heart, so be careful in what you say – never praise some children and not others. Remember that cultures vary in terms of how children are expected to behave with adults, and do not embarrass children.
- **Help children to relax with you:** when you start work with a new group, it is important to spend some time letting the children get used to you, and doing something that will put them at their ease. Put away your notebook and tape recorder until later. Depending on the age group and culture of the children, games, songs, dancing, or drawing may be helpful. Ask them to teach you something of theirs, perhaps. Remember that older children can feel insulted if you assume that they will want to take part in activities they regard as suitable for younger children, like singing and drawing.
- **Preparatory visits:** if possible, it makes a huge difference if you are able to make a visit to the child or children ahead of the time when you want to collect data. It is good if you can then also let the children have a look at your tape-recorder or any other unfamiliar materials you plan to use.

- **Taking time:** there is no substitute for spending enough time with children for them to get accustomed to you. Their confidence will build just by observing that you are willing to invest reasonable time in being with them and learning from them. Wait for them to come to you.

Making yourself clear

- **Language:** Match your conversation to the age and emotional/physical state of the child. Let children talk to you in their own language – do not try to get them to use the terms you are accustomed to. If you are in doubt as to their meaning, ask questions. Take care with the language you use yourself. It is very off-putting to children to be asked questions they do not understand.
- **Consent:** make sure that you explain your research in a way that the children can understand. Research is not an easy thing to explain to children, and it is worth rehearsing what you will say beforehand. Ask them if they have questions, and gently ask questions yourself to find out what they have understood from you. You will usually need to get consent from parents as well as from children themselves.

People in authority over children, for example teachers or managers of institutions, may assume that it is for them to give consent to participation in research for children. Always start by ensuring that children understand that they are under no compulsion to take part in your research. See Chapter 13: Research Ethics and Chapter 15.1 – on consent.

- **Confidentiality:** is very important to children. Make sure you explain what you will do to protect children's identities, and show that you take this seriously.
- **Getting expectations clear:** you need to make sure that children do not have unrealistic expectations of the results of your research project. Having someone take an interest in you can be a powerful thing, and it is your responsibility to make sure that children's hopes are not raised inappropriately.
- **Ground rules:** you may want to agree with the children some ground rules for how you will work together, for example in a group setting. Ask the children for their suggestions of ground rules. Letting people finish what they are saying without interrupting, and letting everyone have their say, are important.

Choice of research techniques

You may need to be flexible about your research techniques in working with children. Expect to think on your feet, to respond to the children's lead, as you learn what they are most comfortable with. You may need to take more time with children to get the right approach sorted out.

While in some situations, formal research methods can be suitable to work with children, there is a danger that structured interview techniques will feel to children like a sort of test. It is helpful to spell it out that there are no right or wrong answers to your questions.

- **Asking open questions:** it is often a good idea to let children tell you their story in their own way. Even if they begin somewhere way off your subject, let them continue and only later, if necessary, guide them back to what you are interested in.
- **More structured approaches:** with children who are reasonably comfortable with reading and writing, it actually grants very good confidentiality to ask children to fill in a self-completion questionnaire, or to write a short essay on a subject. These methods have been used in relation to teenagers' experiences of sexual abuse (Kelly et al, 1995), and to ideas about families (Morrow, 1999). 'Draw and write' is a helpful technique with younger children – see Chapter 17.8.
- **Group work:** it is worth considering working with children in groups, rather than individually, as they may gain confidence from the presence of their friends. The 'strength in numbers' effect can be strong for children, where one-to-one time with an unfamiliar adult may feel threatening. All the same drawbacks of course apply as to group work with adults (see Focus groups, Chapter 17.3), but so do the advantages.
- **Stimulus materials:** children may find ideas easier to grasp if they are made concrete in some way. For example, using drawings or photographs, or offering 'vignettes/scenarios' (very short stories which illustrate or dramatise the issue you are investigating), can be helpful. References to either fictional or factual elements of popular culture (soap operas, news reports) can be useful in focusing a discussion. Young people will often enjoy working on a practical problem you set, and you can then probe for the reasons behind their judgements. Beware, though, of letting your materials take over – they should generally only introduce discussion which moves on to a deeper level in relation to the children's own experiences.

Finishing the research encounter

Research processes can produce strong feelings in children. Children may get upset by the issues you discuss with them, and you need to handle this calmly and naturally. Make sure you finish an interview on a light note – do not leave a child in distress. Make sure that you have time to help children to regain control of their feelings before you leave.

As with adults, it is important to thank children for their contribution, to sum up what you have heard, and to ask for feedback on their experience of the research. Let them know if they will see you again, but do not make promises you cannot fulfil.

Working with Practitioners

Where children have a trusting relationship with professionals, it may be a good idea to ask them to work alongside you. For example, a youth worker can sometimes 'lend' you the trust they have built with young people by introducing you and working with you. However there are of course adults who will inhibit children. It may be best to avoid working closely with those in direct authority over children, such as teachers or social workers, even if they have a good relationship with the children. It depends on the subject you are looking at.

Child protection

It is generally best to spend time with children in places where you can be seen by others. There is no need, for most research purposes, to be completely alone with individual children. You need to strike a balance to give your respondents some privacy whilst avoiding making them feel isolated and vulnerable, or any possible accusation of abuse.

Researchers are often concerned about what they would do if a child disclosed to them that they or others are at risk of significant harm. See Chapter 13 on ethics for discussion of these issues.

CHECKLIST   On effective communication with children

✓ Listen and observe
✓ Show respect
✓ Let the children set the agenda and use their own language
✓ Take time to let the children get used to you, and to relax
✓ Ensure that the children themselves have consented to their involvement in the research – explain its aims carefully, and do not raise false expectations
✓ Choose methods which these particular children will find comfortable

---

14.6 Working with People whose First Language you do not Share

This is obviously a challenging situation, and carrying out successful research where you cannot speak directly with people requires considerable care and preparation. Language is of the greatest importance to all kinds of research. Wherever possible, it is best to work alongside an experienced researcher who shares a mother tongue with your respondents. There is no doubt that working through a third party impedes communication. But at times this is inevitable.

It is worth noting, however, that if you have some understanding of the language in question, even if you cannot speak it well enough to conduct an interview yourself, this will be helpful. You will be able to follow how questions are being asked, and to get the gist of the replies.

In many parts of the world people may speak several languages, with more or less skill. Their own mother tongue may be one of a group of languages spoken in the local area, and they may also speak the 'national language', which is sometimes that of the old colonial power. We are all most able to express ourselves in our mother tongue, and research which relies on respondents communicating in a language of which they have only partial command will not get the best out of its respondents.

It is well worth investing some time in making sure you have good arrangements for interpreting, as it is easy to waste a lot of time and money trying to do research without adequate assistance with translation.

Working with an interpreter

When you involve someone else to assist you in communicating with people, it is important to be clear about the capacity in which you wish them to act. They may be a research assistant, an interpreter, or an advocate, and each of these roles brings with it different expectations. A professional interpreter will simply translate exactly what you say to the person, and their responses. They will also explain their role to the respondents. A research assistant may take a more active role, asking their own questions, or perhaps leading interviews, once it is clear that they fully understand the purpose of the research. An advocate may see it as their role to draw out the respondent, encouraging them to put forward their views. You need to negotiate what to expect from one another. It is best to use professional interpreters, not colleagues, or professionals with other roles. Where this is not possible, you may need to spend time training someone in the role you need them to fulfil.

It is important to encourage the person interpreting for you to let you know how questions will be understood in their language. Often concepts (including common terms like 'household', 'work', or 'child') do not simply translate directly from one language to another, and you should discuss with them exactly what the issues are that you are investigating. They will be able to help you to ask questions in an appropriate way, with their knowledge of the language and culture. If you do not do this, you may find they alter your questions in any case, to avoid the embarrassment of asking what seem to them to be stupid questions.

However you also need to make it clear that you want to know exactly what respondents are saying, and you do not want your interpreter to censor or edit what is being said, whatever their own views on it. At times interpreters feel a responsibility to represent their people to you in a particular way, or may disapprove of respondents' points of view. Inexperienced interpreters may feel that they should explain what is being said, or even edit it if they feel it is politically sensitive. If they are unused to research, they may find your questions stupid, or question why you are asking the same question of different people. You may need to explain that you will be repeating questions, and that some questions may appear stupid, as you have to double-check your information.

It is worth noting a further complexity, which is that an interpreter from their own community may not seem to offer much confidentiality to respondents, particularly in small or closely knit communities. Depending on the subject to be discussed, it may be best to use an interpreter from a little further away if sensitive topics are to be raised.

In some areas where many communities co-exist, you may wonder how to involve people from a number of different language groups. Bringing together too many different language groups will not work.

EXAMPLE

Too many languages – research on escaping domestic violence in London

A London research project set up focus groups with women on their experiences of help in escaping domestic violence. One group included four women who needed interpreters for different languages – and of course their interpreters. The discussion was very difficult. Given the complexity and emotional sensitivity of the topic area, having participants speaking so many different languages was not a successful strategy. The point of focus groups is to allow discussion amongst the participants, and language problems made this impossible. Individual interviews or groups organised by language group might have been better.

Remember though that if you group people by language, this may mean that there are people from very different backgrounds in your group – and people whose attitudes towards each other are far from straightforward. For example another London focus group, this time on breast cancer and conducted in Turkish, included women from Cyprus, Turkey, and Kurdistan, and some hostile comments were made, arising from political tensions between these communities.

Sometimes, where a number of different languages are spoken, you will not be able to find an interpreter who can talk directly to all your respondents. For example, your interpreter speaks the national language and her own local language, plus English, but your respondent belongs to another language group. Is it worth proceeding in a situation where you need two stages of translation to communicate – someone who can translate into the national language, for example, and then someone else who can translate into English? It depends on the skills of the interpreters, and what type of information is required. It is always a problem to exclude groups of respondents on the basis of their language group, as they may have particular experiences which you should hear about, as members of a specific ethnic group. But of course you cannot gather subtle and sensitive information with a room full of interpreters!

In choosing an interpreter, experienced researchers say that they would favour someone with good inter-personal skills (tact, an interest in what people are saying) over someone with better language skills. Exact translation is helpful, but the interpreter is the person the respondent is looking at during the interview, and if they do not look as if they are interested, respondents will be discouraged from speaking freely.

CHECKLIST   For working successfully with an interpreter

- ✓ Spend time with the person explaining the purpose of the research and how you like to work
- ✓ Clarify the role the interpreter is to play – are they a researcher? Or primarily an interpreter?
- ✓ Discuss the questions you want to ask, and find out how they work in their language. Ensure the interpreter is comfortable to ask these questions.
- ✓ Ensure that the interpreter understands that you want them to tell you exactly what the person or group is saying, and not edit or censor it
- ✓ Choose interpreters with good interpersonal skills as well as good language skills
- ✓ Learning to work with an interpreter is a skill in itself and takes time to perfect

---

CHECKLIST   For good communication

- ✓ Make sure your non-verbal signals demonstrate listening and respect
- ✓ Take time to build rapport and observe how people usually communicate before asking questions
- ✓ Adapt your ways of communicating to the group of people in question, and don't make assumptions about their abilities
- ✓ Use simple language and avoid jargon
- ✓ Visual materials can help focus discussions
- ✓ Never pretend to have understood when you have not
- ✓ And check that your respondents are understanding you by asking for feedback

Further Reading

McCrum, S. and Hughes, L. (1998) *Interviewing Children: A guide for journalists and others*. London: Save the Children.

Useful booklet, accompanied by an audio tape.

Boyden, J. and Ennew, J. (eds) (1997) *Children in Focus: A manual for participatory research with children*. Stockholm: Rädda Barnen.

Ward, L. (1997) *Seen and Heard: Involving disabled children and young people in research and development projects*. York: Joseph Rowntree Foundation.

15 How to Ensure Quality in Data-Gathering

In the next chapter, the most important techniques used in research for development work are described. But the quality of research depends as much on the way in which a technique is applied in practice, as on which technique is chosen. This chapter looks at the key issues that need to be considered in assuring good practice in fieldwork.

The issues discussed in this section are at the heart of the matter of doing research properly. They are greatly emphasised to researchers in their training. Making sure your tape recorder is working, making sure your respondent realises you are not able to give them practical help, making sure the questions you are asking make sense to people – not very exciting, but crucial. Some of the advice may seem obvious, but experience shows that all the kinds of mistakes that can be made will be made!

Some principles: 'rules for making rules'

The following rules are derived from Boyden and Ennew (1997) in relation to participatory research with children:

- Discover your own ignorance
- Look before you leap – observe and listen before starting to do any formal research
- Respect respondents
- Do nothing without permission
- Do no harm
- Be prepared to change

15.1 Consent

We have already discussed the importance of getting genuine consent from respondents to participate in research in Chapter 13 on ethics. This may be a particular issue for development workers where potential respondents may associate them with benefits they hope to gain from programmes their agency carries out, and may think that participating in research could affect their likelihood of so benefiting. The issue of how to explain research to respondents so that they really understand is a practical one which needs to be addressed in every research project.

It is important to remember that people may have no experience of the kind of research you are doing, and may jump to unexpected conclusions. For example, a respondent I approached recently thought that I was making a TV documentary, even though she had already had two conversations and a detailed letter about the research.

Rehearse what you will say to people in explaining the purpose of the research, and eliminate all jargon from your account. It is also crucial to be clear that people will not personally benefit from taking part, nor suffer any ill consequence from not taking part. It is helpful to be specific about this – for example, if the research was to collect their views of an aspect of health care, it would be helpful to say something like 'whether or not you partici- pate in this research will not in any way affect your medical treatment'.

You need to ask specific permission to record what people are saying, whether you are taking notes or using a tape recorder. If you want to tape the interview or focus group, people will sometimes refuse consent for this, and you need to be prepared to cope (ie be ready to take notes instead). In asking permission, it can be helpful to emphasise that only you and perhaps one or two other people (who can be named) will hear the tape. People sometimes imagine themselves on national radio when they see a tape recorder!

15.2 Confidentiality

Again, this is discussed in general terms in Chapter 13, but the practicalities are of the essence. First, you need to decide what sort of undertakings about confidentiality to make. For some sorts of research, where community involvement is central, confidentiality is irrelevant, and no undertakings should be made to protect people's identities. In these situations, the whole process, in effect, needs to be a matter of public record, and people are not able to contribute unless they can stand by their evidence publicly. However in many situations it is appropriate to enable respondents to tell their story with the reassurance that identities will be protected, and their names will not appear in any final report.

Disempowered people generally have realistic concerns about what is known about them, whether known by their landlords, social security, or social services officials. There may be real risks for them in trusting you with sensitive information. You need to be prepared for people to be sceptical of your ability to keep information confidential, and willing to explain why you think you can do so.

Be as specific as possible in explaining to people exactly how you will protect their identities. It is best to avoid ever writing names and identifying details on questionnaires, and you can show respondents that their names are kept on a separate card and a code number assigned to them. Tell people exactly who will see or hear the material they give you. And again, be specific, for example, in a health care setting, explain that 'the doctors and nurses who look after you will not know whether or not you have taken part in this research' – or equivalent. However of course in a village, people will often know who has taken part in research, whatever you try to do as researchers.

With qualitative research, it can be worth saying that you will disguise stories you are told, if you think that they are so unusual that they might identify the respondent to others. You may want to offer respondents the chance to look over the information they have given you and check that they are happy for you to use it. It is easy for people to get carried away in telling their tale, and forget the purpose of an interview. Consent is a process, not a one-off event – people need to be able to withdraw it at any time. You could either read back the notes you have made at the end of an interview, or show the respondent a draft of your report, and then ask them to confirm that they are happy for you to use the material you are quoting from them.

Having assured respondents of the confidentiality of data, you must then follow this through by being scrupulous about office procedures which will actually make it so. Identifying details should be kept separately from data, and data should be locked away. It is also important, of course, to be rigorous about not verbally breaking confidentiality. Surprisingly often, professionals who are used to sharing personal information about people they are involved with will expect researchers to similarly tell them what people have said – you need to tactfully remind them of the different rules which apply to research information. As noted above, there will be times when you cannot guarantee confidentiality, and it is important then to make that clear too.

CHECKLIST   For ensuring confidentiality

✔ Never write names on questionnaires etc
✔ Ensure office procedures protect people's identities
✔ Change details of stories which may identify respondents

15.3   Recording

It is crucial to the success of your fieldwork that you choose an appropriate method of recording the information you set out to collect. Even methods which are to some extent self-recording, like participative mapping, require you to record the discussion which takes place while the work is going on. Recording for research should be as complete as possible – you should summarise and analyse later, not as you note what people are saying. Details whose importance you do not see at the time may come to the fore later on in your research process. This is where not jumping to conclusions comes in – keep an open mind, and simply record as much as you can.

TIP   It is really worth writing on only one side of the page, for your own notes and for recording interviews, etc – it helps you not to get in a muddle when analysing the material

There are a number of different ways of recording interviews, focus groups, and observations – first these will be briefly described, and then their strengths and weaknesses summarised.

Making notes during the interaction

This is sometimes the only option, and one gets better at it with practice. It is important to learn to make notes as unobtrusively as possible. It can be difficult to maintain eye contact with a respondent sufficiently to make them feel at ease while furiously scribbling notes.

One of the problems of semi-structured and depth interviewing is that you need to be thinking about the next question at the same time as writing notes from the last one – you inevitably miss some material.

Making notes after the interaction

This is obviously the least intrusive method of recording fieldwork events. However it relies on the memory to store a large amount of information and reproduce it accurately. You will inevitably lose some. If working in this way, it is essential to do your note-making as soon as possible after the event. We forget a lot very quickly, and by the next day a lot of information will have gone forever. In this situation it is helpful if you are able to return to the respondent after you have written up your notes to check any matters you found you were uncertain about.

Whilst it may often be a good thing if respondents are not made aware of your recording their words, it is important in terms of ethics to ensure that they understand that they are taking part in research.

Using an observer to make notes

This is common practice with focus groups, where an observer can free the facilitator to concentrate on the group process. It means introducing a non-participating person into the group, and this may put some people off, but if they are unobtrusive they are soon forgotten. The observer can note non-verbal communication as it happens.

It is also possible to use an observer in an interview situation. One person leads the interview and the other writes notes – this is freeing for the interviewer. This practice, for interviews or focus groups, also has the bene-fit of giving a second person a role in the fieldwork setting without 'throw-ing them in the deep end'. They can observe how a more experienced person carries out an interview, and can discuss how it went afterwards. Similarly, novice interviewers can be supported by someone more experienced.

Flipchart notes

Writing flipchart notes produces a summary of what has been said – it is not the same as a detailed record. However it is helpful in enabling participants to see the picture being built up from what they are saying. This can rein-force their sense of being heard, and can reduce repetition of key points. It can mean that a summary is agreed by the group by the end of the session. Where a summary is needed, this is good practice, as it avoids distortion of the group's intentions through analysis by the researcher – however it can implicitly give the message to the group that they are expected to agree with each other about what is important, which may suppress minority views. You may like to say, 'one point of view was this, another was that'.

Tape-recording

Tape-recording creates a complete record of what has been said. This avoids the problem of the interviewer getting distracted from the interview by the process of recording it. It captures people's own way of saying things, which can bring a report to life. However it has several drawbacks. Taping can make people self-conscious, though if you present it in a clear and low-key way, people will usually soon forget the tape is there. Transcribing tapes is a lot of work, and generates much detailed information which can be difficult to analyse. It depends on whether you need the details of people's points of view or only the gist.

As mentioned above, you need to be prepared to cope if people refuse to let you tape-record the interaction. You also need to be mentally prepared that occasionally tape machines fail, and you may need to write notes quickly after the event. Always check that the tape has worked.

It is best to use 90-minute tapes (45 minutes on each side) – the 15-minute ones you get in office dictating machines will stop just when your respondent has settled down to talking. There are now small, good quality portable machines. You can get a small microphone which lays flat on the ground, which is useful for taping group sessions, and another with a suction pad if you need to tape telephone interviews, as well as the standard kind which points towards one person.

EXAMPLE

When respondents are afraid: ex-child soldiers in Liberia

A qualitative study in Liberia of ex-child soldiers' views of help they received when they were demobilised planned to tape-record some interviews. Local people advised the researchers that using a tape recorder, or indeed writing notes in front of the respondent, would make people nervous. The civil war lasted a long time, there is still considerable fear of repression, and people are naturally suspicious.

Transcribing

Before deciding to rely on tape-recording, do think ahead about transcribing. This is a skilled task for which you need to be able to type well and quickly. Transcribing one hour of tape-recording takes anything up to five hours for an experienced transcriber. Focus groups are more difficult to transcribe than interviews. There are freelance professional transcribers, who are good value if you need a large amount of transcribing done.

Do not assume that an administrator can easily do transcribing – experience shows that this is not the case. You need to give detailed instructions about how you want the work done (ie you want every word as it is said), and it is always important to check transcripts against the tape.

If you want to do a substantial amount of transcribing in-house, it is worth getting a transcribing machine, which controls the tape by a foot pedal

Table 15.1   Different recording methods – advantages and disadvantages

Recording method	PROS	CONS
Making notes at the time	– Can be fairly accurate – Encourages you to summarise as you go along	– Difficult to do at the same time as interviewing – Some details will be missed – May put off respondents
Making notes afterwards	– Avoids making respondents aware of recording process, which can lead to freer discussion	– Quality depends greatly on skill of note-taker and how quickly notes can be written after the event
Using an observer to make notes	– Frees lead researcher to concentrate on the interview/focus group – Observer can note non-verbal communication too – Enables learning	– A silent person in the group might be off-putting for some – Observer needs good note-taking skills to capture everything that is said – Need a second researcher to be available
Flipchart notes	– Shows participants what is being recorded – enables them to disagree – Begins the process of analysis in the group	– Can collect only limited, superficial information – May discourage minority voices
Tape-recording	– Creates a full record of what has been said – Allows discussion to flow uninterrupted – Frees researchers from taking detailed notes – easier to give eye contact etc	– Time-consuming and expensive to transcribe and analyse – Need tape recorder, tapes, batteries, etc – May put off some respondents

to free the hands to type. Each time you stop the tape, it bounces back a little way, so you can check what you have just typed.

It is possible to use a tape to keep a record, but also to take notes at the time. Or rather than fully transcribing the tapes, you can listen to them and take notes. You can then use the tape to get important quotations accurate, or to check on that point when the dog barked and you got distracted. Tape recorders have little counters which enable you to make a note of where you were on the tape, as you do the interview, when something is said that you'd like to hear again, and then go back to it later.

Whatever method you use to record fieldwork interactions, you should also write notes as you go along recording your observations of the context you are working in, any interactions which occur 'behind the scenes' that may be relevant, and your own thoughts about what you find.

Recording and Interpreting

Working with interpreters adds another dimension to the recording process. Ideally you could tape the whole interaction. In one case, a researcher working in London only found out that the interpreter (actually a community worker without specialist training in interpreting) was not translating what her elderly Chinese respondents were saying, but was putting her own point of view, by getting another Chinese speaker to transcribe the tape. However it is to be hoped that you have worked out an excellent relationship with your interpreter, and this sort of thing could not happen! See Chapter 14.6 for how to do this.

It is important to spend time with the interpreter immediately after each interview, going through your own notes and checking anything you were not sure about. Matters may have been taken for granted between the two people sharing a culture, which could usefully be made explicit for you at this point. Equally you may simply not have understood exactly what was meant from a short translation of a complex statement.

CHECKLIST   For recording data

✓ Choose an appropriate method
✓ Check that it actually works in the conditions you are working in
✓ Check it is acceptable to each respondent, and be flexible if not
✓ Be scrupulous about recording everything you can as fully as you can

---

15.4 Ensuring 'Trustworthiness'

One big challenge to qualitative research, in particular, is the charge that we find what we set out to find – in effect that we select only those parts of respondents' testimony which suit our argument. And indeed the same is sometimes said about quantitative work – for example, it is true that doctors generally only publish the results of drug trials when the results are positive. A key way of keeping traditional scientific research 'honest' is the principle that it should be possible to replicate (copy) exactly what was done in the research, and come up with the same findings. This is the reason why the exact methods used are always given in research reports. Although for some sorts of research replication is impossible or irrelevant, the principle that it should be possible to trace exactly what was done is an important one.

You should leave a 'paper trail' which could be followed by someone else, documenting important processes and decisions. This is important in relation to sampling, data collection, and particularly analysis. It should be possible to see why you have arrived at the categories you use – or at least at which point these decisions were made. This discipline can also be useful if someone else needs to pick up your work from you.

15.5   Piloting Materials

In research we are always inventing new questionnaires, topic guides, interview schedules, observation schedules. You are urged throughout this manual to pilot these first, and this point cannot be emphasised too often. It is simply very wasteful to collect data from large numbers of people in such a way that you do not get the information back that you need. And even if, for example, you are carrying out only one focus group interview, you still need to test out your topic guide carefully. You will have only one go at getting it right – if people cannot follow your questions, you are wasting everyone's time.

The best pilot test is to try it out on a small group of people who are potentially part of your sample. If you cannot organise that, at least try it out on some friends or colleagues. Reading over a questionnaire is not at all the same as actually trying to fill it in. Ask people to use the materials as they are intended, not just to glance through the text. See also below, Chapter 17.1, 'Evaluating your draft questions'.

At times, even with good piloting, problems with a questionnaire become clear only after you have the first batch of proper interviews completed. It is still usually worth making changes, to ensure that you get the most useful information from the majority of your respondents. You may then have questions for which there are missing answers, from the first batch – this can be reported as such.

15.6   Logistics and Timing

A lot of research projects hit serious problems as they move from the planning stage into real fieldwork. This is where it is important to be flexible and learn from your experience. At times such practical barriers arise to carrying out data collection in the ways you imagined, that you have to regroup and try a completely different approach. For example, if people are not showing up for your focus group discussions, should you try individual interviews instead? If you can't get access to a suitable list to sample from, is there another way entirely of contacting your respondents, eg advertising in the local paper or on local radio, putting up a notice in a public place? Obviously you will need to look back at your aims and objectives and research questions to establish whether any change in tactics will be in keeping with the purpose of your project.

Timing can be a key issue in a whole series of ways. You obviously need to allow time to travel to remote villages, possibly by unreliable transport, and perhaps a little time to recover from the journey! Seasonal changes in workload can be important in terms of respondents' ability to spend time with you. Adverse weather conditions or national or religious holidays can make travel impossible. The time of day when you aim to carry out fieldwork also needs careful thought – many factors need to be considered, and it is definitely worth consulting respondents about what would be best for them.

15.7   Reflecting on Your Work

Finally, an important way of maintaining quality in research work is to pay attention to your own feelings and actions, and how others respond to you, and to reflect on their impact on the research process. At the most obvious level, do you think that people are giving you answers they think you want to hear? But equally, are you hearing more from some people than from others because you are a man or a woman, because of your age, your ethnic background, your perceived status? Are you feeling frustrated with your work, and is this coming through in how you deal with respondents?

As you carry out fieldwork, it is a good idea to write notes about how things went after each interaction with people – what went well? What might you do differently another time? And you might want to write some notes too about what you expected to find, and what actually happened.

If the research is a large part of your work over a period of time, it is really useful to keep a research diary, where you write notes regularly, recording your thoughts about the research – the content and the process – as you go along. This develops the habit of reflection, and can be therapeutic, if you feel alone with your problems! But it also creates a record of your expectations and struggles which can be used as data later on in the process. An ethnographic project would include this diary writing as part of a more intensive process of recording observations of all relevant aspects of daily life.

Finally when you are part of a research team, reflection should be built in to your work process. Each phase of the process should be discussed together, and suggestions for improvements made. However do not rush to criticise, when people are finding their feet. When opening up discussion of how a piece of work has gone, first ask the person who, for example, led the interview under discussion, to give their own reflections on how it went, and what might have been better. Only then allow others to give their opinions, and temper negative comment with praise for what was good.

CHECKLIST   For quality in data-gathering

✓ Find an appropriate method of recording your data, and use it systematically and consistently

✓ Keep notes of all research decisions you make and the reasons for them

✓ Pilot-test all questionnaires, focus group topic guides, observation guides, etc

✓ Be very careful to ensure that you are getting genuine informed consent to participating in your research

✓ Ensure that your agreed procedures to protect respondents' confidentiality/anonymity are consistently carried out

✓ Be aware of your own strengths and weaknesses in relation to data-gathering skills

✓ Reflect on fieldwork experience continually, and make improvements as you go along

---

Further Reading

Denscombe, M. (1998) *The Good Research Guide for Small-Scale Social Research Projects*. Buckingham and Philadelphia: The Open University Press.

Includes useful practical guidance on how to use a number of research methods and approaches.

16 Choosing Methods

This chapter aims to assist you in deciding which methods to use for your project. You need to make decisions of two kinds – first of all, which overall approach you intend to take to your research, and secondly, which techniques (such as interviews, observation) you will use within that. We will look first at some issues involved in choosing your broad approach, and then at factors to consider in deciding on specific techniques to use. There are many factors to consider in choosing methods, but your decisions should be guided primarily by the aims of the research. It is often best to use more than one technique within your investigation, to 'triangulate' the evidence you collect, so you are not here engaged in a search for one perfect technique.

16.1   First, Step Back

Before you start to choose methods, you need to get the purpose of the research as clear as possible in your mind:

- the research focus (see Chapter 5.3)
- the aims and objectives (see 6.2.2)
- the research questions (see 5.4), and
- the audience/s (see 6.2.3).

Look back at Chapters 5 and 6, and if need be have another go at clarifying the brief for the project. Writing out some precise research questions or identifying a hypothesis are the steps most likely to help you in establishing which methods you will need to use. Are you asking 'how many?' type questions? Or do your questions tend to concern 'how' or 'why' people do things? Look at the questions you are writing, and try to imagine what kinds of answers you might find to them – then consider what methods might lead to this sort of information.

> **COMMON PITFALLS 16.1**   Deciding which methods you will use before you are clear on the purpose of the research

16.2   Choosing a Research Approach

The following are some of the key issues to consider in deciding on the general approach you will take to your work:

- Purpose/audience?
- Positivist or social constructionist?
- Quantitative and/or qualitative?
- Individual or collective methods?
- Level of participation of community members and other stakeholders?
- Short- or long-term research?

Look back at Part One, especially Chapters 2, 3 and 5 and recall which approach you are intending to take, within these broad frameworks.

Each of these issues will be discussed briefly below. It may be helpful also to look at Chapter 18, which discusses various packages of methods commonly used in development work, such as action research, case studies, peer research, PLA, and so on.

Purpose/audience?

The distinction made in Chapter 2.3 between programme-focused and policy-focused research is important here. You need to decide what will be good enough evidence for you to rely on, given the purpose you have in mind. Think not only about the quality you require, but also the nature of the information you will need, and the kinds of processes which will be helpful to your project.

Who needs to have confidence in the findings of your research? What are their values, and ideas about what is valid evidence? Are they interested in community members' views? Or do they only recognise traditional 'scientific' approaches?

Having said this, we know that most decision-makers the world over will tell you that they favour what they like to call 'hard facts', usually meaning large surveys, for more or less any purpose. However remember that it is not the case that this type of research is in practice necessarily listened to. It is clear that in practice, participatory styles of research can influence decision-makers. A strong case study which explores relevant themes in a convincing way is also influential. So don't necessarily take what people say about the kind of research they trust at face value.

In making this choice, consider the political issues around the case you want to make as well. There is no point in trying to make a highly controversial point through a style of research which is also seen as highly controversial. Your substantive point will be lost in the chorus of voices denying the validity of your work.

Positivist or social constructionist?

Traditionally, research has often been divided into quantitative and qualitative methods (see below), but the prior decision to make is really whether you are aiming to work within the positivist scheme of things, or whether to work within a social constructionist framework, which challenges positivism. This distinction was discussed in Chapter 2.2. Positivist approaches see research as ideally an unbiased investigation of reality, which is 'out there' to be observed. Social research should in this view be as like the natural sciences as possible.

Social constructionist approaches maintain that there is no one 'right answer' out there waiting to be identified. Research should accept that the researched are actively engaged in constructing their world, as is the researcher. There will always be different ways of seeing things and a range of interpretations that can be made.

It may be helpful to look back at the example given in 2.2, which showed how a study of the situation of children in a refugee camp might be undertaken differently within each of these traditions. Each has its strengths and weaknesses, and much research in practice draws on both traditions. What really makes for bad research is to fail to decide which sets of rules you are playing to, and therefore produce work which meets the criteria for neither approach. One example would be to ask open questions of respondents you have gathered in a haphazard way, and to then start adding up their responses and reporting percentages as if they were taking part in a survey.

Quantitative and/or qualitative?

The choice between research that gives you numbers and research that produces mainly words has long been seen as a key issue in social science. However it is not helpful to feel that you need to 'pick sides' on this. Very often you do need qualitative information, but you also need some sense of the scale of things, some element of quantification.

Semi-structured interviews, a common technique, typically collect both qualitative and quantitative information. However it is not OK, for example, to start quantifying focus group data – counting how many people mention a particular issue, for instance. Because it is part of a group discussion, you cannot place any great significance on whether or not people mention particular issues. If you want to collect some information on an individual basis alongside your group work, you could, for example, ask participants to fill out a questionnaire before or after the focus group.

Many of us are prejudiced in one way or another by our past experience in relation to quantitative or qualitative methods. Leedy (1997) counsels that 'avoiding statistics or hating maths is not a good reason for choosing a qualitative study'. Equally, fearing the complexity of the answers you may get is not a good reason to avoid qualitative work. Your own skills come into the decision as to whether you undertake the research yourself, and what types of help you may need to buy in, but they should not restrict the kinds of information you are able to consider collecting.

Individual or collective methods?

Some research methods are focused on individuals, others on groups of people – village communities, interest groups, or households. It is important to be clear what type of information, and what kind of process, you need for your project. Traditional positivist research (see Chapter 2.2) has tended to focus on the individual, aiming to collect information in as private and confidential a way as possible. Participatory approaches, and PLA in particular, tend to be more interested in the collective level. There are problems with both approaches – as ever, it depends on the purpose of the research as to which one is best.

It is well-known that people do respond differently depending on the context in which they are asked questions. The impulse to give 'socially acceptable' answers may be an issue in any research, but is stronger when working with groups. However it may also be argued that in closely knit societies, people are more likely to be able to misrepresent their situation, for example in relation to their economic resources, when interviewed individually, than in a group.

One particular issue to look out for is the problem of inequalities within the household. In assessing the well-being of members of a household, it cannot be assumed that men, women, children, younger and older people share their resources in an equitable way. Or that they do not. However it may be unacceptable to ask to talk to people separately from other family members – it will often be assumed that the head of the household should answer for the others. This has been a big concern for researchers (Pratt and Loizos, 1992). One approach is to assign someone in your team to talk to the men of a household, while another goes around to the kitchen and talks to the women, or out into the yard to see the children. The question for your piece of research is – what do you really need to know? What information can you actually use?

A combination of methods will make it possible to get information of both kinds. And you can work with groups in different ways. Whole-village meetings will inevitably to some extent be dominated by whatever local groups hold the most power – men, the better-off, those with most education. However it is possible to specifically convene group discussions with people whose view you are interested in, but who might not otherwise speak up – younger women, landless labourers, minority ethnic groups. To counteract group bias, it may be best to ensure that some data is also collected from individuals, as some information is unlikely to be shared in front of any of one's neighbours, however close the relationship.

The key point is to be conscious of the choices you make. When you get to analysing the data, it will be important to be clear whether you have information relating to individuals or groups. Data from group and individual discussions are quite different types of material, and need to be analysed differently.

Pratt and Loizos (1992) identify some more pitfalls which can cause problems in development-related research:

- *Avoid false certainty about people's class*
- *Do not assume solidarity* – 'to share a characteristic is no guarantee of a sense of having "something in common"'
- *Do not assume community* – 'living near to each other [does not] automatically lead to something called "community spirit"'
- *Do not read rural patterns into urban contexts (or vice versa)*
- *Avoid over-reliance on particular informants*

Level of participation of community members and stakeholders?

There are many issues to consider here, discussed at length in Chapter 3. If community members are to be involved in deciding on which methods to use, it is important for them to be able to practise a range of methods, so that they have a real choice. Otherwise they are likely to pick whatever is most familiar to them – in the South perhaps PLA methods, in the North perhaps questionnaires or interviews.

Short- or long-term research?

Some research methods inherently take a long time. Major surveys are usually in this category, as are complex case studies. Other methods may look quick and simple, but turn out differently. For example, it can be quick to run a focus group with an existing community group, but if you are bringing people together specially, the process of organising the group meeting can be time-consuming. Analysis and writing are rarely as quick as anyone hopes.

Much research in development work is done to extremely tight time-scales. In some cases so little time is taken that it is hard to see how there could be much reflection on the data collected. Perhaps this is where research overlaps with consultancy, and what is really happening is less a process of data collection and analysis than one where the consultant's theoretical framework is tried out on a new situation, as described by those involved in the project.

At times, of course, there are very good reasons for undertaking research in a hurry. However sometimes it seems to be assumed that only very rushed research can be attempted, perhaps because of the importance and urgency of the issue under consideration. But working fast has real costs in terms of the quality of the research which can be done. In particular, the process of building trust with both community members and other organisations is inherently slow, and if it is not done, sources of data available to you will be severely limited.

Many of the issues which require investigation in development are actually deep-rooted and long term. Where this is the case, it is unlikely that research conducted at a breathless pace will get to the bottom of the matter. It might be better to invest in a solid piece of research that can produce more reliable results than to expect several short-term projects to add up to substantial evidence.

Some of the most powerful research designs involve comparisons over time. In evaluation research, collecting information before and after an intervention, or at stages throughout its life, greatly strengthens the ability to draw conclusions from what is found. The same applies to studies of the impact of a particular policy change. To follow the fortunes of a group of people in the context of the AIDS epidemic or after economic liberalisation, for example, a series of 'snapshot' studies at intervals over a number of years, could be much more convincing than a study carried out at one point in time only.

The use of multiple methods can sometimes allow for an early report on the findings of elements of a piece of research, enabling action to proceed in light of these, while the more in-depth research proceeds more slowly.

It is also worth saying again here that with policy-oriented research, it is important not to 'miss the boat' by failing to produce your evidence in time for the relevant decision-making process.

16.3   Choosing Research Techniques

Once you are clear about the broad approach you want to take, you need to move on to choose specific techniques. These can be selected from the seven key techniques described in the next chapter, or you may use other less common ones or invent new ones. In deciding on specific techniques, you need to take some further issues into account.

Good communication

Your research will only be as good as your communication with the people you are working with. Consider carefully what types of communication the people you are concerned with find most comfortable, and those for which they may have only negative experiences.

Obviously some people cannot read or write, and some will also be unfamiliar with drawing – though people can learn some new techniques, they will be most at home just talking to you (See also Chapter 14). Though verbal communication is most comfortable for many people, this should not be assumed. Where people are used to it, for example for some groups of school children, asking respondents to fill in a questionnaire is a very confidential and straightforward way to collect data. On the other hand some people will associate forms with threatening dealings with officialdom.

Group work is familiar to some people, but they may be used to using it for different purposes. For example, for a research-oriented focus group, you would need to brief participants that they do not need to agree with each other, or to come to any consensus on the issues in question. Other people will not be accustomed to speaking up in group settings, and will not find it easy to participate.

Remember that in any group of people, in addition to those who obviously have disabilities, there will be some with some communication impairment – those who are deaf or hard of hearing, those who do not see well, those with speech difficulties, eg who have had a stroke. And of course those who had a more limited education than their neighbours. If you think carefully about communicating with all these people, and aim positively to include disabled people, you will also make life easier for everyone else, who might have struggled through anyway. More guidance on this is given in Chapter 14.4.

Another problem can be how to get people's attention, and sometimes choosing an unusual, attractive research method can make a real difference. Use your imagination. Another way is to use valued technology. Some researchers who need to collect information from busy officials have found that sending questionnaires by fax leads to higher response rates!

Language issues are discussed in Chapter 14.6.

Recording and analysis

When you are deciding on which techniques to use, consider the whole process you will follow in collecting and analysing the material, not just the face-to-face situation. In choosing ways of recording the data, for example, if you choose to ask people to fill in questionnaires themselves, check that they are actually giving you the type of responses you need, before committing yourself to this method. (See Chapter 15.3, on recording methods.) Piloting generally identifies problems of this kind.

Do also pilot-test your methods of analysis. This is most important, as it is only when you try to analyse the material you collect that you are forced to connect the material you get from people with the questions you set out with. The other reason to worry about analysis early is that you need to establish whether you can do the analysis yourself, or whether you will need help. Both quantitative and qualitative analysis can be tricky, in different ways. And if you are going to involve someone else in analysing the data, it will be greatly beneficial if you get their advice on the approach and techniques that you are using, as soon as you can.

If you plan to undertake large-scale survey work or any research where you aim to use a representative sample, it is crucial to consult a statistician about the size and nature of the sample you need for your purposes.

Sensitive subjects

Sometimes research for development work concerns issues everyone is happy to talk publicly about, but often we are trying to open up issues which are traditionally kept hidden. Issues around sexuality, domestic violence, family planning, HIV/AIDS are obvious examples, but in many cultures people are reluctant to talk directly about their income, too. Money can be a more sensitive subject than sex! If you work closely with community members, they can guide you as to what people may have difficulties with.

People's fears are likely to be based on a rational calculation of the risks involved – for example, a violent man is likely to be provoked by his wife taking part in research he disapproves of. Researchers need to be careful that their intervention is worthwhile in terms of the risks to which it potentially exposes respondents.

Choice of appropriate methods can help a great deal in approaching difficult subjects in an acceptable way. Other factors, like ensuring that you have proper consent from respondents (see Chapters 13.3 and 15.1) are also of course important, whatever methods you use. But do not jump to conclusions about which methods people will find most suitable. What seems private and safe to one group may seem threatening to another.

Focus groups have been used successfully for a wide range of issues which might be assumed to be too private to discuss in a group. If people feel that the others in the group are in the same position that they are in, they will often greatly enjoy sharing experiences which attract stigma in the broader society. Groups have discussed HIV prevention, and the care for terminally ill cancer patients, without difficulties, for example. However there are limits. The student who was planning to undertake a focus group in an English hospital with men and their partners where the men were receiving medical treatment for sexual problems had to be persuaded that questionnaires might make it easier for respondents to express their views!

The use of some sort of stimulus material, or a warm-up exercise, can be helpful in encouraging people to talk openly about subjects they may find difficult. However don't beat about the bush! If you are embarrassed, you will convey your embarrassment to your respondents.

Experience or opinion?

It may be helpful to consider whether the material you need to tap is essentially a matter of gathering information about people's experiences, or whether you want to encourage them to give their opinions. When collecting views, it is important to realise that people may not have fully-formed views on the issues you are investigating. This is why simple yes/no questionnaires can be so frustrating on issues like this. What weight can you give to which box people tick if it is not likely that they have really thought through the issues?

There are two points to make here. First of all, if you want to gather both types of material, make sure you allow time for people to properly tell their story, so that you do not short-cut the process of understanding people's experiences, in your haste to get on to asking their opinions. Experience is the more solid thing – opinions may change, as people think further about the issues.

Secondly, in gathering opinions, there can be a problem of people having limited experience, and hence only limited ideas about what might improve their lives. Group work can give 'strength in numbers', and enable more creative thought, where one person will build on another's ideas. Whether in a group or in individual situations, if you want imaginative answers, you need to give people time to think, and not just tack on questions about what might be better at the end of an interview.

Pilot-testing your methods

It is important to try out questionnaires and other research tools in order to check that all the details are right, eg questions asked in the best way. However when you pilot your research materials you should also be checking whether *the technique itself* is right for the exercise. You may want to change more radically than just rewriting parts of an interview schedule, perhaps realising that including an element of observation might be a good idea, or even that you are asking your questions of the wrong people. Pay attention within the pilot stage to how difficult it was to contact respondents, how they reacted to the materials you used with them – ask them their views directly. They may be able to guide you towards more effective approaches.

A common problem is that of trying to do too much at once. If the materials you are using seem unwieldy, consider breaking down the research process you are undertaking into smaller elements. This makes the whole thing much more manageable.

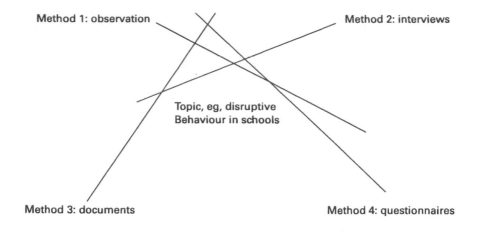

Method 1: observation

Method 2: interviews

Topic, eg, disruptive
Behaviour in schools

Method 3: documents

Method 4: questionnaires

Figure 16.1 Methodological triangulation

Get advice

The choice of methods is another very important point in the research process to ask advice from one or more experienced researchers. When you have worked on several research projects you get a much better 'feel' for what data is generated by which research methods, and many researchers will be interested to give you their view on this, knowing that this may be the last opportunity to get it right.

16.4   Triangulation – Using More than One Technique

Triangulation is an important concept to understand in planning research. The term comes from surveying, where it is a method of finding out where something is by getting a 'fix' on it from two or more places. A calculation is then made, using the known properties of triangles to work out distances. As this image suggests, the idea is to look at the same thing from different points of view and in different ways. Triangulation in social research can be done by using multiple and different sources (for example informants), methods, investigators/analysts, or theories (Denzin, 1988).

The idea of triangulation is used within the Participatory Learning and Action (PLA) tradition, referring to the use of different techniques, asking questions of different groups of people, and to the involvement of a range of investigators, perhaps with different kinds of training or different sensitivities.

EXAMPLE

Triangulation in practice: studying drought in Malawi, Zambia, and Zimbabwe

A Participatory Learning and Action study of the 1992 drought in Malawi, Zambia, and Zimbabwe used a range of methods in 24 villages in each country. Mapping, calendar tables, interviews, and scoring techniques were used with men, women, and children from three different wealth categories. Several cross-checks were used to validate the results: internal consistency within one household; internal consistency between several households; checks between answers given by individual households and those given in the group discussions; secondary data; direct observation. In addition six of the villages were visited in a follow-up study. The objectives of this study were to discuss and check the results and policy conclusions with smallholders. In all six cases they endorsed and in some cases enlarged upon the findings and recommendations (Eldridge, 1993).

Why is it thought important to collect information in different ways within one project? Essentially it is because we have to accept that the means through which data is collected has an effect on the findings. Therefore if we want to build confidence in the trustworthiness of our research, it is helpful to collect information in different ways. Of course this links for development workers to the familiar process of taking account of the views of all stakeholders. For example if you were investigating water use, you might want to do some observation, as well as detailed interviews with different types of people (women, children, men, those with land to irrigate, those without), to supplement people's account of the community's needs as given in a group session.

As noted above, it is likely that you will want to include some element of quantitative data-collection alongside qualitative methods. But the key to triangulation is to see the same thing from different perspectives, and thus to be able to confirm or challenge the findings of one method with those from another. The sequence in which methods are used is important, and there should be opportunities to reflect on the meaning of any apparent contradictions.

The image of triangulation can, however, be questioned. A social constructionist approach would suggest that there is no one social 'thing' which can be seen from different angles – but that the accounts collected from different perspectives may not match tidily at all. There may be mismatch and even conflict between them. A mismatch does not necessarily mean that the data collection process is flawed – it could be that people just have very different accounts of similar phenomena. You need to critically examine the meaning of any mismatches to make sense of them.

> **CHECKLIST**   For choosing methods
>
> ✓ Methods must be chosen in the light of the research focus, aims and objectives, research questions, and the hypothesis (if there is one)
> ✓ It is usually best to use more than one research technique in any project, to 'triangulate' the information you collect
> ✓ The audience you want to influence is a factor to consider in your choice of methods
> ✓ Think ahead about how you will record and analyse your data when you choose a method
> ✓ Take account of what you know about communication with this group of people in choosing techniques
> ✓ When you have chosen a technique and are pilot-testing it, if you find major problems, consider changing to a wholly different technique

Further Reading

Pratt, B. and Loizos, P. (1992) *Choosing Research Methods*, Oxfam Development Guidelines, No. 7. Oxford: Oxfam.

Written for development workers, based on field experience. Includes discussion of factors to consider in choosing methods, and a summary of some possible approaches.

Leedy, P.D. (1997) *Practical Research: Planning and design*, 6th edition. New Jersey: Merrill, Prentice Hall.

Includes direct discussion of how to choose methods – primarily written for researchers, but clear and interesting to read.

Wadsworth, Y. (1997) *Do It Yourself Social Research*, 2nd edition. St Leonards, Australia: Allen and Unwin.

Written for community organisations, helpful in resisting pressures about what constitutes 'proper research'.

Craig, G. (1998) *Women's Views Count: Building responsive maternity services*. London: The College of Health.

Written to assist in identifying appropriate methods for assessing satisfaction with UK maternity services, this is a very thorough and helpful presentation of a range of different research methods. Includes a useful section on choosing a method.

<table>
<tr>
<td>

17

</td>
<td>

Seven Key Research Techniques

</td>
</tr>
</table>

This chapter focuses on seven of the most useful methods in research for development work. Since there are many other books which give detailed guidance on methods, each technique is briefly described here, along with comments on its strengths and limitations. This chapter needs to be read alongside those on how to choose a method (16), sampling (19), and negotiating access (8.3). It is important to make sure that you are clear on the aims and objectives, and the research focus and key research questions for your study, before you begin to choose methods for it (See Chapter 5). There is no 'good method', just methods fit for their purpose.

Chapter 18 goes on to look at some packages of methods used in development-related research, for example needs assessment, action research, case studies, and so on. These all require the use of one or usually more of the techniques described in this chapter, in different combinations.

After a short general section on how to ask questions, this chapter concentrates on giving guidance on seven key research techniques:

- interviews,
- focus groups,
- documentary sources,
- observation,
- questionnaires,
- ranking exercises, and
- visual methods,

plus a short final section mentioning some other options. This manual aims to recommend tried and tested approaches, rather than emphasising new and experimental ways of working. There are many, many others, but you can get a long way with these few techniques. Learn to do an effective interview, and you will be a good way on the path to becoming a competent researcher.

17.1 How to ask Questions

This section offers guidance on how to develop good questions for use in research, whether they are for an interview, a focus group, or a questionnaire.

Some specific guidelines for the particular techniques are given in the different sections below, but there is much in common, and these core rules are described here.

CHECKLIST   For writing good questions

Questions need to be:

✓ Necessary to the research
✓ Clear and completely unambiguous
✓ Simple, one thing at a time
✓ In everyday language – no jargon, no technical language
✓ Interesting to respondents
✓ About things respondents will have information about – it's not a test
✓ Directed to the respondent – better not to ask one person to answer for others
✓ Questions should be asked in a neutral way – see below for types of question to avoid

---

Types of questions to avoid

- Leading questions – eg 'would you agree that education should have high priority for government spending?'
- Vague questions – eg 'what do you think about the education you have received?'
- 'Presuming' questions – eg 'what qualifications did you leave school with?'
- Multiple questions (two or more questions in one) – eg 'why did you leave school and what have you done since?'
- Hypothetical questions – eg 'if you had been able to complete your schooling, what would you be doing today?'
- Questions which contain value judgements – eg 'were you forced to drop out of school at an early age?'
- Offensive, irritating or insensitive questions – eg 'why do you not think it important to pay for your child's schooling?'

How to avoid asking leading questions

Leading questions encourage the respondent to answer in a particular way. They make it difficult to disagree, by the way they are expressed. For example, asked in a group setting:

'Who agrees that capital punishment is wrong?'

is a leading question. Questions must be reworded in a more neutral way, for example:

'Do you think that capital punishment is right or wrong?',

could still lead to yes or no answers; or if you wanted to hear more about the respondents' views you could ask:

'What do you think about capital punishment?'

If you allow leading questions to slip through, it makes it easy for opponents of your point of view to discredit your research. It can be surprisingly difficult to spot leading questions, on issues close to your heart, so ask someone who is not involved in your work to check your questions with this in mind.

Questions need to be placed in a logical order. Make sure to start with an interesting but straightforward question, to which everyone will have some answer. This will get you off to a good start, helping respondents to feel confident. Keep more challenging questions till later.

In terms of the process you follow:

- Draft your questions early, and expect to redraft them many times.
- However you can leave collecting any 'boring details' to the end, as these can remind people of 'official', assessment-type interviews and put them on the defensive. But do remember to collect any details you will need later.
- Think about how you are going to analyse the answers you may get to your questions, and change them if this throws up problems.
- Pilot-test your questions – first by asking a number of people to read them over, and then, with corrections made, by getting some people to work through them and try to answer them. Finally, test them out on a small group from your final sample, to see how they work in 'real life'. Each of these stages can reveal major issues which can then be sorted out.

Evaluating your draft questions

It is easy to get carried away with all the interesting things you could ask. And it can be surprisingly difficult to work out how to ask the questions that will really answer your key research questions. But it is important not to load down the questionnaire or interview schedule with inessential questions, and to ensure that you do include those which will be key in shedding light on your research problem.

When you critically read your draft questions, think about the following points:

- Look back at your research focus, and your key research questions, (see Chapter 5) and check that it gets at answers to these.
- Think about what kinds of reply you anticipate getting to your questions, and try to imagine how you will use this type of information in making

your arguments in the final report – what is the story you want to tell? Will this material enable you to do so?

- How do you see the analysis of the data working? Read Chapter 20 before finalising your questions, and think through how the replies to each question will be analysed. Consult anyone you hope will help you in the analysis at this stage.
- Analyse which type of question each one on your questionnaire/topic guide is, and check that it is right for its purpose.
- And just check – you are asking the right group of people, aren't you?

Sometimes we assume that we must research the powerless, when actually our problems lie in understanding the thinking and behaviour of the powerful.

Experienced researchers do get skilled at seeing which are good and which are bad questions for a particular purpose, and it is always worthwhile showing a draft to at least one researcher.

17.2   Interviews

What is an interview?

This section will look at one-to-one interviews, where a series of questions are addressed to an informant, and their responses recorded. Group interviews (focus groups) will be considered separately, as will self-completion question-naires. For a general discussion on how to achieve effective communication in research, especially relevant to interviews perhaps, see Chapter 14.

All sorts of professional workers undertake interviews as part of their daily work, but a research interview follows quite different rules from these. It may be necessary to consciously un-learn some of the habits you have developed for interviewing in other contexts. As we shall see, the 'rules' for research interviews also depend upon the type of interviewing involved.

The rest of this section focuses on individual semi-structured and depth interviews. Guidelines for highly structured interviews are more akin to those for questionnaires, see 17.6 below.

When should you use interviews for research?

Interviews are most useful when:

- You need to know about people's experiences or views in some depth.
- You are able to rely on information from a fairly small number of respondents.
- The issue is sensitive, and people may not be able to speak freely in groups.
- Your respondents would not be able to express themselves fully through a written questionnaire.

Table 17.1 Some types of interview

Structured	Semi-structured	Depth/unstructured
Useful when research questions are very precise, and quantified answers are needed	Useful where some quantitative and some qualitative information is needed	Useful to help set the research focus, or to explore new or sensitive topics in depth
Questions must be asked in a standard way	Questions may be asked in different ways, but some questions can be standard	More like a conversation – no standard questions, just topic areas
All questions must be asked	Questions can be left out and others added	Follow (or ask) the respondent to establish what is important to discuss
Most questions have pre-set answers to choose between	Include a mix of types of question – some open and some closed	Avoid questions which can be answered by 'yes' or 'no'
Results easy to analyse	Analysis is fairly straightforward	Analysis requires time and skill
Follow many of the same rules as questionnaires		Follow many of the same rules as focus groups

Continuum of structure in interviewing

Conducting an interview

Preparing for the interview

Please see section 17.1 above, on how to ask questions.

- Ensure that your recording method (note-taking, taping) is workable in the context in which you will be doing the interview.
- Eliminate all but the absolutely necessary questions – and then go back and eliminate some more!
- Be prepared that some respondents will not be able to be interviewed when you have arranged to do it – expect to have to call back for some of them. Their time is pressured too.

Opening up the interview

- Begin with an appropriate greeting and suitable small talk.
- Take enough time to introduce the research properly, and encourage discussion of its purpose. This is often not as simple as it sounds. It is well worth rehearsing before trying any interviews.

- Having explained about the research, give another opportunity for the respondent to withdraw their consent if they wish to. You should be clear with people that they will not directly benefit from participating in the research (though see also Chapter 19.3, on incentives), nor will they suffer any adverse consequence by not participating.
- Early questions should be as straightforward as possible – make sure all respondents will have a ready answer.

Monitoring progress

- Keep an appropriate level of eye contact, and note any non-verbal signals which might help in understanding what has been said.
- Encourage the interviewee to tell their story the way they want to, only later checking through your questions to make sure that their account contains the information you need.
- Look for the underlying logic of what the respondent is telling you.
- Ask sensitive questions only when the person seems to be at their ease with you.
- Look for apparent inconsistencies in what people are saying, and probe to discover the thinking behind them.
- Be on the lookout for the kind of answer which seems designed to distract you – probe further if you are unconvinced by answers you are hearing. But of course beware of seeming to interrogate your interviewee!
- Keep a discreet eye on the time.

Closing down the interview

- You may want to ask how the respondent has felt about the interview, and if there is anything else they would like to say.
- Repeat assurances of confidentiality.
- Give sincere thanks for the time the respondent has spent talking to you.
- It can be helpful to summarise the gist of what you think the person is saying back to them, so that they can check that you have got it right.
- After the interview, make notes for yourself about the context of the interview (eg small children present, respondent feeling unwell), and of any non-verbal communication you observed.

In Table 17.2 (below) a researcher comments on how he conducted a real interview.

How many people are involved?

Often, a research interview is literally one-to-one. However there are good reasons at times to have a third or even a fourth person present:

- Of course at times an interpreter is required.
- A second researcher can write notes while the first interviewer concentrates on asking questions.

Table 17.2 Interviewing by conversation. Reprinted by permission of Simon Dyson, from 'Interviewing by Conversation', *Sociology Review* 3 (4) April 1994.◆

Interviewing by conversation

ONE POSSIBLE METHOD of obtaining information for project work is by conducting an unstructured, in-depth interview, or as they are sometimes called interviews-as-conversations (Burgess, 1984). Interviewing is arguably a skill best acquired with practice; but some guidance may be derived from looking critically at actual interviews in order to debate their good and bad features. We have therefore asked Simon Dyson, Senior Lecturer in Health Studies at De Montfort University, Leicester, to introduce extracts from an actual interview. The interview is with Ben – a young man who suffers from a serious inherited blood disorder called sickle-cell anaemia. Sickle-cell primarily (although by no means exclusively) affects people of African-Caribbean descent. The interview itself lasted about 50 minutes and was videotaped. Also videotaped were a preliminary five minutes where the ground rules for the interview were negotiated, and a final five minutes debriefing after the interview was over. The extracts are presented in three columns. Firstly, there are the actual words of the interviewer Simon Dyson (SD) and of the respondent (Ben). In the second column there is a commentary from Simon Dyson on features of the interview. In the third column there are suggested issues for debate, questions to ask yourself if you intend to try to carry out some interviews by conversation, and ideas for further reading.

Interview transcript

SD: The next thing is whether I could check if I have your permission to use the videotape and the material in particular ways: firstly for teaching health studies students and other students about sickle-cell anaemia; secondly, for teaching a range of students about research methods including doing interviews; thirdly, whether I could use what you say anonymously if ever I come to write up

Author's commentary

This is part of a wider set of initial negotiations about the interview. Ben was asked to read through the checklist of questions to see if there were any proposed topics he objected to discussing. He was asked if he preferred to be anonymous (he did – Ben is therefore not his real name). He was reminded that he could change his mind at any time in the interview and ask for information not to be used. And he was asked for permission to use the

Issues and questions

This stage of interview negotiations is every bit as much part of the social situation of the interview as the interview itself, although it is a stage not always reported on in analysing the interview data. Indeed even this account excludes the real beginning, as there clearly had to be preliminary discussions about getting to the stage of sitting before a video camera. Further questions you may wish to debate are:

Continued

Table 17.2 Continued

Interview transcript	Author's commentary	Issues and questions
research articles about sickle-cell anaemia and people's experiences. Finally how you would feel about the local support group having access to the video for their educational purposes?... I know that's a lot of things to ask ... BEN: (laughs) SD: ... but would you be happy with all of those potential uses of the video and material? BEN: I don't see why not. Might as well go the whole hog. SD: Right. That's very good of you. Thank you. Obviously, if during the course of the interview I ask you a question you are unhappy about, please do say: 'well, I don't feel I can answer that, that question'. And of course, obviously you've got the right to withdraw and say: 'well I don't really think I can continue'. You know, that would be fine. BEN: OK. SD: I anticipate that, depending on how the interview is going, that the main interview might last between 45 minutes and an hour. So that's why I've got the water in, in case we die of thirst meanwhile.	interview for a number of specified purposes, as can be seen from the text of the interview. Other features to note about this section are: ▪ the way I adapt my initial question and add the phrase 'I know that's a lot of things to ask' in response to a short pause when I realise immediately that I may have asked too much of Ben; ▪ the way I give Ben some guidance about the amount of time I am hoping to spend with him. In fact I had already given him these time estimates before the day when the interview took place; ▪ how an interviewer's knowledge of a topic may help sensitivity towards the respondent. Having water available was important not only as a courtesy, but because people with sickle-cell anaemia need to keep up their intake of fluids.	▪ Should the interviewer have given Ben the opportunity to say yes or no to each of the four uses of the interview material, rather than yes or no to all four taken together? How might this have affected the chances of obtaining Ben's permission? ▪ Is the current use of the material as part of an article about research methods adequately covered by the second point on the list (i.e. 'teaching a range of students about research methods including doing interviews')? What effect might there be on the conduct of the interview arising from the respective statuses of interviewer (university tutor) and interviewee (university student)? ▪ In this example the interviewer is white. Ben is of African origin, and was in fact born in Nigeria. Try to find out what implications this 'social distance' in terms of 'race' may have on the interview according to existing literature. Write a 200 word summary of how the 'race' of interviewer and interviewee may alter the outcome of an interview.

SD: Ben, perhaps I could begin by asking you when it was that you were first aware that you had sickle-cell anaemia?

BEN: Well, I came over here when I was six years of age from Nigeria.

SD: Right.

BEN: And I don't think I'd have really been aware of anything until the age of about eight, nine years of age when my mum would be taking me to the sickle clinic at St Joseph's hospital.

SD: Right, right. What did you think was happening to you at the time? What was your understanding of what was happening to you?

BEN: I don't think I understood what was going on. But I knew there was something wrong with me. And I'd been told I had sickle-cell anaemia. But that didn't mean anything to me.

This is an extract taken from the beginning of the main interview. Features to note here are:

- The use of short words like 'right' (or in other parts of the interview 'OK', 'yes', or nods of the head) to signal that the interviewer is listening, interested and has understood what has been said to them.
- The opening question is only possible because I already knew that Ben knew he had sickle-cell anaemia. In other circumstances I should proceed by asking the respondent firstly to describe what is happening to them in their own words (to describe the pain, the ulcers, the tiredness or whatever). And secondly to ask for their own understanding of what is happening to them, as they might not know they had sickle-cell anaemia or they might know they had been given that medical label but not know what it meant. In fact I do know of at least one young person who suffers severe pain with sickle-cell anaemia but where neither the parents nor the health professionals have directly explained this to him.

- How would you phrase an opening question to a young person with sickle-cell anaemia (there are no doubts about his medical status since the condition is genetic) who did not know they had sickle-cell, or whom you were not certain they knew?
- Would it be ethical to interview such a person without telling them what you knew about their illness?

Simon Dyson had to address a similar problem when interviewing parents of children labelled 'mentally handicapped' when the parents do not agree with the label.

FURTHER READING

Dyson, S. (1987) *Mental Handicap.* Croom Helm.

Continued

Table 17.2 Continued

Interview transcript	Author's commentary	Issues and questions
SD: Had you been told or heard anything about sickle-cell anaemia before you came to Britain? Had it affected you before you were six years old? BEN: (pause) SD: As far as you can remember? BEN: Absolutely not. Absolutely not.	A poor choice of words. I have asked three questions in one – has he been told? Has he heard? Has he been affected? Little wonder that Ben hesitates to give a reply. However the extract does arguably illustrate two more positive features of the questioning: ■ the use of data gained earlier in the interview to help phrase questions; ■ the way that lengthening the question ('As far as you can remember?') can help encourage a reply.	For some suggestions about improving interview technique, particularly when interviewing about health-related issues. **FURTHER READING** Oyster, C., Hanten, W. and Llorens, L (1987) *Introduction to Research: A Guide for the Health Service Professional*: Pennsylvania, USA: Lippincott.
SD: You say she's [Ben's mother] sometimes a little overprotective. How does that show itself? What kind of things does she do? BEN: Well, I'm supposed to keep warm when it's really cold outside because I'm pretty sensitive to that. And she's always asking me, you know, 'Have you got a jumper on?' 'Have you taken your coat?' It's really cold outside.' If I've anything slightly wrong with me, I won't want to go to the doctor's but she'll be urging me to go to the doctor's in that sense. And she probably spoils me compared to my sisters basically.	An example of a question which probes for further information and seeks clarification of a term Ben introduces himself. I reflect back to Ben the actual word I think he has used ('overprotective'). Whilst I might have my own perception of what this concept means, I try to put this to one side and ask Ben for his understanding of 'overprotective'. Note that I do not ask for an abstract definition, but for specific categories of behaviour which he feels represent this concept.	See Chapter 5 in Burgess (1984) below, for a discussion of asking questions which help show the mental categories people have for their behaviour, and for useful guidance on reflecting back to the respondent what they have said. **FURTHER READING** Burgess, R. (1984) *In The Field*. Unwin Hyman.

SD: Could you describe for me Ben any time in your life when you've had physical or painful problems arising out of sickle-cell?

This proves to be a particularly well-received question. It produces a reply in which Ben speaks without interruption for 4 minutes 15 seconds and covers a whole range of issues listed below:

- what parts of the body he gets pains in;
- the impact of pain on his student career;
- the first time he had pain;
- a five-day period spent in hospital;
- his reduced participation in sports;
- exams as a stressor causing pain crises;
- his visual impairment from sickle-cell;
- 'Why is this happening to me?';
- his sisters' statuses as carriers;
- his feelings of depression;
- his feelings that he is more fortunate than other people with sickle-cell anaemia who have more frequent painful crises than he does.

This is arguably where interviewing by conversation comes into its own. I tend to judge the relative success of such an interview by whether the transcript of the interview contains more of the interviewee than the interviewer. Clearly quantity is not the only, or even the primary, measure of success, but it does give an indication that the interviewee has had an opponunity to:

- Express themselves fully on their own terms;
- use their own words;
- take the conversation in directions that are important to them.

However, can you think of any problems with giving people space to express themselves verbally? Think about respondents from different social classes or educational backgrounds or different genders.

Continued

Table 17.2 Continued

Interview transcript	Author's commentary	Issues and questions
SD: Were there any other periods when you had to be in hospital for a painful crisis after the initial one when you were seven or eight years old? Ben: Err ... yes, there was. I'm surprised. I actually nearly forgot about that. That would have been quite near to my 18th birthday.	An example of a relatively successful question, in which I try to make sure that the category in question (painful crises) is exhausted before moving on to the next. An example of what Whyte (1984) calls probing an idea earlier in an interview before the immediately preceding block of conversation. **FURTHER READING** Whyte. W.F. (1984) *Learning From the Field: A Guide From Experience*. Sage.	Whyte (1984) suggests that in a 'non-directive interview' there are actually gradations of directiveness: ■ encouragements (nods of the head, words like 'right', 'OK', 'yes') – to encourage the speaker to continue; ■ reflecting back to the respondent his/her own words to encourage them to continue and/or elaborate on their train of thought; ● probing the respondent's last remark; ● probe an idea before the last remark, but within the previous block of talking; ■ probe an idea from an earlier part of the interview, before the immediately preceding block of conversation; ■ introduce a new topic.

SD: What about the nursing staff at the second hospital? Was there anything that you feel you need to say about them, compared to say the nursing staff at the first hospital?

BEN: ... not really, not really. Because I think that in both cases they're just following the doctors' orders.

A truly dreadful question, in which I let my own preconceptions influence my line of questioning to the extent that I appear to be pushing Ben to be critical of the nurses. I had been misled by my experience of interviewing others with sickle-cell anaemia who had been extremely critical of staff's lack of sympathy with the pain they were in.

SD: Can I ask you about some of the tests? You mentioned the kind of pre-natal test. Urn ... How, as someone with sickle-cell anaemia. how does the whole situation in which some people do make the decision, when they know that they have a ... a possible child who has sickle-cell, to abort that child. How does that make you feel? What feelings do you have about that?

This is arguably the question dealing with the most sensitive issue in the whole interview. That as the interviewer I know how sensitive it is may be judged from the hesitations in the phrasing of the question. However, my chances of obtaining an answer to such a question were helped by a number of factors:

- the question is sited approximately 40 minutes into the interview, when some

If you have access to a video camera or to an audio-cassette player, try carrying out an interview by conversation with a friend or colleague. When you play the tape back try to spot your own mistakes in leading your respondent. Or let other colleagues point out your mistakes for you!

- what kind of issues and topics do you feel that respondents might be reluctant to talk about at interview? Why might they be reluctant?
- try to make a list of any topics or issues that you feel should not be asked of someone during an interview by conversation;
- what do you think the interviewer should do when asked for their own opinion on a sensitive topic?

Continued

Table 17.2 Continued

Interview transcript	Author's commentary	Issues and questions
BEN: Well... I can't really say that I blame them. And I'm not one to judge because I don't know until I'm in that actual situation what I would do myself. But I can only say that it does hurt a bit. If you've got sickle-cell anaemia and they decide to abort that's their decision. You know what someone with sickle-cell anaemia actually has to go through. And I know that I'm one of the lucky ones, because I've had relatively few – compared to some people – actual incidents from having the disease. So I'm not one to judge at all.	opportunity has been had to build up rapport with Ben; ■ Ben himself has raised the issue of the testing of foetuses in the womb for sickle-cell anaemia – the question of abortion is implicitly linked to this issue; ■ lengthening the question may help prepare the respondent for a sensitive topic.	**FURTHER READING** Oakley, A. (1981) 'Interviewing women: a contradiction in terms?' in Roberts, H. (ed.), *Doing Feminist Research*. Routledge and Kegan Paul.

*Dyson, S. (1994) Interviewing by Conversation, *Sociology Review* 3 (4) April 1994, pp 21–3. [ISSN 0959 8499. Philip Allan Publishers Market Place, Deddington, Oxford OX15 OSE] The interview is also on an hour's videotape.

Table 17.3   Strengths and limitations

Interviews – strengths	Interviews – limitations
• Depth of information – you can gain insights into why people act as they do, and the feelings behind an issue, from interviews	• Time-consuming
	• Analysis can be difficult with less structured interview data
• The individual respondent is able to tell their own story in their own way	• Interviewer effect – who the interviewer is will have an effect on the responses you get
• Can reach people who would not be happy to take part in groups or fill in questionnaires	• Interview data tells you what people say they do – you may need to check how this relates to what they can be observed to actually do
• Respondents usually enjoy interviews – people like the rare opportunity to be listened to at length	• For questions about what people would like to see different, a group setting may give more confidence, and an interplay of ideas, which is not available in a one-to-one situation
	• There is potential for invasion of privacy – tactless interviewing can be upsetting for respondents

- If you are learning to do interviews, working in pairs makes it possible to observe each other and improve practice.
- Some research teams have members with different perspectives, who might ask different types of question.

You might wish to interview a person alone, but this is not always acceptable or appropriate, where other household members expect to be present. It may be best to accept this, or you can try and find a time when others may not be around, if this is acceptable to your respondent.

Telephone interviews

Where respondents have a reasonably reliable telephone service, using the phone for interviews reduces the costs in terms of researcher time enormously. The problems are, of course, that even in relatively well-off communities, not everyone has a phone, so you must not exclude some respondents on that basis, and that you cannot build rapport so easily as face-to-face. There may be confidentiality issues. But for some purposes, for example in collecting reasonably straightforward information from professionals, using the phone is a very efficient method.

> CHECKLIST   **For good practice in interviewing***
>
> ✓ Ensure that the respondent understands the purpose of the interview and has given informed consent to take part
> ✓ Listen carefully – be attentive to the respondent, avoiding getting distracted by note-taking, background noise, and so on
> ✓ Be sensitive to the respondent's feelings
> ✓ Don't wear your respondent out – interviews should take 45 minutes or less, ideally, and an hour and a half at most. For depth interviews on complex subjects, it may be good to meet twice or more times
> ✓ Where appropriate, probe the meaning behind people's statements
> ✓ As you go along, check your understanding of what has been said – it can be useful to offer a summary of what you think has been said for the respondent to check
> ✓ Be non-judgemental
> ✓ Respect the rights of the respondent – accept it if the person does not wish to tell you something, and know when to stop or back off if they become distressed
> ✓ Always pilot questionnaires before use

17.3   Focus Groups

What is a focus group?

A focus group is a group interview, where 6 to 12 people are brought together for a discussion. Often they have experiences in common, but not always. They may be strangers to each other, or drawn from an existing community group. It is not a series of individual interviews conducted in a group – the interaction between group members is part of the process, and should be encouraged.

In planning focus group work it is important to distinguish between focus groups in which the participants share some important characteristics or experience from those where a diverse group of people is brought together, perhaps seen as representing a wider population. The focus groups famously used by political parties to test their 'messages' are generally diverse groups, and are sometimes criticised as leading to 'lowest common denominator' responses. However a focus group where people are similar in relation to the subject under discussion – for example they all farm similar land, they have all had breast cancer, whatever – is different. Being in a group with others 'like you' can give people confidence to speak about their experiences in a way which may not occur in one-to-one interviews, especially, perhaps, when the subject under discussion is in some way stigmatising.

---

* There is further reading on each technique at the end of the chapter.

How many people are involved?

A focus group requires an experienced facilitator. It is crucial that this person enables everyone to talk, and is not tempted to join in the argument. Someone not directly involved in the issue under discussion is best.

Many researchers also work with an observer, and this has several benefits. The observer can take notes/deal with the tape recorder, observe non-verbal communication, and help the facilitator in putting people at ease before and after the session. This frees the facilitator to concentrate on listening to and steering the group.

When should you use focus groups for research?

Focus groups are useful when

- You need in-depth information about how people think about an issue – their reasoning about why things are as they are, why they hold the views they do.
- You need guidance in setting a framework for some larger-scale research, about what people see as the issues for them.
- You want people's ideas about what would be better.

Conducting a focus group interview

Please also refer to the guidelines on individual interviews – many points are relevant. Focus groups are similar to in-depth interviews. And please see also Section 17.1 above, on how to ask questions.

Preparing for the focus group

- Prepare a topic guide, well ahead of time, with up to ten questions to focus the discussion.
- Questions should be open and straightforward – closed questions will stop the group dead.
- Test the topic guide out on a pilot group of colleagues or friends – this will also give practice in facilitating.

Opening up the focus group

- Brief the group that they do not need to come to any agreement, and that everyone's views are valued.
- Make sure your first question encourages everyone to speak – it should be straightforward, but open (ie cannot be answered by 'yes', 'no', or 'three years'). For example: 'What were your first impressions when you arrived in this area?'

Table 17.4   Focus groups – strengths and limitations

Focus groups – strengths	Focus groups – limitations
• The group interaction can produce invaluable data on how people think about an issue – their own explanations and understandings	• Do not produce statistics
	• Data can be complex to analyse
• Accessible to people who cannot read or write	• Groups can be 'led' by dominating individuals, and controversial or different views suppressed
• Particularly good when you want people to think about what changes they would like to see – support from others like them can enable people to think more creatively	• A skilled (preferably independent) facilitator is needed
	• May be difficult to recruit to – asks a lot of the respondents in terms of time and effort
• The group situation can reduce the power of the researcher, with participants feeling some 'strength in numbers', and having greater control of the process	• Can exclude people who are not comfortable (or accepted) to be speaking in public, so minority voices may not be heard
• Enjoyable for participants	
• Very rich data is generated	
• Sometimes group members are motivated to take action as a result of sharing their stories	

- Ask 'how' questions first, and move on to any 'why' questions after the group has got going.
- It may be helpful to agree some ground rules with the group at the start, by asking them for suggestions and writing them up, to engage group members with the issues of confidentiality, not interrupting, and so on.

Monitoring progress

- Be attentive to everyone in the group, and attempt to draw out those who are quiet, in a sensitive way.
- Do not allow individuals to dominate.
- Check whether group members are in agreement with statements being made, 'is that what everyone thinks?' 'does everyone agree that xyz?'

Closing down the focus group

- Towards the end of the session, summarise what you have heard said, and check with the group whether that is what they thought was said (the observer can do this if you have one).
- Thank people for their time – coming to a focus group is quite a commitment.

- Ask if participants have any questions they want to ask you – they will often ask what will be done with the findings, so have your reply prepared!
- Ask how people have felt about taking part in the focus group.

CHECKLIST   **For good practice in conducting focus groups**

✔ Find a suitable location for the group – somewhere quiet and comfortable for participants

✔ Put people at ease with an informal, open approach – ensure they do not feel that they are under scrutiny

✔ Make sure everyone gets a fair chance to speak

✔ Encourage interaction between group members, but keep them on the subject

✔ Prevent group members from pressuring others to agree with them

✔ Do not rely on one focus group to represent a whole group of people's point of view – it is much better to do more, to guard against a 'rogue' group going off at a tangent

✔ Remember that the data collected relates to the group, not the individuals in it

---

17.4   Documentary Sources

What is a study of documentary sources?

Most research projects require some sort of literature review. But sometimes a study of documents (also called using secondary sources) is central to the research, either by itself, or combined with other methods. Documents are treated as sources of data in their own right.

It is sometimes possible to re-analyse existing data sets to ask new questions.

EXAMPLE

Statistics with children as the unit of analysis – Vietnam

Using information from the Vietnam Living Standards Survey, it was possible to re-analyse the data to examine the proportion of children living in poverty. The re-analysed data showed that while the numbers (and proportion) of adults living in poverty had gone down, the proportion and numbers of children in poverty had increased.

EXAMPLE

Difficulty reading and writing – a study across two generations

The Basic Skills Agency in the UK commissioned an analysis of data from the National Child Development Study, which showed very clearly how the children of parents with difficulty with reading and figures tend to have similar difficulties. The NCDS is a major study, where detailed information is collected from a large sample of people at seven-year intervals throughout their lives, and it is now studying the children of its first cohort. The data on education had been collected but not analysed. This research gave strong support to the case the agency wanted to make about the importance of offering literacy and numeracy teaching to adults as parents.

This type of analysis is pretty technical, and development agencies would be well advised to commission such work from experienced researchers.

When should you do documentary research?

Documentary research is useful when:

- It is one element of a larger study.
- Some of your research questions may be (even partially) answered by existing data.
- Reasonably reliable data exists on the population you are interested in.

Conducting a study of documentary sources

Please see also Chapter 12, which gives detailed guidance on locating and working with documents of every kind, since this is also needed for a literature review which is part of any research project.

Locating relevant documents

- Much important material may be unpublished – you need to ask people what exists, and seek it out.
- Be persistent.
- Make guesses about what 'ought' to be available (see Table 12.4), and see if you can find it.

Analysing the documents

- Once you locate a relevant document, always make full notes, especially of its bibliographic details, before you hand it back – you may never see it again.

Table 17.5   Using documents – strengths and limitations

Using documents – strengths	Using documents – limitations
• Can add authority to your study • Can avoid wasteful duplication of research which has already been done • To influence policy, you need to show that you are aware of the current work in the field, especially any which appears to contradict your argument	• Usefulness depends upon the quality of information available for your area of concern • The data will have been produced for another purpose than yours, so it will rarely fully meet the objectives of your own investigation • Can be difficult to keep a clear focus on your own research questions • Documents cannot be treated as objective reflections of reality – they represent the point of view of those who produced them

- If you hope to use statistics quoted in documents, ensure that you note down full details of exactly how, when and by whom the data was gathered, and what definitions were used.
- With important figures, if possible, talk to those who produced them to get further insight into their status (ie how much weight can be put on them).
- Read critically, keeping your own questions in mind.

Writing up your study

- Give complete references for all sources (see Chapter 12.1).
- If citing others' figures, note any obvious criticisms which could be made of them, and explain what level of credibility you would give them.

CHECKLIST   **For good practice in using documents**

  ✓ Keep your own research focus clearly in mind as you work on the documents
  ✓ All information must be carefully assessed for credibility – look for possible sources of bias or error
  ✓ Look out for what is not there
  ✓ Any re-analysis of existing data should be undertaken with advice from a statistician in the case of figures, and an experienced researcher in the case of qualitative data

17.5   Observation

What is observation?

Observation plays a role in all research. For example, noticing children drinking from a stream when there is a well nearby, or noticing recently destroyed areas of forest, might suggest questions to ask. By directly observing what happens, the researcher can check whether what people say they do or think is reflected in their actual behaviour. The two main types of observation research are very different from each other.

Participant observation is a key method of anthropology/ethnography. This is not a technique but a whole approach to research, involving living alongside those you are studying, and will not be discussed in detail here. See Pratt and Loizos (1992), and other sources more aimed at research students for guidance on this approach (for example, Burgess, 1982; Hammersley and Atkinson, 1993). Development workers may be able to learn from this tradition in terms of mobilising what they understand through their daily work (Goodell et al, 1990), and also by realising that what you get to observe is thoroughly conditioned by the role in which you operate. For example, you may meet only people who are interested in engaging with the programme you are seen as being identified with, and may miss other groups' insights altogether, unless you take special steps.

Systematic observation involves observing objects, processes, relationships, or people, and recording these observations. You need to identify indicators that are important to your research questions, and which can be assessed by direct observation. For example, if you were studying an institution caring for disabled people, you could observe numbers of interactions between residents and staff, between different residents, and between staff themselves. A study of access to clean water might involve observations of how people use different water sources.

Table 17.6   Some types of observation

Systematic observation	Participant observation
Observers look for specified behaviour at specific times and places	Observer learns from living and/or working alongside those they are studying
A checklist of items to be observed is required	The observer notes everything they can
Quantitative data is generated	Qualitative data is generated in large quantities
Observers are open but unobtrusive in making their observations	Consent can be an issue, if people forget that you are a researcher
Easy to analyse	Difficult to analyse

The rest of this section advises on the use of systematic observation.

When should you use systematic observation for research?

Observation is useful when:

- The information you want is about observable things.
- You need to cross-check people's account of what happens.

Conducting an observational study

Preparing for the study

- Draft an observation checklist which identifies the indicators which will be sought.
- Always pilot observation checklists and procedures (times of day chosen etc).
- When observing a complex event, eg a local celebration, different observers could concentrate on observing different groups of people, such as women, men, children, tourists.

Carrying out the observations

- Observations must be carried out in a systematic, consistent way, to allow comparisons across time and sites.
- The observer should disturb the setting they are observing as little as possible, by placing themselves somewhere unobtrusive and avoiding interaction with people (can be easier said than done!).

Table 17.7 Observation – strengths and limitations

Observation – strengths	Observation – limitations
• Directly records what people do, as distinct from what they say they do	• Focuses on observable behaviour and therefore sheds no light on people's motivations
• Can be systematic and rigorous	• Danger of leading to over-simplification, or distortion of the meaning of the situation
• Can produce large amounts of data in a fairly short time	
• Can generate data which can then form the basis for discussion with those observed	• The presence of the observer cannot help but influence the setting they are observing to some extent

CHECKLIST **For good practice in systematic observation**

✓ Observation is best used alongside some other method/s – the meaning of observed behaviour cannot be assumed to be obvious, and people should be asked to interpret it themselves

✓ Observations can be based on:

 – Frequency of events – how often does the event on the checklist occur?
 – Events at a given point in time – observer logs what is happening, eg every 30 seconds, or every 20 minutes
 – Duration of events – instances are timed as they occur
 – Sample of people – individuals can be observed for predetermined periods of time, after which attention switches to another person

✓ Items may be included in the checklist if they are

 – Overt – observable in a direct manner,
 – Obvious,
 – Context-independent – context does not affect interpretation,
 – Relevant,
 – Complete – should cover all possibilities,
 – Precise – no ambiguity between the categories, and
 – Easy to record

(Taken from Denscombe, 1998)

17.6   Questionnaires

What is a questionnaire?

A questionnaire is a written list of questions, either given or posted to respondents, who fill it in themselves (this is called a 'self-completion questionnaire'). Information is gathered directly from people through a series of questions, many of which are likely to offer the respondent some possible ('pre-coded') replies to tick.

Questionnaires are also used by researchers who ask the questions verbally and then fill in the answers – the process then becomes a type of interview, though the questionnaire itself may look very similar to a self-completion questionnaire. This is more common practice in the South, due to low literacy rates. For this type of research, much in this section will be relevant, but see also Section 17.2 on interviews.

When should you use a questionnaire for research?

Questionnaires are useful when

- You need information from large numbers of respondents.
- You know exactly what data you need.

- The information you need is fairly straightforward, and you want it in a standardised format.
- Your respondents are able to read and write, and comfortable with filling in a questionnaire.

Conducting a questionnaire survey

Hang on! Make sure, before you start drafting a questionnaire, that the aims and objectives, research focus, and research questions for your study are clear and agreed (see Chapters 5 and 6).

Preparing the questionnaire

Please see also Section 17.1 above, on how to ask questions.

- Questionnaires should be very carefully prepared – small mistakes in wording a question can make the responses useless, and you have only one chance to get your replies.
- Consider carefully the order of the questions.
- Ask around to see copies of questionnaires people have used in your agency, or on the subject area you are working in, to get ideas.
- Pilot any questionnaire carefully, including timing how long it takes to answer.
- Be sure to give information on the questionnaire as to who you are and the purpose of the research.
- The sample must be chosen with care (see Chapter 19).

Pre-coded questions

When researchers talk about 'coding', they are referring to the process of assigning categories to data. So pre-coded questions give the respondent a choice between a set of categories determined by the researcher. Open questions allow the respondent to write whatever they please.

For example, an open question might ask:
How long have you lived in this area?

Whereas a pre-coded question would ask:
Have you lived in this area for:
Less than six months □
Between six months and one year □
Between one year and five years □
More than five years □

Pre-coded questions are much easier to analyse than open questions. However using them does mean that you are obliging respondents to fit their reply into your categories, and you need to make sure that the categories you offer are right. For example, if you used the open question in the example

Table 17.8 Seven types of question that can be used in a questionnaire

VERBAL OR OPEN	The expected response is a word, a phrase or an extended comment. Responses to verbal questions can produce useful information but analysis can present problems. Gives respondents a chance to give their own views on the issue.

More structured questions are easier to analyse. Youngman (1986) suggests that there are the following broad types:

LIST	A list of items is offered, any of which may be selected. For example, a question may ask about types of crop grown and the respondent may grow several types of crop.
CATEGORY	The response is one only of a given set of categories. For example, if age categories are provided (20–29, 30–39, etc), the respondent can only fit into one category.
RANKING	In ranking questions, the respondent is asked to place something in rank order. For example, they might be asked to place qualities or characteristics in order of importance to them.
SCALE	There are various scaling devices (nominal, ordinal, interval, ratio) which may be used in questionnaires, but they require careful handling.
QUANTITY	The response is a number (exact or approximate), giving the amount of some characteristics.
GRID	A table or grid is provided to record answers to two or more questions at the same time.

Source: Bell, 1993, quoting Youngman, 1986 (reproduced with permission).

above, some answers might to some extent mirror the options we thought of, eg 'four months'. But others might say 'since my child was born', or 'since the earthquake in my home village', or 'all my life'. With open questions, you allow the respondent to use their own categories – these are less easily comparable, and are usually not quantifiable, but they may be more meaningful.

If you used the pre-coded example, and many respondents replied 'Less than six months', you do not have the option to find out whether that means two weeks or five months – very different in terms of how a person feels. You also cannot then find out whether they moved before or after an event you later guess may have had an impact.

If you use open questions, you have to 'code' the replies – group them into categories – after the event, as part of your analysis. This is worthwhile for important questions where detailed qualitative information is needed, but very time-consuming compared to the simplicity of adding up replies to a pre-coded question.

Table 17.9   Questionnaires – strengths and limitations

Questionnaires – strengths	Questionnaires – limitations
• A relatively cheap way of collecting information from large numbers of people • Easy to analyse, if mainly pre-coded questions are used • Self completion questionnaires remove any 'interviewer effect' from the picture, so respondents are reacting to a standard package	• Response rates can be low • Pre-coded questions can slant the findings towards the researcher's view of the world rather than the respondents' – the questions asked determine the range of responses which are possible • 'Tick boxes' can frustrate respondents, and put them off participating – on the other hand, some people will find them easier to deal with and more attractive • Can take substantial time to draft and pilot, and for people to complete and return • People who cannot read or write can only be included by making special arrangements • There is little opportunity to check the truthfulness of responses, especially with postal questionnaires

See Section 17.1 above for guidance on how to evaluate a draft set of questions.

Practical matters – in setting up the questionnaire

Doing a questionnaire is a major administrative task. It requires organisation, persistence, and attention to detail to carry out successfully. Some essential matters to consider are:

- Background information to include: whose research is this; any official backing you have; the purpose of the research; return address and date; confidentiality; voluntary response (that is, there is no obligation on the respondent to complete the questionnaire); thanks.
- Instructions to the respondent – give very exact instructions, and preferably an example, to show how to fill in the questionnaire.
- A serial number – can be used to distinguish date and place of distribution etc, to establish which questionnaires are returned. But beware – if the data are to be anonymous, you need to ensure that any coding system does not compromise this by identifying the individual.
- Coding boxes: if you want to use a computer to analyse the data you collect, it is helpful to include boxes in which to write the codes you will use in entering the data onto the computer.

- Ensure that you include 'don't know' as an option, and that you can also record it clearly when an answer is missing.
- Appearance: make sure the questionnaire is as attractive and well set out as you can make it – this will increase the response rate. It will also help you when you get to analysing the data.

Carrying out the survey

- Make sure you are meticulous in keeping track of paperwork – keep a record of what goes out and what comes in.
- Plan to do some follow-up on people who have not been contacted – this will increase your response rate.
- Think about anything else you can do to improve the response rate (see Chapter 19.3 on increasing response rates amongst hard-to-reach groups).

CHECKLIST   **For good practice in questionnaire research**

✓ Allow enough time to:
  - plan and design a first draft of the questionnaire,
  - show it to people,
  - revise it,
  - pilot it,
  - revise it again in light of the pilot, and then
  - print and distribute the final version

✓ Make sure you have obtained any official approval you need to distribute the questionnaire (see Chapter 8.3 on negotiating access)

✓ Allow resources for the production and distribution of the questionnaire

✓ Some follow-up of people who have not responded is essential to increase your response rate – this takes time and effort

✓ If you plan to analyse the responses on a computer, you need to think about how you are going to prepare the data for this

---

17.7   Ranking and Scoring Exercises

What are ranking and scoring exercises?

Ranking or scoring means placing something in order (Theis and Grady, 1991). These are useful methods to learn about the categories people use to understand their worlds, and the values they place on things. Ranking means putting things in order, scoring relates to the weight people give to different items. These exercises can be used as part of an interview or separately, or in some cases as the basis of a group discussion.

Table 17.10 Some types of ranking and scoring exercises

Type	Useful for
Preference ranking (ranking by voting)	To determine quickly the main problems or preferences of community members. The priorities of different individuals can easily be compared. Voting is also a form of preference ranking
Direct matrix ranking	To identify lists of criteria for a certain object, and the reasons for local preferences
Wealth ranking	To investigate perceptions of wealth differences in a community, discovering local criteria for wealth and well-being

These techniques are an important element of PLA work, giving an accessible, visual way of initiating discussion of possibilities in the local situation. Wealth ranking has been widely used in PLA and other types of work, and enables discussion of relative wealth without asking about people's wealth directly.

Ranking exercises of many sorts are also widely used in more traditional research to understand people's preferences and values. Ranking questions are one type of question that can be used in a questionnaire or an interview.

These techniques can be used either with individuals or in a group. For some exercises it would be best to ask a number of individuals to carry out the ranking independently, for example of community members' wealth, and then to put the results together in a table. You could then discuss the results, without revealing who gave which scores, with a group of community members. A quicker but perhaps less reliable method goes straight to the group setting.

When should you use ranking and scoring exercises for research?

Ranking and scoring exercises are most useful when:

- You want to engage with community members in deciding priorities for action.
- You need to understand community members' ways of categorising things.

Conducting ranking and scoring exercises

First some general guidelines, then we will look at each of the three types of exercise in turn. These exercises can be done using visual images to represent the items to be ranked, and stones or beans for people to 'vote' with.

How to carry out preference ranking

1. Choose a set of problems or preferences to be prioritised. This could be, for example, farming problems or preferences for tree species.
2. Ask the interviewee to give you her favoured items in this set, in order of priority. Get a list of three to six items from each interviewee.
3. Repeat for several interviewees.
4. Make a table of the responses.

Example of preference ranking

Constraints to Agricultural Production

Problem	Respondents						Total Score	Ranking
	A	B	C	D	E	F		
Drought	5	5	3	5	4	5	27	A
Pests	4	3	5	4	5	4	25	B
Weeds	3	4	4	1	3	3	18	C
Costs of inputs	2	1	2	2	2	2	11	D
Labour shortage	1	2	1	3	1	1	9	E

This exercise needs to be carefully adapted to the local situation, and relevant items for ranking identified by the participants. This may happen naturally through other fieldwork, but it will often be a good idea to start the process with a brainstorming discussion about what items should be included – in this case, what are the main problems for farmers here? The table above has been constructed by putting together preferences from individuals. You could also work in a large group, which has the advantage that you will also learn by hearing people debating the relative importance of different factors or items.

Choosing priorities is obviously a key step in the move from research to action – this exercise can be used to structure that process. But remember that if you work together in a large group, less powerful members of the group may find it difficult to get their priorities heard.

How to carry out direct matrix ranking

1. 'Choose, or ask people to choose, a class of objects which is important to them (eg tree species, cooking fuel types, fruit)
2. List the most important items (3 to 8 items)
3. Elicit criteria by asking:
   'What is good about each item? What else?' (Continue until no more replies)
   'What is bad about each item? What else?' (Continue until no more replies)
4. List all criteria

   • Turn negative criteria into positive by using the opposite (eg 'vulnerable to pests' becomes 'resists pests')

5. Draw up a matrix (grid)
6. For each criterion ask which object is best:

   • 'Which is best, then next best?'
   • 'Which is worst, then next worst?'
   • of the two remaining ask 'Which is better?'

7. Ask: 'Which criterion or factor is most important?'
8. Force a choice: 'If you could only have one of these, which one would you choose?'

(Taken from Theis and Grady, 1991)

How to carry out wealth or well-being ranking

The term 'wealth' suggests a focus on material assets or income, and so has been questioned as a Eurocentric approach. The term 'well-being' is used instead to orient questions towards a broader concept of 'quality of life'.

This type of ranking can also be used to find the 'best' and the 'worst' of anything. This system is more effective in groups or communities of about 50 to 150 members. However it does not work well in heavily populated areas as it is too difficult to get everyone's name and to find sorters who know everyone, or in cultures where discussion of inequality is taboo.

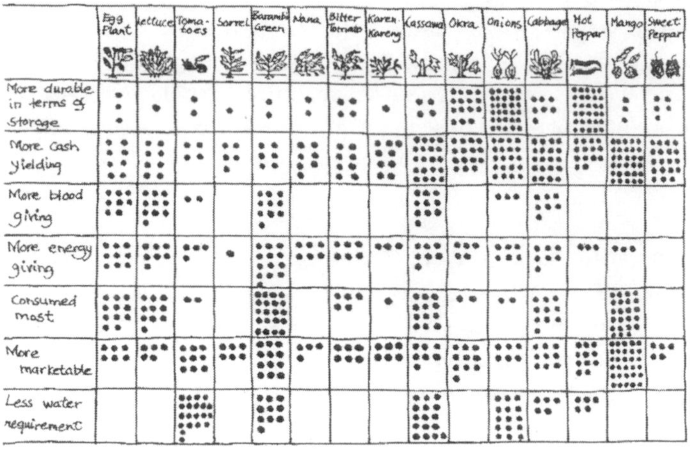

After ActionAid, 1992: 56.

Figure 17.1 Direct matrix scoring and ranking of vegetables grown (young women). Reproduced with permission from Mikkelsen, 1995.

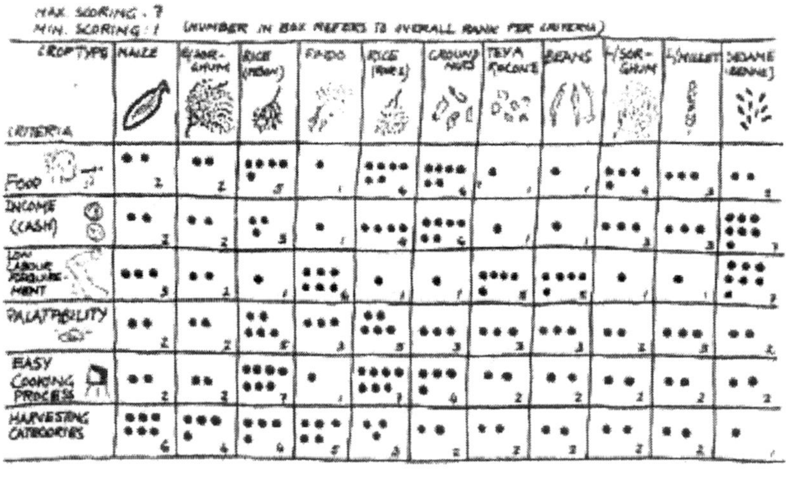

After Action Aid, 1991: 17.

Figure 17.2 Direct matrix scoring and ranking of crops grown (old women). Reproduced with permission from Mikkelsen, 1995.

Steps for wealth ranking

1. Make a list of all the households in the community and assign each household a number. The name of each household head and the number from the master list are written on a separate card.

With the informants:

2. A number of key informants who have lived in the community a long time and who know all the households are asked independently of each other to sort the cards into as many piles as there are wealth categories in the community (using their own criteria). If the informant is not literate read the name on the card and then hand it to him and let him choose the pile in which to place it.
3. Use numbered baskets or small boxes. This helps the sorter remember which is which, and it helps you record the scores without mixing the baskets. Also, shuffle the cards between sorters.
4. After sorting ask the informant for the wealth criteria for each pile and differences between the piles. Assure the sorters of confidentiality and do not discuss the ranks of individual families, so as not to cause bad feelings within the community. List local criteria and indicators derived from the ranking discussion and examine differences between informants.

Putting together the information:

5. After the informant has sorted all cards into piles, record the score of each household on a score sheet according to the number of its pile. If a sorter is not able to place a family because she doesn't know them or cannot decide where to put them, leave a blank by that household's name for that informant. Have at least three informants sort all households in the community independently to make sure results are reliable.
6. If the number of wealth categories used by the informants differ from each other, divide each household's score by the number of wealth categories used by the particular scorer and multiply by 100. For example, a household in the third out of five piles would receive a score of 60 (3/5 × 100 = 60). This procedure is necessary in order to compare the different scores of different sorters with each other (unless they all use the same number of wealth categories).
7. After the scores of each informant have been recorded on the form, the scores are added up and divided by the number of sorters. For example, if there were four scorers but one did not know one of the households, then that household's total score is divided by three rather than four. Check the sorter scores for consistency. If one scorer's results are greatly different from the others, he may not have understood the directions or

got the baskets reversed. If this happens, disregard all of that scorer's scores and ask another informant to do the sorting.

8.   Finally, arrange households according to wealth categories. If the informants used a different number of piles take the average number of wealth categories (eg if four informants have 4, 4, 7, and 6 piles respectively, divide the community into five wealth groups).

9.   Using this system, rich households in the community will have low scores while the poorest will have high scores.

(Theis and Grady, 1991)

Wealth ranking can be useful for a number of reasons, but a key issue is to understand what people use as criteria for wealth, status, and power. Linked to this are the constraints mentioned as impeding the less well off. A wealth ranking exercise in Mongolia (Mikkelsen, 1992), for example, identified first productive assets, ie the numbers and species mix of private animals, self-sufficiency in meat and dairy products. In addition a number of other material wealth indicators were mentioned – jewellery, utensils, saddles, bank savings, furniture, motor cycle, generator, quality of snuff, and possession of Chinese silk. Some important distinctions between households in terms of their level of vulnerability were revealed, for example 'the more articulate herdsmen have friends in high places, they can get help whenever they need it.'

In terms of production constraints, indebtedness and availability of labour, dependency burden, and school children away from home, emerged as issues. These were followed up using other research methods.

In many parts of the world, land would of course be a key factor in wealth creation, but it is always useful to find out people's own analysis of these issues. Skills can also be important, as can other kinds of asset.

Although it is a useful tool, practitioners have warned against the inappropriate use of wealth ranking:

'Wealth ranking is a means to target the poorest of the poor. It can encourage an attitude change within agencies better to consider who they can realistically help: those with direct welfare needs and/or those with development possibilities. However, in communities where everybody is subject to considerable stress such as is the case with refugees, wealth ranking seems to provide irrelevant details. There, the differences in well-being would seem to be increasingly marginal and wealth ranking less suitable. Its use for people in distress should probably be avoided. Beyond a certain limit, attempting to pick out variations in stress, malnourishment and misery would appear to be irrelevant [and unethical, we may add].'
(Mikkelsen, 1992)

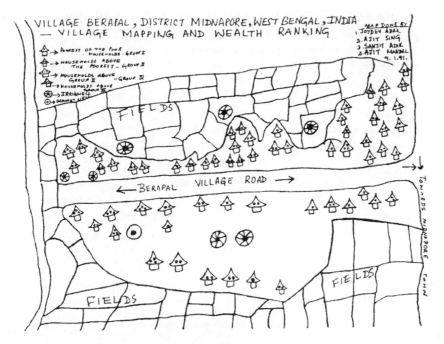

Figure 17.3   Village map with wealth ranking of Berapal (reproduced with permission from Mikkelsen, 1995)

Figure 17.4   Ranking and scoring – strengths and limitations

Ranking and scoring – strengths	Ranking and scoring – limitations
• These methods give a practical, visual focus which can encourage participation by those who might not readily take part in verbal discussion • Draw out the categories used by community members • Useful for sensitive information, especially for income and wealth – respondents are more willing to provide information on relative wealth than absolute figures • Can be done relatively rapidly, and in a form available to the local community • Reading and writing skills not essential to participate	• Bias can be introduced if only some people are consulted – eg women and men may be aware of different needs in relation to which crops are grown • Some methods, such as matrix scoring, can be difficult and tiring for participants, and there can be confusion about the scoring system (Mikkelsen,1992) • Wealth ranking relies on people all knowing each other, so is not workable in larger communities

> **CHECKLIST   For good practice in ranking and scoring exercises**
>
> ✓ The key first step is to discover and learn to use community members'
>   own ways of categorising things – their own units of measurement and
>   names for things
> ✓ Adapt exercises to the requirements of the study and the environment
> ✓ Discuss any ideas you have about what to focus on with knowledgeable
>   people first
> ✓ Let people do it their own way
> ✓ Make sure you get the perspectives of different groups of people on any
>   ranking process you do: women and men, young and old, etc will have
>   different points of view
> ✓ Probe people's reasons for the order of the ranking, and their criteria in
>   giving importance to items

17.8   Visual Methods: Maps, Diagrams and Drawings

What are visual methods?

A wide variety of visual methods have been used in research for development
work. They are an important feature of PLA methodology, enabling participation by all types of people, and have been developed also for research with
children, building on many children's familiarity with drawing. Visual methods can be used either with individuals or in groups, where the group, for
example, draws a map based on suggestions from all participants.

It is a central feature of these methods that they be used creatively, and
adapted to find the information you need. The options are too many to
discuss – just a few examples are given below.

Some types of visual methods:

- Maps

    - participatory mapping
    - social maps
    - mobility maps
    - transects (a cross section of an area)

- Diagrams

    - daily routine diagrams
    - seasonal calendars

- Drawings

    - draw and write technique
    - body mapping

When should you use visual methods for research?

Visual methods are most useful when:

- You want to learn quickly about 'how things work here'.
- You are interested in issues relating to the physical environment, eg farming problems, access to water, etc and how they relate to social issues.
- A focus is needed to encourage group discussion of the issues.
- Used with care, they can be an effective way of opening up sensitive or embarrassing topics.
- When people relate better to visual representations than to verbal discussions.

Carrying out studies using visual methods

In PLA, maps and diagrams are often drawn on the ground, using locally available materials to build up the picture. This means that everyone can see what is being made, and can chip in with their ideas, using familiar things to show what they mean. The discussion around the mapping process is part of the data.

Steps for participatory mapping

This allows you to discover the 'mental maps' of community members. It is usually important to get more than one group of people (women/men, old/young) to draw a map, and then compare them.

1. Decide what sort of map should be drawn (social, natural resources, farm, etc).
2. Find people who know the area and the topic of the mapping exercise, and who are willing to share their knowledge.
3. Choose a suitable place (ground, floor, paper) and medium (sticks, stones, seeds, pens, pencils) for the maps.
4. Help the people get started but let them draw the map by themselves. Be patient and don't interrupt. It's *their* map.
5. Sit back and watch, or go away!
6. Keep a permanent (paper) record including the mappers' names to give them credit.

Social mapping

Social mapping is closely related to wealth ranking, see above 17.7, Figure 17.3. In social mapping, an outline map of the area is prepared, and then a group of local people is asked to show where the poorest households are located. A discussion follows on what constitutes wealth and well-being, and the

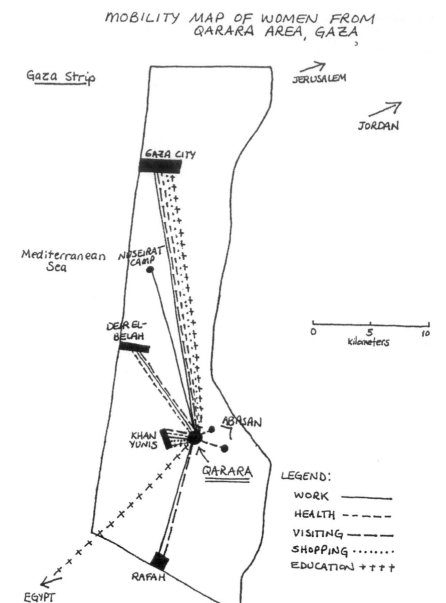

Figure 17.5 Example of a mobility map (reproduced with permission from Theis and Grady, 1991)

main criteria are agreed upon. Next, each household is assessed using well-being criteria, for which symbols are placed on the map, starting with the poorest of the poor, and working up through three to five social groups. The group themselves 'hold the stick' to draw the map.

Mobility maps

Spatial mobility can in many societies be used as an indicator for a person's contact with, and knowledge of, the outside world and his/her authority in the community. It may also indicate freedom, wealth, empowerment, education, or consciousness. The mobility map allows us to record, compare, and analyse the mobility of different groups of people in a community (eg men, women, children, older/younger, educated). Again the discussion surrounding the process of drawing the map may be as informative as the map itself.

People being asked to draw mobility maps need to be given a certain time period to which it should relate (week, month, or year). Maps could be drawn individually, and then compared, or drawn by a group in discussion. Different colours could be used to show different activities, and different frequencies of journeys could be shown with thicker and thinner lines.

Transects

A transect is a diagram of main land use zones, helpful in research relating to natural resources, and in learning quickly about a new place. It compares the main features, resources, uses, and problems of different zones. First, you ask community members to participate in a walk through their village, showing you the important factors about the area. Walk the transect, observing, asking questions, and listening. Then you can make a sketch of what you have seen, and discuss it with the participants. Transects do not have to be walked in a straight line. It is important to take transect walks with different community members, such as men, women, and children, and listening for what they think important in their environment.

Draw and write

This technique has been developed within health research as a way of learning about children's perceptions of health and ill-health issues. For example, children in inner city Manchester in England were asked to first draw something – for example 'you find a bag with drugs in it – draw what you found'. Then they are asked to write around and alongside it about what their picture showed. They were then given a short series of tasks, drawing and writing in response to different suggestions. The study on drugs went on to ask the children to draw the person who might have lost the bag they had found, and then to write what you would like to say to them. Some of the children drew a drug dealer looking good in his fashionable designer-label clothes and trainers.

Body mapping

Has been used internationally to get people to draw their images of how bodies work. It can be used to find out people's names for different parts

Figure 17.6 Child's drawing identifies his problems

and functions within the body, and to open up discussion of all kinds of health-related issues. For example, women can be asked to draw their own reproductive organs, and discuss their drawings, which can produce useful information about how they understand them to work (Johnson and Mayoux, 1998). However, it should not be assumed that drawing is familiar to people – in the example from Zimbabwe quoted by Johnson and Mayoux (Cornwall, 1992), several of the women had never drawn anything before.

Figure 17.6, a drawing by a 9-year-old Peruvian boy of the street where he lived, showed the route he had to take across a busy road to collect water from the only tap available to his family.

Without either an explanation or knowing the context, this line could be meaningless or misinterpreted.

Using children's drawings

Much research with children, especially psychological research, has used drawings, but they have been used in different ways within different disciplines. Virginia Morrow (1999) comments:

Figure 17.7   Reproduced with permission from Boyden and Ennew, 1997

'Development psychological research in particular has tended to use children's drawings as ways of emphasising children's different competencies in perception and pictorial representation at certain stages of development; psycho-analytic approaches have tended to use children's drawings as ways of projectively interpreting children's inner emotional states.

'One of the benefits of the draw-and-write technique is that it enables all children to participate, including young children; the drawbacks are essentially ethical ones, to do with consent, ownership of drawings ... and more importantly, interpretation (Pridmore and Bendelow, 1995). Both developmental psychological and psychoanalytic approaches are problematic, from a sociological point of view, because unless a researcher is prepared to sit and listen to a child talking about and explaining their drawing then the dangers of mis-interpretation and over-interpretation are very great indeed.' (Morrow, 1999)

Figure 17.7 drawn by a 12-year-old street boy in Addis Ababa, is difficult to interpret without the boy's own explanation. An adult might not see the significance of the most important feature – the hat.

The boy explained that he had drawn himself eating rotten fruit. He had drawn himself wearing a hat because he was ashamed to be seen by other people.

Table 17.12 Visual methods – strengths and limitations

Visual methods – strengths	Visual methods – limitations
• Most people enjoy taking part in research using visual methods	• Interpretation is inherently tricky with visual images – there is a danger of misinterpreting what is meant
• Mapping or drawing can create a good focus for group interaction	• It may not be culturally appropriate – and you need to be familiar with local 'ways of seeing' to make sense of the images
• Some people may find it easier to communicate if they do not have to use words	• Some people may see the use of visual methods as patronising, or be inhibited by the method, for a variety of reasons
	• It is crucial that there is opportunity for respondents to explain or interpret the images they have produced – this should not be rushed
	• There can be problems about ownership and reproduction of images

CHECKLIST   **For good practice in using visual methods**

✓ Pictures need interpretation – listening to and recording what people say about the images they make is as important as the images themselves
✓ Do not comment on the artistic merit of any product – it's not the point
✓ People own their drawings or maps – ask permission if you want to take them away or use them in a larger group, and make copies for yourself if people want to keep the original
✓ Do not assume that all children, especially older children and young people, will be happy to express themselves through drawing – some will see it as 'for younger children' and be insulted

17.9   Some Other Ideas

The methods described above are the basic tools of research for development work – they are frequently needed, often useful, tried, and tested. However there are many, many other ways of working, and it is important to experiment with new ideas. This section gives brief details of a few methods which have been found effective – I hope readers will be inspired to invent more.

Music and drama

Music can be a wonderful ice-breaker, for example in work with children. Some children may find it more comfortable to sing songs, than to immediately start to talk to a researcher. Making up your own songs can be a good way of expressing difficult feelings in many cultures.

EXAMPLE

Making up songs – Nepal

Nepali children made up songs about the emotional impact of floods on their lives. They sang

'Khola Pari Ma Maya Laundina Barkha Lagyo Airana Paundina' (I don't want to fall in love across the river because in the rains there is no possibility of getting a message to him.)
'Tala Tala Didiko Ghara Barkha Lagyo Aundaina Khabora'
(The flood has prevented getting a message from my dear sister because I am on top of the hill and she is in the plain.) (Johnson et al, 1995)

Drama can be used with groups to draw out and illustrate what is important to community members. It was used effectively with a group of London children who invented a play about the local park, which was under threat from developers.

EXAMPLE

Making a play – children working in gold mines in Burkina Faso

A theatre company worked to develop a play with children (aged 13 to 17) who were miners and gold processors in the gold mines of Burkina Faso. Although it was seen as development work rather than research, the process revealed a great deal about how they saw their problems, the origins of their problems, and what changes they wanted for the future. For example, much became clear about power relations and the use of force against the children.

Video

Video can be used in a number of ways in research:

- as a creative tool to use with community members,
- as a means of recording, or
- as a stimulus for discussion.

In participatory work, video may be used with a group of people who want to express important issues through this medium, and who plan and make a film. Video can also be used as an alternative to tape-recording, to record research interactions. However of course using a video camera increases the sense of exposure felt by participants, and consent may be refused.

EXAMPLE

Using video with young children

In a study looking at how young children in London responded to dolls representing disabled people, the researchers videoed children playing with various dolls. We were concerned that the video camera would be disruptive to the environment, but the children took it very calmly. They were clearly familiar with video cameras from family weddings etc, even though this was a group of children facing great disadvantage. We allowed the children to have a look through the camera, and play with the equipment a little, until they were used to it. Video did make a good record, but we were not able to use the recordings more widely, eg to illustrate presentations, because we had not sought permission from parents and children to do so when we got consent to their participation in the research (Pettitt and Laws, 1999).

Videos are also one type of stimulus material which could be used to open up sensitive areas for discussion. Their use in this way should be piloted carefully – video is an emotive tool.

Photography

Respondents can be given cameras and asked to take photos of subjects that will illustrate the issues under investigation. As with drawings, it is important to get a commentary from the person or group who took the photos to explain what they mean to them. Photography has been used as an element of participatory needs assessment in a number of situations, for example with women in China to assess public health needs (Wang et al, 1996; Wang and Burris, 1997), and with hearing-impaired children in Vietnam (Save the Children, 1999). Visual images have great power, and can facilitate discussion of issues which might be difficult to gain attention for through more traditional means.

In one project, the young people worked as a group:

EXAMPLE

Children using cameras, Orissa, India

Sanjit Patnayak has been a community level worker in a tribal area of Orissa for some years. During classroom-based learning in New Delhi he was extremely sceptical about the ability of the children he works with to use cameras. But he was persuaded to include taking photographs in the methods he used for field-based learning and took some disposable cameras as well as his own auto-focus camera with a supply of film.

By the time he was visited by the facilitator in the field Sanjit was a convert. But when the facilitator saw the photographs taken by the children she at first refused to believe the children had taken them. The pictures were a record of their daily lives. Perfectly framed and focused, each one told a story. They appeared to have been taken by experts. And, in the sense that the children were the experts on their own lives, they were.

Later, the facilitator saw the children taking photographs. First a group discussed what they wanted to record, then one child actually took the photograph, with advice from others, so that the photographs were a purposeful group statement as well as being technically good. She was also able to see the pleasure the children took in seeing (and individually owning) developed photographs of themselves, as well as the way Sanjit was able to use these images as the basis for focus group discussion about the children's work within the community (Boyden and Ennew, 1997).

Market research

Market research surveys can be useful in advocacy work, where you want to argue something about the views of the general public, or where you need information about large numbers of people in the general population in Northern countries. In the North there is a huge, complex industry of market research companies, which carry out many surveys of different population groups, often segmented, eg, by age, location, etc. One type of these is called an omnibus survey, where questions from a whole number of different clients are asked of respondents, so that they are asked, for example, about their preferences in relation to shampoo, car tyres, and TV soap operas. It is possible to get these companies to add one or more questions for your purposes, for example 'what do you think about calls to write off the debts of the poorest countries?'

EXAMPLE

Using an omnibus survey

Save the Children wanted to argue that there is too little play provision for children in the UK during the school holidays. It arranged to add questions to an omnibus survey to parents, just before the summer holidays started, asking them what their children would be doing in the holidays and what they thought about provision. It was then possible to quote a high percentage of a good sample of parents agreeing that this was a problem to them.

This method can be used with straightforward issues which can be framed in an unambiguous way. Get advice on exactly how to word your questions. Market research companies are commercial operations, but the costs can be worthwhile, especially compared to the costs of doing your own research.

The Delphi technique

This term refers back to ancient Greece, to the oracle at Delphi, a wise woman whose views were sought on important decisions. Essentially the Delphi technique involves collecting views from experts in a field, and generating discussion amongst them to interrogate these views. It could be used in advocacy, to test or strengthen your case, in needs assessment, or in sorting out your research questions.

It can be done in various ways. Robson (1993) suggests that for generating good research questions, you might identify a group of people who are knowledgeable about the issue in question – preferably people from different disciplines. Each individual is then asked to generate independently up to three specific research questions in the chosen area. They may be asked also to provide additional information, perhaps giving a justification for the questions chosen. The responses from each individual are collected, and all responses are passed on in unedited and unattributed form to all members of the group. A second cycle then takes place. This might involve individuals commenting on other responses, and/or revising their own contribution in the light of what others have produced. Third and fourth cycles might take place, of either similar form or seeking resolution or consensus through voting, or ranking, or categorising replies.

Further Reading

Interviews

Denscombe, M. (1998) *The Good Research Guide for Small-Scale Social Research Projects*. Buckingham and Philadelphia: The Open University Press.

Has a chapter covering interviews in detail.

Theis, J. and Grady, H.M. (1991) *Participatory Rapid Appraisal for Community Development*. London: IIED and Save the Children Federation.

Has a good section on semi-structured interviewing.

See also further reading recommended in Chapter 14 on communication, especially for work with children.

Focus Groups

Morgan, D.L. and Krueger, R.A. (1998) *The Focus Group Kit* (6 volumes). Thousand Oaks, California: Sage.

This is a very full account of how to use focus groups, but is well set-out and easy to use. Borrow it.

Krueger, R.A. (1994) *Focus Groups: A practical guide for applied research*. Newbury Park, California: Sage.

Morgan, D.L. (1997) *Focus Groups as Qualitative Research*. Thousand Oaks, California: Sage.

Documentary Sources

Pratt, B. and Loizos, P. (1992) *Choosing Research Methods*. Oxfam Development Guidelines, No. 7. Oxford: Oxfam.

Includes discussion of the use of secondary sources in development work.

Levitas, R. and Guy, W. (eds) (1996) *Interpreting Official Statistics*. London: Routledge.

Interesting collection of essays, looking at the issues in relation to a range of UK official statistics.

May, T. (1997) *Social Research: Issues, methods and processes*. Buckingham, UK: Open University Press.

Includes two relevant chapters: 'Official statistics: topic and resource', and 'Documentary research: excavations and evidence'. UK-oriented, but the general approaches discussed are relevant anywhere.

Observation

This section has drawn on Denscombe (1998) and Theis and Grady (1991).

Denscombe, M. (1998) *The Good Research Guide for Small-Scale Social Research Projects*. Buckingham and Philadelphia: The Open University Press.

Theis, J. and Grady, H.M. (1991) *Participatory Rapid Appraisal for Community Development*. London: IIED and Save the Children Federation.

Questionnaires

You will find guidance on questionnaire design and administration in most books on how to do research. If you need detailed guidance for a major questionnaire exercise, Oppenheim and Moser and Kalton are classic textbooks, and still useful – will be found in many libraries. For simpler exercises, Denscombe and Bell give excellent advice.

Denscombe, M. (1998) *The Good Research Guide for Small-Scale Social Research Projects*. Buckingham and Philadelphia: The Open University Press.

Drawn on in writing this section – gives good guidance on questionnaire research.

Bell, J. (1987) *Doing Your Research Project*. Buckingham, UK: Open University Press.

Helpful advice for designing simple questionnaires. Also drawn on in preparing this section.

Oppenheim, A.N. (1992) *Questionnaire Design, Interviewing and Attitude Measurement*, new edition. London: Pinter.

Moser, C.A. and Kalton, G. (1971) *Survey Methods in Social Investigation*, 2nd edition. London: Heinemann.

Ranking and Scoring Exercises

The following texts have been drawn on in writing this section, and all contain more help on ranking and scoring exercises.

Mikkelsen, B. (1995) *Methods for Development Work and Research: A guide for practitioners*. New Delhi, Thousand Oaks, London: Sage.

Theis, J. and Grady, H.M. (1991) *Participatory Rapid Appraisal for Community Development*. London: IIED and Save the Children Federation.

Boyden, J. and Ennew, J. (eds) (1997) *Children in Focus: A manual for participatory research with children*. Stockholm: Rädda Barnen.

Visual Methods: Maps, Diagrams, and Drawings

The following texts have been drawn on in writing this section, and all contain more help on visual research methods.

Theis, J. and Grady, H.M. (1991) *Participatory Rapid Appraisal for Community Development*. London: IIED and Save the Children Federation.

Mikkelsen, B. (1995) *Methods for Development Work and Research: A guide for practitioners*. New Delhi, Thousand Oaks, London: Sage.

Boyden, J. and Ennew, J. (eds) (1997) *Children in Focus: A manual for participatory research with children*. Stockholm: Rädda Barnen.

Some Other Ideas

Boyden, J. and Ennew, J. (eds) (1997) *Children in Focus: A manual for participatory research with children*. Stockholm: Rädda Barnen.

Discusses a number of creative approaches to research with children.

Robson, C. (1993) *Real World Research*. Oxford, UK and Cambridge, USA: Blackwell.

Describes the use of the Delphi technique.

18 Some Packages of Methods for Research for Development Work

This chapter considers some ways of putting together the methods described in the last chapter to apply them to development processes. The chapter will include discussion of: needs assessment, stakeholder analysis, action research, consultation, baseline studies, peer research, case studies, PLA and PPA, and household food economy assessment tools. These different approaches generally use similar basic tools, such as interviews or group discussion, but apply them in different ways, and within different philosophical frameworks.

18.1 Needs Assessment

When development workers were consulted in preparing this manual about what they use research for, the most common reply was 'needs assessment'. It is this process which development workers particularly wanted to do better. There is a feeling that resources are sometimes wasted on badly designed or inadequately targeted needs assessment work.

Much of the material in this manual should help practitioners to improve their needs assessment work – all the sections relating to the planning and management of programme-focused research (Chapters 2 to 9) are very relevant. Needs assessment processes should draw on many of the techniques of data collection and analysis described here – interviews, surveys, observation, focus groups, and the mapping and ranking approaches which were specifically developed within the PLA tradition for undertaking needs assessment in the South (Chapters 14 to 17).

Different organisations have different traditions and expectations in terms of needs assessment requirements. Obviously some systematic assessment of need is important to justify the direction of resources to one purpose rather than another. But the fact is that we all know that there is plenty of 'need' out there – it can be as important to identify opportunities and to assess ideas about ways of meeting needs, as to identify needs themselves. Needs assessment must include work on the organisation's own strategy, and those of surrounding agencies, as well as on collecting information about the potential beneficiaries of any programme.

Large-scale surveys are quite widely used in needs assessment work, and this may be appropriate for some types of programmes. But in recent years various types of participatory appraisal processes (PLA, PRA, PPA, see below, 18.7) have become increasingly popular in international development work. These involve the active engagement of local people in setting the agenda for future work and beginning a process of change. Data collection is combined with a process of discussion within the community in question.

However it is carried out, needs assessment can be seen as part of a project cycle, and it should be done in such a way that the information collected can be used later to evaluate changes brought about by the project intervention. Thus needs assessment or appraisal forms the basis for project planning, and then once the project is in place, the information is also used to structure monitoring and evaluation activity.

It is worth thinking ahead to how you might want to monitor your project work, when carrying out needs assessments. What factors would you hope to see change in light of your intervention? Can you collect data which can serve as a baseline, from which change can be observed? (see below, Section 18.5). It may also be a good idea to think about *how* data is collected with evaluation in mind. If you are able to involve practitioners who will later either deliver or monitor any services you put in place, they gain very useful learning from the process.

Joachim Theis, former Programme Director for Save the Children in Vietnam, writes:

'In the past we often started with a general needs assessment. These often turned out to be rather unwieldy and unfocused exercises that did not necessarily bring us closer to making programme decisions. The next step would be a problem analysis. This may or may not require further data collection. Following the problem analysis we prepare a project strategy. This forms the key part of each programme or project. A project without a strategy won't go very far. The project proposal or description takes the strategy as its starting (and end) point.

Once all of this has been done needs for further data collection and analysis become clear. Further research is likely to be much more focused than the initial assessment and may include: KABP (Knowledge, Attitudes, Beliefs and Practice) surveys (used in HIV prevention work), quantitative baseline surveys, establishing quantitative monitoring systems, research on specific topics (eg sexual practices and gender relations among adolescents; nutrition survey). I find short and very focused research activities most useful at this stage (as part of a project strategy). Since this work generally involves partners and communities, the process aspects become very important.'

There is a big difference between large-scale, general needs assessment processes, which look at whole areas of need (eg health, housing, environmental issues), and smaller-scale exercises which look specifically at an area the agency plans to work on. Experience suggests that the more targeted the research is, the more satisfactory its outcomes.

EXAMPLE

Problems in 'needs assessment'

A group might say: ' We want to know the needs of the people of Ballywallop', when in fact they already reckon Ballywallop needs a youth refuge, and they hope this will emerge from a general needs study. This will be a waste of time, and might not actually even come up with a mention of a youth refuge, though lots of residents may recommend more police, higher security at the local schools to prevent break-ins, and reminisce about the good old days when children did what they were told and went out and got reliable work when they left school.

The genuine question for this study would be:

*   What makes us think Ballywallop needs a youth refuge?
    The answers to that provide part of the evidence that makes up the research study. The group would probably find they had already done a lot of small 'r' research. The need is to document that, and then ask:
*   Are these good enough reasons?

Now the task is to see if there is enough evidence, and to check against blind spots – that is, check whether they can be refuted, or whether a refuge is the 'answer' or whether something else might be better. For example, if the problem turns out to be youth unemployment, and parents can't tolerate or afford an unemployed adult in the home, better 'answers' might be employment opportunities for youth, parent education as to why their children can't find work, or higher unemployment benefits to ease the financial strain. (Wadsworth, 1997).

What is a need?

It is not actually possible to read off from a broad assessment of people's situation what interventions are needed and possible. There are a number of reasons for this. One is about the nature of 'need'. It may be useful to distinguish 'felt' or 'expressed' need – that which people themselves put forward – from 'normative' need (based on standards) – that which is socially/culturally accepted as necessary for a decent life.

It is important for needs assessment work to take account of these differences in choosing appropriate methods to use – whose view of needs is important here? In an ideal world, perhaps, the potential beneficiary's view would be paramount, but in real life it may not be so central to arguing your case.

Participatory methods will naturally produce an account of needs which depends largely on people's own perceptions. This will therefore be limited by people's experience, knowledge, and expectations. For example, a PLA might not pick up on a particularly high rate of infant mortality, if the community itself was so accustomed to this situation that people did not think to raise it.

On the other hand, surveys and the use of secondary sources generally focus on measuring needs which the researchers have identified as important, concentrating on normative need. One drawback to this is that the survey may get us no further in knowing how to go about addressing the needs which are identified. Questions will only be asked in the area of life the researchers have identified as important, and may completely miss key issues as perceived by the community.

People's own lack of experience and low expectations can be an issue in both surveys and more participative approaches. People know about their own problems, and have ideas based on their experience about how to address these. But in developing new projects, there is often a search for exciting new ideas about how to address a particular problem. Creative ideas are not typically found in responses to questionnaires. People often produce responses based on what they feel they are entitled to (eg help they used to receive in the past) rather than any sort of ideal.

Group processes, where people grapple together with analysing their problems and looking at potential solutions, are likely to generate more helpful responses. However remember that those who will come to group meetings may not fully represent those who will not (eg differences could be linked to gender, ability/disability, confidence speaking in public, etc).

People are naturally somewhat cynical and suspicious when asked what they want to remedy their problems. Giving them information about exactly what the status of your work is, in relation to any help that might be forthcoming, can be useful. But you may also need to frame questions in such a way as to ask people to think more imaginatively than they usually do: 'in an ideal world, what would you like to see done about ...?' 'If you could have your way, ...?' And you will need to spend time building up confidence in the process you are undertaking.

Include resources as well as needs

All communities have strengths and resources as well as needs, opportunities as well as problems. It is important to take these into consideration in needs assessment processes (Hawtin et al, 1994). PLA does this naturally, as local people take such an active part in the process. Disadvantaged communities often feel that stigma is one of their key problems, and assessments that emphasise only their problems can contribute to lowered collective self-esteem.

EXAMPLE

Caring and coping strategies of families of people living with AIDS

A study aimed at finding ways of minimising the impact of HIV on children in East Hararghe, Ethiopia, focused part of its fieldwork on the caring and coping strategies adopted by families of people living with AIDS.

Assessing resources may mean looking at infrastructure, physical resources, but it may also concern the more intangible strengths of the community. People very close to a community often forget to inform outsiders of basic facts about people's situation, because they are so obvious to them, and to all 'insiders' that they forget other people will not know. You may not need to research these matters, but you should include them in your analysis and reporting.

Obviously in targeted exercises, where the aim is to assess the likely appropriateness of a particular intervention, it is essential to collect information about what services or organisational structures currently exist to meet the needs in question. Such services may have monitoring or evaluation data of their own which could be useful to you. Tact will naturally be required in approaching staff in existing services.

CHECKLIST   **For good practice in needs assessment**

✓ Broadly based, unfocused needs assessments are rarely effective – target the process as precisely as you can

✓ Consult the community before, during and after – whether or not you plan to use participative data-collection methods

✓ Include consideration of strengths, resources, and opportunities as well as problems and needs

✓ Think ahead about data you may need for project monitoring and evaluation – and consider this in how you collect the data as well, eg involving people who will stay with the project

---

18.2   Stakeholder Analysis

This term refers to a process closely allied to needs assessment, which is carried out as part of programme planning. Stakeholders are people, groups, or institutions with interests in a project or programme. It is helpful to distinguish between primary stakeholders, who are those directly affected (either positively or negatively), and secondary stakeholders, who are the intermediaries in the aid process, or those not so directly affected (Rietbergen-McCracken and Narayan, 1998). For example, in a reproductive health project, local people are the primary stakeholders. Secondary stakeholders are people who also have an interest in the issue, like direct service-providers, the Ministry of Health, district authorities, religious leaders, and so on.

The uses of stakeholder analysis are to:

1. identify various groups that have an interest in a project or proposed project;
2. better understand client/beneficiary interests, needs, and capabilities;

3. understand the interests, needs, and capabilities of other groups and identify opportunities and threats to implementation;
4. assess which groups should be consulted or directly involved in project planning and implementation.

The process followed is essentially one of analysing information about the various stakeholders to assess their likely responses to the project, and thus to plan a strategy to win people over or at least reduce their resistance to an innovation. The information you need to base this on could be collected through all the usual methods – interviews, survey data where available, institutional appraisals, observation. Carrying out an analysis like this could at least prove a useful way for a team to share its knowledge of the different groups involved. The analysis can lead into an inclusive planning process.

The process followed can be summarised as follows:

1. Identify and list all stakeholders (divide primary stakeholders into relevant sub-groups; consider the poorest; consider gender issues).
2. Draw out the stakeholders' interests (what benefits may they gain? What resources may they commit? Do they have other interests which may produce conflict?).
3. Assess stakeholders' power and influence.
4. Assess which stakeholders are important for project success.
5. Identify the assumptions which must be made about what role each stakeholder group will play for your project to succeed – and consider the risks if there is a negative response.

Assessing stakeholders' power and influence requires some thought. Table 18.1 suggests some factors to consider.

Table 18.1   Assessing stakeholders' power and influence

Within and between formal organisations	For informal interest groups and primary stakeholders
Legal hierarchy (command and control, budget holders)	Social, economic, and political status
Authority of leadership (formal and informal, charisma, political, familial or cadre connections)	Degree of organisation, consensus, and leadership in the group
Control of strategic resources for the project (eg suppliers of hardware or other inputs)	Degree of control of strategic resources significant for the project
Possession of specialist knowledge (eg engineers)	Informal influence through links with other stakeholders
Negotiating position (strength in relation to other stakeholders in the project)	Degree of dependence on other stakeholders

You might like to map out the influence and importance of the different stakeholders on a matrix like the one shown in Table 18.2.

Table 18.2   Stakeholder influence/importance matrix

High importance/Low influence	High importance/High influence
A	B
C	D
Low importance/Low influence	Low importance/High influence

Stakeholder analysis is essentially a strategic planning tool – it should not be seen as some sort of scientific process. As with all such tools, the quality of the decisions you make will depend upon the quality of the information you are able to feed into the process. Check your information carefully, where possible drawing on more than one source.

A note of caution

'... "lip service" to proper consultation is a major problem. Stakeholder analysis is too often an academic/desk exercise. The common practice of external experts briefly consulting stakeholders then going away and writing up project proposals and project framework "based on findings of wide-ranging consultation". This acts against ownership, particularly recipient group ownership' (Bilateral aid donor).[1]

18.3   Action Research

Most of the research discussed in this manual could be called action research. Action research recognises explicitly that it is concerned about change, and that the people who need to implement the change should be directly involved in investigating the issues surrounding it. Traditional research sees its process like Figure 18.1 overleaf.

Action research sees data collection, analysis, and reflection on it as part of a cycle, of which action is a key element (Figure 18.2).

It is recognised that research questions arise originally from the experience of people working in the field and reflecting on their work. Action

---

[1]Quoted in Open University text for course TU870, Capacities for Managing Development 1999.

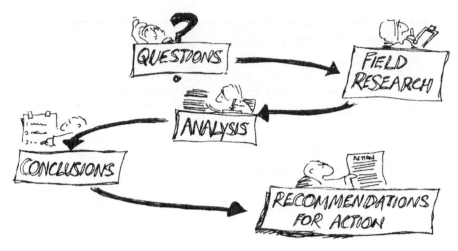

Figure 18.1   Traditional research

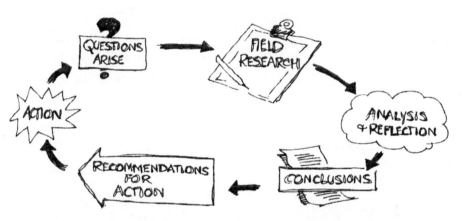

Figure 18.2   Action research (reproduced with permission from Wadsworth, 1997).

research usually involves introducing new practice, and then testing how well it goes. It is seen as a kind of experiment, in a real-life setting. And in action research, implementation is the real test. Action research is usually about finding a local solution to a local problem – solutions which are fully owned by the key participants. The people most directly concerned with the issue have been seen as the people most important to involve in action research processes.

Action research has developed within education (Carr and Kemmis, 1986), health and social care (Hart and Bond, 1995) in Europe and the United States, as a practice of professionals who want to introduce new ways of working. It has also been influential in management (Gill and Johnson, 1991). Reflective practice in social work research is a similar tradition (Broad, 1999) – in the UK there are a number of networks promoting this type of research, for example the Participatory Inquiry and Action in Social Practice Network.

In many ways development work could be seen as action research. There is perhaps more concern for systematic recording in action research. The emphasis on participation is very similar to a development work approach. The same group of methods are used as in other types of research. The fact that such research involves as researchers only those who are already directly involved in the setting could be seen as a strength or as a limiting factor. From the development point of view, participation of people beyond the professional realm would usually be important.

It should be noted that action research is, naturally, criticised by traditionalists as bad research. For example, Adelman (1989) considers much educational action research to be 'inward looking and ahistorical' and of poor quality. As we have seen, criteria for good research are not shared across the different traditions, and it is not to be expected that research focused on practical outcomes would satisfy the academics, who are preoccupied with theory.

18.4   Consultation

As we saw in Chapter 2.4 it may not be helpful to think of consultation as a type of research. Consultation is a directly political process – it should have a life of its own, and not be constrained by the conventions of research. However the research techniques described in Chapter 17 can often make a very useful contribution to consultation exercises. It should be noted that there are of course many other methods which can be used for consultation work that are not covered in this manual. Direct discussion, public meetings, participative work with small groups, and debate in local or national media are some traditional methods.

More recently in the UK, some interesting new methods have been developed which aim to assist public bodies to more effectively consult the public on public policy issues (Barker et al, 1997). This was driven in part by the new Labour Government's concern to be seen to be more answerable to the public in its decision-making (Sykes and Hedges, 1999). There may also be a wish to engage the public more deeply in the problems of prioritisation of spending, for example in relation to health services, in the hope of reducing demands on them.

Citizens' Juries have now been used quite widely and with some success. A Citizens' Jury is a model of public participation developed in Germany and brought to the UK by the Institute for Public Policy Research (IPPR). The jury consists of 12 members of the public who are paid to attend as a jury member for four days and then make a decision on a question. People participate as citizens, not as people with a particular stake in the issue. The jury may undertake investigations, and will call witnesses who give evidence to it. These processes are found to be costly to run.

EXAMPLE

A Citizen's Jury on models of palliative care, Walsall, England

Walsall Health Authority in England asked a Citizens' Jury to answer a question about palliative care (care of the dying), choosing between four alternative models:

- palliative care at home;
- inpatient hospice;
- acute hospital; and
- nursing home.

Health panels have also been used by UK health services for planning and prioritising decisions. One type of panel involves eight to ten people, reflecting, for example, a range by age, sex, or locality, who meet for a number of sessions to discuss set topics and give their views. Members of the panel may rotate so that at any one time there is a balance of 'old' and 'new' members.

Another type of panel is a postal panel. These would be made up of a larger representative group of people who may be sent questionnaires on particular issues.

These are deliberative processes, meaning that the people involved discuss and deliberate on an issue, and reach a decision. This is obviously different from individual-focused research methods such as questionnaires, as it involves group discussion. But it is also a very different process from a focus group, for example, where people are asked to draw on their specific experience and put forward their views, but are specifically briefed that they need not reach agreement with the others in the group. Thus these are not the same as research processes.

There are also of course many ways of consulting communities which are more familiar as part of the community development worker's repertoire (Hadfield, 1998).

CHECKLIST   **Some principles for community consultation**

- ✓ Recognise community members' competence
- ✓ Allow enough time to build up trust and to carry out the consultation work
- ✓ Be flexible about the process you follow
- ✓ Find a balance between collecting information and a positive process for community members
- ✓ Ensure that all sections of the community are consulted, taking account of factors which mute some voices

> ✔ Engage other agencies in the consultation process
> ✔ Involve people who are good at communicating with the community group in question
> ✔ Ensure that you have the support you need
> ✔ Ensure that community members' views are heard
>
> (From Laws, 1998)

18.5   Baseline Studies

'A common problem with baseline studies is that they attempt to collect so much data that it cannot be analysed. Another problem is that programmes often change their areas of emphasis as they develop, so data collected in an initial baseline study may not be relevant later on. It is essential to analyse what information is required as a baseline and be selective.' (Gosling with Edwards, 1995)

Baseline research crops up in conversations more often in its absence than in its presence. Human nature being what it is, we are more often well into a programme before someone thinks about evaluating it, and there is wringing of hands over the lack of a baseline study to compare with, to see whether there have been changes. The evaluation of development programmes would be much more effective and convincing if baseline studies were more often undertaken.

Baseline research should take place before a programme starts. It is aimed at understanding the nature and extent of a problem so that planning can be informed by this information. It would also look at any existing legislation, policies, and interventions which are relevant to the problem. At this point it may overlap with a stakeholder analysis (see above, 18.2). (It is certainly essential to consider who are the key stakeholders, and of course whose reality/ies you need to reflect.) And a baseline study aims to provide a reference point against which changes can be measured so that the impact of the programme, or of external factors (eg new policy implementation processes) can be measured.

It should be noted that baseline research should not be a sort of census process! Spending obviously needs to be in proportion to the benefit to be gained from the study. But at a minimum the collection of existing research data, a systematic look at what is at present being done to address the problem, and some small-scale fieldwork to get basic information about how the issue is experienced in the community, should be undertaken. For large and important programmes, which are seen as demonstration projects whose learning should inform practice very widely, a more rigorous study will be needed. Consider what are the key factors which the planned intervention should change – what can be used as observable, quantifiable indicators for these? Logical framework analysis refers to these as 'verifiable indicators'.

There can be a 'chicken and egg' problem – how to finance a baseline study before spending the resources on a baseline study to show that it is needed? This is probably why these studies are relatively rare, but funders are becoming increasingly interested in evidence of effectiveness. A good balance between cost and benefit/learning is needed.

Critical questions in baseline assessment

- What kind of issue or problem is giving us cause for concern?
- How serious or widespread is this problem?
- What are its exact dimensions?
- What are the existing policies and programmes that affect these community members?

A range of research techniques may be used in baseline research, but if the aim is to create a basis for a later evaluation process, it will be important to include indicators which can be used in a quantitative way to assess the success of the programme.

EXAMPLE

A baseline study of rural water supply schemes in Tibet

Since 1991, Save the Children's Environmental Health Project has developed about 130 rural water supply schemes in Tibet. Its second phase started in September 1999. Due to lack of sustainability of the previous approach, more focus is now required on increasing community involvement and health promotion. The purpose of its logical framework is: 'Improved livelihoods for poor people in Lhasa valley through sustainable water and sanitation improvements.'

Fifty-four villages from 4 counties of Lhasa Prefecture are to benefit from the project within the next 5 years. In order to assess the impact of the project it was proposed to carry a baseline survey on related Objective Verifiable Indicators (OVIs). The aim of this baseline survey was to measure them in 12 sample pilot villages (3 in each county) before work starts, after one year, and again after two years of project activities completion. The first survey would represent a benchmark to be compared with the two later surveys in order to evaluate the impact of the project and in order to get feedback from the new project approach. The links between the baseline survey and the two following 'evaluation' surveys is presented in Figure 18.3 (Lorillou, 2000).

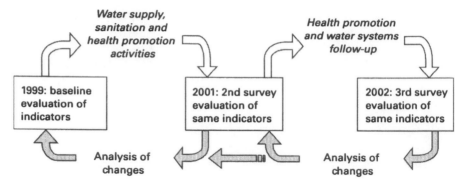

Figure 18.3   Use of the baseline survey for future evaluation of Environmental Health Project indicators

18.6   Case studies

Case studies are widely used in development work. However the term is used to describe many different things. At times it refers to a paragraph written about a particular project or individual, which will be used to make a particular argument, perhaps for policy influencing or for fund-raising. Here, the 'study' element is generally pretty minimal! For the purposes of this section, we are looking at more in-depth case studies where there is direct investigation of the case or cases in question, using multiple sources of evidence.

Case study research is effective when it is rooted in theory – that is, an idea about why things happen as they do. Simply describing what happened can only be of interest to a very narrow audience. It is possible to carry out an effective case study on one project or programme, but it requires much more than an account of the project's development from the point of view of those running it to enable it to travel beyond the local area.

Robson (1993) identifies different kinds of case study:

1. Individual case study
2. Set of individual case studies – of a small number of people with some features in common
3. Community studies, eg a town, a village
4. Social group studies, eg families, occupational groups
5. Studies of organisations and institutions
6. Studies of processes, events, roles, and relationships.

EXAMPLE

Use of case studies – health sustainability

Save the Children's Health Sustainability study looked at the way in which primary health care in developing countries was financed and organised through five case studies in countries with different characteristics. The study had a strong theoretical framework, and a standard set of information was gathered through substantial fieldwork in each country.

The study used a definition of health sector sustainability as: 'the capacity of the health sector to function effectively over time with a minimum of external input', although problems were identified with this definition. In each case study country an analysis was undertaken of the historical development of the health sector, an appraisal of the key factors (political, organisational, and economic) which determine the context of health sector operation and development, and an analysis of the role of government, donors, and communities.

One element of the theory behind the project was that health care in poor countries would be best served by long-term support to government health systems to create a sustainable infrastructure, rather than project-based short-term funding targeted at specific health issues (eg immunisation, HIV/AIDS prevention, family planning, etc). Sustainability comprises two features: effectiveness and continuity. The study concluded that 'Increased aid flows will be essential if progress is to be made towards comprehensive basic health care in the poorest countries ... the traditional view of aid as "catalyst" must be modified in the light of the limited [resources] of many beneficiary countries.'

Different kinds of case study

It will be seen that the 'case' under consideration, the unit of analysis, may be any of a number of things. Studies of particular decisions or policy implementation processes are common in development work, as are studies which look at projects and programmes or at households or villages.

The other important distinction is between the single case study and multiple case studies. It should be noted that although research is always strengthened by some element of comparison, you would not be able to think of multiple case studies in the same way as you might the results of a study of a representative sample. However you may be able to build a very convincing case based on theoretical generalisation – trying out your theory on different cases and seeing how it works out in practice. By theory I mean a guess about what is happening in the world. For example, we might think that certain categories of children are at increased risk of being recruited into the armed forces in a conflict situation – this proposition could be tested in relation to a number of countries. Or we might think that inter-agency projects addressing domestic violence will be more effective if they succeed in involving the police as an active partner, than if the grouping only includes welfare agencies.

In relation to single case study designs, Yin (1994) suggests three main rationales:

- the critical case (which may be a test of theory or a way of comparing theories or ideas);
- the extreme (sometimes unique) case; and
- the revelatory case (where the researcher gains access to a previously unavailable situation).

Case studies concerned with 'good practice' are common in development work. It is worth thinking about in what way a particular example of practice is special – is the setting particularly challenging? Is it in fact testing a particular theory or approach? For 'good practice' case studies to be persuasive to the reader, it is important to analyse what exactly are the features of the work which constitute 'good practice', and how we know it is effective. The reader wants to know what key principles or practices have been followed which could be replicated elsewhere. It may be useful to think of it like this: the challenge to counter is that any positive outcomes have arisen because of the presence of exceptionally charismatic or committed staff, rather than from a particular way of working.

Undertaking a case study project

It is important to set out a formal plan for your case study – its aims and objectives, and the methods you intend to use. You may need to revise these as you go along, but making your assumptions explicit at the start will be very helpful. Case studies need to be based on a clear theoretical framework, and a set of research questions that are capable of being investigated. These will guide not only the choice of cases to study, but also your decisions about what is the important data to gather on your cases. Case studies are usually undertaken to investigate 'how' and 'why' questions, and you need at the start to set down on paper your ideas about what cause explains what effect.

Choosing cases for a multiple case study

It is worth first carrying out some exploratory work, in which you work out a preliminary typology of the cases you aim to consider. What are the important principles you want to follow in classifying your cases? Once this is done, the following steps could be followed to build up a more complete list of possible cases for consideration:

1. Use obvious differences (age, size, geography, etc) to form a preliminary typology.
2. Tell 'experts' about the cases you are looking at and ask them to suggest others which might uncover different types.
3. Use multiple sources, eg not cases known to one organisation only.
4. Ask people involved in one case about the existence of others, perhaps cases where a different strategy is being tried.
5. Think of logical alternatives.
6. Look in different social and political environments.

(From Thomas et al, 1998)

Once you have used this process to map out all the possible cases of the phenomenon you are considering, you will need to select from them those you intend to study in depth. Having done the process of looking broadly at the field in general, you should be able to work out a logical structure to guide your choice of cases for detailed study.

It should be noted that this is a completely different process from sampling for a survey. You probably do not know the extent or nature of the total population you are sampling from and you may not have enough information about the possible cases 'out there' to draw a meaningful sample. This means that you should not imply at any point that the cases you select can be seen as statistically representative or comparable with each other.

Methods for case studies

In carrying out a case study, you may want to use any or all of the techniques described in Chapter 17. It would be wrong to assume that only qualitative methods are appropriate to case study research – some case studies require the collection or re-analysis of quantitative data. It depends upon the research questions. Usually a combination of methods is best, enabling a look at the issues from various points of view.

Let us take a study of an organisation or a decision-making process as an example. Typically you would start with a look at documentary evidence and some exploratory interviews with key individuals. Then you would need to negotiate access (see Chapter 8.3) for more detailed work, and would probably undertake more focused interviews with a number of people. There might be data already existing which could shed light on the questions you are asking, and you should use any material you can locate which is relevant to your research – but not any which just happens to be around, but is not relevant, of course.

Finally, as you work towards presenting your case, it will be important to sharpen your focus on the theoretical questions you started with. Case studies can be tedious to read if you do not keep a very tight rein on the amount of detail you include, and constantly return to the questions at the centre of your investigation.

Case study research is potentially vulnerable to the charge that the investigator has looked only to see what they wanted to find. To make your work rigorous and defensible, it is important to 'triangulate' the research process by looking at the same issue in different ways, collecting data of different kinds from different people. Thus a more convincing picture can be built up. It is also necessary, as discussed in Chapter 15, to keep detailed records of your work, for example by making careful notes of interviews as you go along. This should create a record which would enable someone else to follow your trail of reasoning to see how you arrived at the conclusions you reached.

As we have seen, case studies are an attractive option for some types of research for development work. However they need to be done properly to have persuasive power, and this takes considerable resources.

EXAMPLE

Case studies – children and domestic violence in the UK

In the UK the Children's Society, funded by the Joseph Rowntree Foundation, wanted to study ways of offering support where there is concern for children in relation to domestic violence in their family. In order to identify what is good practice in relation to this issue, a number of voluntary agencies engaged in relevant work were given £5000 each to enable them to produce a case study on the practice or policy intervention they were involved in. The agencies also met and debated amongst themselves what constitutes good practice, and consulted their service users on the issue. The intention was to establish an evaluative framework, informed by the views of the children and women concerned, which could be used to assess interventions in this area in future, as well as to describe existing models of good practice.

CHECKLIST   **For good practice in case study research**

- ✓ Write a brief for case study research, as you would for any other research (see Chapters 5 and 6)
- ✓ Case study research needs a clear theoretical basis – a framework which links the research questions to the data you collect
- ✓ Choose cases carefully, linking their selection to your theoretical framework – but do not think of this as the same process as sampling for a survey
- ✓ Case studies use multiple methods for data collection
- ✓ Studies of more than one case are always more persuasive

18.7   Participatory Learning and Action

Participatory Learning and Action (PLA) used to be known as Participatory Research and Action (PRA) and before that Rapid Rural Appraisal (RRA). PLA is an important approach to needs assessment and feasibility studies, which has been very influential on work in the South over the past 15 years or so. It constitutes an important alternative to the tradition of big surveys, and overturns the emphasis on experts making technical assessments and prescribing remedies, in favour of placing community participation at the core of the process. For a broader discussion of participatory approaches, please see Chapter 3.

PLA is fully described in the companion volume to this one, Save the Children's *Toolkits* (Gosling with Edwards, 1995). There is also useful guidance in the training manuals by Joachim Theis and Heather M. Grady (1991) and by Pretty et al (1995).

Some of the techniques used in PLA are described in the last chapter – ranking and scoring and visual methods are important in PLA. But PLA is much more than a bundle of methods, and practitioners are concerned to point out that the methods used are less important than the attitudes and beliefs of those carrying out the work. The checklist below gives a summary of the key principles behind PLA. The most important tenet of PLA is the 'one-sentence manual':

'Use your own best judgement at all times.'

CHECKLIST   Principles of Participatory Learning and Action (PLA)

- A reversal of learning – 'experts' learn from ordinary people
- Learning rapidly and progressively
- Offsetting biases
- Optimising trade-offs – 'optimal ignorance' – knowing what is not worth knowing, and 'appropriate imprecision'
- Triangulating – using a range of methods to cross-check information
- Seeking diversity
- Facilitating – 'they (community members) do it', 'handing over the stick'
- Self-critical awareness and responsibility – welcoming error as an opportunity to learn to do better; using one's own best judgement at all times
- Sharing of information, ideas, resources

(Chambers, 1992)

Development workers and researchers in the North should have a look at this material – it brings a strong creative energy into the search for appropriate methods. Many of the methods are particularly useful for working with people who do not read or write confidently – which applies to plenty of people in the North as well as the South. There are examples of PLA being used in the North (Cresswell, 1996), but the practice has not been developed very far. Some of the techniques could certainly be adapted to a range of different settings.

PLA grew out of the needs of the type of work this manual calls programme-focused research – as a more effective approach to village-level appraisal processes. In the mid- to late nineties there has been an interesting debate about to what extent PLA approaches can be successful in influencing policy more broadly (Holland with Blackburn, 1998).

An important initiative in this field has been the development of Participatory Poverty Assessments (PPAs), where PLA-type methods are used within a process which aims to describe and analyse poverty issues in whole countries or districts. The World Bank sponsored a series of these PPAs in a wide range of countries. Many of the lessons learnt (Robb, 1998) are typical of efforts of every kind to influence policy – that it is crucial to engage those with real power over policy decisions in the process from the beginning and as closely as possible. Management support and follow-up are essential if the findings of this kind of process are to be put into practice.

The popularity of PLA has led to a wave of critiques, which tests the claims made for it. PLA tends to deal with 'the community' as a group, although it may collect data from sub-groups separately. This means that it can perpetuate power differences within the community. Those with the strongest voice are most likely to be heard. This may mean that those with more power – men rather than women, adults rather than children, majority rather than minority ethnic groups – or those who know what they want, perhaps the somewhat better off farmers (Ashby and Sperling, 1995), are more able to get their issues taken seriously (Mosse, 1994).

These problems may to some extent be addressed by PLA research teams having a strong consciousness of social inequalities and how they work, but to a degree they may be inherent in the PLA process. Issues like domestic violence, for example, are very unlikely to be prioritised, or indeed even mentioned, within whole-community groups. Where stigma is attached to a condition or problem, it will be difficult to raise, as it will be for issues constructed as 'private'. Where the issues relate to inequalities within the family, or within the local community itself, participation by all may actually work against less powerful individuals being able to raise their problems within the process.

18.8   Frameworks for Specific Issues: Risk Mapping and the Household Food Economy Approach

This section introduces one approach to a specific type of development problem. There are other such frameworks available, such as living standards surveys, poverty analysis, and gender analysis (for example, Scoones, 1998).[3] If it seems likely that such a framework may have been developed for a piece of work you are planning, it will be worth investigating this before you 'reinvent the wheel'. You will of course need to critically assess the relevance of any framework you adopt, and customise it to your particular context and purposes. Using an off-the-shelf framework can bring many benefits, in directing you towards specific questions, but it could also limit your thinking.

Much study has been directed towards the important issue of how it is best, in times of crisis, to identify areas and households most vulnerable to food shortage, and the necessary amount of food or other aid required to avoid famine or protect livelihoods. The difficulty is to predict the possible impact of changes arising from a range of sources, climatic change, deteriorating security situations, and economic changes such as falling commodity prices on a particular area.

Experience has shown that even a combination of 'shocks' of this sort rarely gives rise to disaster as people demonstrate a remarkable ability to revise the ways they make ends meet – their livelihood strategies. Outright famine has actually been rare in recent years and related more often to warfare than climatic factors. The link between crop failure and starvation is, then, indirect. To understand it you need a detailed picture of how households meet their food needs in a 'normal' year, and the many strategies they use to lessen the impact of crises (selling or consuming assets, migration for employment, eating wild foods, etc).

Save the Children UKs Household Food Economy Approach (HFEA) aims to provide a framework to create a picture of household economy and its relationship to markets and employment opportunities. It is useful for answering the question 'what will be the effect of some event, or combination of events, on the economy of defined types of households in defined areas?'

HFEA in action

The household is used as the basic unit, and information is collected, following a line of questioning producing increasingly focused information. This is done by using a range of rapid and participatory approaches to work with groups of 'key informants'. The following steps are taken:

---

[3]The World Bank Household Budget Surveys and Living Standard Measurement Surveys are well-tested survey instruments for assessing living standards. The World Bank's website (see Appendix 1) includes full details of how to access these materials, and where they have been used.

A good place to look for other frameworks relating to food security is the Eldis web page on 'Technical guides for operationalising household food security in development projects', produced by the International Food Policy Research Institute, 1999. *http://nt1.ids.ac.uk/eldis/tech.htm*. (See Appendix 1)

1. Identifying Food Economy Areas and populations.
2. Identifying wealth groups, and a 'normal' year.
3. Describing households' access to food and cash income.
4. Understanding links to markets.
5. Clarifying potential coping strategies.
6. Problem specification – calculating the likely impact of shocks on each wealth group and the likely impact of different interventions.

So, information is gathered through a range of methods, and this is then analysed either manually or using a spreadsheet, or for larger areas, using the RiskMap computer programme, which has been developed by Save the Children to store all this information and work successively through a range of problem specifications.

This model has been used primarily in rural Africa, but its application is potentially global. In addition to identifying the need for food aid, it is increasingly being used to look at alternatives to food aid, as a training tool to increase understanding of household economies, and as a tool to aid development planning. Save the Children has been working to establish baseline information in countries most likely to experience crises. In Africa Save the Children holds information ranging from the Eritrea/Ethiopia border in the north to Swaziland in the south.

Further Reading

Needs Assessment

Gosling, L. with Edwards, M. (1995) *Toolkits: A practical guide to assessment, monitoring, review and evaluation*, Development Manual 5. London: Save the Children.

Contains a short section on needs assessment, and tools which can be used to carry it out.

Mikkelsen, B. (1995) *Methods for Development Work and Research: A guide for practitioners*. New Delhi, Thousand Oaks, London: Sage.

Though needs assessment is not used as a term, much of the book concerns these issues.

Stakeholder Analysis

Rietbergen-McCracken, J. and Narayan, D. (1998) *Participation and Social Assessment: Tools and techniques – module 2: Stakeholder analysis*. New York: The World Bank.

This resource kit also includes modules on social assessment and other participatory methodologies.

Overseas Development Administration Social Development Department, *Guidance Note on how to do Stakeholder Analysis of Aid Projects and Programmes,* (July 1995); *Note on Enhancing Stakeholder Participation in Aid Activities* (April 1995); and *Guidance Note on Indicators for Measuring and Assessing Primary Stakeholder Participation* (July 1995).

Action Research

Hart, E. and Bond, M. (1995) *Action Research for Health and Social Care: A guide to practice.* Buckingham, UK: Open University Press.

Written for practitioners, to encourage them to research their own work.

Denscombe, M. (1998) *The Good Research Guide for Small-Scale Social Research Projects.* Buckingham UK and Philadelphia USA: The Open University Press.

Contains a good chapter on action research as an approach.

Wadsworth, Y. (1997) *Do It Yourself Social Research.* St Leonards, Australia: Allen and Unwin.

Whole book is in the spirit of action research, without using the term.

Consultation

Barker, J., Bullen, M. and de Ville, J. (1997) *Reference Manual for Public Involvement.* London: Bromley Health, West Kent Health Authority, and Lambeth, Southwark, and Lewisham Health Authority.

Very well-presented manual, aimed at UK public authorities, especially the health service. But much more widely relevant – describes many different methods clearly, as well as the broad issues involved. Gives pros and cons of different approaches.

Sykes, R. and Hedges, A. (eds) (1999) *Panels and Juries: New government, new agenda.* London: Social Research Association. (Website listed in Appendix 1)

A collection of short papers discussing the pros and cons of various methods of consultation with the public.

Hadfield, M. (1998) *Community Consultation: Power, politics and policies.* Booklet and video. Nottingham: The Urban Programme Research Group, University of Nottingham.

This pack aims to assist people in thinking through the 'political' aspects of community consultation work. It includes accounts of three different approaches in practice.

Coote, A. and Lenaghan, J. (1997) *Citizens' Juries: Theory into practice.* London: Institute of Public Policy Research.

The results of the pilot series of citizens' juries. This report sets out the reasons for the experiment, describes and analyses the pilot project, and makes recommendations for the future.

Baseline Studies

Boyden, J. and Ennew, J. (eds) (1997) *Children in Focus: A manual for participatory research with children*. Stockholm: Rädda Barnen, Swedish Save the Children.

Case Studies

Thomas, A. (1998) 'Challenging Cases', in Thomas, A., Chataway, J. and Wuyts, M. (eds), *Finding Out Fast: Investigative skills for policy and development*. London: Open University/Sage.

A helpful article on case studies, within a collection aimed at development practitioners.

Robson, C. (1993) *Real World Research*. Oxford, UK and Cambridge, USA: Blackwell.

Discusses case study research as a typical 'real world' approach.

Yin, R.K. (1989) *Case Study Research*, Applied Social Research Methods Series Volume 5. Newbury Park, California: Sage.

A thorough and authoritative text that offers a clear conceptual framework within which to think about case studies.

Participatory Learning and Action

Theis, J. and Grady, H.M. (1991) *Participatory Rapid Appraisal for Community Development*. London: IIED and Save the Children Federation.

Training manual for PLA.

Pretty, J.N., Guijt, I., Scoones I. and Thompson, J. (1995) *A Trainer's Guide for Participatory Learning and Action*. London: IIED.

Designed for both experienced and new trainers, provides a comprehensive background to the principles of adult learning, as well as detailed guidance on facilitation skills and the principles of PLA. Describes the process of organising training both in workshops and in the field. Includes 101 games and exercises for trainers, and helpful examples from real life.

Selener, D., Endara, N. and Carvajal, J. (1999) *Participatory Rural Appraisal and Planning Workbook*. Ecuador/Phillipines/USA/Kenya: International Institute of Rural Reconstruction.

The only PRA manual to include Latin American experiences. Presents and analyses two case studies, and aims to go beyond information gathering to show readers how to use the information generated by participatory appraisal.

Gosling, L. with Edwards, M. (1995) *Toolkits: A practical guide to assessment, monitoring, review and evaluation*, Development Manual 5. London: Save the Children.

Gives an account of PLA methodology.

Mikkelsen, B. (1995) *Methods for Development Work and Research: A guide for practitioners*. New Delhi, Thousand Oaks, London: Sage.

Includes a good discussion of PLA in theory and practice.

Blackburn, J. with Holland, J. (eds) (1998) *Who Changes? Institutionalising participation in development*. London: Intermediate Technology Publications.

Holland, J. with Blackburn, J. (eds) (1998) *Whose Voice? Participatory research and policy change*. London: Intermediate Technology Publications.

These two collections reflect on a whole body of PLA-inspired work.

Risk Mapping and the Household Economy Approach

Seaman, J., Clarke, P., Boudreau, T. and Holt, J. (2000) *The Household Economy Approach: A resource manual for practitioners*, Development Manual 6. London: Save the Children.

The RiskMap computer programme itself can be obtained from Malcolm Newdick on mail@riverbank.co.uk, or write to Malcolm at Manor Cottage, Little Milton, Oxford OX44 7QB. Runs on Windows 3.1 or 95 to 98, cost is £30.

19 Talking to the Right People – Choosing a Sample

The decisions you make about from whom to collect information will be one of the important elements shaping your research project. This chapter explains some different ways of approaching sampling for various types of research. Quantitative and qualitative research have different requirements in terms of sampling, and a good sample is a key criterion for quality research of any sort.

In this chapter we will first discuss a variety of different types of sample, which fall into two groups – random or probability samples, and purposive or non-probability samples. Sampling for qualitative research has particular requirements, which are different from those for quantitative studies, and this is discussed next. The chapter concentrates mainly on sampling people, but will look briefly also at choosing time, places, and events for study. A short section looks specifically at site selection for participatory policy research. Then we will look at a number of ways of increasing your response rate – the proportion of those you approach who agree to take part in your research. In particular we will consider ways of including traditionally 'hard to reach' groups of people. Finally the question of whether or not to use incentives is discussed.

The sample you use is of the greatest importance for any piece of research. It is always important to look carefully at the sample involved when you are evaluating a piece of research someone else has done – and you can be sure readers will do the same with your research.

EXAMPLE

Assessing levels of need: refugees in Rwanda

In 1982 when 50,000 displaced people from Uganda arrived in neighbouring Rwanda, the Red Cross reported that 20 per cent of children under five were in a state of serious malnutrition. This figure was accepted by UNHCR and by the government, neither of which had reason to doubt the Red Cross findings. The data were transmitted to NGOs, and plans were made for a massive response based on emergency feeding procedures.

An Oxfam doctor managed to reach the camp within a couple of days and pointed out that the 20 per cent figure was unusually high and, if it were true, was an indicator that the whole refugee population was in a very bad way indeed.

Further enquiries revealed that the Red Cross data had been collected at the emergency health post in the camp. In other words, the sample was severely biased because the only children to be taken to the health post were children who were already ill, many of them with intestinal complaints. A random nutritional survey was put into operation and within a short time reliable data were available which put the nutritional status of under-fives at a figure which was normal for southern Uganda at that time of year. The nutritional status of the whole population was therefore not of acute concern. Plans for emergency feeding were scrapped (Pratt and Loizos, 1992).

Table 19.1   Some terminology

Technical term	Definition	Examples
Population	The complete set of units about which generalisations are to be made	All adults in Peru All villages in a district Children attending a school
Sampling frame	A complete list of all the units in the population	Electoral register for Peru[1] List of villages School register
Sample size	The total number of units selected from the population	A sample of 60 students drawn from a school population of 400 – sample size = 60
Response rate	The proportion of all those who are eligible to respond who do actually respond	Of a sample of 100 households, contact was made with 78 households – a response rate of 78%
Non-response	Failure to provide data by some of those in the sample. Runs risk of causing bias in the achieved sample	Respondent is out when you call at their house. Person unwilling to take part in your research

Source: Taken from University of North London teaching pack on research methods.

What Does Sampling Mean?

Researchers always talk about 'sampling', on the principle that you usually cannot gather data from everyone you might be interested in, so you select a sample which can represent the larger group. The image this conjures up may seem rather remote from your experience. Frequently development workers are interested in groups who are not tidily listed anywhere, who may not have fixed addresses and may not appear in official counts for a

---

[1]There are of course often problems with the quality of a sampling frame.

variety of reasons. You might feel your sample has chosen you, rather than the other way around.

Whatever approach is taken, it is likely that some negotiation will be needed to get access to respondents – this may mean talking to the chief of a village; writing formal proposals to public bodies; or meeting with a hospital manager or head teacher. This process comes before choosing a sample, though it is involved with it, and is discussed in Chapter 8.3.

However the process of selecting respondents is done, it is still called sampling, and it still requires thought as to how best to minimise bias in the sample, and clarity about what can be claimed for which type of sample. We will talk first of all about sampling of people, which is how the term is most usually used, but remember there may also be sampling issues in relation to location, time, and events that you study – see Section 19.3 below.

The key decision

There are essentially two main types of sample: probability or random samples, and non-probability or purposive samples. Basically if you want to claim that your data are statistically representative of a larger population, you need a probability sample. Quantitative research requires a reasonably representative sample to be convincing.

Purposive samples are more likely to be appropriate to qualitative approaches. The term 'purposive' refers to selection linked to the purpose of the research. For example, if your research is about the needs of HIV-positive mothers of young children, no one is going to give you a list of these people, but you can build up a sample by working through service-providers and direct appeals to the relevant communities. Those you are able to contact may be in some important respects different from those you cannot contact, but you will still learn a great deal from them in relation to your research questions.

The most common types of sample can be grouped as follows:

Random

- Simple random sampling
- Systematic sampling
- Stratified sampling
- Cluster sampling.

Purposive

- Quota sampling
- Snowball sampling
- Judgement (purposive/theoretical) sampling
- Convenience sampling.

We will now discuss these different types of sample in more detail, starting with random-type samples.

19.1   Random/Probability Samples

Table 19.2   Some types of probability sample

Type of sample	Definition	Example
Simple random sample	A sample designed so that each unit in the population has an equal chance (probability) of selection	Names (or numbers) drawn out of a hat; choose from a numbered list using random numbers generated by a computer
Systematic sample	A version of simple random sampling in which the sampling frame is arranged in order, then every nth unit is selected	Pick a number between 1 and 100 (say 9), then select the 9th unit, 109th unit and so on from your list, or else the 4th, 8th, 12th, etc ... Visit every third house in a village
Stratified random sample	A version of simple random sampling which is used when there is a need to represent all groups of the population in the sample	Divide target population into strata, eg males/females, urban/rural, etc. The defining feature of the strata must be identifiable from information you hold. Select simple random or systematic sample from each group or strata. Merge samples into one
Cluster sample	Instead of selecting individual sampling units, you select from clusters of units, and then choose units within that on some systematic basis. This saves travel costs and time, and you only need a sampling frame for the clusters, not for individual units	To sample households in an area where they are grouped together in isolated settlements, interview all the households in a number of randomly selected settlements Caution: because you are concentrating your sample in small areas, you can miss out some important sub-groups completely
The random walk	Fieldworkers are given a standard set of detailed instructions to follow a set route, interviewing households at regular intervals	From the starting point, go north as directly as possible. Take the first road on your right. Interview at the second plot on your left. Continue along the road in the same direction. Pass ten plots and interview at the next, and so on. Only works well in neatly laid out, dispersed settlements

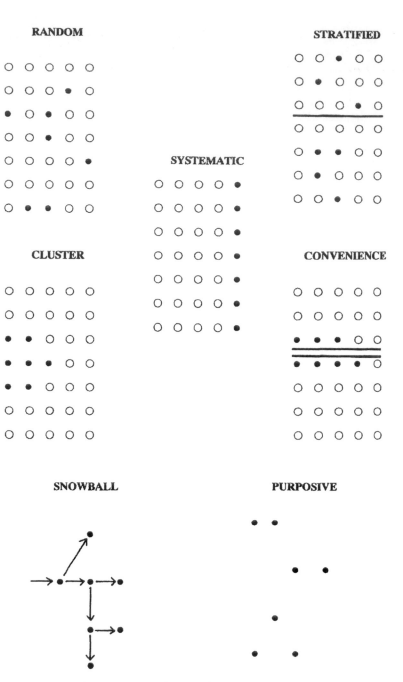

Figure 19.1   Sampling strategies illustrated
Reprinted with permission from Blaxter et al (1996).

The first thing to get clear is that a random sample is not a haphazard, arbitrary, careless sample – quite the opposite. The reason for using a random sample is to avoid bias. There are many ways in which bias can creep into a sample to give a misleading picture of the population. Robert Chambers gives some classic examples of sources of bias in development research, for instance 'tarmac-road bias', when researchers tend to keep close to major roads or paths. People living in the most remote places – often the poorest – will be under-represented. 'Dry season bias' refers to fieldwork done only in the dry season – not likely to give a representative picture. 'Project bias' occurs where only people in areas where projects are already under way are included. Of course it is easier to study people who are in touch with your organisation, perhaps using its services. But unless you reach beyond these, you cannot know whether their views and characteristics are in any way representative of the wider community.

If a sample is truly random it will usually be unbiased. So long as the sampling frame lists the complete target population and there are few refusals or missed contacts, every unit has an equal chance of being selected. However it is important to ensure that fieldworkers call back when people are out, and make every effort to contact the person or household who actually falls into the sample, otherwise you may get bias towards types of people who are for some reason easier to make contact with.

In random sampling, you must carry out your fieldwork absolutely consistently. It is not acceptable to avoid households with dogs, up steep hills, or with other unattractive characteristics, unfortunately!

It should be noted that a random or systematic sample of reasonable size from a general population will automatically include people representing the important sub-groups within it, in roughly the proportion that they are present. So you should get a spread by, for example, educational experience, economic category, ethnic group, or whatever, without specifically selecting for this. However unless your sample is very large you may miss some small minorities. One approach, if you are particularly interested in a small group (for example elderly people over a certain age, or from a particular minority ethnic group), and want to ensure you include enough from this group, is to first draw a random sample, and collect data from them. Then you check that you have enough who fall into the categories you are interested in, and if need be, carry out some purposive quota sampling (see below 19.3). Stratified sampling is an alternative approach.

> **COMMON PITFALLS**   Saying you have taken a random sample when really you chose people in a haphazard way

If you are undertaking a major research project for which you want a good random sample, it will be worth getting advice from an experienced researcher, probably a statistician, on exactly what the issues are to consider, and in particular on how large a sample you need. Don't leave it until it is too late to adjust your strategy in the light of advice.

> **TIP**   Proper probability sampling is a technical business – get expert advice from a statistician at an early stage, or you will almost certainly be wasting your time

The next sections offer some more advice on how to carry out some types of sampling described in Table 19.2 above.

How to take a systematic sample from a list

Some lists are naturally grouped into sections, and if you take every nth unit, you will automatically get a sample which represents every section or class. Sometimes information is available to arrange a list in a useful order before you choose a sample. For example, you could arrange a list of villages in order of size, using census data. Then, with a systematic sample, you will be sure of including examples for each category of village size.

The main disadvantage of systematic sampling, like random sampling, is that you need a detailed, accurate sampling frame for the full target population. You also get a sample of widely dispersed units, making field-work expensive.

How to take a stratified random sample

This is helpful where you want to ensure that sub-groups are accurately represented within the sample. Using existing information, you divide the target population into non-overlapping sub-groups, and then take a random sample from each of the sub-groups. Some characteristics which researchers often use to divide up a population are settlement size, ecological zone, housing area; distance from a central point; presence or absence of key facilities (such as a health centre).

However you need a great deal of information about your target population to divide it into sub-groups.

How to take a cluster sample

This method does not rely on complete lists of the population, but the more information you have, the better. In a rural study you could select a sample of villages (the clusters) in a random way from a census list, and hold all the interviews in these selected villages. Stratify the list of clusters before you select areas for interview. For example, group villages by size and select one or more villages from each size grouping.

A cluster sample is only a probability sample when you sample your clusters from a list which represents the whole population of clusters. If you use your judgement to choose clusters it becomes a purposive, non-random sample.

The rules for cluster sampling are:

- Before you choose the sample, arrange a list of clusters into similar sub-groups of about the same size.
- Use many small clusters rather than a few large ones.
- Number each cluster.
- Using random numbers, select a sample of complete clusters. The exact total sample size depends on the clusters selected, but if clusters are roughly equal in size, this is not a problem.
- Fieldworkers interview every household/individual in the selected clusters.

(Nichols, 1991)

The key problem with random sampling is the need for a good quality sampling frame or list from which to select.

EXAMPLE

Off the map?

In Israel there are within its agreed borders Arab villages which are not recognised by the government. Known as 'unrecognised villages', they lack basic services like water and sanitation which are supplied to other villages, often on the next hill. If you took a sample from a government list of villages, you would inevitably exclude the inhabitants of these villages. Your sample would be biased in a particular way, as the experiences of these villagers will be systematically different from those of people living in recognised settlements.

What if there is no list?

Very often development work takes place in contexts where lists which could be used for random sampling simply do not exist, or are so flawed as to be unusable. You may be able to use maps or the more general information about the population which does exist to attempt some kind of random-type sampling. A systematic approach to cluster sampling, for example, can produce a sample which avoids the most obvious sources of bias. Or it may be better to accept that you need to work with a purposive sample. It is worth looking for ways to reduce bias in your sample, whatever approach you take. It is a matter of doing the best you can in the circumstances.

Often, research for development work sets out to explore issues which are not at all well understood. Sections of the population that face particularly acute problems are involved. Purposive sampling is perfectly acceptable when it enables the investigation of issues about which little is known. As long as you explain clearly exactly how sampling has been done, and acknowledge any sources of bias you are aware of, the reader is able to judge for themselves what weight to put on your findings. The danger with small purposive samples is that your evidence may be dismissed as merely anecdotal.

Panel studies

Panel studies are surveys where information is collected from the sample units two or more times. Though people use the term 'panel' to mean many things, in survey research, a panel is a group of respondents who are surveyed periodically over time. This type of research lends itself to studying changes over time, but is also used for other reasons. For example, the UK National Child Development Study has conducted studies of a sample of people at seven-year intervals, asking a wide range of questions about health, education, employment, and so on. The children of the original sample are now being studied. Panels are also being used in the UK as a form of public consultation. For example, Nottingham City Council set up a panel of 1000 residents who are sent questionnaires every so often asking for their views on Council policy issues, such as transport, social services, or refuse disposal. A panel of this kind would be selected by random or stratified sampling.

19.2   How Large a Sample do you Need?

'How many people must we interview before we can do any statistics on it?' This definitely counts as a 'frequently asked question' in social research! And wouldn't you know it, there is no simple answer. I used to know a public health department which generally gave the answer 100, but this is really just a figure plucked out of the air. If you wanted to make claims about a very large population, for example about residents of London (population around 7 million) you would need a sample in proportion to the whole population.

The problem is that it all depends on what you are studying, the population in question, and the issues you are investigating. What is important is not only the total number of respondents, but how many people would be found in any sub-group of respondents – and then on how much those sub-groups matter to the issue in question.

For example, in the area where I live in North London, any study where ethnic origin was an important factor would find a very diverse population yielding small numbers of people of more than 25 different backgrounds. Then there is gender and age. To do a statistically valid study, for example of access to health care for people of different backgrounds, the problem would be that in each sub-category, the numbers would become very small. Your main sample might be 100, but there could be only 3 female Somalis between 16 and 45. And any differences found would be based on too small a number to be meaningful. (Not to say that qualitative data from such a study would not be extremely valuable – just not statistically representative.)

So – it all depends. Sorry!

Response rates

It is important to realise that it is not enough to declare that you will work with a large sample, and attempt to include them, for example by posting out a questionnaire to 3000 households, if very few are actually returned. This is what is referred to as your response rate – the proportion of respondents who actually take part in your research, relative to those you approached.

You are aiming for a response rate well over 50%. A very low response rate casts doubt on the quality of your research, because there may be systematic differences between those who took part in the research and those who did not. It is worth putting quite a lot of work into getting a good response rate: expect to call back, send reminders, make new appointments to replace missed ones, etc.

19.3   Purposive/Non-random Sampling

A good random sample enables you to claim with some confidence that your data are representative of the wider population. However in many situations the sampling frame you need from which to draw such a sample is simply not available. Cost may also be a factor.

Non-random sampling is any form of selection based completely or partly on the judgement of the researcher. For this reason, these methods can produce bias unless they are used with care.

How to draw a quota sample

First decide what characteristics dividing the population are important in relation to the aims of your study. You can really only use features which can be observed such as age, sex, location, etc. It is important to remember that getting a balanced sample for some characteristics does not guarantee that there will be a representative sample on other factors, such as social and economic differences. For example, a quota sample of fathers of teenagers in an inner-city part of London included no minority ethnic men, and no unemployed men, as the fieldworker had not been instructed to take account of these factors. For that area, this produced considerable bias.

To design a quota sample you must know, at least approximately, how the target population is divided up according to the factors you are concerned with. You must check against census or other data what proportion of each 'quota' you need in order to reflect the make-up of the broader population.

Quota samples are quick and cheap to organise. However the method can produce bias, and you should clearly state that the representativeness of such a sample cannot be relied upon. Quota samples are different from stratified samples, in that they are not drawn randomly from a known population. Therefore they are not a probability or random type of sample.

Table 19.3   Some types of purposive sample

Type of sample	Definition	Example
Judgement (purposive/ theoretical) sample	The researcher chooses respondents, trying to obtain as wide a representation as possible, taking account of likely sources of difference between individuals. The danger is you have no way of knowing how typical your sample is	In a small rural case study, choose one or two villages with 'typical' health problems
Quota sample	Uses information about the target population to describe the types of units to be included in the sample. Individuals are then sought who fit these characteristics, eg by age, sex, housing type, or location	In a study of informal water sellers, specify a small quota of informal sellers in each housing area, based on the number of on-plot water supplies (available from water authority records). Fieldworkers locate their quota through talking to those carrying water
Snowball sample	Start with one or two respondents, and ask them to refer to you others who share characteristics with them. And so on	A study of illicit drug use started with a few contacts and asked them to invite friends who also use drugs to take part
Matched sample	To compare two sub-groups which are similar in some way. Units (whether a whole settlement or an individual) are matched to share as many relevant characteristics as possible	Choose a matched pair of villages with similar populations and services, where only one of the pair experiences a new project, and look at changes in both villages
Convenience sample	Sample includes whoever happens to be around at the time. Not possible to generalise from	Clinic users attending on a particular day

> **TIP**   Remember that you may need to use more than one type of sample within your research project, just as you may use more than one data-collection technique

Sampling for qualitative research

It is important to remember that most of our ideas about sampling relate to quantitative research, where claims about statistical representativeness are central to its validity. Qualitative research works to different priorities, and usually uses purposive samples. The concept of theoretical sampling is a useful one to understand, as it gives a completely different perspective on sampling.

Theoretical sampling 'is the process of data collection for generating theory whereby the analyst jointly collects, codes, and analyses his (sic) data and decides what data to collect next and where to find them, in order to develop his theory as it emerges. This process of data collection is *controlled* by the emerging theory' (Glaser and Strauss, 1967).

The initial decision of where to begin collecting data is not based on a preconceived theoretical framework but from a general sociological perspective on a subject area. When a category emerges from the data, the researcher looks for information which would elaborate the category further. This process continues until no new aspects of the category emerge. The category is then said to be saturated (like a sponge filled up with water). So in 'theoretical sampling', data are collected as long as they are adding to the development of a particular category. Unlike statistical sampling, the sample cannot be predetermined numerically – it has to be worked through.

A study of a new issue, such as how young people use mobile phones, might see its purpose as to generate hypotheses (ideas) about what are the important issues in this field. It might carry out observation in a number of different sites; seek out young people to talk to through a snowball sample, moving through informal networks; carry out group discussions in schools and other settings. Ideas would be generated, perhaps for instance that mobile phones give young people privacy from their parents, which could then be tested by targeted observation and discussion. Fieldwork would cease at the point when it seems to the researchers that they are not hearing anything new from their respondents.

Selecting case studies

Where your project consists of a group of case studies, you need to think of their selection in a different way again. Case studies cannot be, and do not claim to be, representative of the wider situation in any statistical sense. You cannot usually know to what extent they may be representative, because you do not have information about the whole 'population' of cases that is out there. See Chapter 18.6 on case studies for discussion of how to choose cases for a multiple case study.

Selection for location, time, and events

The discussion above has focused on selecting people to talk to. However most studies involve at least an element of observation as well as interview-type methods, and it is certainly the recommendation of this manual that this should be so. In undertaking observational work, important choices are made as to exactly what you will observe. Make these as explicit as possible.

Selection of location

Sites for study obviously need to be selected in the light of the aims of the research. In addition to seeking some sort of representativeness (see above), you need to take account of:

- Accessibility – in the sense of the degree of access/entry given to the researcher.
- Unobtrusiveness – a situation where the researcher can take a relatively unobtrusive role.

Remember that your choice of site is likely to determine many other things about the research process, and don't jump to conclusions too quickly about what is possible or desirable.

Selection of time

If one is studying a community or an organisation, it is important to understand its rhythm, by looking at:

a) the range of activities/events over a 24-hour period;
b) the activities which take place during the day as opposed to the night; the week as opposed to weekends; any day of rest or prayer as opposed to ordinary days;
c) seasonal changes in activity;
d) imposed patterns like shift systems for work.

Selection of events

Events can be classified as:

a) routine – situations that regularly occur
b) special – but anticipated, eg Christmas, Ramadan, etc
c) untoward – emergencies, crises.

The researcher aims to observe a spread of events over a time-scale which takes account of important variations in activity. In research that makes great demands on respondents, for example participatory assessments, it is essential to schedule the work at times of year and times of day when hard-pressed people are most able to spend time on this sort of activity.

Site selection in participatory research

Often with participatory research, the project grows out of the site, rather than there being any question of selection by some outside agency. However in wider exercises such as Participatory Poverty Assessments, a balance has to be struck between working in areas where there is some infrastructure to facilitate ongoing participation, and the claims the PPA needs to make about the applicability of its findings to a wider area.

Holland and Munro (1997) suggest that it may be helpful to think in terms of 'nesting' areas you want to work in within a cascading series of spatial levels, from the national down to the sample site level. You would then try to reconcile diversity with representativeness at each level by:

1. Selecting a small but sufficient number of regions: small in order to retain richness and depth of analysis, but sufficient to arrive at a range of regional profiles that are representative of national level diversity. Extreme cases should, however, be avoided – ie regions from which insights could not be transferred to any larger area – unless they are specifically needed as a contrast.
2. Within each sampled region, purposively sampling a small number of sub-regions that represent a range of contexts that can be pre-identified in the region: again, avoiding extremes.
3. Selecting a 'typical' site profile in order to provide a regional level reference point for examining the implications (for analysis and policy recommendations) of the diverse elements within each site profile. In other words a 'control-group' type population to which the analysis of the diverse profiles can be compared.

So you could represent a profile of the areas involved at each spatial level in a matrix, setting out various community characteristics. This then makes it possible to see where the sites you study fit into the wider picture. You will build confidence in the importance of your findings by putting the particular communities you work with into this wider context.

Including 'hard-to-reach' people

In planning your sampling strategy, remember that some kinds of people may be systematically easier to contact than others. Having power in a society gives people greater ability to choose to participate or avoid participation in public processes like research. You will probably need to make special efforts to talk to some of the people who most need to get their voices heard.

If you work primarily through public group discussions, in many cultures women will simply be absent, and in many others will not be expected to speak. Equally if you visit households and do not specify who in the family you want to talk to, male family members will probably present themselves first – depending on the subject of your enquiries. In most cultures, to enable women to be able to get their views heard, it is a good idea to hold separate group discussions, and separate interviews, with women.

Disabled people are also often excluded from public discussions. Unless you specifically ask, you may not meet disabled people at all, even if they are living nearby – it will not be assumed that their views would be of interest. Where disabled people are segregated into institutions, you will need to make particular efforts to include their perspective.

Children and older people are also of course groups whose views are often not considered important. On the other hand in some cultures, where elders are highly respected, younger people may not be comfortable giving their views in front of older people. Other groups likely to be excluded are people belonging to ethnic minority groups, and those with a lower educational achievement than average. Think about the community you are interested in, and the particular inequalities that affect it. See also Chapter 14 on communication issues.

Remember though that your intervention may have consequences beyond the life of your project. Take advice, for example, from local women on how you handle gender issues. But do not settle for accepting the status quo:

EXAMPLE

Achieving the 'impossible'

A woman evaluator from India, who was used to working with women in a semi-closed society, was able to achieve in Sudan what she was told would be impossible. She succeeded in holding meetings with large numbers of poor women, and getting them to speak openly about their views on their economic role. Previously the women project staff had accepted the traditional view that women would not and could not meet for such discussions, because inevitably the project staff were themselves a part of the same tradition, despite their professional roles (Pratt and Loizos, 1992).

Some interesting approaches have been developed by those addressing the HIV/AIDS epidemic with communities around the world. To tackle this obviously sensitive topic, one programme in Ghana started with group discussions using PLA techniques, in a single sex group of 6 to 12 married or unmarried people. The groups later suggested that women and men should meet together as well. The researchers comment:

'The use of participatory learning approaches in exploring sexual health concerns can radically change the development programmes in the villages concerned in a number of ways. For the first time groups of men and women, older and younger people are sitting together to talk about sexual issues of great importance to them. People can communicate more easily with their spouses and men in a particular are pleased and relieved to be involved in what has been seen as "women's business"'. (Save the Children, 1997b)

CHECKLIST   Improving response rates – a checklist

✓ Get the backing of people or organisations who are known and respected by the community you wish to work with who can lend their support to the study
✓ Get groups of 'the researched' actively involved at the start of the study
✓ Consider whether you will need to use interpreters or advocates to overcome language or cultural barriers or serve as a point of contact
✓ Make any direct approaches to people personalised – address them by name
✓ Explain clearly what the aims of the study are and why it is important that people participate
✓ Make sure you give a contact name and a way of contacting them to potential respondents

✓ Ensure that information about the study is presented appropriately taking into account problems with literacy, language barriers, and disabilities – expect to repeat verbal information many times

✓ Give respondents a choice of ways of participating – some may lack the confidence to take part in a group discussion, for example

✓ Choose accessible neutral venues for fieldwork, away from service provision (eg hospitals) – somewhere people will feel at home

✓ Consider employing outreach workers who know the community you wish to work with to recruit participants and publicise your research

✓ Think creatively about recruiting participants – eg go to relevant work places, places of worship, community centres, etc

✓ Consider using researchers from the community you wish to study to collect face-to-face data

✓ Use pre-existing groups to recruit participants where appropriate – eg tenants' associations, self-help groups etc

✓ Consider offering some incentive to those who participate – at least meet their expenses and offer some refreshment – see below

✓ Expect to have to ask some people more than once

(Reproduced with permission from Craig, 1998)

Incentives – what are the issues?

One way of increasing your response rate is to offer some kind of incentive to respondents to take part in the research. This is a hotly debated issue, with some saying it is unethical to offer incentives in any circumstances, and others arguing that it is unethical not to! Increasingly in the UK, mainstream researchers are offering some kind of vouchers or even cash, to people who take part in interviews or focus groups. However incentives are not allowed in health services research. Offering incentives is much less common in the South, and the problems of sustainability and creating expectations exist everywhere.

There are many different types of incentives which can be used – some are more a question of meeting people's expenses in taking part. Researchers should expect to meet expenses people incur, and help with travel costs, for example, will often make a key difference in whether or not people can take part. Offering food and drink creates a comfortable atmosphere. Incentives are usually not paid in cash. Sometimes a local business will donate vouchers for this purpose.

Some types of incentive

- Food and drink.
- Expenses repaid, for

- travel;
- childcare provision;
- replacement care for disabled people, for example.

- Offering useful information at the end of the session.
- Gift vouchers for the cinema, shops, etc.
- Telephone cards (especially useful to homeless people).
- Goods relevant to the project, eg seeds for farmers; pencils to children.
- A gift to a community organisation rather than to individuals, eg a blackboard for a school.

Benefits of paying incentives	Drawbacks of paying incentives
Sample may be distorted by people being unable to take part without gaining any financial benefit	Sample may be distorted by people taking part to gain financial benefits
Can encourage more people to take part	Could create a sense of obligation, and hence compromise informed consent
Recognises the value of respondents' time and contribution	Can create expectations of recompense for other participation in the future
	People might take part for the money and then answer with a view to pleasing you
	And of course cost!

The UK National Children's Bureau's policy is to make a small payment, but not to advertise it, and to pay it only at the end of the interview. This means that they are recognising the value of the child's time, but they are not gaining the advantages of using the payment as an incentive.

Little research has been done on respondents' views on the payment of incentives, though there is no doubt that it increases response rates in commercial market research. This is why the practice is spreading. One study looked at the issue in research with injecting drug users, and the researchers emphasise that for all respondents their motivations in participating will include many factors, especially seeing the research as interesting, relevant, and worthwhile. They quote some respondents' different views:

'Phil: … when you said you get a five pound voucher that's why I said [yes]. It was for the money but not only that – it helps you doesn't it … To be honest mate if I hadn't have had that … I wouldn't come, because I've got to go ahead and make some money.'

And by contrast:

'Kieran: yeah, it's all right but I'd do it for nothing. It doesn't really bother me talking about it.'

'Robert: I mean I didn't come here knowing that. You've just told me
today. I will accept it, thanks a lot. I'll get something for the little
lass, thanks very much.' (Hughes, 1999)

An incentive payment will make only a marginal difference to people's decision whether or not to participate in research, but it may tip the balance for
some people, perhaps especially those under financial pressure.

EXAMPLE

Not offering incentives has costs too

In the peer research project with UK young people using mental health services, there were
unforeseen difficulties in recruiting respondents for interview. The peer researchers were not
able to locate suitable respondents through their friendship networks, as had been assumed. If
incentives had been offered it may be that more young people would have participated, greatly
improving the scope of the research. Any cost incurred would have been easily outweighed by
the wasted costs of staff time spent failing to recruit respondents without the aid of incentives.

Issues to consider in deciding on use of incentives

- The state of the local economy.
- How much trouble are you putting people to? For example, a focus group
takes more effort than an interview in your own home.
- How important is the issue to your respondents?
- Will the respondents have to forgo any income in order to take part in
your research?
- What is standard practice for research in your area?

A related set of dilemmas presents itself in peer research projects in relation to
the question of whether or not to pay people who actually carry out research
alongside professional researchers. This issue is explored in Chapter 3.4 on
peer research.

CHECKLIST   **On sampling in research for development work**

    ✔ Expect to spend time and effort negotiating access to your sample
    ✔ Make a clear decision as to whether you are going for a random/
probability sample or a purposive/non-probability one
    ✔ Be clear whether you are sampling for quantitative or qualitative
research
    ✔ Once you have chosen a sampling method, stick to it and carry out
selection of respondents in a consistent way

✔ In choosing an appropriate sample, consider:

    – how good a sampling frame you have available
    – what response rate you anticipate
    – logistical problems
    – costs and, as ever,
    – the purpose of the research and its audiences

✔ Make a special effort to reach out to those normally excluded from research processes

Further Reading

Blaxter, L., Hughes, C. and Tight, M. (1996) *How to Research*. Buckingham, UK: Open University Press.

Clear account of all types of sampling.

Nichols, P. (1991) *Social Survey Methods: A fieldguide for development workers*, Development Guidelines No. 6. Oxford: Oxfam.

Strong on sampling methods for surveys in the South.

20 Analysis

Analysing the data from your research project can be very interesting and rewarding – you get to really step back and look at all the issues. It can also be overwhelming, fiddly, and frustrating. Development research projects have been known to grind to a halt at the point when a huge heap of data has been collected, which no one can quite face dealing with.

The aim of this chapter is to help you to analyse your data in the most convenient way for you, and to an adequate standard for your project. Quantitative and qualitative data have very different requirements in terms of methods of analysis, and so these will be dealt with in separate sections. Both require the analyst to be sensitive to questions of interpretation, and the first section of this chapter will discuss these issues.

Data analysis has traditionally been seen as the lonely burden of a single researcher, but it is important to involve stakeholders in analysis as well as in other stages of the research process. The process of analysis is crucial in terms of determining what the research will be said to have found. If community members are to have control of the research process, it is necessary to work out ways of involving them in data analysis. Guidance is given in Section 5 of this chapter.

Methods of analysis are discussed next, first in general terms (getting organised) and then separately for qualitative and quantitative data. The emphasis in these sections is on straightforward techniques which can be used with confidence by the inexperienced researcher.

The final section looks at the idea of synthesis – the process of drawing out the key important points from your findings. Your analysis is not finished until you have answered the question: so what?

20.1 Methods of Analysis

This section starts with a general consideration of how to get organised for data analysis, including discussion of the broad issues involved in the decision whether or not to use a computer. Then techniques for analysing qualitative data are described – first the core process and then four different ways of actually carrying it out. Finally, ways of ensuring rigour in qualitative analysis are discussed. The last part of the section looks at quantitative analysis: some essential techniques, ways of describing your data statistically, and again how to do this work rigorously. Both of these sections include further details on software for each type of analytical process.

The processes you follow to analyse quantitative and qualitative data are very different. It is helpful to be clear what kind of information you are looking for in your data, and to separate out material which will be looked at primarily to find numbers, from material you will analyse qualitatively.

For example, sometimes we use a semi-structured questionnaire, which includes both quantitative and qualitative questions. It might ask first: 'How long have you used xyz service?' and then it might ask 'what have you found helpful about xyz service?' In analysing the answers, you will have numbers for the first question, and words – perhaps whole paragraphs – for the second. It is easiest if you separate these two types of question, when analysing the data, and work with the quantitative material separately from the qualitative. Quantitative data includes all yes/no type questions, and rating scales, for example 'How satisfied were you with xyz service?', with a pre-coded set of answers such as 'Not satisfied/somewhat dissatisfied/somewhat satisfied/ satisfied' – anything where the answers are very simple and pre-determined. Following this last question, you might then ask 'Why?', and this will lead to another set of qualitative responses.

When you are working with qualitative data, you may still want to quantify to some extent. For instance, you might analyse the answers to this type of 'why' question, making a set of categories from the various answers you receive (see below, 20.6). You could then count how many respondents gave each answer. However you should not place too much reliance on this type of figure. In mentioning certain issues, for example responding to the question 'Why were you satisfied with xyz service?' with mentions of the location of the service and of friendly staff, a respondent has not disagreed that other factors may be important, such as cost. They may just not have thought of them at that moment. If you had offered a list of possible reasons for satisfaction or dissatisfaction, and respondents were asked which were important, the numbers would have more meaning.

In general, it is important to remember that the power of qualitative data is in the concepts it conveys, its inherent meaning. It is best to think in terms of themes which emerge, and not worry too much about how many respondents said one thing or another. You do need to distinguish a single anecdote from themes which are meaningful for many people, and also to take note of what kinds of people bring up what kinds of issue. But counting heads is usually inappropriate in qualitative work.

For this reason, and for convenience, it is best to deal separately with the two kinds of data – then you can process each in a different way without getting confused. However you then need to reintegrate the data, to make sense of it. It would be inappropriate to report the findings separately, so you need to put it all back together again once you have analysed responses to each question.

Getting organised

The first phase of analysis is all about getting the paperwork under control. As data comes in, make sure it is at least listed somewhere, so that you know exactly what you have got. If there are not already code numbers on questionnaires etc, add them now, and record these along with the date they arrived in the office and any other information which may help you later. A recording sheet might look like this:

Date received	Code number	Type of data	Area data originates from
	1	(eg interview by x; notes of observation of y; focus group transcript)	Or other key factors which may be useful to you
	2		
	3		

Do not put this off! It is really worth doing it as you go along, as otherwise you can quickly lose track of what you have got. For example, you might pull out some notes you need for another purpose, and then forget to put them back. If everything is numbered and dated, you will have more hope of tracing any missing material.

COMMON PITFALLS 20.1	Allowing a huge pile of disorganised paper to accumulate, with no record of what is (or should be) there

Perhaps this is stating the obvious, but you must page number all your data. If you did not do it before collecting it, do it now. Thus, you will be able to identify where someone said something by at least a page reference as well as the code number for their questionnaire. If you are using lengthy transcripts, you may also want to number the lines, for reference. Word-processing packages can do this automatically. Catalogue all photos, drawings, etc as well.

Activity 20.1   Thinking about your data

What forms of data have you collected:

- Questionnaires?
- Interview notes, recordings or transcripts?
- Notes of readings?
- Copies of documents?
- Notes or videotapes of observations?
- Measurements of behaviour?
- Charts, maps, tables or diagrams?
- Photographs?
- Art work?
- The notes in your research diary?
- Other forms of data?

Make a note of the different forms of data you have collected, and work out roughly the amount of each sort of data you have.

Think about where your different sorts of data have come from, how they have been collected or produced, and how reliable they might be. Think also about how much you will need to reduce the volume of your data in order to present it within the space you will have available.

(Reproduced with permission from Blaxter et al, 1996)

Table 20.1   Is it worth putting it on a computer?

	Pro	Con
General	Speed of processing data	Requires access to expensive technology
	Enables flexible handling of large quantities of data	Can exclude others from the analysis process
	Your data is held in a form which enables you to return repeatedly to find things, and to try out different ideas	May require time to learn to use program
	May impress people	You will usually need some human help to get started with a new program
		You will know the data less well than if you analyse it by hand
		May create an illusion of accuracy!
Quantitative analysis	Ability to return to calculations and recalculate easily if changes are made	If you lack experience, it can lead to feeling you have 'lost control'
	Can draw graphs directly from the data	
	Better control for human error, though you still have to get the data entry right	
Qualitative analysis	Enables handling of large quantities of qualitative data	Requires a lot of text to be typed into the computer
	Easy to re-code data when you change the categories you want to use, encouraging a flexible approach	

Using computers

It is obviously a key decision whether or not to use a computer to analyse your data. There are now packages that assist with qualitative analysis, as well as numerous options for quantitative work. You should make this decision early on in the process, as the way in which you prepare your data for analysis will depend upon what methods you are going to use to analyse it.

The computer packages that are now available for data analysis are much easier to use than they used to be. If you expect to go on doing research in your professional life, it is likely to be worth getting access to, and learning to use, a computer package for at least the quantitative elements of the analysis. But it is quite possible to do the work by hand. And there can be good reasons to do it like this – for example if you want a number of people, whether community members or staff, to be able to participate in the analysis process.

Computers can enable you more easily to move text around, order text, copy it, add up figures, compare different sets of figures, prepare diagrams and tables, and more. They can do all kinds of calculations with numerical data, and can also sort text in many different ways. It is important to understand that computers are 'very high speed idiots' – they cannot do any thinking for you, but they can effectively organise and re-organise large quantities of data very quickly.

After your own degree of access to the necessary technology, probably the next most important issue to consider will be the scale of the research you are undertaking. With very large projects it could be madness not to use computer technology, if you possibly can. With very small ones, it depends on your familiarity with the software – it is not worth learning new tricks that are not strictly necessary, if this feels stressful, but you could decide to analyse a small project on the computer as a way of learning the ropes.

EXAMPLE

Data analysis by hand: livelihoods and land use in Belize

Research on livelihoods and land use patterns in southern Belize used semi-structured questionnaires to generate qualitative and quantitative data from about 100 respondents in three villages. The data was analysed by hand because the team had no computer, and also both members of the research team could do the work together. Tables were drawn up on paper to contain the answers to each question. All the data was then entered onto these sheets and added up accordingly. Questions included, for example, enquiries about problems faced in agricultural production, producing a range of answers around: limited markets for specific products, lack of credit, and limited access to land in some places.

We will return to these issues in the sections below that look specifically at computer software for quantitative and qualitative analysis.

20.2   What is analysis?

Data analysis is a process of taking things apart and putting them together again. This is why I have included a section on 'synthesis' – to direct attention to the importance of drawing together the meanings you gather from your material.

In the process of analysing the data you have collected, you need to work out the links between the material you have from respondents, and your original questions. What does it all mean?

Remember that analysis is something we all do in daily life, not a wholly new trick you have to learn. For example, suppose a colleague has not turned up in the office one morning. People begin to make guesses (hypothesise) about why this could be. Have they gone to a meeting somewhere else? Are they ill? Perhaps they had booked a holiday and everyone else has forgotten about it. Or have they just overslept?

The guesses we make will be tested when the person turns up – or when new evidence comes to light, such as a colleague arriving for a meeting they had arranged with the missing person. Or we may make decisions based on our hypotheses, knowing there are uncertainties. What will we tell the person who expects to meet our colleague? So we analyse all the time, and we question the evidence in front of us – are things what they seem? It is the same with data analysis – using all your knowledge, you guess at links between data, at explanations – and you always keep in mind that all your ideas are provisional. New data may change your conclusions.

There are three distinct elements or stages to the analysis of research data:

1. Organising and cataloguing your data.
2. Breaking it down into its constituent elements, identifying themes.
3. Bringing it back together – deciding how different elements relate to each other, and clarifying the meaning of the data.

The central task in analysing data is to seek out patterns, trends within the data. Are different people telling you the same thing? Or are there clear patterns of difference, for example when women have one point of view and men another? At times you have to actively pull the meaning out of the data – it may not jump out by itself. For example, it is important to think about what is not there, which you might have expected to find, for instance did the girls similarly disagree with the boys, or not?

When you have identified patterns, then check exactly what data fits this pattern, and whether there are exceptions. Perhaps some women did agree with the men. What are some possible explanations for the patterns you find? Were men present while these women were interviewed? Do they come from a different income group from the other women?

At the same time as looking for patterns, you need to be questioning the data – making sure you can have confidence in it.

Three aspects of accurate analysis – questioning the data

- **Check the trends – where the same information appears in different places:**

  - Do they fit in with what you expect?
  - Are they surprising? Do they contradict your expectations?
  - Are they the result of researcher bias?
  - Do they reflect the way the methods were used?
  - Does this mean that the research has uncovered new information and ideas?

- **Check the contradictions – Are they the result of:**

  - Working with different groups?
  - Using different methods?
  - External factors affecting data collection at different times?

- **Check the gaps – where information you expected to see is missing:**

  - Did you forget to collect some important information? If so, is it possible to return to the field, or use secondary data, to fill in the gaps?
  - Is there a social silence about this topic? If so, why?

(adapted from Boyden and Ennew, 1997)

So, for example, if findings from observation conflict with what people say to you, what does this mean? If you are using a small number of key informants, how much weight can you give their views? How representative are they? Why do they see things like this? Can you base an argument on this data? How able were people to say exactly what they thought during your data collection? If their employer came into the room during an interview, could respondents talk freely about their work situation?

EXAMPLE

Looking again – the Child Labour Project, Sialkot, Pakistan

In the Sialkot study, many people in the community told researchers that they thought it was acceptable for children to work stitching footballs. But researchers made a second check on the data, to see whether the mothers of children actually doing it agreed with this, and also whether the poorest families, those who were really struggling, were equally happy with the situation.

TIP   Look for patterns, develop ideas about trends in the data, but keep in mind that your ideas are provisional – they need to be tested against the data as a whole, and others' interpretations of it

---

There is no one universally correct approach to analysing research data, and you need to find a process you are comfortable with, given your skills, phobias, and general disposition. For example, computers are very useful for analysis, but if they make you feel anxious, remember that people managed very complex analyses without their aid for many years. You can too.

Having said there is no single right way of doing analysis, it has also to be said that there *are* wrong ways of doing it, and this chapter aims to help you avoid these pitfalls. Perhaps the greatest temptation of analysis in development-related research is to claim more from the research than can really be justified by the data – it is crucial to check all along that you are not over-interpreting your material.

It is essential to approach data analysis in a critical spirit. You need to question the meaning of the data you have collected at every level, starting with your own assumptions.

EXAMPLE

Avoid jumping to conclusions

A training exercise with UK health service staff learning qualitative analysis asks them to analyse a number of statements from patients about their experience of services. The quotations from patients describe various incidents of inadequate care, for example an elderly man having his spectacles and his false teeth taken away, and then being left in a hospital corridor for hours, while awaiting some procedure. Trainees often produce a category of 'staff shortages', into which they sort some of these statements. But what they are doing is bringing in their own assumptions about why such problems occur – there is no reference to staff shortages in the data. The effect of introducing such categories at this stage in the analysis is in fact to block off consideration of exactly why these problems occur. There may be all kinds of other explanations.

It is important to realise that analysis is not really a separate process from data gathering – we analyse as we go along, trying to make sense of what we are hearing.

WHEN to carry out qualitative analysis

The analysis process can begin before the data is even collected. You need to think about how you are going to organise your material, what themes you will be looking for, as you design your research. But beware – your initial ideas will be provisional, as you will need to make revisions in the light of what people actually tell you.

Analysis can begin during an interview or focus group:

- Probe to check your understanding of what the respondent really means.
- Check one person's experience or views against another's.
- Ask for suggestions for explanations, where people's views diverge.

At the end of an interview or focus group:

- Ask respondents to identify the main topics of concern to them.
- Summarise what has been said and ask for confirmation.

This process ensures that you are clear about what are the respondents' priorities, rather than your own. It also enables respondents to explain further any ambiguous comments they may have made.

Immediately after the interview or focus group:

- Ensure that you have either full notes or a tape recording from the inter-action – if not, write notes as soon as possible.
- Write any field notes recording your thoughts about the interaction – main themes, what was surprising/expected?
- Researchers should discuss together any observations they may have made, and record their conclusions.

After a few interviews you begin to build a theory as to what is happening. You may well change it as time goes on – or you may not.[1]

Styles of analysis

In preparing this manual, I looked at many texts describing the analysis of research data. Some were impenetrable – many described extremely complex processes. This was all rather intimidating. Do not be put off. Bear in mind that your analysis needs to be fit for its purpose. Leave the elaborate statistics and the subtle linguistic analyses to the academics. In research for development work, the information you need to get from your data is generally fairly straightforward, at least in principle, if not in practice! Think of your audience and ensure that your approach to analysis would

---

[1]Adapted with permission from College of Health Training Materials, 2001.

make sense to them, and meet the aims of your project. It needs to have integrity, and be convincing to others – keeping it simple is the best approach.

One key element of most academic approaches is that they see the process of analysis as essentially about bringing theory to bear on the data. This is often also the case in practical research for development work. For example, we want to know what impact a change in policy towards a group of people has had on their behaviour and views – and we have some kind of theory about what this might be at the start of the project.

However sometimes data analysis basically just describes what was found. For example, if you are consulting a group of people about their views on issues related to a government service, it would be inappropriate for you to bring in your own theories to make sense of what they have said, at least when you first report it.

For most research for development work, the analysis you require is quite straightforward, and should not be mystified. Consider the aims of your study to establish what level of sophistication of analysis you require.

20.3   Interpretation

As we have seen, questions of interpretation are central to the quality of the analysis you carry out. You have to interpret it, but at the same time you need to ensure that you are not introducing your own ideas into the analysis when they were not there in the data.

NGOs naturally sometimes set out to do research to 'prove their point'. Mayer warns against this mindset – her advice is:

> 'Do not claim that your data prove something – this makes your use of data much easier to attack' (Mayer, 1998).

Because we all understand the world through the filters of our own life experience, and because the way in which data is gathered vitally affects what is found, you can never convince everyone of the truth of any statement. This is not to say that evidence is not important – just to say that we have to be very careful about the claims we make for our work. Even in the natural sciences it is impossible to definitively prove something – but data can nonetheless suggest a particular explanation.

What is meant by a rigorous approach? One key element of the definition is that you must have considered the alternative explanations for anything you claim to be true. Thus you need to show that you have done this, taking account of the likely arguments of those you aim to convince of your interpretation. It is useful to put yourself in the shoes of someone critical of your position, and try to imagine how they would challenge your interpretation. Within the research group, have a good argument, with someone 'playing devil's advocate' (arguing the other point of view for the sake of debate), and check that you can defend the way in which you have interpreted your data.

An important mistake to avoid is that of claiming that you can show a causal relationship between things (that one factor directly explains changes in the other factor), when what you can show is actually only that the two appear to relate to each other in some way. For example, if long-standing illness is found to be more common amongst unemployed people, which comes first? The individual's illness and resultant inability to work due to physical or mental impairment, or is unemployment itself leading to illness?

EXAMPLE

Cause or effect? Size of land holding and household size in Tanzania

A good example of this problem is given by Mukherjee and Wuyts (1998). Table 20.2 shows the relation between the average size of land holdings (in acres) and household size for a sample of 600 Tanzanian peasant holdings in 20 villages (Collier et al, 1986). The authors argue that in Tanzania, 'other than their own labour, Tanzanian peasant households have only a limited range of assets', of which 'undoubtedly the major assets are land and livestock'. But 'in most of Tanzania land is abundant and so we would expect [land] distribution to be determined predominantly by the availability of household labour'. The data in Table 20.2 are given to support this hypothesis.

Table 20.2   Average farm size versus household size

Average land size (acres)	Mean household size	% of households
0.8	3.5	6.6
1.8	3.5	12.3
2.7	4.4	20.5
3.7	5.1	15.0
5.2	5.6	22.5
7.1	6.7	10.9
10.0	7.6	9.4
16.7	9.9	2.8
Source: Collier et al, 1986.		

It is clear that the authors' view is reasonable in light of this evidence. The point, however, is whether this is the only hypothesis that the data support. The authors did not explore other possible explanations but merely gave the evidence in support of their hypothesis. Can you think of any other hypothesis which fits the data just as well?

A plausible alternative explanation could be based on the following argument. The authors assumed that household size is fixed and, hence, land size adapts to the number of hands available and mouths to feed. But is it correct to see household size as fixed? Perhaps the authors reasoned that household size depends on the number of children a couple chooses (or happens) to have, and therefore, in this sense, is given. But, even so, children may leave a household for a variety of reasons and, similarly, others (mainly close relatives) may join the household. So, what then determines household size itself? Is it just a matter of chance, or does it depend on the assets a household holds? For example, a poor household may be more subject to fragmentation: children leave home in search of better fortunes or are sent to live with better-off relatives. Similarly, a rich household not only may be more cohesive (ie less subject to fragmentation) but also may be able to draw upon the labour of poorer relatives. It is plausible, therefore, that assets (including, but not only, land) matter, even if, on average, Tanzanian peasants have few assets at their disposal. Differences in ownership of assets among households may well be a determining factor which explains differences in household size.

The data in Table 20.2 support this hypothesis equally well and, hence, do not allow you to decide between these rival explanations. To do so, you would need additional data, possibly including qualitative evidence about individual cases.

So in this example, a correlation appears to be present, but we cannot tell which factor can be seen as causing the other. This is quite a common situation. This is not to say that you cannot make any claims from your data, but that you need to be careful to leave open the chance that another explanation could be better than yours. The more evidence you can show for your point of view, the more likely you are to convince others.

The key charge to guard against is that you have made a biased interpretation of your data. This can occur in a number of ways, which are discussed throughout this manual. At the point of data collection, it is the reason why researchers are always keen to make notes which are as detailed and as close to verbatim – how the person actually said it – as possible. As soon as you start to summarise, there is a risk of introducing bias. People accustomed to summarising situations for a different professional purpose (such as social workers or health professionals) will have to work hard to avoid introducing their habitual ways of seeing things, in describing what respondents have said. The aim is to be very conscious of when you are making your own interpretation, and to ensure that the data is available in its 'raw' state, so that checks could be made of when any interpretation came in.

Getting others' perspectives on the data

Having advised you do the work yourself, I am now strongly advising you also to involve others! Everyone with any involvement in your research project will have been making their own interpretations of what you have found. This is a rich resource to draw on, and you should not waste it. To learn from others' ideas will improve the quality of your analysis. It will also ensure that everyone is able to feel that their contribution has been valued, which will increase their commitment to implementing any action which may arise from the results of your research.

The other very important point about this is that you will need to ensure that you have looked at possible alternative interpretations of your data. Your report should take account of obvious alternative approaches, and show why you have decided on yours.

It may also be useful to involve others in the detail of the analysis. You might ask one or more other person to do some of the analysis in parallel with you. This is one of the ways of checking whether personal bias is being introduced into the analysis process. If you work alongside others when collecting data, they will be part of the ongoing process of analysis that naturally accompanies data-gathering.

You may want to hold analysis/interpretation workshops – first among the core team members, and then with the wider team, perhaps including partner agencies. Another useful thing to do, at a later stage, is to ask someone who is expert in the field you are studying to read a draft, to check on your conclusions in terms of how they fit in with existing knowledge. How consistent are they with general trends? How strong is your evidence, if it is unexpected?

CHECKLIST   **Principles of data analysis**

✓ Interpretation must be accurate and honestly reported
✓ Avoid introducing your own preconceptions into the data
✓ Take into account all possible explanations, including those which conflict with your own
✓ Avoid generalisations which cannot be supported by the data
✓ Where appropriate, your analysis may be strengthened by reference to other existing research findings

---

20.4   The Process of Data Analysis

What is the process of analysis like?

It depends very much on the type and quantity of data involved. If your project was entirely quantitative, it may be a very simple matter of counting up totals, or feeding figures into a computer, and then reading the results. The actual analysis is done electronically in seconds. You still need to decide how meaningful these results are, but the basic data sorting can be very swift. You will have done most of the thinking at an earlier stage, when you set the questions.

However few development-related research projects depend only on numbers. Qualitative analysis is a very different process. When there is a lot of data, it can be a major undertaking to get on top of the information you have collected. Some researchers advise expecting to spend as long doing the analysis as you did collecting the data. And I have certainly never heard anyone saying their analysis went more smoothly than they expected!

A word of warning: it will be very difficult to get the analysis done unless you can get at least some time when you can concentrate solely on this task. It is simply too complex to do in fits and starts – you lose such a lot every time to have to start again. Your own brain is your essential tool – no amount of card indexes, tables, or computer files can substitute for your overall grasp of what is significant in your data.

Who should do the analysis?

In qualitative analysis, it is best for those who undertook the fieldwork to analyse the data. They can bring their direct learning from the process of the fieldwork to bear on the analysis – this will help in a variety of ways, especially in understanding what was most important to the respondents. If they are not experienced in analysis, they should get help from someone who is.

In some quantitative research projects in development work, data is handed over to a consultant to be analysed. This is only a good idea where:

–   they have been involved in designing the study;
–   they have a good understanding of the aims and ethos of the study;

or

–   where the analysis required is quantitative and straightforward, but involves big numbers.

It is generally best to either contract out the whole project, or to do it all in house.

When involving someone new, it is crucial that those leading the project set out a clear list of questions to which they wish to find answers from the data.

CHECKLIST   **If you 'farm out' your data analysis**

If you really do need to get help with your analysis, and there are situations where you certainly must, here is some advice.

• Write down a list of the questions you want answered by the data
• Consider asking up to three people or organisations to tell you how they would handle this task (ie to tender for it informally) before you decide who should do it
• Get a clear explanation of any method or computer programme the consultant intends to use, what it does and why they think it is suitable to the task
• Find out what experience they have of analysing other similar datasets
• Make sure the agreement you set up with the consultant is clear in all its details, and written down:

    – Who is responsible for entering the data – you or them?
    – Who of their team will actually do the work?

- What format will they give you the analysis in? (what will it look like, and can they give you a disk as well as a printout?)
- Can they provide graphs, charts, etc?
- Are you willing for them to use your data for any other purpose than your own project?

- Ensure that there is clear agreement about the confidentiality and ownership of the data
- If at all possible, keep a copy of the whole data set

20.5   Participation in the Analysis Process

Analysis is an important stage of any research project – some would say it is the most important stage, as this is when key findings are identified and conclusions drawn. So how can a wider group of people be involved in data analysis? Before we move on to the practical techniques involved in data analysis, these issues will be discussed. There are a number of models to draw on here, although it is not uncommon for participation to break down at the point of data analysis.

To create a robust process, and to increase the chances of action following from your research, you may want to engage in the analysis not only community members themselves, but also co-researchers or staff from agencies that will be involved in implementing findings. However be prepared to mediate between different views – staff of other agencies must be prepared to listen to community members. It is important to avoid putting disadvantaged people in a difficult position.

The PLA approach offers important guidance here. In PLA, the aim is for analysis to be integrated with the data collection process. As local people reply to questions, take part in exercises or group discussions, they are asked to choose priorities – to identify the key issues for them – and to draw conclusions. Analysis occurs as the process unfolds, in dialogue with local people, not at the end. Because PLA is undertaken over a brief intensive period, it is possible, for example, to check on apparent contradictions which emerge from the data. If people say that time spent fetching water is not a problem, but women and children can be observed spending a large part of their days doing this work, it would be possible to ask what this means.

Most research books, including this one, present analysis as if it was a separate stage taking place after the fieldwork. But actually the PLA approach reflects the reality of how analysis really gets done in many projects. Researchers begin to identify key themes, and form and test opinions about 'what is going on' as they carry out fieldwork. The difference with participatory research is that emerging theories are developed and shared with community members and immediate feedback obtained. Action may be taken as a result of understandings gained while the process is under way, and it may in fact be necessary to guard against people jumping to conclusions.

But this approach relies on the research team being easily assembled in one place, and community members readily available for discussions. Not always the case. Other projects have involved participants in analysis in a variety of ways.

EXAMPLE

Local women carry out quantitative analysis – Newcastle, England

In the community-led study of local people's experience of health services in Cowgate, Newcastle, the local women researchers did much of the work of a large quantitative study themselves. Having insisted on gathering data from all the households in a small area (500 questionnaires were returned), they themselves did the coding and data entry. This meant that community members made all those small decisions that are part of the analysis process, such as what to do about ambiguous replies, missing answers, and so on – what researchers call 'cleaning the data'. It was demanding and at times tedious for the women, but led to a great sense of pride in the work, and of course of ownership of the findings. They later used them to campaign successfully for changes in health service provision for their area.

It may be worth considering what impact the techniques and technology you use for data analysis may have on your ability to involve a wider group of people in the analysis. Unless there is particularly good access to computers for your group, it is likely that using a computer for analysis will tend to centralise the process in one or two people's hands. If you can use simpler technology, this may be helpful. However if the data set is large, you may still need to use a computer!

It is more difficult to share the detailed process of qualitative analysis, but by no means impossible. One approach, where working with a group of community members as co-researchers, is for one person to identify key themes coming out of the material, and any problems they see in its interpretation, and then to feed that back verbally to the group. Everyone can then discuss the issues raised, using their own experiences as well as their fieldwork experience to help make sense of the material.

Another way, making more demands on participants, is to decide on the key themes together and then organise the material relating to each theme. Each participant takes one theme and looks at the key issues coming out of the data relating to that issue. One lead researcher may need to co-ordinate this process.

It is, of course, important to show drafts of reports to participants, but experience shows that many people find the process of commenting on long documents daunting (and tedious!). Much confidence and a critical disposition are required to 'see into' a completed text and suggest changes. Professional staff often find this difficult, and it is of course all the more difficult for those whose education is more limited. Nonetheless, people should be shown drafts, but work may need to be done to encourage comment – for example pointing out the parts which are particularly important.

A much more participatory process is described in the next example.

EXAMPLE

Participative analysis – bringing together PPA data, Tanzania

An interesting approach to participative analysis in a major policy-oriented study was devised by those bringing together the findings of a set of eight Participatory Poverty Appraisals (PPAs) which had been undertaken around Tanzania (Gaventa and Attwood, 1998). The intention was to enable staff who had taken part in the fieldwork to work on a synthesis report which could make recommendations at national level.

Eighteen participants met together at a six-day-long workshop. On the first day, each participant was asked to list on 3–5 cards the most important things which he/she saw, felt, learned in the fieldwork experience, as if they were sharing the experience with close friends. The researchers say that 'This process gave a certain feeling to the analysis.' The group then discussed the meaning of synthesis, and aims of the exercise. On subsequent days, each of the six research teams in turn presented their case study (a local PRA), taking questions. Everyone else was asked to be 'active listeners', and write down on cards key themes as the presentations were being made. They were to note down everything they felt should be included in the synthesis report.

The cards produced (over 800 of them) were then sorted by groups of participants, and categories developed. Eventually chapter headings were identified and a proposed report structure presented back to the whole group for discussion. After that, the research teams were asked to index their PRA reports, using the categories which had been developed. Finally a smaller team was identified to finish writing up the report.

The benefit of this process was not only in the quality of the analysis produced, but also that it engaged the participants in complex debate about the issues raised. This was of great value as many participants were government employees with a real influence on policy. They went back to their jobs influenced not only by their own fieldwork, but also by comparing their experience with that of others, and of grappling with the issues directly. Reading a report by someone else never has the same impact.

This example describes presentations of already analysed local projects. You could, however, use a similar framework to hear from people who had undertaken fieldwork (observation, interviews, group discussions), asking them to present their impressions back to the group, as a basis for discussion. This is a good process to do for many reasons, including encouraging reflection on how an interview has gone. A framework of categories can be developed in such a process and then tested against the detail of the data at a later stage.

> **CHECKLIST   For participation in data analysis**
>
> ✓ Ask participants how they would like to be involved in analysis, offering some ideas
> ✓ Community members can take part in analysis during data collection – ask them to prioritise amongst issues they raise, to explain contradictions you find in your data, etc
> ✓ Co-researchers can give verbal presentations and other research group members identify themes from these – or brainstorm initial categories together
> ✓ Make sure that the techniques and the technology you use does not exclude wider participation unnecessarily
> ✓ Discuss together possible explanations for the findings – what causes what?
> ✓ Researchers should not impose their own categories or explanations without good reason, but at the same time should situate the analysis within a broader framework where appropriate

20.6   Qualitative Analysis

This section will first describe the core process involved in qualitative analysis, and then will explain four ways of carrying it out, including using computer software. The last part of the section looks at how to ensure rigour in qualitative analysis.

There are a number of ways of setting about qualitative analysis, and you need to decide which of these is most suitable to your project. Some are quite crude; others enable very subtle and careful handling of the material. This section aims to give you practical guidance in using some of the most common approaches. If you were to look at the desk of someone who was carrying them out, these look different – but they are different practical ways of doing essentially the same job. These are some common approaches:

1. Cut and paste
2. Charting – by hand
3. Card index
4. Using computer software for qualitative data analysis.

More will be explained about each of these below. But in all cases the same core process is going on. We will first examine that process more closely.

Qualitative analysis – the core process

Essentially the task is to draw from the data a set of key themes which summarise the important categories within the data, and to look at how these relate to each other. However you plan to handle the data, the following steps will be needed:

1. Familiarise yourself with the data: read and reread your notes, interview schedules, transcripts. Begin to make notes of themes you see arising.
2. Make a preliminary list of themes or categories you can see in the data.
3. Go through the data, making notes in the margins of the text as you go along, as to what theme is being dealt with where.
4. Look again at your list of categories, before, during and after this second reading of the materials, and make changes as problems emerge.
5. Set out your list of categories in some clear format (separate sheets, charts, file cards – see below) where you can link them with notes, quotes, or references direct from the data.
6. Go through the data again, and note all material that you find relating to each category under its heading (crucial here to make detailed references to the data with any quotes or notes, so that you can trace them back). Researchers often call this process 'coding' – that is, locating material in the data which relates to the codes, or categories, you are using to analyse it. It is best to work through the material once, looking for all your categories at once – it is too slow to go through it searching for each category in turn.
7. Then you can look at each category and see what you have got, and it will be easy to make sense of the material you have collected.

The categories you choose to use will come out of your specific project. For example, a study of a lesbian and gay youth group had as some categories – comments on the group itself (positive and negative); other sources of advice and information; overcoming isolation; experiences of prejudice from others; coming out (disclosing one's sexuality) to parents; coming out to friends; and self-esteem issues. A further categorisation was made within the comments about the group itself, around the issues the young people identified as important to them.

> **TIP**   Write 'memos'
> As you go through the process of analysing qualitative data, many ideas will occur to you. Make sure you keep track of these – some of them will be useful. Write yourself memos, either on cards, or in a notebook, or on a large piece of paper – whatever suits you. Keep them, and read them over at intervals while you are working on the analysis

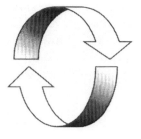

Reading the data, trying to categorise it		Thinking of categories which make sense to you

Figure 20.1   The iterative process

As is clear, the identification of categories within the data is an *iterative* process, as shown in Figure 20.1. This means that it is crucial not to set out a rigid set of categories at the start and then stick to them through thick and thin. You want the data itself to help you to form the categories you use. They should arise from the data, not be imposed upon it.[2]

One of the issues which is always faced in this process is of deciding about how your different categories relate to each other – is one a sub-category of another, or a separate one? You will probably change your ideas on this a couple of times. Some people find it helpful to draw out a diagram of the categories they are using, to see how they fit together.

For example, in a study of the experiences of women who have reported a rape to the police, you have respondents identifying negative attitudes from health service staff as a problem. Do you create a category relating to health care, or do you include this material within a category covering attitudes of all types of professional staff? Or is there a category covering stigma towards rape victims more generally? Or does this issue require a category of its own?

Where do categories or themes come from?

- Your original research questions, aims and objectives.
- The questions you asked respondents.
- The data itself – the way in which respondents think about things.
- Your theories about what is going on.

If you are able to, the best way of checking on categorisations you are making, and ideas about how they relate to each other, is to go back and do some more fieldwork, perhaps directly asking people's views on the framework you are developing.

---

[2]Some approaches to research, of course, take the opposite view, and see the categories you use as pre-set by you at the start. But these are approaches that generally emphasise the use of quantitative methods – they make for weak qualitative research.

Please note that I have not suggested simply grouping the answers to the questions you have asked under each question. Of course you can do this, but you are likely to find a good deal of repetition and overlap in the themes which come out from the material. For example, what people say when you ask 'What did you find helpful in the way in which xyz authority dealt with you?' might well overlap with what they say when you ask 'What advice would you give xyz authority to improve their services?' It would be better to draw the themes from both sets of replies and use these as your headings.

> **COMMON PITFALLS 20.2** Reporting your data in exactly the order of your questionnaire, simply describing people's answers under each heading – very tedious for the reader

> **TIP** Before you start doing any analysis, but after you have put it in good order and put reference codes on it, photocopy the whole of your data set and put away the original. Loss of data would be a disaster

This may seem extravagant of resources, and tedious to do, but think of the waste of resources if you lose, or accidentally deface, the data from just one of your interviews. Or even worse, the whole pile of original data gets caught in a flood or a fire. Having copied the material, you can literally cut up the text and stick it down under different categories, if you want to work like this.

> **TIP** Always keep an identifying code number and page or line number alongside any quotation or other direct reference to the data – you will soon forget who said what!

Analysing focus group data

In some ways, focus group data looks much like other qualitative data drawn from individuals. But if it is treated as such, there is a danger of losing its unique value. The great strength of the focus group is in the interaction between the participants – the way in which people work together, or argue with each other, to make sense of an issue. It is good to try to preserve this process in the analysis, perhaps by quoting a chunk of text which includes important discussion between participants.

Focus groups should not be analysed as if they were a series of individual interviews. For example, it would generally be inappropriate to add up responses from individuals to a question asked during a group discussion. The group process is so likely to influence people that only limited confidence could be felt in these figures. People may not have spoken about an issue simply because someone else had already made the point. While some analysts do quantify references to issues by group participants, it is not clear what status should be given to the number of times an issue is mentioned in a discussion. Another approach, which may be more appropriate, takes the group as the unit of analysis, and counts in how many different groups an issue comes up.

EXAMPLE

Adding up focus group data: the Child Labour Project, Sialkot, Pakistan

In the Sialkot study 46 focus groups were held with a range of people. Researchers counted how many of the groups mentioned issues like poverty, education, or concerns about unemployed young people running wild, etc. They could then report, for example, that 75% of the focus groups mentioned improving the quality of education as an important step in improving the quality of life for these communities.

We will now look in more detail at some of the practical methods used to analyse qualitative data, which are all essentially aiming for the same goals.

Some techniques for qualitative analysis

This section describes how you practically organise the process we have just looked at. There are a number of different ways of doing this, which can be suitable for different types of project. Table 20.3 overleaf shows the different techniques, and they are further described below.

Cut and paste

A crude approach, but perfectly effective when you are in a hurry, your study is small and your data pretty simple. It can be done by hand or using the word-processing package of your computer.

Cut and paste – by hand   Here you absolutely must photocopy the whole of your data set, as you are going to literally cut it up and paste parts of it onto other sheets. First you need to follow the core process described above to arrive at a set of categories into which you want to sort your data. These may

Table 20.3 Techniques for qualitative analysis

Technique	Can it be done by hand?	Can a computer help?	Suitable for ... ?
Cut and paste	Yes	Yes, using word processing	Small, simple projects
Charting	Yes, this is the usual method	Yes, you can set up tables in word processing or on a spreadsheet	Any size of project
Card index	Yes	No	Any size of project, when you have time for careful analysis
Computer programs for qualitative analysis	No	Essential – needs a special program	Projects requiring detailed analysis of large quantities of textual data

derive very simply from the aims of your study, but you should keep a look out for any themes that arise from the data, which you had not anticipated.

Make an A4 sheet for each category you have identified, and then go through and cut out all the important material from your data, and stick it on the various sheets. Stick it with blutack or paperclips, so that you can move things around easily. Here you need to be careful to write on each note or quotation where the item comes from, so that you can trace it back and, for example, be sure that all your quotes do not come from one person.

An alternative approach would have you just writing a very short note and a reference to the data on each sheet, but to actually take whole statements means you have the material very handy to work from. Only possible with small data sets.

What you end up with is a set of sheets with a jumble of statements for each category, and you will need to organise these carefully – new subcategories may emerge naturally. Once this is done, you can look within each category for the themes of people's statements about it.

Cut and paste – by computer This is essentially the same process, but carried out in the word-processing package of your computer. It requires that the data you want to analyse be typed into the computer. Once this is done, you can either make a word-processing file for each category, or give each category a page in one large file, and then copy and paste items of data across from the data files to the analysis one. Again, be sure to keep track of which item comes from which interview or set of notes, and do copy rather than cut and paste, so that you retain a complete data set in the original file.

Doing this in word-processing allows you to move the material about very flexibly. Also, importantly, you can put the same material under more than one heading, which may be helpful where there is overlap.

Although you can do this with any word-processing package, there is a special software package called Hypersoft that gives you more help, and a book which explains the method (Dey, 1993).

(Hypersoft – requires Macintosh with System 6.0 or later and Hypercard ver. 1.2 or higher. From: Professor Ian Dey, The Department of Social Policy, The University of Edinburgh, AFB, George Square, Edinburgh, EH8 9LL.

Charting – by hand

This method has been described as particularly well-suited to research for applied policy research (Ritchie and Spencer, 1994). It is known as 'Framework', and was developed by the UK research institute Social and Community Planning Research (now the National Centre for Social Research). It is not as technical as this might suggest – you do it by hand on big pieces of paper! However it enables you to handle much bigger data sets than the simpler techniques described above. It was developed in part in response to a need to formalise qualitative data analysis in order to build confidence in the validity of its results. In this approach, you do not directly sort quotations from text, but create a set of codes which enable you to map the whole of the data onto a series of charts.

Again, the same core process is followed, although in familiarising yourself with the data, you can only look at a sample of the material, if there is too much to read it all. Then you set up a framework of categories, referred to as an index. Some researchers give each category and sub-category numbers for reference, others make short descriptive textual 'labels' to apply to the text.

So you have an index of categories, with a short code set beside its definition. Now go through the data and label it in the margins with these codes. Some passages may relate to a number of different codes.

Next, you create a number of charts, where your categories and sub-categories read along the top of the page, and your cases (whether these be interviews, focus group transcripts, or observation notes) read down, always in the same order. Use large sheets of paper for this – at least A3.

Table 20.4 overleaf gives an example of the way in which a subject chart is built up. This is a real example, from a study of UK maternity services by the College of Health. There were also charts covering antenatal and postnatal care. And for each of these stages of the childbirth process there were three charts: one for things women liked, one for things they disliked, and one for improvements they suggested.

You will need a number of charts, which can bring together your categories in a coherent way. It is worth giving some thought to the way in which you arrange the categories, as this will either help or hinder you in writing up the material.

It is essential to be consistent in entering data from each case in the same order for each chart. This enables you to read easily across and see the whole story for this case – often essential in making sense of what people

Table 20.4   Example of subject chart
Maternity Services
Labour and delivery: what women particularly disliked

	(I) Information	(F) Facilities	(M) Monitoring	(SS) Staff busy shortage/no staff to assist/left alone
Focus group 1	Conflicting information because of busy period (276–279) Conflicting advice/ information from doctors (333–338)	Theatre cramped (286–288) Beds too high (297–307) Lack of privacy (309-326)	Frequent monitoring (241–246)	Too busy compared with previous birth (235–240) Have to ask for assistance (240–241) Have to get your own tea (252–253) Staff rushed 'conveyor belt' delivery (283–284)
Focus group 2	Lack of information when in labour (134–136)	Lack of privacy in delivery rooms (199–216)		Midwives running between delivery rooms (222–234)

Reprinted by permission of Gill Craig/The College of Health, 2001.

have said, even if you do not intend to report cases individually. If you like, you can group your cases in such a way as to make it easy to investigate differences between groups. For example, you could enter information from people living in different geographical areas together.

Once the charting is complete, you need to look down each column and decide what is important to report from the data you have in each category. You can also read across, to check how an individual respondent's answers fit together. This makes it straightforward to write your report.

Card index

A more traditional approach in some disciplines is to use index cards to hold references to the data. A card is created for each category, and then you write on it notes of material you have collected relating to this category, including cross-reference information to enable you to trace it back to its source. It is best not to write on the back, so that you can lay out the cards and see their contents easily.

The joy of index cards is that you can sort them in any order you like, so it is easy to try out different ways of organising your material. One problem is that they are small, and can only show limited information before they are

> Sources of income: trading by women
>
> Interviews with women: earn 'own' money – Int. 5 p 9 [Interview Number 5, page 9]; took over selling cloth from mother – Int. 21 p 3; sells farm produce – Int. 23 p 6
>
> Observation notes: Market in town (detailed notes) 5 May; also 12 May; stalls by roadside – 2 July.
>
> Interviews with men: useful contribution to family income – Int. 3 p 10;
>
> See also: Markets

Figure 20.2   Example of index card used for qualitative data analysis

full of writing. It is also tempting to keep adding more cards, for more categories, without checking how they relate to each other. To stop things getting out of hand you need to regularly review your categories and either merge some or divide some.

To locate direct quotations from people, as with charting, you need to go back to the data itself, directed by your references on the card.

When you come to writing up, you can arrange and rearrange your cards into whatever patterns you like, probably laying them out on the floor to do so.

Using computer software for qualitative data analysis

In recent years, some computer programs have been developed to facilitate the process of qualitative data analysis. These are now widely used by professional researchers, and are felt to be very useful. In particular they make it easier to change categories, and re-label one's data, as ideas change in the course of the work. They make it possible to handle large bodies of qualitative data.

Some popular programs are NUD*IST, and The Ethnograph, and there are many others on the market. Essentially these packages help with both of the main stages of analysis: identifying and listing the themes coming from the data, and organising these themes into a coherent picture. The big issue for the researcher in a hurry is that all of your data needs to be on the computer to make this process work.

It is only worth buying and learning to use these programs if you have a large amount of qualitative data to analyse – and probably only then if you think you will do this type of work again. However they are now quite user-friendly, and they do bring great benefits in terms of handling the administrative side of this process conveniently.

It is possible to teach yourself to use these packages, or else you can go on a course run by the manufacturers or a university.

For more guidance, it is worth contacting a centre at the University of Surrey which has specialised in helping researchers on this matter.[3] This

---

[3]CAQDAS Networking Project, Department of Sociology, University of Surrey, Guildford GU2 5XH. Tel: Ann Lewins 01483 259455. Email: a.Lewins@soc.surrey.ac.uk

centre will give free advice by email, phone, etc. They have a good website which includes discussion groups, lists of software, demo software that can be downloaded, etc, at *http://caqdas.soc.surrey.ac.uk*. This site has links to all the companies which produce this kind of software, and is a very good place to start.

There is also good information on the company's websites, for example, for NUD*IST, the market leader: *http://www.qsr.com.au* You can also get help from Sage, which distributes much qualitative data analysis software including Atlas, NUD*IST, Winmax, and Ethnograph, on +44 (0) 207 330 1222 (a Sage helpline number for all its software) – or try the website: *http://www.sagepub.co.uk*

Rigour in qualitative analysis

The purpose of qualitative approaches to research is not to provide statistically reliable information for which representativeness can be claimed. However for such research to be persuasive, it is important to show that the methods and conclusions of the research are reasonable and justifiable. To enable readers to make a judgement about this, we need to give as much information as possible to enable them to understand how the research has been carried out.

It is important to include in research reports a full account of how the data was collected and how it was analysed. This is sometimes referred to as an 'audit trail'. The idea is that another researcher should be able to follow through your process and see where decisions were made and why.

As we have seen it is accepted in the social constructionist tradition of research (see Chapter 2.2) that the identity of the researcher, or analyst in this case, has an inevitable impact on the analysis. For example, a European man would probably have a different perspective in a study of the effects on children of the conflict in Angola from an Angolan woman researcher. So it can be appropriate to give some biographical details about the researcher as part of the analysis. You can say in what ways you feel your own background, values, and experience prior to the research project, may have influenced the research. The reader is given some information on which to judge how reasonable the writer's claims are. This is referred to as 'reflexivity' – rather than claim to have no 'vested interests', we declare them and let the reader make their own judgement.

Validity

Denscombe (1998) suggests the following checks be made to assess the validity of the findings:

- 'Do the conclusions do justice to the complexity of the phenomenon being investigated and avoid "oversimplifications", while also offering internal consistency?

- Has the researcher's self been recognised as an influence in the research but not a cause of biased or one-sided reporting? This is a difficult tightrope to walk, but vital in the context of such research.
- Have the instances selected for investigation been chosen on explicit and reasonable grounds as far as the aims of the research are concerned?
- Have alternative explanations been explored?
- Have the findings been 'triangulated' with alternative sources as a way of bolstering confidence in their validity?
- Have the research findings been fed back to informants to get their opinion on the explanation being proposed?
- How far do the findings and conclusion fit with existing knowledge on the area, and how far do they translate to other comparable situations?'

It is most important in qualitative work to present research findings in context – and avoid, for example, taking out 'quotes' from an interview in such a way as to twist their original meaning. The context includes not only the words on either side of a particular statement, but also the situation in which the words were produced – for example was it said in a public group setting? In front of the respondent's family, or her boss? The day after some significant event?

CHECKLIST   **For qualitative analysis**

✔ Has an analysis method been selected which allows an appropriate level of sophistication?

✔ Do the categories or themes identified reflect the research questions and the data?

✔ Has the topic been approached with an 'open mind'?

✔ Have alternative explanations been explored?

✔ Has the data been presented in context?

✔ Are the findings of one technique or group of respondents triangulated with those from another technique or group?

✔ Have the conclusions of the analysis been checked back with respondents?

✔ Have existing relevant research findings been used to support your data?

✔ Has the process followed in the research and the analysis been made explicit?

20.7   Quantitative Analysis

This section aims to give guidance in some straightforward techniques for analysing quantitative data. If you need complex statistics, such as tests of significance (only appropriate with large, representative samples), get advice from an experienced researcher, preferably a statistician. But for most research for development work, only a limited number of procedures are needed.

The first part of this section looks at some ways of carrying out simple analysis of number-based data, moving on to discuss using percentages and how to describe data statistically using averages and measures of spread. Then we look at how to find correlations within the data, and at computer software for quantitative analysis. Then we consider how to ensure a rigorous approach to quantitative analysis. The last part of the section looks at ways of presenting quantitative data such as tables and charts.

Some techniques for quantitative analysis

The data matrix

You may find it helpful to think of the data you have collected in terms of a matrix – a table with rows and columns (Table 20.5). You set out all the information from each respondent along one row, with a column for each question. Then the next respondent, then the next.

Table 20.5   A data matrix

Respondents	Questions			
	1. Age	2. Sex	3. Housing type	4. etc.
A				
B				
C				
D				
Etc				

For example: with small simple questionnaires, it may be possible to do your calculations directly from a data matrix, but usually things get too complicated, and you need to work on each question on a separate sheet. This is similar to the charting method for qualitative analysis described in 20.6 (2), but you are entering numbers rather than words.

TIP	A data matrix (on paper or on a spreadsheet) is a really good way of holding your data safely, even if you will use different methods to analyse it later

Coding

Some data naturally presents itself in the form of figures, but often the first process we have to think about is that of turning the information you have from words into figures. With luck, most of your questions will have contained 'pre-coded' answers – see Chapter 17.6, on questionnaires. This means that you have decided before you asked the questions what groups of answers you expected, and have given respondents limited options. You will now need to group and 'code' your questionnaires – meaning, here, to assign numbers to the different answers you have received.

Missing data and 'other'

It is important to record missing answers clearly. There is a difference between people who have made no reply to a question, for whatever reason, and those who said they did not know. The interviewer may have simply forgotten to ask a particular question, leading to a missing answer – but replies coded as 'other' (and the reply 'don't know'), on the other hand, are meaningful responses. Make sure to include a category for missing data in all your coding schemes. Where appropriate, 'don't know' and 'other' should also be included.

Traditionally, where they are creating a numerical coding scheme for a data set, researchers use 8 or 88 for 'Other' and 9 or 99 for 'Answer missing'.

Counting up the totals

The most common calculation we make is to simply add up how many people answered in which way to closed questions. Researchers tend to call these 'frequency counts', referring to the frequency with which different types of answer occur. The most straightforward way of carrying out this kind of calculation by hand is to set out a tally (reckoning, counting) sheet like that in Table 20.6.A (Hall and Hall, 1996). You can use a blank questionnaire, if numbers are small and there is space, or else use a separate sheet and create a table for each question. You fill in the tally sheet by going through the questionnaires and entering a mark in the correct category for each answer.

Table 20.6.A   Example of a simple tally sheet
Do you own a refrigerator?

Response		Number
Yes	JH+ I	6
No	JH+ JH+ JH+ II	17
No answer	III	3
Total		26

This is a perfectly good way of doing this sort of analysis for small numbers of questionnaires. A refinement, which enables you to go back and check your information, if you find, for example that your totals do not add up correctly, is to enter onto your tally sheet the code number for each questionnaire instead of just a tally mark (Table 20.6B). You can still count them up in the same way.

Table 20.6.B Example of a tally sheet using code numbers
Do you own a radio?

Response		Number
Yes	①⑥⑧⑩	4
No	②③⑤⑦⑨	5
No answer	④	1
Total		10

The numbers in circles are code numbers referring to respondents.

> **TIP**   This method is really useful – consider using it BEFORE you spend days using the simple counting method only to find you have one missing answer and don't know where it should have come from

In addition to enabling checking, this method has the advantage that if you also have qualitative data, for example about why people said they did or did not own radios, you can turn to that material directly from your tally sheet.

Percentages

Percentages are of course a most useful way of presenting data.

You can see in Table 20.6.C how much easier it is to get the basic gist of the information contained in numbers when they are worked out as percentages.

Table 20.6.C Example of a tally sheet with percentages
Do you own a refrigerator?

Response		Number	(%)
Yes	ʜʜ I	6	(26)
No	ʜʜ ʜʜ ʜʜ II	17	(74)
No answer	III	3	
Total		26	
Total valid replies		23	(100)

This table shows one convention for presenting actual numbers and percentages, which is to give the actual number followed by the percentage figure in brackets. You then could write in the text, for example: '6 (26 per cent) said they owned a television'.

However beware, percentages can be misleading, especially if the total number of respondents is low (certainly if fewer than 40). This is because percentages tend to magnify the actual differences between groups – one individual can make a big difference to how the figures look. For example, if your sample is only 25, each individual accounts for 4% of the total. If your total number of respondents is low, it is good practice always to give the actual number alongside any percentage you mention.

Percentages are calculated after excluding missing answers – this is why there is no percentage shown in the row for 'No answer' (Table 20.6C). It may be important to show the actual numbers as well, so that the reader can decide what importance to put on your figure, knowing exactly how many people were involved. What you are reporting is the *percentage of those who gave a reply* and you need to make this clear.

EXAMPLE

Identifying meaningful figures: maternal and child health in Liberia

A Save the Children study of maternal and child health in Liberia asked about families' experiences of diarrhoeal illnesses in children, and about mothers' knowledge of how to make a rehydration solution using sugar and salt. It was more meaningful to report percentages in relation to the knowledge of the mothers whose children had experienced diarrhoea than in relation to the whole sample, which included a lot of missing answers. About 40% of the sample had experience of diarrhoea in their children. Only a small proportion of these mothers (15%) gave correct information, and this was an important clue that health workers need better training on how to communicate this information effectively.

It is best, again with small samples, not to give percentage numbers calculated to one or more decimal points, as this gives a false impression of precision. Round the numbers up or down as appropriate. For example, if 9 out of 17 people said x, you might quote a figure of 54.94%. But with such small numbers, this is over-exact. Round it up to 55%. With very small numbers, perhaps including this example, it may be best not to give percentages at all, to avoid the appearance that you are trying to make wider claims than your data will support.

Working out percentages

To handle percentages confidently, make sure you understand how they relate to fractions of things. When you are using a calculator, always make a guess by working it out in your head, to check that your answer is in the right general area.

To find a percentage of a number:

It can be easier to ignore the % button on your calculator. To answer the question 'What is *something* per cent of *something else*? Remember that x per cent of y simply means x divided by 100 multiplied by y.

Example: find 15% of 240

Rewrite it like this: 15/100 × 240

And calculate: 15 ÷ 100 × 240 = 36.

To express something as a percentage:

This is where we change a fraction or a ratio into a percentage. Use this technique where you are trying to answer a question which basically says 'what is *something* as a percentage of *something else*?' The answer is always a percentage. The basic technique is to divide the top by the bottom and multiply the result by 100 to make a percentage.

Example:

60 out of 130 students on the course are female. What percentage is this?

Rewrite the question as: 60/130 × 100

And calculate: 60 ÷ 130 × 100 = 46.1538...

Give the answer as 46% since a whole number is probably accurate enough (from University of North London teaching pack on research methods).

Grouped data

It is often useful to put together raw data into groups. For example, it would be tedious to present all the ages of people in your sample in turn, so you might consider grouping them into, for example, 0–18, 19–29, 30 to 59, 60 plus, or some such set of groupings. However be careful when you do this. If you do offer your respondents only a set of groups to tick (a common way of collecting age data), you are stuck with the groupings you choose for any analysis you may want to do. So if you later decide that under and over 16 would have been a better grouping, then you do not have the information.

You can of course collect your data in its most basic form – eg ask for age in years – and then group it together as part of the analysis process – this leaves you more flexibility. It could be helpful to list out all the data in order, for one variable, so as to see where natural groupings might arise. This will also be apparent if you look at the basic frequencies for the variable.

Analysis of open-ended questions in a questionnaire

This is a common task, and one which falls between qualitative and quantitative analysis (see comments above, in Section 20.1). You have asked a question which invites comments, and then you want to make categories within the replies, and add up how many respondents made a comment within each category. You may also want to directly quote some typical comments for some categories. For example, you might have asked school children taking part in a particular programme what they hope to gain from it.

The first process is similar to the core process for qualitative analysis described above in 20.6. You need to bring together all the responses – perhaps by listing them on a separate sheet, either on the computer or by hand. If you have a very large data set, you can take a sample, eg every nth questionnaire, and make a preliminary categorisation from that. As ever, keep track of which statements come from which questionnaire – put the identifying code number beside each comment. This will help you if you need to recode any category later on. Some respondents may have made several comments and their code number will appear repeatedly.

Having listed out the comments, make a suitable set of categories for the data, and expect to revise it as necessary, as described above. Take another sheet of paper, and write these categories along one side of the paper. Then enter the code number for each questionnaire where this type of comment was made under each category. Then you can add up total numbers who made each type of comment.

It is also important to keep track of how many respondents answered these questions at all. This information could be kept with your main quantitative analysis. So you might create a table (on paper or on the computer) which just notes 'comment' or 'no comment' against questions which ask for this sort of response.

Describing the data statistically

Averages

It is often useful to find the mid-point or average amongst a set of values. The bad news is that there are three types of average in mathematics – these are known together as 'measures of central tendency'. The good news, however, is that once you have understood these, each will be useful for a different purpose. (Denscombe, 1998)

The mean

This is what most people are talking about when they refer to 'the average'. You calculate the mean by adding up all the values for the respondents in your data set, and then dividing them by the number of respondents (excluding those for whom there is a missing answer).

Consider the following set of values:

Number of children in family

| 2 | 1 | 4 | 3 | 2 | 9 | 3 | 2 | 10 | 1 | 1 |

To calculate the mean of the values above:

1. Add them all together (= 38)
2. Divide by the total number of cases (÷11)

Mean number of children in a family = 3.45.

But perhaps this example shows something of the weakness of the mean as a measure of 'central tendency'. It describes what would result if there were an equal distribution of values – if the total numbers were spread evenly. How well the mean can represent a set of values depends upon:

– how spread out or dispersed the values are around the mean; and
– whether there are any extremely large or small values within the data set.

The mean is strongly affected by any extremely large or small numbers, and where this happens the distribution is said to be skewed. In our example, apart from the two large families, most are quite small. This is often the case with income distribution, for example, where a mean could present a false picture for the majority of cases, if one or two very high earners pulled up the average.

The median (middle point)

The median is defined as the middle value of a set, when the values are arranged in order of size. Half the values fall on one side of the median, half on the other.

For example, using the data set discussed above, let us find its median. First, place the numbers in ascending order.

There are eleven values, and the middle one (the number falling halfway between the highest and the lowest values) is 2 – this is the median.

| 1 | 1 | 1 | 2 | 2 | [2] | 3 | 3 | 4 | 9 | 10 |

What happens if there is an even number of cases, such as 12? Then the median falls between the two middle numbers, and the convention is to take the mean of the two. So, for example, if your series of values went like this: The median is the mean of 2 and 3 – 2.5.

| 1 | 1 | 1 | 2 | 2 | [2] | [3] | 3 | 3 | 4 | 9 | 10 |

The median can be useful when your data is skewed, that is, there are a small number of large or small values. It also works well with small numbers of values, in contrast to the mean. It is easy to understand what the median is – half the values in the set are above it and half below. So in the example, half the families have more children and the other half have less than the median number.

The mode

The third type of average is the mode. The mode is the value which occurs the most often. You find it by counting the number of times each value occurs. The mode can be used with any kind of data – it can be read off from any count of frequencies, as the most common value. Like the median, it is not affected by extreme values.

Going back to this example:

Number of children in family

2	1	4	3	2	9	3	2	10	1	10

It will be seen that both 1 and 2 occur three times, so these are the modes for this group of families. There can be two or more modes.

Measures of spread

Measures of spread are logically linked to averages. They describe the way in which the data are arranged around the mid-point – how they are dispersed.

The simplest measure of spread is very easy to work out! This is called the range, and is found by simply subtracting the lowest value from the highest one.

Thus in the example we have been using, the smallest families had one child, and the largest had ten, so the range is nine. However in this case it might be best to simply give the information about what the highest and lowest values are. This is meaningful information, especially if combined with information about the average – either the mean, which should be expressed as between three and four children, or the median of two children.

The range is, however, strongly affected by extreme values, so should be used with caution. For example, if only one family has nine children and everyone else has one or two, the range is still 'between 1 and 9'. There are a number of other ways of describing spread, including the shape of the distribution in relation to the standard deviation. While for large data sets these may be relevant, you would be well advised to find help from a statistician in working out this type of calculation, and in explaining its relevance. You also need to be sure that your audience will understand the meaning of any statistics you use.

Finding connections – tests for correlation

We are often interested in how two different sets of data relate to one another. For example, you have done a survey and you want to know whether people on low incomes are more likely to have problems of access to clean water than people on higher incomes. Or you want to know if men are more likely to hold a certain view than women. This is called a correlation or a cross-tabulation.

Table 20.7   Cross-tabulation: Illness during last four weeks by age – adults

Health status	age	18 to 40	40 to 60	Over 60	Total
Yes (illness present)		10 (17%)	8 (15%)	14 (47%)	32 (23%)
No illness		50 (83%)	44 (85%)	16 (53%)	110 (77%)
Total		60 (100%)	52 (100%)	30 (100%)	142 (100%)

Some terms

A variable: Age and income can be variables, and so can people's opinions on issues. The term is used to refer to any quality or characteristic of a number of individuals which has different degrees of magnitude or different categories, so that individuals vary in the extent to which they possess this quality, or fall into this category. In effect, each question you ask usually relates to one variable.

Correlation: The degree to which changes in one variable are associated with changes in another variable. Does income increase or decrease with age?

Cross-tabulation: A technique where you create a table of data including two variables, each of which is divided into two or more categories. The cross-tabulation shows the number of cases that occur jointly in each combination of categories of the variables under investigation. They answer the questions:

– Is there any association or relationship between two variables?
– If there is, how strong is the relationship?

A very important note of caution: When we set up cross-tabulations, we usually have an idea in our minds about what the relationship between the data will mean. But there is always the possibility that any relationship is simply the result of chance. That is, it would probably not recur if you did the research again. This is why *tests of significance* are used. These enable us to establish what degree of confidence we should have that our findings are reliable.

And another note of caution: You cannot be sure, even if you find a correlation which is statistically significant, in which direction causation goes (what is the cause and what the effect). For example, if there are more charges brought in areas where there are more police officers, is a higher level of crime the explanation, or are more officers simply able to prosecute more cases? We have already discussed this issue above in 20.3, as it is very important.

You can work out basic cross-tabulations by hand. Set out a large table like Table 20.7, with lots of space in the boxes, and go through the data (preferably using the data matrix you prepared earlier, (see Table 20.5)), entering code numbers as in Tally sheet type B above (Table 20.6.B). This is advisable as you can so easily get in a muddle entering simply tally marks. Then add up the totals for each box.

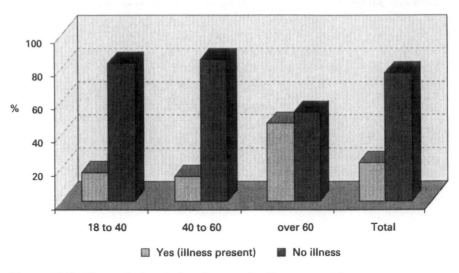

Figure 20.3 Illness during the last four weeks disaggregated by age group

However if you are doing cross-tabulations, it is more likely that you are dealing with a large data set, and using a computer is a very much easier way of working out cross-tabulations for large numbers. The statistical pro-gramme SPSS does this easily.

The difficulty with all this is not so much in the calculation, but in what it all means. Unless you are working with a large, reasonably representative sample, it is unlikely that any correlation you identify will be statistically significant. It is bad practice to publish correlational data unless it reaches a reasonable level of significance. If you do so, you can seem to be misleading readers.

> **COMMON**   Wasting time running dozens of cross tabulations when your data set is not
> **PITFALLS**   big enough to have confidence in any statistics generated
> **20.3**

If you do cross-tabulations, you need to investigate whether any correla-tions you find could have arisen simply by chance. This involves using tests of significance. I am not going to explain here how to undertake signifi-cance tests. Any book on statistics will do this. However you definitely need advice from an experienced researcher, probably a statistician, to use these competently. SPSS will calculate some tests for you automatically, and many others on request, but you still need to be able to interpret the information correctly.

> **TIP** Consult a statistician or qualitative researcher now

Having got advice, your key task is to think about which cross-tabulations you want to look at. Even with quite a small data set (ie not too many respondents or too many questions), there are a vast number of cross-tabulations which could be run. What you need to do is to go back to your theories about what is going on, and see what relationships you would expect to see in the data. Then look for them. Then question any you find! But also remember that a correlation which might be expected but is *not* found may be important to report as well. For example, if girls and boys do equally well in a set of examinations, this could be an important finding. Most people's expectation would be either that gender would affect performance in different ways in relation to each subject – or that girls (or indeed boys) would simply do worse at everything.

What statistics you can reasonably use for your project depends on the size and type of sample you have used. See Chapter 19 on sampling for more discussion of this issue.

Using computer software for quantitative analysis

There are a number of options available in terms of computer software for quantitative analysis.

Specialist statistical packages

These are specifically designed for this task, and will therefore give you the most help with your project. They are set up to expect survey data, and will easily carry out all the calculations you need (and many more!).

- A commonly used package is SPSS (the Statistical Package for the Social Sciences). This is a powerful program which allows you to analyse large quantities of data. Data is entered using a spreadsheet format where each column is a variable (for example, a question – male/female; region) and each row represents a case (eg a respondent; a village). It allows you to put in labels which keep the information about the meaning of the data close to the numbers involved, and can produce high quality tables and graphs. The latest versions are quite user-friendly. You may have to buy it specially, and learn to use it of course, but if you expect to do more than one substantial survey (perhaps 60 or more respondents) with a quantitative element, it might well repay its cost (for guidance on how to use SPSS, see, for example, Bryman and Cramer, 1997; Einspruch, 1998).[4]

---

[4] SPSS is available from SPSS UK Ltd, St Andrews House, West St, Woking, Surrey, GU21 1EB. Tel: 01483 719200.

- Minitab is also widely used, but less user-friendly than SPSS (Cramer, 1997; Mayer, 1998). Also Statview, which is available for the Macintosh as well as for Windows.
- Epi-Info is a package designed for analysing public health data, and is widely used in the South. It is a series of microcomputer programs for word processing, data management, and epidemiological analysis, designed for public health professionals. Epi-Info is easy to use, but also offers programming languages for both data input and analysis so that permanent health information systems can be developed. It can generate a questionnaire as well as carry out analysis on the results. It is public-domain software, and is distributed free by the Centre for Disease Control and the World Health Organisation. Though its reference point is medical, it can be used for other kinds of survey.

  The CDC's Epi-Info home page is at: *http://www.cdc.gov/epo/epi/epiinfo.htm*. You can download the software from there, in English. The package is available in Arabic, Chinese, French, Indonesian, Russian, Spanish, Serbo-Croatian, and Vietnamese. Manuals only have been translated into Czech, German, Hungarian, Italian, Portuguese, and Polish. The website gives addresses to write to for the translated materials.[5]
- Kwikstat is a shareware package running on IBM PC compatibles and does more than enough to analyse your data. Shareware is free software which can be downloaded from the Internet. Search for 'shareware' and you should find it.

Spreadsheets

Excel (part of the Microsoft Office package); Lotus 1-2-3; and Quattro Pro are spreadsheets. These can be used for laying out tables and producing graphs for presenting your data. You could set up a data matrix on one – see Table 20.5 Data is entered in the spreadsheet as one huge table, with each row containing a case (one respondent's answers) and each column containing a single variable. You can then apply various formulae to the data, eg you could work out averages etc. They do everything a calculator does and a lot more. But spreadsheets are not designed for analysing research data, and some tasks, eg cross-tabulation, can be a struggle. In Excel these can be done as PivotTables. An easy-to-use statistical analysis package is more helpful for these purposes. You can generally export data from a spreadsheet to other packages, by putting it into the ASCII format first. Spreadsheets are widely used for financial management, so you may find your organisation already uses one.

---

[5]Alternatively, you can purchase the package from the suppliers by telephone with a credit card, which also includes the users' manual (which is of course helpful): USD, 2075-A West Park Place, Stone Mountain, GA 30087 USA. Tel: 001 770 469 0681. Email: usd@usd-inc.com. Or you can legally copy it from someone else's computer.

Database packages

Access (part of the Microsoft Office package) and others. These can be useful tools to assist in data entry. You can design a set of data entry tables which closely match your questionnaire, so reducing the risk of mistakes. Data can then be exported to other packages for analysis. But databases are of limited value in research, as they cannot carry out the analyses you will need.

Rigour in quantitative analysis

There are well-established criteria for rigour in quantitative analysis, based on the positivist framework (see Chapter 2.2 above). Essentially the rules are those of common sense – to be satisfied of the honesty of the findings presented, the reader needs access to enough information to see what has been done and how. The model is that of a laboratory experiment – it should be possible for another researcher to come along and do what you did, and find the same results. Therefore you need to describe fully the methods you used to reach your conclusions.

Two key concepts need to be understood:

Validity: In relation to research data, this notion refers to whether or not the data reflect the truth, reflect reality and cover the crucial matters. The question is 'Are we actually measuring what we intend to measure (are the right indicators being used) and are we getting accurate results?'

Reliability: Researchers need to feel confident that their measurements are not affected by a research instrument (eg questionnaire) that gives one reading on one occasion and a different reading on the next occasion when there has been no real change in the item being measured. A good level of reliability means that the research instrument produces the same data time after time on each occasion that it is used, and that any variation in the results reflects real variations in the thing being measured (Denscombe, 1998).

The techniques described in the chapter on research techniques (17.1 and 17.6) for pilot-testing questionnaires are important for increasing confidence in the validity and reliability of your research instruments. The pilot-testing you did should be described in your report. Did respondents understand your questions in the way you expected?

Response rates

It is important to report what proportion of your original sample actually took part in the research. If the proportion is very small, it can undermine confidence in the representativeness of the findings (see Chapter 19). If you do have a low response rate, it may be worth checking to see if those who actually took part reflect the sample you aimed to include. You could look at some obvious sources of bias, for example numbers of male and female respondents, area of origin, language spoken, or income levels.

You should describe any sources of bias in your sample that you are aware of, and discuss how important you consider them to be. Equally you should be honest about any problems you see with any analytical procedures you have undertaken – this will not undermine your work, but on the contrary will show that you understand its limitations as well as its strengths.

CHECKLIST   **For quantitative analysis**

✓ Don't panic! For most purposes in research for development work the statistics required are very straightforward

✓ Go back to your original research questions and make sure your analysis is relevant to them

✓ Make sure the way you describe the data makes sense – that you can explain what it means in simple language

✓ If you use averages, select the appropriate type

✓ Don't attempt more elaborate statistical analysis than your sample will stand

✓ You can do quantitative analysis by hand, but you need to allow time for this

✓ For larger data sets computers bring many benefits – especially in speed and accuracy, once you have understood the program

✓ Explain in detail what you have done to increase confidence in the validity and reliability of your findings

---

In the next chapter, on how to write an effective research report, there is a section on presenting quantitative data images.

So what does it all mean? – synthesis

This section draws attention to the crucial final stage of analysis, whatever type of data is involved (qualitative or quantitative), where you need to step back and think about your findings in the context of the questions you started out with. When you are deeply involved with your material, it is easy to lose sight of the bigger picture, and to imagine that people will be interested in every detail of your findings. Sadly they will not. It is up to you to identify what are the most important aspects of your research project in relation to what was previously known, and what were the questions you were setting out to answer.

Analysis is always a taxing process, and one inevitably wants to collapse at the point when the data has been nicely organised to make a coherent picture. But this is the moment when you need to find some new energy, and

look around you again. There are sure to be lots of fascinating details, but what really is the significance of this work? What is the key evidence that you have produced, and what exactly can it be said to show?

If analysis is a process of breaking things down, then this is a process of synthesis, bringing them together again, but in a new form. You may, for example, be able to bring together quantitative and qualitative information in a new way.

So, when you have written the long version, describing the data, setting out the relationships you see between things, or at least when you feel you are on top of the data, sit back. Meet with those who have worked with you – co-researchers, community members, perhaps even funders, and brainstorm the key points that you think come out of your research.

I have found it useful at this point to talk with a press officer or a friendly journalist. Journalists have a 'so what?' mentality, as their role is to fight for the public's attention in a very competitive environment. They will want you to summarise the point of the research in one (or at most three) sentences. This is always agonising for the researcher, but is a good thing to learn to do. It may be that you conclude that your research is really aimed mainly at a knowledgeable audience who will make the effort to understand your more technical version of the findings, but at least have a go at producing a plain-language short statement.

It may be important at this stage to bring in data from other studies, or information from other sources – government statistics, newspaper reports (always being aware of the status of the data you use, see Chapter 12). You can build confidence in the trustworthiness of your data by setting alongside it any findings of other studies which have similar findings. Or if your work appears to challenge the findings of other studies, you need to address what you think are the reasons for these differences in your report.

The next important stage is to test the points you want to make by playing devil's advocate. Imagine all the arguments that could be made to discredit your work, or diminish its importance. Question and criticise your own conclusions and assumptions, from the point of view of those whom you need to influence. You need to 'cover your back', by anticipating the arguments that will be made against you and explaining why you think they are incorrect. Give evidence – you cannot ask your readers to make any leaps of faith. They may not share your value base, so why should they take your word for anything?

Writing recommendations

Practical research usually aims to produce a set of recommendations for action based on the findings of the study. Sometimes ideas for action arise directly from the process of research, and action may start at an early stage, especially in Participatory Learning and Action type projects. However recommendations do not always leap out of the data readily. Respondents sometimes describe the problems really well, but do not have much inspiration about solutions.

At this point you need to be very clear about the status of the research, and your role in relation to making recommendations. Where the research is very much a matter of 'giving voice' to a group of people, it may be a good idea to do some work within the process of the research to directly consult community members on the recommendations they think you should make. Group work can be better than individual interviews at helping people to think into the future and to be imaginative. People can build on each other's ideas, and gain confidence from the process of the group.

You may also want to consult with partner agencies that would be important in implementing any recommendations made, including any which have already been involved with the project. In terms of getting recommendations implemented, it is far more likely that the research will have an impact if those who would need to put them into practice feel some ownership of the project. It may be helpful to present the key findings of the research to a group of managers and practitioners, and ask them to work out what should be done about problems identified. This could be done alongside consultation with community members.

However sometimes when you do this, agencies will produce the same agenda they always do, regardless of the findings of your research. You need to be clear about whether your findings actually support any recommendations people are suggesting. If they do not, there is no problem with agencies publishing their own response to your research, which can bring in new ideas, but these should not be presented as recommendations *of the research*. Your own recommendations must be directly linked to the data you have presented.

As discussed above, no one likes to read about research which directly affects them in the newspapers. You want to build sympathy for the work you have done. It can be a good strategy to send a draft of the research report to agencies to whom recommendations may be addressed and ask them for comments, or perhaps ask for a meeting to discuss their response. Obviously this needs to be part of an agreed strategy for influence.

It is always tempting to call for further research in your recommendations – but do think carefully before you do so. There is a danger that this will be read as a lack of confidence in the work that you have done. And many people will be a bit cynical about researchers who always want to do more research.

CHECKLIST   Synthesis – bringing it all together

✔ Consider the question – so what does this mean?

✔ Look at the bigger picture – what is important about this study, in relation to the key questions in this field?

✔ Look at your findings in relation to other important research in the field – does it support earlier research, or challenge it?

✔ Ensure that your data genuinely gives evidence for the arguments you want to make

✔ Test carefully the claims you want to make, working out how people might argue against you and 'covering your back' – explaining why they are wrong

✔ Consult respondents, community members, and partner agencies about recommendations, *but*

✔ Recommendations must be supported by the research findings

Further Reading

The best two general accounts I have found of data analysis for practical small projects are:

Hall, D. and Hall, I. (1996) *Practical Social Research: Project work in the community*. Basingstoke, UK: Macmillan.

Denscombe, M. (1998) *The Good Research Guide for Small-Scale Social Research Projects*. Buckingham, UK and Philadelphia, USA: The Open University Press.

On more specialised matters:

Ritchie, J., and Spencer, L. (1994) 'Qualitative data analysis for applied policy research', in Bryman, A. and Burgess, R.G. (eds), *Analyzing Qualitative Data*. London: Routledge.

Explains the 'Framework' method of charting qualitative data.

Fielding, N.G. and Raymond, M.L. (1994) *Computer Analysis and Qualitative Research*. London: Sage.

Mayer, S. (1998) 'Critical issues in using data'; and Mukherjee, C., Chandan, and Wuyts, M. (1998) 'Thinking with Quantitative Data', in Thomas, A., Chataway, J. and Wuyts, M. *Finding Out Fast: Investigative skills for policy and development*. Milton Keynes: The Open University/Sage.

Articles on two different aspects of data analysis.

Gilbert, N. (ed) (1996–) *Social Research Update*. Guildford, UK: University of Surrey. Dept of Sociology, University of Surrey, Guildford, GU2 5XH England. Website: *http://www.soc.surrey.ac.uk/sru*

A quarterly series of short papers on practical research issues – for example on analysing qualitative data by computer; secondary analysis of qualitative data. Subscriptions are free to researchers with addresses in the UK, and all back issues are also available on the Internet.

Nichols, P. (1991) *Social Survey Methods: A fieldguide for development workers*, Development Guidelines No. 6. Oxford: Oxfam.

On the analysis of quantitative research in developing countries.

21 How to Write an Effective Research Report

This chapter aims to help you to write about your research – especially to write reports, which are usually necessary to present your findings. We will start by giving some guidance about style of writing, what you need to include, and what you can leave out, from your final report and then will say a little about how to go about the task of writing.

The inclusion of this chapter does not mean to suggest that all research must be reported in a 'long and boring' report. As we have seen in Chapter 10, it is clear that such reports may not be the best way to influence policy or to have an impact on programme planning. Other measures can be more effective, including, for example, face-to-face feedback to community members and/or decision-makers. Sometimes research findings begin to have an influence long before any report is written, where the key stakeholders take action as a result of information they themselves generate.

EXAMPLE

Learning about poverty in Mozambique

The Mozambique Participatory Poverty Assessment team took a long time to produce an overall poverty assessment for the country. But in the mean time they achieved purposeful collaboration amongst a wide group of organisations and government. Two types of policy-relevant information were apparent:

1. The outputs from wealth-ranking and problem-ranking exercises were immediately impressive, and were put to direct policy use, even in rough form and with little analysis. They helped to identify priority problems as perceived by those concerned.
2. Equally important, but more complex, were findings derived from aggregation (adding together) of livelihood analyses. These touched on many areas of life, and had the potential to illuminate the collective and multi-dimensional causes and consequences of poverty. Achieving this required more complex, sustained analysis and study (Owen, 1998).

The report, then, is not an end in itself, and collaborative working should not be sacrificed to achieve tidy outputs on paper. However for most substantial pieces of research, it will be necessary to write a report of some kind, if only in order to decide for yourselves what your findings mean. Once you have done that, it becomes much easier to write short summaries or articles, and to take your message out through verbal presentations, press releases, and so on. Reports are also important to create a permanent record of the information collected, and to prevent future duplication of effort.

Activity 21.1

What makes a good research report?

Brainstorm with a group of colleagues what you look for in a research report. Try to think of real examples that you have admired, and identify why they were effective.

21.1   What to Write

As we have seen in Chapter 10, it is important for reports and articles to be tailored to their audience, and for these to be part of a wider promotional strategy.

Style of writing

Your style should be determined by your own natural way of expressing yourself and the needs of your audience. However bear in mind that while some audiences might be impressed by a complex way of writing, the main purpose of the exercise is to convey information. The crucial thing is to encourage people to actually read it. Clear and simple expression will help people to make sense of the material you present, and therefore to act upon it.

It is important to strike a balance between making your message hit home at a human level, and avoiding seeming to exaggerate or sensationalise. Telling the story through direct quotation of respondents' own voices can be very effective. Be specific and accurate. Do not generalise beyond your data (or existing knowledge from other sources). Avoid emotive words and phrases, jargon and technical terms, and statements which cannot be backed up by evidence. Also avoid describing people in ways which make them out to be helpless victims.

Activity 21.2

Style of writing

This exercise is best done as a group discussion. The facilitator should write the following statements on a flip chart, for participants to criticise. In this box they have been written with the problem words or phrases underlined. On the flip chart the underlining should not be shown.

You may want participants to work individually, in pairs, or to brainstorm together in the group.

(i)   <u>Ribero says</u> that half the <u>children</u> in Peru <u>work</u>.

(ii) <u>Many</u> Ethiopian <u>elderly</u> people <u>suffer</u> from <u>malnutrition</u>.

(iii) <u>UNICEF says</u> that <u>urbanisation</u> in Africa is <u>increasing</u>. <u>More</u> women and children are migrating from rural areas to towns, and this <u>'contributes to the lack of housing infrastructure' (Smithson)</u>. <u>NGOs</u> are also concerned about <u>growing numbers</u> of <u>CEDC</u> and <u>delinquents</u>. The <u>resulting misery can only be eradicated</u> by <u>drastic</u> government action and <u>should be</u> supported by <u>international aid agencies</u>.

(Reproduced with permission from Boyden and Ennew, 1997)

If you are presenting a lot of quantitative data, use charts and diagrams to make it easier to understand. See below for guidance on visual presentation of quantitative information. Some people find diagrams like flowcharts helpful also in understanding how systems work. But do not let charts or diagrams get too complicated – present only essential data in this way. You can use an appendix for charts or diagrams which include necessary information but would disrupt the flow of your argument if included in the main body of the text.

What not to write

What you leave out is as important as what you put in. Do not attempt to include all of your data. Since everyone you are writing for is very busy, and many of them may not much enjoy reading reports, you should include only the minimum necessary to fulfil the aims of your project. If you did some fieldwork which was not very helpful or relevant, you may want to refer to it somewhere in an appendix, but you need not describe it or its findings in your main report.

What must be included

> **CHECKLIST   What to include in your report**
>
> ✔ Contents list
> ✔ A summary
> ✔ An introduction giving background and rationale – why did you undertake this research?
> ✔ Details of funding and partner agencies (with brief descriptions)
> ✔ The original aims and objectives
> ✔ An account of the methods you used (for analysis as well as for data collection) – can go in an appendix
> ✔ A description of the sample, how it was drawn, and any problems you see with it
> ✔ Presentation of your findings
> ✔ Conclusion – overall value of the study
> ✔ Recommendations, where appropriate – already discussed with key players
> ✔ Full references for any research you cite

Note that I am not advising you to create a section headed 'Discussion', 'Analysis', or 'Synthesis', although I have emphasised the importance of bringing your ideas together (see 20.8 in Analysis chapter). This is a process which should inform the whole way in which you present your findings, not necessarily form a separate section which you set out alongside of the data.

Also omitted is a 'literature review' section (see Chapter 12). At times this is a central part of the research, and will need to be included, but if so, then give it a title which explains why the reader should be interested in it. For many research reports, it is better to incorporate insights from the wider literature into the discussion of your own findings. Does other research support or contradict your findings? What light does it throw on them, or they on it?

The best research reports weave together new findings with information about the context of the research and data from existing research. Headings should be closely relevant to the questions the reader has in her or his mind – or to the way in which respondents think about the issues. This is not a report on a scientific experiment where methods, data, and discussion are set out separately.

Remember to include information about issues you looked for but did not find, for example issues you expected community members to be concerned about but which they did not bring forward.

Describing the methods

A brief but complete account of the methods you used is an important ingredient of any research report – part of the accountability of researchers for their work. This enables readers to decide for themselves how much weight to put on your findings. But how much emphasis to put on process as opposed to findings is something to judge in relation to the particular project. If the methods are particularly interesting, do write them up fully – but it may be that different people are interested in the findings than are interested in the methodology. Even if the methods were not innovative, it can save future researchers huge amounts of trouble if you describe clearly what you did, any problems, and how you solved them. You could write two different kinds of report, one for each audience.

At a minimum you should include: which approaches and techniques you used and why (see Chapters 14 to 18); details of your sampling procedure – sample size and how it was drawn; how people were approached, and response rates. It is useful to say how well you felt your methods worked, and whether you would do it differently another time. You should also explain how you analysed the data. For example, did you do any quantitative analysis by hand, or on a computer, in which case which software did you use? Why do you have confidence in the analysis you have carried out? (see also Chapter 20 on Analysis).

The introduction

The introduction is very important, as some readers may never get any further – it needs to draw them in. By this point you are over-familiar with the issues, and probably rather tired of the data. But you need to start at the beginning for the reader, and take them through the logic that led you to design your project as you did. Aim to make them interested in the questions you were interested in.

Include some contextual information, perhaps about the area you are working in, perhaps about your own programme, or about broader initiatives which are relevant to this one. But make sure this is carefully chosen and relevant – too many reports start with context of the 'Mali is a country in West Africa' kind – any reader interested in your findings will already know this. Get quickly to the point of this report, giving broader background later, if necessary.

Forewords or prefaces

A useful device, when you want to add authority to your publication, is to ask someone to write a foreword to it. They lend their support to your message, and this may help politically as well as perhaps encouraging people to read it. Who you ask depends upon what you need: you could ask a well-known person with an interest in your field; a senior manager of your own organisation; or someone who represents the community you have worked with.

EXAMPLE

Ask someone who knows

A Charter for Learning for people with learning difficulties in UK adult education was produced with strong participation by people with learning difficulties themselves. It was introduced by a preface by Eve Rank-Petruzziello, who is a member of the Government's Disability Rights Commission, and is the first person with learning difficulties to sit on this kind of important committee. The editor of the report worked with her to get on paper what she wanted to say about the Charter (Jacobsen, 2000).

The summary

Many people will only read your summary, so it is worth spending some time getting it right. Which means very short and straightforward, using plain language.

Different types of summary are needed for different purposes. It is only really correct to talk about an executive summary when its contents are addressed to an agency that commissioned it, and will be used directly to take decisions. Just call it a summary if what it does is summarise the contents of the report. Obviously the key findings are the core of the summary, but you may also need to include some contextual information; perhaps a few short quotations if that will show the strength of your research; and any key recommendations. It is usually helpful to include aims and objectives.

Academic articles traditionally have a type of summary called an abstract, which is only about 100 words long. An abstract should include the topic or research question; theories and methods used; details of sample; and conclusions reached.

Dealing with hot topics

Sometimes the process of analysis and writing makes issues clear – and sometimes it identifies areas where there are real contradictions between different points of view. When you have conflicting data, one way of dealing with it is simply to set it out, perhaps side by side in two or more columns, and let the readers see the tensions for themselves. Perhaps a group of parents and a group of adolescent young people have produced entirely different versions of the same issue. It is not your role to sit in judgement on them, though you can perhaps usefully put people's views in context by giving information about the situations they face.

In rather the same way, you may find in your analysis that while some issues are clear, others are still hard to see clearly. It is fine to describe dilemmas or tensions as well as to lay out recommendations. This can give a framework for discussing difficult issues tactfully.

And while we are on tact, there is of course the question of how to handle it when your findings are strongly critical of the government or some other agency. This manual has urged you to involve key players in your project from the start, as this is the best way of avoiding a situation where a research report becomes a site of confrontation. Assuming that your aim is to change the behaviour of the criticised agency, rather than to confront them, it is best to approach them directly, before publication, and let them see what you will be saying. It may be appropriate to give them some way of publicly responding to your findings, perhaps by speaking at your launch event, perhaps by writing a short statement of response that you can include in your report. However you should not compromise on the need to present your findings honestly. If you cannot successfully involve your 'audience' in the process of the research, then publishing the report has to be seen as part of a campaigning process.

Do not feel that it is necessarily your responsibility to find a solution to the problems your research exposes. Take the analysis as far as you can, and reflect carefully on whether or not you are confident to give guidance for action. Sometimes the best we can do is to present problems clearly, in context, and invite others to engage with us in addressing them.

Presenting quantitative data

This section offers a little advice about how to present quantitative data within your report. It really is worth trying to present your data in visual form – many people find diagrams and charts much easier to learn from than figures on the page.

With a computer it is a lot easier to produce all kinds of diagrams and charts, as they can easily be produced within all sorts of packages – statistical programs of course but also spreadsheets and even word-processing packages. There are also special packages for the purpose. But you still need to make sure that you use them in a way that makes sense. It is easy to get carried away or overwhelmed!

If you are presenting your data in charts, just pick out key material to discuss in the text – you do not need to describe the complete data set in the text as well as visually.

The important general rules are to:

- Keep it simple.
- Avoid including so much data that the reader is unable to make sense of it.
- Choose an appropriate type of table or chart for your purpose.
- Help the reader with visual clues and clear presentation.

Tables

It is amazing how often people present tables without all the information you need to understand them. Usually this is because the information is over-familiar to the writer – but it may be entirely unknown to reader! Tables need to include the following information:

- A title, fully explaining the point of the table.
- A table number is usually helpful, for reference, and to show where it goes in relation to the text.
- The name of the column variable (eg income), and its categories or values (perhaps income bands), especially any unit they come in (eg £, $, etc).
- The name of the row variable, to the left of the table, reading across and its categories or values and the unit they come in.
- The actual number for the respondents who fall into the relevant categories, in each 'cell' of the table – and for the total sample involved.
- Totals for both rows and columns should be included.
- Percentage figures should appear alongside the actual number, clearly labelled as such – also show the percentage total of 100 for clarity.
- Statistical information such as significance test figures should be included where appropriate.
- The source of the data, if they were originally produced elsewhere.

Bar charts

These are a good way of presenting simple information about frequencies. The bars should be of equal width, and the height of the bars represents the frequency or amount for each separate category. Bar charts are usually used where the item on the horizontal axis (the independent variable) is discrete

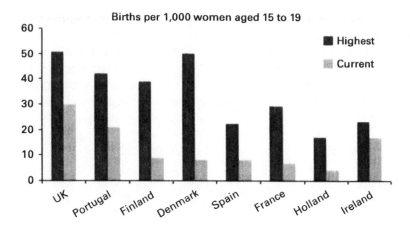

Figure 21.1 Sample bar chart

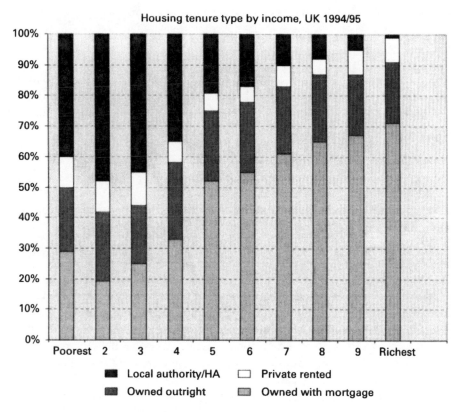

Figure 21.2 Sample stacked bar chart

or categorical – they fall into distinct groups such as countries. They are easy to read, providing you do not include too many categories. Beyond ten categories bar charts tend to get too crowded to read.

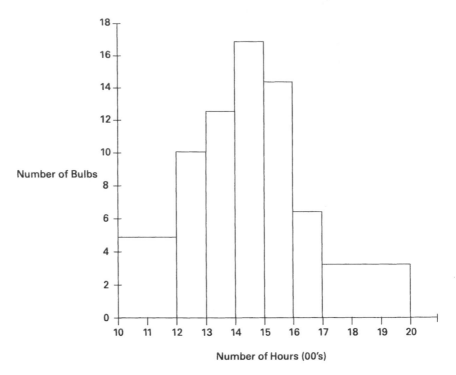

Figure 21.3 Sample histogram

Stacked bar charts make it possible to show the component elements of the total within a category.

Histograms

A histogram looks very like a bar chart. It has bars, normally of equal width, and where they are of equal width, the height of the bar represents variations in the frequencies. What distinguishes a histogram from a bar chart is that the histogram is used where the horizontal (independent) variable is a continuous variable such as age and height. Whereas a bar chart is used for discrete data and separate categories. Histograms show how one variable is distributed over another continuous variable, eg how the incidence of children in poverty differs with age.

Line graph

A line graph is used for depicting development or progression in a sequence of data. It is most commonly used to show change over time, with time

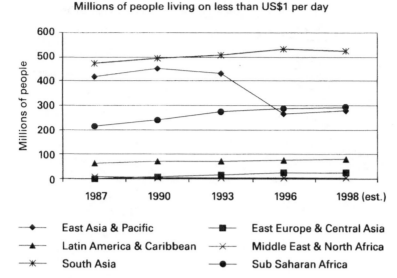

Figure 21.4   Line graph showing millions of people living on less than US$1 per day in different regions[1]

plotted from left to right on the horizontal axis. Line graphs work best with large data sets and big variations.

Pie charts

These present data as segments of the whole pie. They show very clearly the proportions of each category which go to make up the total. Usually the segments are presented as percentages.

To show particularly the size of one segment, you can pull it out from the rest of the pie. For example you could show the proportion of government expenditure on health, or arms, by pulling this out from a pie showing how other expenditure is divided.

Pie charts are visually powerful, but they can only be used to show the values within one category, not to compare two together as with other charts described above. However it is possible to use two or more pie charts, perhaps of different sizes, in proportion to the absolute figures expressed, to make comparisons. It is important not to have too many segments – preferably there should be fewer than seven segments. Segments which account for less than 2% of the total are difficult to see. It is good practice to show the figure for the percentages on the chart, where possible within the segments.

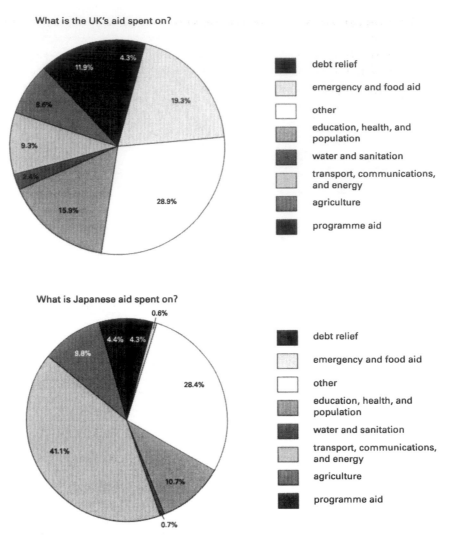

Figure 21.5   What is the UK's and Japanese aid spent on?
From *The Reality of Aid*, 1997/8

Warning

It should be noted that the way in which graphs and charts are presented can be used to mislead the reader. In reading graphs, have a sharp look at the scales on both axes – and look at the ones on different tables in the same report, to see how they compare. In producing your own, make sure you keep control of these matters (sometimes the computer can take over rather), and ensure that you do not distort the way in which data should be understood. It is fine to add footnotes to tables if you think they are needed.

> **COMMON PITFALLS 21.1**
>
> Presenting masses of different charts with little guidance as to what is important and what it all means

> **CHECKLIST**   **On presenting quantitative data**
>
> ✓ Choose an appropriate way of presenting the data – make sure it makes sense
>
> ✓ Keep it simple – do not include too much data in one chart
>
> ✓ Don't go mad with the charts and diagrams – only present important data in this form, and only data you have reasonable confidence in
>
> ✓ Make sure tables and charts have informative titles and labels for all their contents
>
> ✓ Include clear information about the units of measurement for each category
>
> ✓ Make sure the source of any information from another study is clearly given

How to write – process

The task of writing a major report can loom large. It is a very different job from many you undertake, and you will have to make space for it.

- **Get started – don't put it off.** Decide on the day and time you will start, and start then, whatever excuses present themselves!
- **Don't leave all the analysis and writing to the last minute.** You should aim to arrive at the start of the final report with lots of materials to work from. The worst thing is to face a blank sheet with your data disorganised and no part of the material already written up. You should already have:
  - organised and analysed your data;
  - written some sections in first draft, eg from your survey of existing information, reports on elements of the data collection (eg a set of focus groups, some observations);
  - worked on a synthesis – bringing it all together, asking what it means (see Chapter 20.8).

- **Draft an outline early on – you can always change it later**. This is a working document, and can just include headings, or can have some phrases to help you remember what needs to go in each section. It can be useful to consult colleagues on your outline.

- **Break down the task**. Doing an outline will help you with this.
- **Start wherever seems easiest (often in the middle).** Work from some data you are interested in. It is never a good idea to try to write a report from beginning to end. The beginning and the end are the most difficult parts to write, and the most likely to be read. Write them when you are well into your flow, and know what needs to go into them.
- **Think of it as a draft.** Expect to rewrite. Learn to accept others' criticisms and suggestions. Rewriting is very valuable. Occasionally people make comments on drafts which are impossible to make use of, but usually, asking some colleagues or other knowledgeable people to read and comment will improve your text hugely. You do not have to incorporate everything everyone says, but you do need to think about why they have made their suggestions.
- **Keep it simple.** Write as directly and clearly as possible. Don't read too much academic material just before you write your report, so you won't be infected by an obscure style.
- **Picture your audience in your mind.** Choose someone you want to address in this report – not someone hostile, but someone who needs to know what this research says and is interested – and write to them.
- **Remember where your readers are.** Explain why you decided to do this research in the first place, why it is important.

After the first complete draft

Be prepared that a lot of work remains to do, even after you have written your first full draft. If you are involved in any sort of collaborative process, it is essential to show draft reports to others. It may be that community members are involved as partners, and you will want to show them drafts and hear their comments, and probably also set up a verbal presentation of the main points, to enable those who will not read complex written materials to have a say.

Editing processes can be quite problematic where many interests are at work. Sometimes it is only at this point that different participants' expectations are declared, through comments on a draft. This can be difficult to handle. In my experience most authors can improve a document by about 25% in light of comments at this point – not more. If a great transformation is required, think again about how to achieve this – and whether it is wise to try. Go back to the brief and see what it says.

Support and supervision need to be sustained into the writing-up and editing periods. Sometimes what seems to be 'writer's block' really points to issues within the work which need further discussion.

After the final draft

Even once you have sent your text off to be published, there will be further work to do. It is very important for the author/researcher to thoroughly proof-read text, tables, and diagrams. Make sure spelling and grammar are correct. It is easy for mistakes to creep in, even now that printed text is usually taken directly from a disk from the author. For example, a paragraph can simply be lost if it doesn't fit on a page and someone loses concentration. Make a good check at the last minute, before the report is printed.

CHECKLIST   **Before sending a publication to the printers**

- ✓ All the text is where it should be
- ✓ The credits and acknowledgements include everyone they should
- ✓ The publication is dated, and an address included
- ✓ Make sure the title is interesting and communicative – avoid the 'Final Report Of Long And Complicated Project In Obscure Place By Five Organisations With Long Names' syndrome
- ✓ Anonymity of respondents is effectively maintained
- ✓ There is a 'blurb' (short advertising paragraph) on the back which tells readers what the report is about and who it is for
- ✓ Tables, charts, and diagrams are complete and properly labelled
- ✓ References are complete (see Chapter 12.1)
- ✓ ISBN (International Standard Book Number) – see Chapter 12.1

You may think of these as technical tasks for someone else, but new technology means that there are often no technical experts involved in producing a report. In any case, researchers need to remain involved to ensure that the message does not get distorted further down the chain. For example, people may be tempted to try to spread the word further by introducing titles or publicity materials which make generalisations and in effect claim more than can properly be supported by the research.

Using the Report

Finally, remember that you will need to actively use your report as part of a strategy to influence those of whom it is addressed to. Look again at Chapter 10 and ensure that the findings of your research are reported where your target audience will see or hear them.

CHECKLIST **For writing effective research reports**

✔ Write in your own voice, adapted to your audience
✔ Present information in an unemotional way, but let the voices of the respondents come through
✔ Make it as short and simple as possible
✔ Start by planning an outline, giving the report a logical structure
✔ Include:

- an appropriate summary
- a brief description of the methods used and how well these worked
- an account of the sample, how people were contacted, and any problems you see with it

✔ Expect to re-write several times – consult partners, including community members, on drafts

---

Further Reading

Bell, J. (1987) *Doing Your Research Project*. Buckingham, UK: Open University Press.

Contains a useful chapter on writing the report.

Appendix 1 Useful Websites

1. General Information

1.1 Libraries

Libweb
Networks all libraries worldwide.
http://sunsite.berkeley.edu/Libweb/

British Library: Online Public Access Catalogue
Direct access to the vast catalogue of the British Library – very useful.
Recommended. ★
http://www.bl.uk/

COPAC
Unified free access to the catalogues of some of the largest university research libraries in the UK and Ireland.
http://copac.ac.uk/

School of Oriental and African Studies, University of London
Access to this specialist library, which includes material written in Asian and African languages.
http://www.soas.ac.uk/Library/home.html
See under 'development' for more specialist Libraries.

1.2 Newspapers

Many have good websites, indexed by subject and are worth looking at for current information. Find specific newspapers through a search engine. For example, the *Guardian* and *Observer* have a good site.
Recommended. ★
http://*www.guardianunlimited.co.uk*

There are also specific news search engines, for example this one covers 300 newspapers:
http://www.newsindex.com

2. Information on Specific Issues

Please note that often only one website is given on a particular area – there will be others, but they can usually be accessed from each other.

It is also worth noting that this list tends to emphasise 'official' websites of various sorts, rather than those giving an alternative view. Remember to search for (and create) these as well – the great thing about the Internet is that anyone can put material up.

Africa

Index on Africa
'A comprehensive guide to the Continent on the Net'.
http://www.afrika.no/index/

Africa News
For up-to-date information from governments, NGOs and the media on all of Africa.
http://allafrica.com/

Ageing

Age Wise
Site full of links to ageing matters – UK-focused
http://maxpages.com/bromyard

Asia

South East Asia:

Association of South East Asian Nations
ASEAN secretariat home page – includes information on government structures and some statistics for countries in the region.
http://www.aseansec.org

Charities/NGOs

British Overseas NGOs for Development (BOND)
Britain's broadest network of voluntary organisations working in international development. Good links to member and other organisations, searchable database.
http://www.bond.org.uk/

Charity Net
Provides Charities Aid Foundation information on sources of funding, policy materials on taxation and regulation of charities, and an international listing of non-profit organisation links. Link to Funders Online. One way of finding contact information for NGOs – can be searched by country.
http://www.charitynet.org

VOLNET
http://nemo.unl.ac.uk:9999/
This is the VOLNET homepage: the voluntary sector database which you can search for articles and publications on community and voluntary sector issues.

Children

The Children's House in Cyberspace
Based in Norway, this site brings together information and contacts from a wide group of European children's organisations, including 200 European research institutions. Includes a research floor and a very useful information floor, including topics like advocacy and policy, children and war. Good links to other sites. Recommended. ★
http://www.child-abuse.com/childhouse/research/index.html

Childwatch International
Aims to promote, initiate, and disseminate international, interdisciplinary research that leads to a real improvement in the well-being of children, through network activities.
http://www.childwatch.vio.no

Children's Rights International Network
Global network of organisations sharing their experiences and information on children's rights. One section takes you 'Stepping through the UN Convention on the Rights of the Child'. Includes also material for example on the rights of children with disabilities, children living with HIV.
http://www.crin.org

Save the Children Fund
Information on the organization, its publications and news on children's rights.
http://www.scfuk.org.uk

UNICEF
Site includes the text of the latest report on 'The State of the World's Children', and campaign briefings, for example on children and domestic work. Also child-related statistics by country, but no definitions or source are given for the figures.
http://www.unicef.org

International Child Development Centre
Some people find this an easier site to use than the central UNICEF one. Includes research and advocacy digests and portfolios – useful briefings on issues like juvenile justice, inter-country adoption. Also includes a list of documents you can download from the Internet – abstracts and full papers. Some in French or Spanish as well as English. Good links to other sites.
http://www.unicef-icdc.org

National Children's Bureau
Information on the Bureau's work, including participatory projects they are running with young people. Good contacts list.
http://www.ncb.org.uk

Child abuse

Child Abuse Yellow Pages XYZ
http://idealist.com/cayp/

International Child Abuse Network
YesICAN is a non-profit organisation dedicated to ending child abuse and neglect. Limited list of books and articles; good links.
http://www.yesican.org

ECPAT – a global network to protect children against commercial sexual exploitation
Co-ordinates work against child prostitution, and child pornography on the net. Good site with good links.
http://www.ecpat.net/

Development issues

The Institute of Development Studies (IDS) website.
Very good information, plus good gateways to other sites. Cover participation issues, and the website contains free manuals, including material not published elsewhere. A good place to start for many purposes.
Recommended. ★
http://www.eldis.org

Includes a number of very useful sites:

- ELDIS – gateway to information on development or environment.
- The British Library for Development Studies (BLDS) – Europe's largest library on international development.
- IDS – research and advisory work, publications, conferences and facilities, teaching and training.
- ID21 – research reporting service, summarising the latest development research. This website aims to make policy-makers and on-the-ground development managers aware of the latest British development research findings. ID21 offers this service free to users and to contributors.
  http://www.id21.org

Best practices for human settlements database
UNHCS (Habitat) and the Together Foundation. This searchable database contains over 650 proven solutions to the common social, economic, and environmental problems of an urbanising world. Can be used for analysing current trends, networking, capacity-building (material for developing new learning tools and methods), and policy development.
http://www.bestpractices.org/

Europe's Forum on International Co-operation (EuFoRic)
Very useful website for information on development co-operation. Thousands of full-text resources from more than 50 organisations. Also has a list of aid agencies.
http://www.oneworld.org/euforic/index.html

IBISCUS
French-language information retrieval system on developing countries – federates the French supply of information on development topics.
http://www.ibiscus.fr/

International Development Research Centre
A good site created by the Canadian government to help communities in the developing world to find solutions to social, economic, and environmental problems through research. Includes many good links; the centre's own research; and access to two major development databases, BIBLIO and IDRIS. Also in French.
http://www.idrc.ca/

EADI – European Association of Development Research and Training Institutions
EADI promotes development research and training activities in economic, social, cultural, technological, institutional, and environmental areas. EADI's objectives include stimulating exchange of information between European researchers concerned with development issues and developing contacts with researchers from other regions of the world. Searchable database.
http://www.eadi.org

One World Think Tank
Research, debate, policy and practice – a window into governmental, professional and academic material on One World. Includes discussion, documents and links on key issues, for example Aid Management and Policy, Ethnicity and Conflict, Water and Sanitation.
http://www.oneworld.org/index.html

The Panos Institute
An alliance of indipendent organization north and south working to support debate about critical issues in sustainable development. Their website features, for example, meterial on HIV/AIDS and on women's health. Please see also Chapter 12.2.

Disability

Enabling Education Network
Set up to establish an information-sharing network aimed at supporting and promoting the inclusion of marginalised groups in education worldwide. Includes, for example, resources/bibliographies on working with deaf children, and those with learning difficulties.
http://www.eenet.org.uk

Disability Research Unit, Leeds University
Part of the Disability Studies Web Ring, which gives access to many useful sites, including organisations of disabled people, research and information sites.
http://www.leeds.ac.uk/disability-studies

Economics

The World Bank Group website
Gives access to lists of the World Bank's publicly available reports. Includes full text for some World Bank research and policy reports on development topics, including useful statistics.
Recommended. ★
http://www.worldbank.org

The Bretton Woods Project
NGO aiming to monitor and reform the World Bank and IMF. It tracks key policy statements and reports, and provides critiques and early warnings used by non-governmental organisations across the world. The Project's quarterly newsletter, the Bretton Woods Update, summarises key World Bank, International Monetary Fund, and NGO activities and lists available documents and important dates. Website includes full text of its briefing papers and its quarterly Bretton Woods Update newsletter.
http://www.brettonwoodsproject.org/

The Development GAP – The Development Group for Alternative Policies
Aims 'to ensure that the knowledge, priorities and efforts of the women and men of the South inform decisions made in the North about their economies and environments'. Documents on structural adjustment and other economic policy issues. Also carries Our Americas Quarterly 'newsletter of the hemispheric network for just and sustainable trade and development – news from Canada, the US, Mexico and Chile'.
http://www.igc.apc.org/dgap/

Organisation for Economic Co-operation and Development website
http://www.oecd.org

Education

Statistical database on education and literacy world-wide
Based on UNESCO figures.
http://www.unesco.org/en/about

NISS – information for education
National Information Services and Systems
Includes access to libraries; links to bookshops; other useful links.
http://www.niss.ac.uk/

University map
Links to all UK universities, accessed through a map. Good for locating people, searching for a course, or looking at library databases
http://www.scit.wlv.ac.uk/ukinfo/uk.map.colls.html

Open University
UK-based distance learning organisation.
http://www.open.ac.uk

Emergencies

Reuter Foundation Alertnet: a news and communications service for the international relief community
Very useful for current updates. A non-commercial service aiming to be a specialist news supplier and neutral information broker.
http://www.alertnet.org

Relief web homepage
Run by the American Red Cross to promote exchange of information for disaster victims and the disaster relief community.
http://www.disasterrelief.org/

Environment and development

International Institute for Environment and Development
IIED is an independent, non-profit organisation with a mission to promote sustainable patterns of world development through collaborative research, policy studies, consensus building, and public information. The website includes IIED's own research and a collection of documents, for example on Drylands, Sustainable Agricultural and Rural Livelihoods, Human Settlements.

Three of IIED's databases can be browsed: Community Wildlife Management, Environmental Impact Assessment Guidelines Database, and Participatory Action and Learning (see under Research methods).
Recommended. ★
http://www.iied.org/

The Earth Council – Sustainable Development Links
http://www.ecouncil.oc.cr

International Institute for Sustainable Development – Linkages
A multimedia resource for environment and development policy-makers. Links to various environment and development websites.

Includes The Earth Negotiation Bulletin, which provides balanced, objective, and informative summaries of environmental and development negotiations.
http://www.iisd.ca/linkages/

Europe

European Union Information Site
Has links to many useful ones. These are large and busy sites, and if you have trouble accessing them, it can be a good idea to try them at a different time of day.
http://europa.eu.int

Evaluation

MandE News – monitoring and evaluation in development work
A news service focusing on developments in monitoring and evaluation methods relevant to development projects with social development objectives.

Excellent site which accesses many complete documents and relevant links.
Recommended. ★
http://www.mande.co.uk

Scottish Community Development Centre
Home of the Community Development Evaluation Skills project: site carries a training manual on monitoring and evaluation of community development. Good site also includes links to a range of resources for community development and to relevant UK policy and research units.
http://www.scdc.org.uk

Food and agriculture

World Food Programme website
http://www.wfp.org

UN Food and Agriculture Organisation website
http://www.fao.org

Includes FAO statistical databases sustainable development pages, and good links
http://www.fao.org/sd/index_en.htm
News, summary and full text materials on FAO progress and policies on participation.

Health issues

Medline
A huge database of medical references. You can get references and abstracts free on the Internet, but you have to subscribe to one of many possible services to get the full text of the articles.
Recommended. ★
http://www.nlm.nih.gov/medline

World Health Organisation
Good site: includes the full text online of the latest World Health Reports.
http://www.who.int/
WHO statistical Information System – *http://www.who.int/whosis/*
Statistics on the global burden of disease, cause of death, basic health indicators, etc

Healthlink (was AHRTAG)
Healthlink Worldwide 'works to improve the health of poor and vulnerable communities by strengthening the provision, use and impact of information'. Holds 16,000 records on its database, focusing on the management and practice of primary health care and disability issues in developing countries. Many materials are published in developing countries or unpublished. You need to subscribe – but it is free if you live in a developing country.
http://www.healthlink.org.uk/

HIV/AIDS

UNAIDS
The global source of HIV/AIDS information – includes information by country or region, information on best practice, and a research documentation centre.
http://www.unaids.org/

AVERT
Information on HIV prevention.
http://www.avert.org/yngindx.htm

Human Rights

Office of the high Commissioner for Human Rights
The website of the UN High Commissioner for Human Rights. Includes much useful information – texts of treaties and statements and of reports on compliance – but is not easy to find your way around. Persist.
http://www.unhchr.ch

Human Rights Watch
Information by country and by issue internationally: news and major reports available on the site.

Juvenile justice

Justice Center Web Site, Alaska USA
A University of Alaska academic, research, and public education programme. Useful site on an issue which can be difficult to research.
http://www.uaa.alaska.edu/just/

Poverty

World Bank Poverty net
Resourses and support for people working to understand and alleviate poverty.
http://www.worldbank.org/poverty

Government statistics on poverty in the UK
Department for Social Security, Households Below Average Income statistical service 1994/95 to 1998/99
http://www.dss.gov.uk/publications/dss/2000/hbai/index.htm

Refugees

UN Commissioner for Refugees website.
UNHCR Refworld: map- and text-based access to country-specific information on refugees, and to UNHCR documents.
http://www.unhcr.ch/cgi.bin/texis/vtx

Refugee studies programme
Oxford University – their own research papers, plus a documentation centre carrying 30,000 items.
http://www.qeh.ox.ac.uk/rsp/

Research methods

Social Research Updates
Short summaries, published quarterly and available in full-text online, on a range of research issues, eg open and closed questions, elicitation techniques with young people, paying respondents, focus groups, and indeed finding information on the world wide web.
http://www.soc.surrey.ac.uk/sru

Qualpage – Resources for Qualitative Researchers
Developed from a private Canadian website that had been started as a repository of information about qualitative data analysis software, and bibliographic database software. Essentially a set of links to other sites.
http://www.ualberta.ca/~jrnorris/ qual.html

CAQDAS Networking Project
Computer-Assisted Qualitative Data Analysis Software – aims to disseminate an understanding of the practical skills required to use this type of software effectively.
http://caqdas.soc.surrey.ac.uk/index.html

Participatory Action Research
US-based site, networking researchers using this approach.
http://www.parnet.org/

Action Research International – online journal
Papers can be downloaded directly from the web, eg Yoland Wadsworth 'What is Participatory Action Research?' Nov 98.
http://www.scu.edu.au/schools/sawd/ari/ari-papers.html

Participatory Learning and Action
Information on over 2000 documents held at IIED library (see under Environment). Includes material on all major aspects of participatory approaches from around the world, with an emphasis on Africa, Asia, and South America. Mainly unpublished. Also the index with abstracts to *PLA Notes* journal, now also available on CD-ROM. There are charges for access, but it is free to NGOs and libraries based in non-OECD countries.

A briefing and resources list on Sustainable Agriculture and Rural Livelihoods – Participatory Learning and Action is available on the net.
http://www.iied.org/resource/pla.html

Resource Centres for Participatory Learning and Action network (RCPLA)
Network of 14 organisations committed to information sharing and networking on participatory methodologies.
http://www.rcpla.org

ARVAC – Association for Research in the Community and Voluntary Sectors
http://www.charitynet.org/arvac/index.html

This is the home page of the UK Association for Research in the Community and Voluntary Sectors and has links to other relevant sites.

Social issues

Social Science Information Gateway
SOSIG can help you locate high quality sites which are relevant to social science education and research. Resources are selected and described by academic librarians and subject specialists.
http://sosig.ac.uk/

Sociological Research Online
An online journal, based in the UK. 'High quality applied sociology, focusing on theoretical, empirical and methodological discussion which engage with current topics and debates.' Very good links.
http://www.socresonline.org.uk/

Software

Epi-Info
Epi-Info is a package designed for analysing public health data, and is widely used in the South. It is public-domain software, and is distributed free by the Centre for Disease Control and the World Health Organisation. The CDC's Epi-Info home page is at: *http://www.cdc.gov/epiinfo/* You can download the software from there, in English. The package is available in Arabic, Chinese, French, Indonesian, Russian, Spanish, Serbo-Croatian, and Vietnamese. Manuals only have been translated into Czech, German, Hungarian, Italian, Portuguese, and Polish. The website gives addresses to write to for the translated materials. (See Analysis Chapter 20)

Statistics

Statistical links
A link index to country statistics worldwide, developed by the Dutch Statistical Agency. The register provides links to a variety of statistical resources on the Internet.
http://www.cbs.nl/en/services/index.htm

The Economist Intelligence Unit
Produces quarterly country reports, giving pretty reliable general information about a country (eg population, inflation rate, etc). Emphasis is on economic matters. Subscription only.
www.eiv.com

Transition

Trans-MONEE
This is the public-use version of the database from 'Monitoring Social Conditions and Public Policy in Central and Eastern Europe,' also known as the MONEE project, at the UNICEF International Child Development Centre (ICDC) in Florence, Italy. The

database allows the rapid retrieval and manipulation of economic and social indicators for 27 transition countries in Central Europe and the former USSR.

All reports are available in English and Russian, and French versions of summary information will shortly be put on the website.
http://www.unicef-icdc.org/documentation/index.html

United Nations agencies

Website locator for UN organisations
Lists all UN agencies; also enables system-wide searching by subject.
http://www.unsystem.org

UK official publications

Government Statistical Service
The source of UK official statistics.
http://www.statistics.gov.uk/

Social Exclusion Unit
http://www.cabinet-office.gov.uk/seu/index.htm

Department of Health research and development
'Providing a knowledge base for health, public health and social care'.
With the right software, you can download many government consultation documents directly from the website.
http://www.doh.gov.uk/research/index.htm

US government information

Government Information Locator Service (GILS)
Identifies and describes information resources throughout the US federal government and provides assistance in obtaining the information.
http://www.gils.net/

Women's issues

Aviva
Women's World Wide Web monthly news magazine.
Can be searched by region.
http://www.aviva.org

Bridge – information and analysis service on development and gender
Good links.
http://www.ids.ac.uk/bridge/index.html

Feminist activist resources on the Net
Aims to connect to other indexes of information on particular issues, rather than directly to the resources themselves.
http://www.igc.apc.org/women/feminist.html

Womenwatch
The UN Internet gateway to the advancement and empowerment of women.
http://www.un.org/womenwatch/

Glossary

Analysis breaking something down into its component parts. To do this it is necessary to trace things back to their underlying sources, so analysis involves probing beneath the surface appearance of something to discover the component elements which have come together to produce it. Examination of data for trends, comparisons, relationships, and themes.

Appraise to examine something objectively and in detail; to evaluate; to make judgements.

Axis, axes denotes the horizontal (x-axis) and the vertical (y-axis) of a line or bar graph. These are typically used to plot two variables in relation to each other.

Baseline study a collection of data about a population before a programme or project is set up. This data can then be compared with later evidence about the same characteristics in order to see what has changed.

Bias any influence which distorts or unduly influences the results of an investigation – perhaps the result of the research method employed, sampling approaches, or the researcher's presuppositions. It may be argued (eg by social constructionist researchers) that some kinds of bias are inevitable. To avoid accusations of distortion, it is important to identify any factors you think may introduce bias.

Bookmarks (also known as 'favourites') when using the Internet, bookmarks enable you mark a web page that you may want to return to.

Brief (research) (or terms of reference) a plan of action, describing the tasks to be carried out; includes aims and objectives; methods; outcomes. See Chapters 5 and 6.

Category a group that has similarities; a class (in the sense of classification) or set. Categories are generally mutually exclusive groupings – or intended to be so.

Causal relationship a relationship between two variables whereby the presence of one (Variable 1) determines the status of the effect (Variable 2).

Causation from 'cause' – any immediate, or more indirect, factor precipitating an outcome.

Census a government-sponsored, universal, and obligatory survey of all individuals in a geographical area (also used to refer to non-government-sponsored population counts).

Classification aims to place together all instances of a phenomenon whose similarities, and differences from all other types of phenomenon, are such as to justify the classification for particular theoretical purposes.

Coaching on-the-job training, working individually to help someone to learn new skills through the tasks they carry out.

Coding a method of transforming qualitative information into quantifiable information by categorisation. Categorisation is according to particular themes or patterns, and these categories can be numbered so that complex information is simplified into manageable and meaningful groupings. Each possible answer is given a code, and then each person's answer is assigned to the appropriate code.

Cohort a group of persons possessing a common characteristic (eg born in the same year). (See also Longitudinal study.)

Community member used here as a general term to refer to those the development worker/researcher relates to. They might be the people who live in a particular geographical area, or may form part of a different kind of community, such as disabled people or sex workers, for example. It is recognised that community links and support may be strong or weak.

Concept a basic idea. A concept is generally abstract and universal rather than concrete and specific. It is basic in the sense that it cannot be easily explained in terms of or equated with other ideas. A theory might be made up of a number of concepts which are linked to provide a more complex explanation or understanding.

Control group a group matched with the group which will receive an intervention in all aspects except that it is not treated with the intervention whose effect is to be studied. A control group is an essential part of an experimental design, since comparison is needed to establish whether or not any change is due to the intervention. In the social world, looking at complex interventions, it is often difficult to identify suitable control groups, given the number of factors potentially affecting any particular outcome.

Correlation the association between two variables such that when one changes the other does also. A positive correlation means that one variable tends to increase together with another variable. Negative correlation means that one variable decreases as the other one increases. The strength of any correlation can be expressed statistically, and tests can establish whether or not any correlation is statistically significant. Correlation does not prove causation (qv). See Chapter 20.3.

Criterion (pl. criteria) standard of judgement, test.

Cross-tabulation a two-way table which uses the classes of a second variable to further sub-divide each class of the first variable. Cross-tabulation is used to establish the occurrence and degree of relationship of connected variables. See Chapter 20.7

Data used to describe all types of information gathered by researchers. 'Raw data' refers to information which has been collected but not processed or analysed.

Demography the study of human populations, especially statistics of birth, fertility, and death. Includes study of the structure of and changes in populations, eg by sex, age, ethnic origin, etc.

Design, research see Research design.

Disaggregate to break down into smaller units, from 'aggregate', to bring together into one mass.

Discipline refers to different systems of learning, realms of knowledge, eg sociology, anthropology, medicine.

Donors organisations which give funds for development work.

Empirical comes from the Greek word for experience – empirical knowledge is knowledge derived from experience. Experience here means sensory experience – hearing, seeing, smelling, tasting, or touching. However there is a common illusion about empirical evidence. This is the idea that this information is somehow purely given, and then grasped by the senses without any ideas in between ('facts speak for themselves'). Actually sense data are filtered, translated, shaped, and transformed through mental processes. We understand things, even at the most basic level ('hot', 'loud', 'sweet'), through words we have learnt for them, so these concepts shape our experience.

Enumerator interviewer implementing a quantitative survey.

Factor one of the circumstances, facts, or influences which produce a result. Some feature of the situation which must be taken into account when describing or attempting to alter it.

Favourites (Internet) – see 'Bookmarks'.

Field (as in 'fieldwork' 'field research') – refers to any real-world setting where research takes place ('field' research as opposed to laboratory experiments); (in relation to databases) – spaces reserved for specified data; columns of data in tables.

Formative (evaluation) ongoing evaluation or monitoring with continuous feedback and use of information gathered so as to amend and improve or 'form' a service or piece of work. (As opposed to 'summative' evaluation, which looks at the whole picture at the end of a period of time.)

Frequency the number of times a particular item of data occurs – for example, a specific answer to a question. In quantitative research, a frequency count might tell you simply how many people gave a particular response.

Generalisable, from **'generalisation'** the degree to which findings may be expected to apply beyond the specific situation in which they occurred. The case for applying such findings in more general situations. Making a statement about the whole population (or a larger population) on the basis of information about only part of that group.

Grey material unpublished documents produced by various organisations – governmental and non-governmental agencies.

Health gain an objectively measurable improvement in health status of the population (eg fewer babies die in the first year of life).

Hypothesis a hunch or educated guess as to why something occurs. Statement of a predicted outcome which the research will either support or disprove. An initial prediction or statement of results which is tested through research. (See Chapter 5.4.)

Indicators objective ways of measuring (indicating) that progress is being achieved. These must relate to the aims and objectives of the project. Indicators are evidence that something has happened, they are not proof.

Informant see Respondent.

Instrument, research see Research instrument.

Interviewer effect the effect resulting from the influence of interviewers on the answers of respondents, arising from many sources, including behaviour, and characteristics beyond the interviewer's control.

Iterative repeating, doing over again; can be seen as a trial-and-error procedure for solving problems, often represented as a cycle where a proposal is made, then tested, then adjusted, then tested again.

Literature review (study) the process of critically assessing and evaluating published and unpublished information materials which are relevant to your research.

Literature search the process of locating the existing published (and perhaps unpublished) information materials which are relevant to your research.

Literature survey summarises as accurately as possible the published information relevant to your research.

Logical Framework Analysis a project planning tool which analyses a project in terms of means and ends. It aims to clarify how the planned activities will help to achieve the objectives, and make explicit the implications of carrying out the planned activities in terms of resources, assumptions, and risks. Designed for use on practical programmes, not research projects, but can be adapted for them.

Longitudinal study a piece of research that extends over a long period of time and collects data at different, regular, planned points in time. It builds in the assumption that the passage of time is important to understanding the phenomenon being studied. A 'motion picture' as opposed to a 'snapshot', taken at just one point in time.

Market research the study of problems relating to the marketing of goods and services, including the study of customer characteristics and preferences.

Matrix a rectangular arrangement of quantities or symbols, often a table of rows and columns.

Methodology (from the study of methods) correctly used to refer to an overall or underlying theory of research practice – the abstract logical basis of 'finding out' and 'knowing' itself (sometimes called philosophy of science). Includes theoretical rules, guidelines, and principles. Also includes methods used, but if you mean methods or techniques, use the simpler term.

Non-probability (sample) see Purposive sample; see also Probability sample.

Normative (eg need) establishing a norm or standard.

Omnibus survey a research service consisting in a survey conducted peri-odically by a commercial market research supplier, serving a number of clients. Clients insert one or more question/s of their choosing into the survey, which is usually of a representative, national sample of consumers. Reduces data collection costs greatly.

Partner agencies organisations which co-operate in the planning and/or implementation of a piece of work. May include community-based organisa-tions; local or national government bodies; non-governmental organisations; or international organisations.

Peer research involves people participating actively in research with others like themselves, for example young people interviewing other young people. See Chapter 3.4.

Phenomenology a major school of philosophy based on the view that humans are active creators of their own rules. It underpins an important branch of qualitative research, with the primary task of achieving a more essential understanding of the social and personal world. A study of life as it is experienced by self and others.

Pilot test pre-test; try out before putting into general use.

Population in research terminology, refers to the complete set of units about which generalisations are to be made – the whole group you are interested in, from which a sample is usually drawn.

Positivism a form of scientific methodology which believes that there is a single true world 'out there', independent of the observer, and that by detached observation, science can identify causes and laws regarding that world. It proceeds on an assumption that any unverifiable (or unfalsifiable) statements are meaningless. It assumes that the principles of natural science apply equally to investigative methods in the social sciences. See Chapter 2.2.

Post-modernism theories (in the arts as well as in social science) implicated in or accounting for change from modernity to post-modernity. 'Post-modernity' is seen as involving such features as a world of 'flux, flow and fragmentation', without absolute values, an end of the dominance of an overarching belief in 'scientific' rationality and a unitary theory of progress.

Pre-coded questions are 'pre-coded' when the respondent is given a fixed set of alternative answers to choose from. (See also Coding.) See Chapter 17.6.

Probability the likelihood that a particular event or events will occur. Can be expressed numerically as the ratio of the number of equally likely ways in which a particular event can occur to the total number of occurrences possible.

Probability (sample) a sample drawn in such a way that each member of the population from which the sample is drawn, eg households or individuals, has a known probability of being included in the sample. Includes random samples.

Proposal, research detailed research plan proposed, usually to a funding body. Often used interchangeably with 'brief', 'terms of reference'.

Protocol a complete plan for a piece of research, explaining procedures to be followed in detail. See Chapter 6.1.

Purposive (sample) sample chosen on the basis of the judgement of the researcher in relation to the purpose of the study. The researcher tries to obtain as wide a representation as possible, taking account of likely sources of differences between individuals. See Chapter 19.3.

Qualitative describes the nature of answers (evidence) in terms of their verbal, written, word or other descriptive nature. Asks who, which, what, when, where, and why – in contrast to 'quantitative' answers addressing how much or how many. Qualitative research approaches belong to a family of approaches concerned with collecting in-depth data about human social experiences and contexts. See also Chapter 2.2.

Quantitative data that are in numerical form. See Qualitative – the 'how many', 'to what extent', or 'how much' aspect. Involves counting and other computation. Quantitative research is concerned with the collection of data in the form of various measures and indices, and its description and analysis by means of statistical methods.

Random (sample) a representative sample chosen from a population in such a way that every unit in that population is equally likely to be selected. The method of selection is based on chance but carried out in a systematic way. A type of probability sample. See Ch 19.1.

Randomised controlled trial (RCT) a type of experimental study design considered most appropriate for medical research, testing new drugs or other interventions. 'Controlled' refers to the use of a matched control group which does not receive treatment. 'Randomised' refers to random allocation of patients to groups receiving different or no treatment/s.

Ranking placing things in order (for example of importance, or of value).

Reflexivity the idea that our everyday practical accounts are not only reflexive and self referring but also constitutive of the situations to which they refer. Theories which are reflexive are those that refer to themselves. (See Chapter 4.5.)

Reliability the dependability of data collected, or of the test or measurement used to collect it. A reliable measure is one which gives the same results if the same individuals are measured on more than one occasion. Research instruments need to be consistent, so that any variation in the results obtained through using the instrument is due entirely to variations in the thing being measured, not to the nature of the instrument itself. See also Validity. See Chapter 20.7.

Research design the method of planning research to gather the most appropriate information, in the correct way, and to analyse the results effectively. See Chapters 5, 6, and 16.

Research instrument (or research tool) a technique used by the researcher to collect and record data. A global term used to describe the various data collection techniques used – for example interview schedules, observation checklists, questionnaires.

Respondent someone who 'responds', taking part in an interview, questionnaire, or other research activity.

Response rate the proportion of those selected to take part in a study who actually do so.

Sample a selection of units chosen to represent the target population. Often also used loosely to refer to respondents within a study, even if no formal sampling process has occurred (ie people were self-selecting).

Sampling frame a complete list or map of all the units in the target population. The nature of the existing sampling frame is an important consideration in determining the sample design.

Search engines on the Internet, these are tools to find relevant web pages. You enter your search terms, and the search engine searches its database and returns a list of results or 'hits'. Try several different ones. See Chapter 12.2.

Self-completion questionnaire questionnaire completed by the respondent him or herself.

Serials (as in libraries) periodicals, journals.

Significance (statistical) occurs when the probability of a given numerical difference or relationship occurring by chance alone is equal to, or less than, 0.05 ($p < 0.05$). The statistical significance of results increases as their probability decreases. The conventional cut-offs are: significant ($p < 0.05$); very significant ($p < 0.01$); highly significant ($p < 0.001$ or less). Note that a relationship can be statistically significant but have no practical significance – this depends on how meaningful it is in relation to the issue being studied.

Social constructionism a broad term used to emphasise the way in which reality, especially social institutions and social life generally, is socially produced rather than naturally given or determined. See Chapter 2.2.

Spreadsheet computer program which produces a matrix for managing numbers. See Chapter 20.7.

Stakeholder a person, group or institution with an interest in something, eg a project or programme. See Stakeholder Analysis, Chapter 18.2.

Subject (as in research subject) person from whom information is collected. Same as respondent. Word now rarely used in social research due to its connotations of belittling the respondent.

Survey a study that involves a relatively large number of respondents, generally chosen by some form of sampling, and involving formal, usually fairly standardised, data collection procedures. Used to gather a broad range of information about a population.

Synthesis combination of separate things or concepts to form a complex whole; process of re-combining what has been analysed.

Tally count or reckoning.

Terms of reference (see Brief (research))

Theory a general statement about how something works. A theory is a proposition (or idea) about the relationship between things. Any abstract general account of an area of reality, usually involving the formulation of general concepts. In physical science, theories normally start life as hypotheses which are repeatedly tested, gaining strength until they achieve the status of theories.

Tool, research see Research instrument.

Triangulation looking at things from different points of view. The employment of a number of different research techniques, in the belief that a variety of approaches gives the best chance of achieving validity. See Chapter 16.4.

Typology a collection of types, a classification, a set of abstract categories derived from empirical evidence. For example, a typology of families might include the nuclear family, extended family, modified extended, etc.

Validity in a broad sense, validity means that the data and the methods are 'right'. In terms of research data, the notion of validity hinges around whether or not the data reflect the truth, reflect reality, and cover the crucial matters. In terms of the methods used to obtain data, validity addresses the question 'Are we measuring suitable indicators of the concept and are we getting accurate results?' Validity relates to the extent to which research data and the methods for obtaining the data are deemed accurate, honest, and on target. See also Reliability. See Chapters 15.4, 20.6 and 20.7.

Variable any characteristic, quality, or attribute that can vary, and which can be observed and measured (eg age, occupation, income).

Verbatim word for word.

Further reading

Robinson, D, and Reed, Val (eds) (1998) *The A to Z of Social Research Jargon.* London: Ashgate.

With thanks also to Denscombe (1998), Nichols (1991), and Wadsworth (1997), which contain useful definitions.

References

Abebaw, M., Abdi, F., Ahamad, D., Goitom, M., Rehane, A., Tesfaye, D. and Yohannes, B. (1998) *Horn of Africa Youth Scheme, Let's Spell It Out: Peer research on the educational support needs of young refugees and asylum seekers living in Kensington and Chelsea*, written in partnership with Save the Children Fund, London.

Adelman, C. (1989) 'The practical ethic takes priority over methodology', in Carr, W. (ed.) *Quality in Teaching: Arguments for a reflective profession*. London: Falmer Press. Cited in Robson, Colin (1993) *Real World Research*, Oxford, UK and Cambridge, USA: Blackwell, p 440.

Alderson, P. (1995) *Listening to Children. Children, ethics and social research*. Barkingside, Essex: Barnardos.

Anon (1998) For the situation analysis about the Mozambican child. Maputo, Paper to seminal.

Arnstein, S. (1969) 'Eight rungs on the ladder of citizen participation', reprinted in Cahn, E. and Passett, B. (eds) (1971) *Citizen Participation: Effecting community change*. New York: Praeger Publishers.

Ashby, J.A. and Sperling, L. (1995) 'Institutionalizing participatory, client-driven research and technology development in agriculture', *Development and Change*, No 26, pp. 753–770.

Attwood, H. and May, J. (1998) 'Kicking down doors and lighting fires: the South African PPA', in Holland, J. with Blackburn, J. (eds), *Whose Voice? Participatory research and policy change*. London: Intermediate Technology Publications.

Barker, J., Bullen, M. and de Ville, J. (1997) *Reference Manual for Public Involvement*. Bromley Health, West Kent Health Authority, Lambeth, Southwark, and Lewisham Health Authority.

Barrientos, S. (1998) 'How to do a literature study', in Thomas, A., Chataway, J. and Wuyts, M. (eds), *Finding Out Fast*. London: The Open University/Sage.

Bennel, P. (1999) *Strengthening Postgraduate Training – capacity in development policy analysis and management in sub-Saharan Africa*. University of Sussex, Institute of Development Studies.

Black, J. and Laws, S. (1987) *Living with Sickle Cell Disease*. London: East London Sickle Cell Society/London Borough of Newham.

Blackburn, J. with Holland, J. (eds) (1998) *Who Changes? Institutionalizing participation in development*. London: Intermediate Technology Publications.

Blaxter L., Hughes C. and Tight M. (1996) *How to Research*, Buckingham: Open University Press.

Boyden, J. and Ennew, J. (eds) (1997) *Children in Focus – a manual for participatory research with children*. Stockholm: Rädda Barnen, Swedish Save the Children.

BOND Guidance Notes. (1999) *Introducing Advocacy – Monitoring and evaluating advocacy*.

Broad, B. (ed.) (1999) *The Politics of Social Work Research*. Birmingham, UK: Venture Press/BASW.

Broad, B. and Saunders, L. (1998) 'Involving young people leaving care as peer researchers in a health research project: a learning experience', *Research, Policy and Planning*, Vol 16, No 1.

Bryman, A. and Cramer D. (1997) *Quantitative Data Analysis with SPSS for Windows: A guide for social scientists*. London: Routledge.

Bulmer, M. (1982) *The Uses of Social Research: Social investigation in public policy-making*. London: George Allen and Unwin.

Burgess, R. (ed.) (1982) *Field Research: A sourcebook and field manual*. London: Allen & Unwin.

Burton, P. (1993) *Community Profiling. A guide to identifying local needs*. Bristol: University of Bristol, School of Advanced Urban Studies.

Carr, W. and Kemmis, S. (1986) *Becoming Critical: Education, knowledge and action research*. London: Falmer Press.

Chambers, R. (1992) 'Rural appraisal: rapid, relaxed and participatory', Brighton, Institute of Development Studies Discussion Paper 311.

Collier, P. Radwan, S. and Wangwe, S. (1986) Labour and Poverty in Rural Tanzania. Oxford: Clarenden Press.

Cooper, R.G. (1984) *Resource Scarcity and the Hmong Response*, Singapore University Press.

Coote, A. and Lenaghan, J. (1997) *Citizens' Juries: Theory into practice*. London: Institute of Public Policy Research.

Cornia, G.A., Jolly, R. and Stewart, F. (eds) (1987–1988) *Adjustment with a Human Face*. United Nations Children's Fund.

Cornwall, A. (1992) 'Body mapping in health RRA/PRA', *RRA Notes*, No 16, Special Issue on Applications for Health, London, International Institute for Environment and Development, pp 69–76.

Craig, G. (1998) *Women's Views Count: Building responsive maternity services*. London: College of Health.

Cramer, D. (1997) *Basic Statistics for Social Research: Step by step calculations and computer techniques using Minitab*. London: Routledge.

Cresswell, T. (1996) 'Participatory appraisal in the UK urban health sector', *Development in Practice*, Vol, 6, No 1.

Cuninghame, C., Griffin, J. and Laws, S. (1996) *Water Tight: The impact of water metering on low-income families*. London: Save the Children.

Denscombe, M. (1998) *The Good Research Guide for Small-Scale Social Research Projects* Buckingham, UK and Philadelphia, USA: The Open University Press.

Denzin, N.K. (1988) *The Research Act: A theoretical introduction to sociological methods*, 3rd edition. Englewood Cliffs, NJ: Prentice-Hall.

Department for International Development (DFID) (1998) *Evaluation Summary EV621, DDT Impact Assessment Project, Zimbabwe*. Full report also available.

Dey, I. (1993) *Qualitative Data Analysis: A user-friendly guide for social scientists*. London: Routledge.

Dodson, J. and Hares, T. (1994) *Involving the Local Community in Health Needs Assessment*. Newcastle: Save the Children.

Edwards, M. and Hulme, D. (eds) (1995) *Non-Governmental Organisations: Performance and accountability*. London: Earthscan Publications.

Einspruch, E. (1998) *An Introductory Guide to SPSS for Windows*. London: Sage.

Eldridge, C. (1993) A Participatory Learning and Action study on the 1992 drought in Malawi, Zambia and Zimbabwe. Unpublished report.

Fairhead, J. and Leach, M. (1996) 'Rethinking the forest-savanna mosaic: colonial science and its relics in West Africa', in Leach, M. and Mearns, R. (eds), *The Lie of the Land: Challenging Received Wisdom on the African Environment*. Oxford: Heinemann, and The International African Institute with James Currey Ltd.

Finch, J. (1986) *Research and Policy: The uses of qualitative methods in social and educational research*. Lewes: Falmer Press.

Gaventa, J. and Attwood, H. (1998) 'Synthesising PRA and case study materials: a participatory process for developing outlines, concepts and synthesis reports', in Institute of Development Studies, Participatory Poverty Assessments (PPA): PPA Topic Pack, Brighton: IDS.

Gill, J and Johnson, P. (1991) *Research Methods for Managers*. London: Paul Chapman.

Gittings, J. (2000) 'Five million census-takers hope Chinese will tell truth', *The Guardian*, 2 November 2000, p 20.

Glaser, B.G. and Strauss, A.L. (1967) *The Discovery of Grounded Theory*. Chicago: Aldine.

Goodell, G., Andrews, K.L. and Lopez, J.I. (1990) 'The contributions of agronomo-anthropologists to on-farm research and extension in integrated pest management', *Agricultural Systems*, Vol 32, pp 321–340.

Gosling, L. with Edwards, M. (1995) *Toolkits: A practical guide to assessment, monitoring, review and evaluation*, Development Manual 5. London: Save the Children.

Hadfield, M. (1998) *Community Consultation: Power, politics and policies*. The Urban Programme Research Group, University of Nottingham. Booklet and video.

Hakim, C. (1987) *Research Design: Strategies and choices in the design of social research*. London: Routledge, pp 157/8.

Hammersley, M. and Atkinson, P. (1993) *Ethnography*. London: Routledge.

Harper, C. (1997a) The power in participatory practice. Unpublished paper to OECF and World Bank Symposium on Aid Effectiveness.

Harper, C. (1997b) 'Using grassroots experience to inform macro level policy: an NGO perspective', *Journal of International Development*, Vol 9, No 5, pp 771–778.

Harper, C. (2001) 'Do the facts matter? NGOs, research and international advo-cacy', in Edwards, M. and Gaventa, J. (eds), *Global Citizen Action*. London: Earthscan.

Harper, C. (1992) The social life of the green Mong Textile: Commercialisation and Alternative Discourses of Value in Thailand. PhD thesis, London University.

Hart, E. and Bond, M. (1995) *Action Research for Health and Social Care: A guide to practice*. Open University Press.

Hart, R. (1992) *Children's Participation: From tokenism to citizenship*, Innocenti Essays No 4 UNICEF.

Hawtin, Murray, Hughes, G. and Percy-Smith, J. (1994) *Community Profiling: auditing social needs* Leeds: Leeds Metropolitan University, Policy Research Unit.

Hecht, T. (1995) At home in the street: street children of Recife, Brazil. Unpublished manuscript, USA, pp 15 and 20, quoted in Boyden and Ennew, op cit.

HelpAge International (1999) 'The contribution of older people to development: the research process', in *Research Updates Nos 1 to 4*. London.

Hillman, M., Adams, J. and Whitelegg, J. (1990) *One False Move: A study of children's independent mobility*. London: Policy Studies Institute.

Holland, J. and Munro, M. (1997) 'Profiling the purposive: some thoughts on site selection in PPAs', in Institute of Development Studies, *Participatory Poverty Assessments (PPA): PPA Topic Pack*. Brighton: IDS.

Holland, J. with Blackburn, J. (eds) (1998) *Whose Voice? Participatory research and policy change*. London: Intermediate Technology Publications.

Huff, D. (1973) *How to Lie with Statistics*. Harmondsworth: Pelican.

Hughes, R. (1999) 'Why do people agree to participate in social research? The case of drug injectors', *International Journal of Social Research Methodology*, Vol 1, No 4, 315–324.

Jacobsen, Y. (2000) *Our Right to Learn: A pack for people with learning difficulties and staff who work with them based on the Charter for Learning*. Leicester, England: NIACE, the National Organisation for Adult Learning.

James, A. and Prout, A. (1990) *Constructing and Reconstructing Childhood*. London: The Falmer Press.

James, A., Jenks, C. and Prout, A. (1998) *Theorising Childhood*. Cambridge: Polity Press.

Jayaratne, Epstein, T. and Stewart, A.J. (1991) 'Quantitative and qualitative methods in the social sciences: current feminist issues and practical strategies', in Fonow, M.M. and Cook, J.A. (eds), *Beyond Methodology: Feminist scholarship as lived research*. Bloomington and Indianapolis: Indiana University Press.

Johansson, L. (1994) 'Interactive media technology and "instant video" in rural development', in *Forests, Trees and People Newsletter*. Uppsala, Sweden: IRDC, Swedish University of Agricultural Sciences.

Johnson, H. and Mayoux, L. (1998) 'Investigation as empowerment: using participatory methods', in Thomas, A. et al, op. cit.

Johnson, V., Hill, J. and Ivan-Smith, E. (1995) *Listening to Smaller Voices: Children in an environment of change*. Chard, Somerset: Actionaid.

Kelly, L. (1988) *Surviving Sexual Violence*. Cambridge: Polity Press.

Kelly, L., Regan, L. and Burton S. (1995) 'Defending the indefensible? Quantitative methods and feminist research', in Holland, Janet and Blair, M. with Sheldon, S. (eds), *Debates and Issues in Feminist Research and Pedagogy*. Clevedon, Avon, England: Multilingual Matters/The Open University.

Kennedy, A.J. (2001) *The Rough Guide to the Internet 2001*. London: Rough Guides/The Penguin Group.

Khan, S. (1999) Participatory Research with Street Children Incarcerated in Jail or Correction Centre. Unpublished report, Save the Children.

Kirby, P. (1999) *Involving Young Researchers: How to enable young people to design and conduct research*. York: Joseph Rowntree Foundation.

Lafond, A. (1994) *Sustainability and Health Sector Development: A review and analysis of five country case studies, Working Paper 9*. London: Save the Children.

Lao Youth Union Vientiane Municipality, Lao Women's Union Vientiane Municipality, Education Department Vientiane Municipality, Save the Children Fund (UK) and Project Assistants (1998) *Listening to the Voice of Young People*, Vietiane, Laos.

Latimer, J. (1996) *Keying into Development – A guide to using computers for research into development studies*. University of Sussex Centre for the Comparative Study of Culture, Development and the Environment and the Institute of Development Studies.

Laws, S. (1998) *Hear Me! Consulting with young people on mental health services*. London: Mental Health Foundation.

Laws, S., Armitt, D., Metzendorf, W., Percival, P. and Reisel, J. (1999) *Time to Listen: Young people's experiences of mental health services*. London: College of Health/National Lottery Charities Board/Mental Health Foundation/BYPASS/Save the Children.

Leedy, P.D. (1997) *Practical Research – Planning and design*, 6th edition. New Jersey: Merrill, Prentice Hall.

Lees, J., Ojha, S. and Loyd, A. (1996) *The Children Speak: Are you listening?* International Conference on Child Sex Abuse, Bombay, India, quoted in Penrose, A., Ivan-Smith, E. and Thomson, M., *Kids for Hire: child's right to protection from commercial sexual exploitation*. London: Save the Children.

Lewis, M. and Kirby, P. (2001) *Consulting Children and Young People with Disabilities in Hammersmith and Fulham*. London: Save the Children.

Lloyd, E. (1995) *Prisoners' Children: Research, policy and practice*. London: Save the Children.

Lorillou, P. (2000) Water Supply Sanitation Project – Baseline study and micro-research study, Tibet. Tibet: Save the Children, unpublished.

Lowe, B., Cronin, A., Bramwell, P. and Breary, A. (1991) *Human Rights for All? A global view of lesbian and gay oppression and liberation*, Reading, UK: Reading International Solidarity Centre.

Mamdami, M. (1972) 'The myth of population control – family, caste and class in an Indian village', *Monthly Review Press*. London.

March, C., Smyth, I. and Mukhopadhyay, M. (1999) *A Guide to Gender-Analysis Frameworks*. Oxford: Oxfam. Also available in Spanish and Portuguese.

Mayer, S. (1998) 'Critical issues in using data', in Thomas, A., Chataway, J. and Wuyts, M. (eds), *Finding Out Fast*. The Open University/Sage.

McCartney, I. (2000) *Children in our Midst: Voices of farmworkers' children*. Harare, Zimbabwe: Weaver Press/Save the Children.

McCrum, S. and Hughes, L. (1994) *Interviewing Children: A guide for journalists and others*. London: Save the Children/UNICEF.

McKeown, C. and Hedges, C. (1996) *Skills in Community Research: A practical training course that will give people the opportunity to research aspects of their own community or peer group*. Newcastle: Save the Children.

Mikkelsen, B. (1995) *Methods for Development Work and Research: A guide for practitioners*, New Delhi: Sage Publications India.

Mollison, S. (2000) Pratham: A challenge to social development? Nepal: Save the Children (UK), unpublished paper.

Morrow, V. (1999) 'If you were a teacher, it would be harder to talk to you: reflections on qualitative research with children in school', *International Journal of Social Research Methodology*, Vol 1 No 4, pp 297–313.

Mosse, D. (1994) 'Authority, gender and knowledge: theoretical reflections on the practice of participatory rural appraisal', in *Development and Change*, No 25, pp 497–526.

Mukherjee, C. and Wuyts, M. (1998) 'Thinking with Quantitative Data', in Thomas, A., Chataway, J. and Wuyts, M. (eds), *Finding Out Fast*. The Open University/ Sage.

National Children's Bureau (2000) *Guidelines for Research*.

Nichols, P. (1991) *Social Survey Methods: A field guide for development workers, Development Guidelines No. 6*. Oxford: Oxfam.

Norton, A. (1998) 'Some reflections on the PPA process and lessons learned', in Holland, J. with Blackburn, J. (eds), *Whose Voice? Participatory research and policy change*. London: Intermediate Technology Publications.

Oakley, A. and Roberts, H. (eds) (1996) *Evaluating Social Interventions*. Basildon: Barnardos.

O'Laughlin, B. (1998) 'Interpreting institutional discourses', in Thomas, A., Chataway, J. and Wuyts, M. (eds), *Finding Out Fast*. The Open University/Sage.

Open University (1993) *Resources from Organisations*, Winning Resources and Support Book 5.

Open University (1993), 'Resources from organisations', in *Winning Resources and Support Book 5*. The Open University.

Owen, D. (1998) 'Whose PPA is this? Lessons learned from the Mozambique PPA', in Holland, J. with Blackburn, J. (eds), *Whose Voice? Participatory research and policy change*. London: Intermediate Technology Publications.

Parry-Williams, J. (1998) Evaluation, primarily by children evaluators, on the Save the Children Female-headed Households Project, Tajikistan. Save the Children, unpublished

Pettitt, B. and Laws, S. (1999) 'It's difficult to do dolls', *Images of Disability in Children's Playthings*. London: Save the Children.

Phoenix, A. (1991) *Young Mothers*. Cambridge: Polity Press.

Pratt, B. and Loizos, P. (1992) *Choosing Research Methods: Data collection for development workers, Development Guidelines No. 7*. Oxford: Oxfam.

Pretty, J.N., Guijt, I., Scoones, I. and Thompson, J. (1995) *A Trainer's Guide for Participatory Learning and Action*. London: IIED.

Pridmore, P. and Bendelow, G. (1995) 'Images of health: exploring beliefs of children using the "draw-and-write" technique', *Health Education Journal*, No 54, pp 473–488.

Princen, T. and Finger, M. (eds) (1994) *Environmental NGOs in World Politics: Linking the local and the global*. London: Routledge.

Pye-Smith, C. (1999) 'Truth games', *New Scientist*, 9.1.99, pp 16/17.

Qvortrup, J., Bardy, M., Sgritta G. and Wintersberger H. (ed.) (1994) *Childhood Matters: Social theory, practice and policy*. Aldershot: Avebury Press and ViennaEuropean Centre.

Reason, P. (1998) 'Three approaches to participative enquiry', in Denzin, N.K. and Lincoln, Y.S. (eds), *Strategies of Qualitative Enquiry*, Thousand Oaks, CA: Sage.

Rietbergen-McCracken, J. and Narayan, D. (1998) *Participation and Social Assessment: Tools and techniques – module 2: Stakeholder analysis*. New York: The World Bank.

Ritchie, J. and Spencer, L. (1994) 'Qualitative data analysis for applied policy research', in Bryman, A. and Burgess R.G. (eds), *Analyzing Qualitative Data*. London: Routledge.

Robb, C. (1998) 'PPAs: A review of the World Bank's experience', in Walland, J. with Blackburn, J. (eds), *Whose Voice? Participatory research and policy change*. London: Intermediate Technology Publications.

Roberts, H. (ed) (1981) *Doing Feminist Research*. London/Boston: Routledge and Kegan Paul.

Robson, C. (1993) *Real World Research*. Oxford, UK and Cambridge, USA: Blackwell.

Salim, Hanif, Swapan et al, with Khan, S. (1997) *A street children's research*. Dhaka: Save the Children.

Save the Children (1993) *Participatory Needs Assessment – Thanh Chuong District, Vietnam*. Save the Children.

Save the Children, (1997a) *Stitching Footballs: Voices of Children in Sialkot, Pakistan*. Save the Children.

Save the Children (1997b) 'PLA case study 1: Ghana', in *Gender and HIV/AIDS Guidelines*, London: Save the Children.

Save the Children. (1999) *Visions of Children who can't Hear, Hanoi, Vietnam*.

Scoones, I. (1998) *Sustainable Rural Livelihoods: A framework for analysis, Working Paper 72*. Brighton: Institute of Development Studies.

Selener, D., Endara, N. and Carvajal, J. (eds) (1999) *Participatory Rural Appraisal and Planning Workbook*. Ecuador/Philippines/USA/Kenya: International Institute of Rural Reconstruction (also available in Spanish).

Sinclair, R. (1998) 'Developing evidence-based policy and practice in social interventions with children and families', *International Journal of Social Research Methodology*, Vol 1, No 2, pp 169–176.

Smithson, P. (1994) *Health Financing and Sustainability – A review and analysis of five country case studies, Working Paper 10*. London: Save the Children

Stanley, L. and Wise, S. (1983) *Breaking Out: Feminist consciousness and feminist research*. London: Routledge and Kegan Paul.

Stubbs, S. (1999) 'Engaging with difference: soul-searching for a methodology in disability and development research', in Stone, E. (ed), *Disability and Development: Learning from action and research on disability in the majority world*. Leeds: The Disability Press.

Sykes, R. and Hedges, A. (eds) (1999) *Panels and Juries – new government, new agenda*. London: Social Research Association.

Theis, J. (1999) *Children and Poverty in Vietnam: Disaggregating Living Standards Survey data by age*. London: Save the Children.

Theis, J. and Grady, H.M. (1991) *Participatory Rapid Appraisal for Community Development*. London: IIED and SCF Federation.

Thomas A, Chataway, J. and Wuyts, M. (eds) (1998) *Finding Out Fast: Investigative skills for policy and development*. London: The Open University/Sage.

UNICEF. (1996) *Sustainability of Achievements: Lessons learned from universal child immunization*, Report of a Steering Committee.

Wadsworth, Y. (1997) *Do it Yourself Social Research*, 2nd edition. St Leonards, Australia: Allen and Unwin.

Wang, C. and Burris, M-A. (1997) 'Photovoice: concept, methodology, and use for participatory needs assessment', *Health Education and Behaviour*, June, Vol 24 No 3, pp 369–387.

Wang, C., Burris, M-A. and Xiang, Y.P. (1996) 'Chinese village women as visual anthropologists: a participatory approach to reaching policymakers', *Social Science and Medicine*, Vol 42, No 10, pp 1391–1400.

Weiss, C.H. (1977) *Using Social Research in Policy Making*. Lexington: MA.

Weiss, C.H. and Bucuvalas, M.J. (1977) 'The Challenge of Social Research to Decision Making', in C. H. Weiss, op cit.

West, A. (1995) *You're on Your Own: Young people's research on leaving care*. London: Save the Children.

West, A. (2000) Street Children Research in Xinjiang Province, People's Republic of China, Save the Children, unpublished.

Yin, R. (1994) *Case Study Research: Design and methods*, 2nd edition. Thousand Oaks, CA: Sage. Quoted in Thomas, A., Chataway, J. and Wuyts, M. (eds) (1998) *Finding Out Fast*. London: The Open University/Sage.

Youngman, M.B. (1986) *Analysing Questionnaires*. Nottingham: University of Nottingham School of Education. Cited in Bell, 1993.

Index